Lecture Notes in Computer Science

Lecture Notes in Artificial Intelligence   **14693**

Founding Editor

Jörg Siekmann

Series Editors

Randy Goebel, *University of Alberta, Edmonton, Canada*
Wolfgang Wahlster, *DFKI, Berlin, Germany*
Zhi-Hua Zhou, *Nanjing University, Nanjing, China*

The series Lecture Notes in Artificial Intelligence (LNAI) was established in 1988 as a topical subseries of LNCS devoted to artificial intelligence.

The series publishes state-of-the-art research results at a high level. As with the LNCS mother series, the mission of the series is to serve the international R & D community by providing an invaluable service, mainly focused on the publication of conference and workshop proceedings and postproceedings.

Don Harris · Wen-Chin Li
Editors

Engineering Psychology and Cognitive Ergonomics

21st International Conference, EPCE 2024
Held as Part of the 26th HCI International Conference, HCII 2024
Washington, DC, USA, June 29 – July 4, 2024
Proceedings, Part II

 Springer

Editors
Don Harris
Coventry University
Coventry, UK

Wen-Chin Li
Cranfield University
Cranfield, UK

ISSN 0302-9743   ISSN 1611-3349 (electronic)
Lecture Notes in Artificial Intelligence
ISBN 978-3-031-60730-1   ISBN 978-3-031-60731-8 (eBook)
https://doi.org/10.1007/978-3-031-60731-8

LNCS Sublibrary: SL7 – Artificial Intelligence

This Springer imprint is published by the registered company Springer Nature Switzerland AG
The registered company address is: Gewerbestrasse 11, 6330 Cham, Switzerland

If disposing of this product, please recycle the paper.

Foreword

This year we celebrate 40 years since the establishment of the HCI International (HCII) Conference, which has been a hub for presenting groundbreaking research and novel ideas and collaboration for people from all over the world.

The HCII conference was founded in 1984 by Prof. Gavriel Salvendy (Purdue University, USA, Tsinghua University, P.R. China, and University of Central Florida, USA) and the first event of the series, "1st USA-Japan Conference on Human-Computer Interaction", was held in Honolulu, Hawaii, USA, 18–20 August. Since then, HCI International is held jointly with several Thematic Areas and Affiliated Conferences, with each one under the auspices of a distinguished international Program Board and under one management and one registration. Twenty-six HCI International Conferences have been organized so far (every two years until 2013, and annually thereafter).

Over the years, this conference has served as a platform for scholars, researchers, industry experts and students to exchange ideas, connect, and address challenges in the ever-evolving HCI field. Throughout these 40 years, the conference has evolved itself, adapting to new technologies and emerging trends, while staying committed to its core mission of advancing knowledge and driving change.

As we celebrate this milestone anniversary, we reflect on the contributions of its founding members and appreciate the commitment of its current and past Affiliated Conference Program Board Chairs and members. We are also thankful to all past conference attendees who have shaped this community into what it is today.

The 26th International Conference on Human-Computer Interaction, HCI International 2024 (HCII 2024), was held as a 'hybrid' event at the Washington Hilton Hotel, Washington, DC, USA, during 29 June – 4 July 2024. It incorporated the 21 thematic areas and affiliated conferences listed below.

A total of 5108 individuals from academia, research institutes, industry, and government agencies from 85 countries submitted contributions, and 1271 papers and 309 posters were included in the volumes of the proceedings that were published just before the start of the conference, these are listed below. The contributions thoroughly cover the entire field of human-computer interaction, addressing major advances in knowledge and effective use of computers in a variety of application areas. These papers provide academics, researchers, engineers, scientists, practitioners and students with state-of-the-art information on the most recent advances in HCI.

The HCI International (HCII) conference also offers the option of presenting 'Late Breaking Work', and this applies both for papers and posters, with corresponding volumes of proceedings that will be published after the conference. Full papers will be included in the 'HCII 2024 - Late Breaking Papers' volumes of the proceedings to be published in the Springer LNCS series, while 'Poster Extended Abstracts' will be included as short research papers in the 'HCII 2024 - Late Breaking Posters' volumes to be published in the Springer CCIS series.

I would like to thank the Program Board Chairs and the members of the Program Boards of all thematic areas and affiliated conferences for their contribution towards the high scientific quality and overall success of the HCI International 2024 conference. Their manifold support in terms of paper reviewing (single-blind review process, with a minimum of two reviews per submission), session organization and their willingness to act as goodwill ambassadors for the conference is most highly appreciated.

This conference would not have been possible without the continuous and unwavering support and advice of Gavriel Salvendy, founder, General Chair Emeritus, and Scientific Advisor. For his outstanding efforts, I would like to express my sincere appreciation to Abbas Moallem, Communications Chair and Editor of HCI International News.

July 2024   Constantine Stephanidis

HCI International 2024 Thematic Areas
and Affiliated Conferences

- HCI: Human-Computer Interaction Thematic Area
- HIMI: Human Interface and the Management of Information Thematic Area
- EPCE: 21st International Conference on Engineering Psychology and Cognitive Ergonomics
- AC: 18th International Conference on Augmented Cognition
- UAHCI: 18th International Conference on Universal Access in Human-Computer Interaction
- CCD: 16th International Conference on Cross-Cultural Design
- SCSM: 16th International Conference on Social Computing and Social Media
- VAMR: 16th International Conference on Virtual, Augmented and Mixed Reality
- DHM: 15th International Conference on Digital Human Modeling & Applications in Health, Safety, Ergonomics & Risk Management
- DUXU: 13th International Conference on Design, User Experience and Usability
- C&C: 12th International Conference on Culture and Computing
- DAPI: 12th International Conference on Distributed, Ambient and Pervasive Interactions
- HCIBGO: 11th International Conference on HCI in Business, Government and Organizations
- LCT: 11th International Conference on Learning and Collaboration Technologies
- ITAP: 10th International Conference on Human Aspects of IT for the Aged Population
- AIS: 6th International Conference on Adaptive Instructional Systems
- HCI-CPT: 6th International Conference on HCI for Cybersecurity, Privacy and Trust
- HCI-Games: 6th International Conference on HCI in Games
- MobiTAS: 6th International Conference on HCI in Mobility, Transport and Automotive Systems
- AI-HCI: 5th International Conference on Artificial Intelligence in HCI
- MOBILE: 5th International Conference on Human-Centered Design, Operation and Evaluation of Mobile Communications

List of Conference Proceedings Volumes Appearing Before the Conference

1. LNCS 14684, Human-Computer Interaction: Part I, edited by Masaaki Kurosu and Ayako Hashizume
2. LNCS 14685, Human-Computer Interaction: Part II, edited by Masaaki Kurosu and Ayako Hashizume
3. LNCS 14686, Human-Computer Interaction: Part III, edited by Masaaki Kurosu and Ayako Hashizume
4. LNCS 14687, Human-Computer Interaction: Part IV, edited by Masaaki Kurosu and Ayako Hashizume
5. LNCS 14688, Human-Computer Interaction: Part V, edited by Masaaki Kurosu and Ayako Hashizume
6. LNCS 14689, Human Interface and the Management of Information: Part I, edited by Hirohiko Mori and Yumi Asahi
7. LNCS 14690, Human Interface and the Management of Information: Part II, edited by Hirohiko Mori and Yumi Asahi
8. LNCS 14691, Human Interface and the Management of Information: Part III, edited by Hirohiko Mori and Yumi Asahi
9. LNAI 14692, Engineering Psychology and Cognitive Ergonomics: Part I, edited by Don Harris and Wen-Chin Li
10. LNAI 14693, Engineering Psychology and Cognitive Ergonomics: Part II, edited by Don Harris and Wen-Chin Li
11. LNAI 14694, Augmented Cognition, Part I, edited by Dylan D. Schmorrow and Cali M. Fidopiastis
12. LNAI 14695, Augmented Cognition, Part II, edited by Dylan D. Schmorrow and Cali M. Fidopiastis
13. LNCS 14696, Universal Access in Human-Computer Interaction: Part I, edited by Margherita Antona and Constantine Stephanidis
14. LNCS 14697, Universal Access in Human-Computer Interaction: Part II, edited by Margherita Antona and Constantine Stephanidis
15. LNCS 14698, Universal Access in Human-Computer Interaction: Part III, edited by Margherita Antona and Constantine Stephanidis
16. LNCS 14699, Cross-Cultural Design: Part I, edited by Pei-Luen Patrick Rau
17. LNCS 14700, Cross-Cultural Design: Part II, edited by Pei-Luen Patrick Rau
18. LNCS 14701, Cross-Cultural Design: Part III, edited by Pei-Luen Patrick Rau
19. LNCS 14702, Cross-Cultural Design: Part IV, edited by Pei-Luen Patrick Rau
20. LNCS 14703, Social Computing and Social Media: Part I, edited by Adela Coman and Simona Vasilache
21. LNCS 14704, Social Computing and Social Media: Part II, edited by Adela Coman and Simona Vasilache
22. LNCS 14705, Social Computing and Social Media: Part III, edited by Adela Coman and Simona Vasilache

https://2024.hci.international/proceedings

Preface

The 21st International Conference on Engineering Psychology and Cognitive Ergonomics (EPCE 2024) is an affiliated conference of the HCI International Conference. The first EPCE conference was held in Stratford-upon-Avon, UK in 1996, and since 2001 EPCE has been an integral part of the HCI International conference series. Over the last 26 years, over 1,000 papers have been presented in this conference, which attracts a world-wide audience of scientists and human factors practitioners. The engineering psychology submissions describe advances in applied cognitive psychology that underpin the theory, measurement and methodologies behind the development of human-machine systems. Cognitive ergonomics describes advances in the design and development of user interfaces. Originally, these disciplines were driven by the requirements of high-risk, high-performance industries where safety was paramount, however the importance of good human factors is now understood by everyone in order to not only increase safety, but also enhance performance, productivity and revenues.

Two volumes of the HCII 2024 proceedings are dedicated to this year's edition of the EPCE conference.

The first volume centers around a diverse array of interconnected themes related to the interplay between human physiology, cognition, performance and assisted decision-making. From examining the impact of sleep deprivation and the impact of startle reflex on human performance and mood to evaluating the competence of pilots as well as workload and cognitive control, each paper sheds light on performance in demanding and high-stress environments. Furthermore, papers explore the effects of individual factors on working memory, the role of personality in errors, and the impact of stress on cognitive tasks. A considerable number of articles in this volume explore the complexities of decision-making, resource management and operation safety, while showcasing innovative systems to support and empower decision-making in complex situations. From adaptive pilot assistance and advisory systems, to resource management in remote and distributed teams, to task allocation in cooperative aviation operations, and multiple probability judgement, these systems are designed to enhance safety and efficiency in high-pressure environments.

The second volume offers a comprehensive exploration of the role of engineering psychology in user experience and the impact of human factors on aviation. Papers, through the lens of engineering psychology, provide insights to designers and engineers into users' cognitive processes, perceptual capabilities, and ergonomic preferences, allowing them to create solutions that are intuitive, efficient, and satisfying to use. The prominence of human factors in aviation is addressed in a number of papers, discussing research and case studies for a wide range of aviation systems, including ground operations, air traffic controllers, and piloting tasks, and exploring users' perceptions and perspectives. These works also deliberate on aspects of safety, automation, awareness, and efficiency, highlighting the importance of human factors, ensuring that technology, procedures, and personnel are aligned to support safe and effective flight operations.

The papers in these volumes were accepted for publication after a minimum of two single-blind reviews from the members of the EPCE Program Board or, in some cases, from members of the Program Boards of other affiliated conferences. We would like to thank all of them for their invaluable contribution, support and efforts.

July 2024

Don Harris
Wen-Chin Li

21st International Conference on Engineering Psychology and Cognitive Ergonomics (EPCE 2024)

HCI International 2025 Conference

The 27th International Conference on Human-Computer Interaction, HCI International 2025, will be held jointly with the affiliated conferences at the Swedish Exhibition & Congress Centre and Gothia Towers Hotel, Gothenburg, Sweden, June 22–27, 2025. It will cover a broad spectrum of themes related to Human-Computer Interaction, including theoretical issues, methods, tools, processes, and case studies in HCI design, as well as novel interaction techniques, interfaces, and applications. The proceedings will be published by Springer. More information will become available on the conference website: https://2025.hci.international/.

General Chair
Prof. Constantine Stephanidis
University of Crete and ICS-FORTH
Heraklion, Crete, Greece
Email: general_chair@2025.hci.international

https://2025.hci.international/

Contents – Part II

Human Factors in Aviation

Contents – Part I

Decision-Making Support and Automation

Engineering Psychology and User Experience

Evaluating User Experience for Intelligent Connected Vehicles: A Qualitative Study

Mengxia He[1,2], Jingyu Zhang[1,2(✉)], Liang Zhang[1,2], and Rong Zhang[3]

[1] CAS Key Laboratory of Behavioral Science, Institute of Psychology, Beijing 100101, China
zhangjingyu@psych.ac.cn
[2] Department of Psychology, University of the Chinese Academy of Sciences, Beijing 100101, China
[3] LiaoningNormal University, Dalian, China

Abstract. Intelligent and Connected Vehicles (ICV) are rapidly advancing and have become the strategic focus of global automotive enterprises. Gaining an in-depth understanding of the psychological experiences of ICV users is crucial to ensure widespread user acceptance and recognition of product development and iterations. However, most user experience studies still primarily focus on the features of traditional vehicles. This study attempts to initially develop a comprehensive evaluative framework to evaluate the user experience of ICVs. By utilizing literature analysis, user interviews, and expert evaluations, we extracted 28 key sub-dimensions of the psychological experiences of ICV users. The findings from this research will provide a framework to evaluate the user experience of ICVs. Future studies may develop the ICV user psychological experience questionnaires based on this study and conduct further validation studies. This, in turn, will assist automotive enterprises in optimizing industrial design for enhanced user experiences.

Keywords: Intelligent and Connected Vehicles(ICVs) · User Experience · literature analysis · user interviews

1 Introduction

Intelligent and Connected Vehicles (ICVs) represent a paradigm shift in the automotive industry, leveraging Vehicle-to-Everything (V2X) technology to enhance information acquisition and sharing. These vehicles are equipped with advanced functionalities such as environmental perception, decision-making capabilities, assisted driving, and cooperative control, culminating in a safer, more comfortable, and efficient travel experience [1]. This convergence of artificial intelligence, communication technologies, and modeling is propelling a new era of innovation within the automotive sector, presenting opportunities for market expansion and industry transformation [2]. Concurrently, the integration of "vehicle-road-cloud" technology and the widespread adoption of ICVs are poised to revolutionize individual travel efficiency, optimize transportation network operations, and catalyze the evolution of intelligent transportation systems (ITS) [3].

The ICV industry is experiencing rapid growth driven by technological advancements and escalating market demand. In China alone, data from the Ministry of Industry and Information Technology indicates that by the first half of 2023, 42.4% of new passenger cars were equipped with integrated driving assistance functions [4]. Globally, numerous companies have entered this competitive arena, with established automotive giants like Audi, BMW, and Mercedes-Benz leveraging their industry expertise and technological prowess to lead the ICV sector. Meanwhile, emerging brands such as Tesla, NIO, and Li Auto are adopting user-centric strategies to carve their niche in the market [5]. Projections from IHS Markit suggest that by 2025, the global penetration rate of ICVs will reach 59.4%, with China spearheading this adoption with a penetration rate of 75.9%.

The widespread adoption of ICVs promises to revolutionize the driving experience by integrating innovative interactive features into vehicle designs. Companies are incorporating interactive technologies such as responsive touchscreens, voice recognition, natural language interaction, gesture control, Heads-Up Displays (HUD), edge interaction, and virtual reality (VR) to not only meet functional needs but also deliver immersive entertainment experiences. Vehicles are evolving into the "third living space" after homes and workplaces, where human-machine interaction performance plays a pivotal role in user satisfaction and purchasing decisions.

Despite the promising advancements in Intelligent and Connected Vehicles (ICVs), ensuring positive psychological experiences for users amidst fierce competition presents a formidable challenge. Traditional usability studies, while valuable, may not readily apply to the complexities of intelligent systems. The introduction of numerous new features in ICVs not only caters to emerging needs but also significantly increases the demands on information processing. This necessitates a reevaluation of fundamental usability metrics such as learnability, usability, and accessibility to ensure that ICVs meet user expectations effectively. Moreover, the increased intelligence and autonomy of ICV systems demand a new level of human-system collaboration. A well-designed intelligent system must effectively express its state and intentions, and allocate functions appropriately between humans and machines to prevent issues such as takeover problems, where the human driver is unable to regain control effectively. Failure to address these challenges may lead to user frustration, decreased trust in ICV technology, and ultimately hinder widespread adoption and market success.

Furthermore, advancements in information entertainment, power, and control systems are reshaping the social and emotional dimensions of the driving experience. Features such as voice interaction can significantly engage younger family members, while advanced infotainment systems and automatic parking functions not only fulfill individual functional needs but also contribute to the satisfaction of social status. As ICVs become more integrated into daily life, understanding and enhancing user psychological experiences are paramount for manufacturers to gain a competitive edge and foster greater user acceptance and satisfaction.

In response to these challenges, this study seeks to fill a critical gap in research by establishing a comprehensive framework for understanding user psychological experiences in the context of human-machine interaction in intelligent connected vehicles. By delving deeper into the nuances of user experiences, including emotional responses, social interactions, and cognitive processes, this study aims to provide valuable insights for ICV manufacturers to design more intuitive, user-friendly, and emotionally engaging systems. By addressing the limitations of previous studies and focusing on the holistic user experience, this research not only contributes to the advancement of academic knowledge but also offers practical implications for enhancing ICV design and promoting user acceptance and satisfaction in an increasingly competitive market landscape.

1.1 Users' Psychological Experience in the Automotive Context

User psychological experience, also known as User Experience (UX or UE), is defined by the International Organization for Standardization (ISO, 2019) as the perceptions and responses evoked by users when utilizing (or anticipating the use of) systems, products, or services. In the realm of driving, user psychological experience encompasses the subjective awareness of drivers during interactions with intelligent vehicles. It encapsulates all cognitions, emotions, and perceptions of anticipated driving behaviors shaped through the interaction between drivers and intelligent vehicles [6]. Despite its inherently subjective nature, commonalities in user psychological experience among user groups with well-defined characteristics can be unveiled through interviews, large-scale surveys, or meticulously designed experiments.

In the fiercely competitive automotive market, it has become increasingly pivotal for car manufacturers not only to meet but also to exceed customer expectations to gain market penetration and achieve sustainable growth rates [7]. Achieving a high level of satisfaction and eliciting positive product evaluations are crucial for attracting customers to make purchases and fostering their loyalty. While previous research has highlighted usability as a significant factor in user satisfaction evaluations for a particular product [8], it's imperative to include additional UX factors in assessments to ascertain whether a particular application or in-vehicle device meets or even surpasses users' expectations to become the preferred choice.

Furthermore, delivering a gratifying psychological experience confers a substantial competitive advantage to brands. It directly influences users' purchase intentions, brand loyalty, willingness to recommend, and overall market competitiveness. A positive psychological experience can bolster users' inclination to make purchases, encourage repeat purchases from the same brand in the future, and prompt active recommendations to others. Moreover, users' psychological experience significantly shapes their behavior in using Intelligent and Connected Vehicles. When users experience pleasure, safety, and comfort while driving, they are more inclined to consistently utilize related features, thereby elevating overall satisfaction levels. By deeply understanding users' psychological experiences, car manufacturers can effectively discern market demands and implement product enhancements tailored to user preferences. This iterative feedback loop fosters the creation of products that better align with user expectations, consequently enhancing market competitiveness.

1.2 The Structures of User Psychological Experience

User psychological experience in the automotive context can be broadly categorized into two higher-level dimensions: instrumental and hedonic experiences. Instrumental experiences relate to the pragmatic aspects of product usage, focusing on functionality, efficiency, and task performance. This dimension conceptualizes the product's value in assisting users in achieving their objectives. On the other hand, hedonic experiences pertain to the emotional and affective responses elicited during product interaction, encompassing enjoyment, pleasure, and aesthetic appeal. The two dimensions have their roots in the singularity theory of user psychological experience, which either encompasses a utilitarian approach emphasizing usability or an experiential aesthetic approach rooted in hedonism.

While some scholars attempted to emphasize the pivotal role of only one dimension [9], it is widely believed that satisfaction of utilitarian value is deemed a prerequisite for pleasurable experiences. Moreover, it became evident that user psychological experience encompasses both perceptions, rendering the singularity theory inadequate [10]. In fact, it has been found that both aspects collectively unveil the holistic panorama of user psychological experience, and the neglect of any dimension is problematic [11, 12]. Consequently, Hassenzahl et al. (2003) synthesized the tenets of the singularity theory, elucidating user psychological experience through the lenses of both utilitarian and hedonic value. This synthesis provides the general basis, which can be considered the dual structure of user experience theory.

In essence, when exploring the user psychological experience of Intelligent and Connected Vehicles, it is imperative to comprehensively examine both utilitarian and hedonic value experiences. However, the current understanding of the sub-dimensions within each dimension might not be sufficient to capture the intricacies of user interactions with advanced technologies and AI integration. As automotive systems become increasingly complex and interconnected, a deeper exploration of new experience sub-dimensions is essential for a more comprehensive understanding of user psychological experience.

In the context of instrumental experiences, for example, while usability assessments traditionally focus on ease of use and task completion, they may overlook the cognitive load imposed by advanced driver assistance features or the adaptability required for seamless integration with evolving AI algorithms. Similarly, within the realm of hedonic experiences, sub-dimensions like emotional engagement, sensory appeal, and perceived enjoyment play a pivotal role in shaping user perceptions and preferences. However, existing frameworks may fail to fully capture the nuances of these sub-dimensions in the context of emerging technologies. For instance, while studies may assess the perceived enjoyment of in-car entertainment systems, they may not adequately address the impact of personalized content recommendations powered by machine learning algorithms, which can meet more needs of humans such as understanding me, promoting social elevation, etc. In summary, while the higher-level dimensions of instrumental and hedonic experiences provide a framework for understanding user psychological experience, a nuanced exploration of the sub-dimensions within each dimension is essential for comprehensive product evaluation, particularly in the context of advancing technologies and AI integration. By acknowledging the potential limitations of current understanding and adopting a more holistic approach to sub-dimension assessment, car manufacturers can better cater to user needs and preferences, driving innovation and enhancing competitiveness in the automotive market.

1.3   Taking Some Important Antecedents into Consideration

To effectively explore the new subdimensions of user experience, it is important to consider several key antecedents. These antecedents include product features (both physical and software system characteristics), user characteristics (such as demographic variables, personality traits, and prior user experience), and the interaction environment (including socio-cultural factors and the physical environment). Previous research has demonstrated that these factors can significantly influence user experiences across various types of products [13–18].

By taking these antecedents into account, we can better identify the specific target product, user groups, and scenarios that need to be examined within the context of Intelligent and Connected Vehicles (ICVs). This, in turn, enables us to identify new subdimensions more efficiently and with greater precision. For instance, when considering software systems, it's crucial to factor in the autonomy of new AI systems, which may introduce novel experiences such as perceived command understanding or perceived control over the system. Additionally, in eliciting experiences, incorporating scenarios involving social interactions within the vehicle can be valuable. Recognizing voices from different locations in the car may not only fulfill functional needs but also necessitate more socially sensitive services.

In summary, to uncover potential new subdimensions of user experiences with ICVs, a comprehensive consideration of product features, user characteristics, and the interaction environment is essential. Conducting a thorough analysis of psychological experience differences among users with varying characteristics will facilitate the design of more targeted products and enhance user satisfaction for greater benefits.

1.4   The Present Study

Previous research on the psychological experiences of users of Intelligent and Connected Vehicles (ICVs) has primarily focused on traditional usability measures [19]. While there is emerging research attention on the psychological experiences of automotive users, a comprehensive and up-to-date analysis of the specific characteristics and constituting dimensions of the psychological experiences of ICV users is lacking. Additionally, there is a gap in the development of a tailored psychological experience assessment tool for ICV users. This gap makes it challenging for designers to accurately grasp user psychological experiences and precisely identify pain points in the psychological experiences of ICV users. This study aims to better serve the establishment the psychological experiences of ICVs. This will be achieved through combined methodologies including as literature analysis, in-depth interviews, and expert evaluations. The goal is to provide a theoretical and empirical foundation to propel further research into user psychological experiences and broader user survey initiatives. Consequently, the study aims to advance the development and iterative design services of ICV products by addressing user psychological experiences more effectively.

2 Methods

2.1 Literature Review

To establish the initial items, we initiated a literature search using keywords such as "psychological experience", "Intelligent Vehicles (ICVs)," "driving experiences," "vehicle purchase and usage" and "vehicle user evaluations". We conducted searches on databases like Google Scholar, Web of Science, and other journal databases. Relevant research articles were identified through abstracts and keywords. Subsequently, we screened and selected 33 key articles through a thorough reading of their full texts. These selected articles guided the formulation of interview content for the questionnaire and contributed to the preliminary development of psychological experience characteristic items.

2.2 User Interviews

User interviews were conducted using the Critical Incident Technique [20], delving comprehensively into the psychological experiences of users during vehicle usage by focusing on key events.

Interview Participants. To identify interview subjects, we posted recruitment posters targeting users of L2 and above Intelligent and Connected Vehicles (ICVs). Using a combination of online and offline approaches, we invited a total of 20 ICV owners to participate in the interviews (15 males, 5 females). Due to some interviewees unwilling to disclose age information, age reporting is not available. The vehicles used included brands such as Tesla (8 individuals), Volvo (8 individuals), and Roewe (4 individuals)

Interview Content. Interviews followed a self-developed outline for Intelligent Vehicle User Psychological Experience and were conducted on a one-to-one basis, lasting approximately 60-75 minutes, either in person or online. The outline was developed through discussions involving a psychology professor and several user experience experts. It consisted of two parts:

1 Basic Driving Information: Including driving experience, self-assessment of driving skills, ICV model used, reasons for purchasing, etc.
2 ICV Usage Experience: Covering desired feelings upon purchasing, most memorable experiences/events during vehicle use and associated emotions, elements or experiences satisfying or dissatisfying during usage, and areas for improvement. Afterward, participants were invited to carefully review the psychological experience feature descriptions derived from literature research, providing feedback to ensure the readability and clarity of each description

2.3 Expert Evaluation

Two experts in engineering psychology were invited to assess elements such as the wording of the names and detailed description of each experience dimension i. Based on the feedback and suggestions provided by the experts, further modifications were made. The questionnaire underwent several rounds of discussion and refinement, resulting in the final version of the list, which can be used for future questionnaire development.

3   Results

After analyzing the content of the 33 papers, we extracted key user experience dimensions, resulting in the preliminary list of 17 experience items, as shown in Table 1. Subsequently, through in-depth interviews with 20 Intelligent and Connected Vehicles (ICVs) owners, we obtained 20 audio recordings. The content, transcribed, amounted to a total of 244,675 words. On one hand, we coded the interviews based on five categories: reasons for purchase, key events, satisfaction and dissatisfaction experiences, and explicit improvement suggestions. On the other hand, we coded the original interview text data and, based on the structure theory, preliminarily classified the psychological experiences of ICV users into two core categories: utilitarian value experience and hedonic value experience.

Following this, we extracted the user experience characteristics and formulated the items for the Intelligent and Connected Vehicles (ICV) Psychological Experience Questionnaire. Based on the interview results, participant suggestions, and the evaluations from two engineering psychology experts, adjustments were made to the psychological experience characteristics of Intelligent Vehicle Users developed after the literature review: ① Flexibility was specified into two items: Environmental Sensitivity and Demand Insight. ② Intelligent was adjusted to Comprehension of Commands, Predictability to Reasonableness of Feedback, Timeliness was specified as Timeliness of Response, Dominance was adjusted to Sense of Control, Innovation was adjusted to Technological Appeal, and Excitement was adjusted to Stimulus Appeal. ③ Additional items were added: Operability, Driving Sensation, Economic Efficiency, Ease, Health Benefit, Stability, Environmental Friendliness, Sense of Speed, Freedom, Power. Combining the results from the preliminary literature review, a final Intelligent and Connected Vehicles (ICVs) Psychological Experience Survey Questionnaire was formed, comprising 28 items (see Table 1). The conclusions drawn from the study can be utilized for the subsequent questionnaire research phase.

Table 1. Summary of ICVs User Psychological Experience

Characteristic	Explanation	Source	Times mentioned in the interview
Command Understanding	The ability to accurately understand or even anticipate user-operated commands	Interview; Lindgren et al. (2020)	5
Convenience	The degree to which the vehicle brings convenience and speed to the user's life	Interview; Pakusch et al. (2018); Steg (2005)	24

(continued)

Table 1. (*continued*)

Characteristic	Explanation	Source	Times mentioned in the interview
Environmental Sensitivity	The ability to make reasonable adjustments based on the environment (road conditions, weather, lighting)	Interview; Lindgren et al. (2020)	19
Demand Sensitivity	The ability to promptly meet user needs based on their state (e.g., automatic door opening, fatigue reminders)	Interview; Lindgren et al. (2020)	2
Safety	Vehicle safety performance, such as the effectiveness of safety protection and collision avoidance	Interview; Dogan et al. (2011); Steg (2005)	35
Ease of Use	Easy to operate, not prone to operational errors	Interview; Steg (2005); Sun (2021)	14
Feedback Reasonableness	Whether feedback on various vehicle condition/environmental information, such as speed and temperature, is sufficient and easily accessible	Interview; Lindgren et al. (2020)	6
Response speed	Whether the operation response is timely and smooth	Interview;Schölkopf et al. (2021)	8
Comfort	The degree of comfort in riding	Interview; Pakusch et al. (2018); Sun (2021)	27
Aesthetic Pleasure	The extent to which the user feels pleased based on their own aesthetic sense	Interview; Ranscombe et al. (2019)	22
Excitement	The degree to which the user feels excited, mentally stimulated, and not bored	Steg (2005)	0

(*continued*)

Table 1. (*continued*)

Characteristic	Explanation	Source	Times mentioned in the interview
Sense of Control	The extent to which the user feels effective in controlling and dominating the vehicle and environment	Interview; Hegner et al. (2019); Pakusch et al. (2018)	3
Superiority	Giving the user a sense of being in a high social status	Lindgren et al. (2020); Steg (2005)	0
Sensation Technology	The user experiences a sense of full new technology and innovation	Interview; Sun (2021)	14
Amusement	The existence of interesting features or experiences, even surprises	Interview; Sun (2021)	4
Uniqueness	The user experiences a satisfying feeling of being different from others	Steg (2005)	0
Personality Fit	The user feels matched with their own personality, even as an integral part of themselves	Sun (2021)	0
Warmth	The user feels supported and loved	Tasoudis (2019)	0
Operability	Feeling in control when manipulating the steering wheel, brakes, and accelerator	Interview	2
Driving Sensation	The user can experience the joy of driving	Interview	2
Economic Efficiency	Relatively low costs in terms of purchase and use compared to performance	Interview	11
Ease	Feeling relaxed during use, not prone to fatigue	Interview	10
Health Benefits	The vehicle makes the user feel environmentally friendly and healthy	Interview	7

(*continued*)

Table 1. (*continued*)

Characteristic	Explanation	Source	Times mentioned in the interview
Stability	The vehicle's equipment has few faults, and there are few shutdowns	Interview	9
Environmental Friendliness	Minimizing external environmental pollution	Interview	11
Sense of Speed	Fast acceleration or top speed	Interview	6
Sense of Freedom	Feeling free and unrestricted while driving	Interviewed	3
Sense of Power	Feeling powerful while driving	Interview	2

4 Discussion

Through a comprehensive analysis of core literature and in-depth interviews with owners of Intelligent Connected Vehicles (ICVs), this study delved into the psychological experiences of users of smart cars. Based on the integrated analysis, we distilled the key characteristics of the psychological experiences of ICV users, ultimately forming 28 sub-dimensions. The results of this research will provide robust support for the compilation and validation of the Intelligent Connected Vehicles (ICVs) Psychological Experience Survey Questionnaire in the subsequent phase. It will assist the automotive industry in conducting more extensive user research efficiently, enabling designers to grasp user psychological needs quickly and accurately. This, in turn, will aid companies in planning resource allocation more effectively, addressing user needs comprehensively, and better serving users to achieve greater benefits, ultimately enhancing customer loyalty and willingness to recommend.

However, due to time constraints and limited participant resources, the study has not undergone further validation for effectiveness and more extensive user research. Future research could further validate the measurement tool's reliability and validity through additional user surveys, establishing a questionnaire with robust reliability and validity to effectively measure the psychological experiences of users of Intelligent Connected Vehicles (ICVs). Additionally, the study solely analyzed the psychological experiences of users from their perspective during the use of Level 2 to Level 3 Intelligent Connected Vehicles. In the future, combining user research analysis with in-vehicle functional design could provide further insights. This could help clarify the prioritization of in-vehicle functional iteration design to enhance the dimensions of user psychological experiences with Intelligent Connected Vehicles. This approach could offer new perspectives for designing around "user psychological experiences.

附录: 智能网联汽车用户心理体验汇总

特征	解释	来源	在访谈中被提及的次数
指令理解力	对用户操作指令（如触屏、语音信息）准确理解甚至预判的能力	访谈; Lindgren et al.(2020)	5
便捷性	给使用者的生活带来方便和快捷的程度	访谈;Pakusch et al.(2018); Steg (2005)	24
环境敏感性	根据环境（路况、天气、照明）自动做出合理调整的能力	访谈;Lindgren et al.(2020)	19
需求洞察力	根据使用者状态及时满足需求的能力（如停车自动开门，疲劳提醒）	访谈; Lindgren et al. (2020)	2
安全性	车辆的安全性能，如安全防护和避免碰撞的好坏等	访谈;Dogan et al. (2011); Steg (2005)	35
易用性	操作容易上手，不容易发生操作错误	访谈 Steg (2005);Sun (2021)	14
反馈合理性	速度、温度等各种况况对动信息的反馈是否充分易获取	访谈 Lindgreret al. (2020)	6
响应灵敏性	操作响应是否及时流畅	访谈 Schölkopf et al. (2021)	8
舒适性	乘坐是否舒适	访谈 Pakusch et al. (2018);Sun (2021)	27
审美愉悦	能纵使用者感到符合自身审美感到愉悦的程度	访谈 Ranscombe et al. (2019)	22
刺激感	让使用者感到兴奋、精神愉悦，不无聊的程度	Steg (2005)	0
掌控感	让使用者感到可有效控制汽车到环境的程度	访谈 Hegner et al. (2019); Pakusch et al. (2018)	3
优越感	给使用者带来身处高社会地位的感受	Lindgren et al. (2020); Steg (2005)	0
科技感	使用者体会到充满科技和创新的感受	访谈 ;Sun (2021)	14
趣味性	存在有趣的功能或结构，甚至是惊喜	访谈 ;Sun (2021)	4
独特感	使用者体会到与众不同的满足感	Steg (2005)	0
个性符合感	使用者感到与自身个性匹配，甚至是自己重要组成部分的感觉	Sun (2021)	0
温暖感	使用者感到受到支持和被爱的感觉	Tasoudis (2019)	0
操控性	操纵方向盘、刹车及油门等时感到控制自如的感觉	访谈	2
驾驶感	使用者能体会到驾驶操作的乐趣	访谈	2
经济性	相对于性能、购置及使用成本低廉	访谈	11
轻松感	使用过程轻松省力，不容易疲惫	访谈	10
有益健康	车辆让使用者感觉环保、健康	访谈	7
稳定性	车辆的设备没有故障，停机次数少。	访谈	9
环境友好	对外部环境污染较少	访谈	11
速度感	加速或最高速度快	访谈	6
自由感	驾驶中感到无拘无束自由自在的感受	访谈	3
力量感	驾驶中感到自己充满力量的感受	访谈	2

Acknowledgments. This study was supported by Natural Science Fundation of China (T2192932, U2133209, 52072406), the Fundamental Research Funds of CAST (x242060302218), and the key project of Chongqing Technology Innovation and Application Development (grant no. cstc2021jscx-dxwtBX0020).

References

1. Li, K., Dai, Y., Li, S., Bian, M.: Development status and trends of Intelligent Connected Vehicles (ICV) technology. J. Autom. Saf. Energy **8**(01), 1–14 (2017)
2. Ministry of Industry and Information Technology, Ministry of Public Security, Ministry of Natural Resources, Ministry of Housing and Urban-Rural Development, 17 January 2024. https://www.miit.gov.cn/zwgk/zcwj/wjfb/tz/art/2024/art_b236a25edf9f4a8f9b60dbcd a924753b.html
3. Liu, J., Liu, J.: Intelligent and connected vehicles: current situation, future directions, and challenges. IEEE Commun. Stand. Mag. **2**(3), 59–65 (2018). https://doi.org/10.1109/MCO MSTD.2018.1700087
4. Equipment Industry Department I: The 2023 World Intelligent Connected Vehicles Conference opened in Beijing. The Ministry of Industry and Information Technology of the People's Republic of China, 21 September 2023. https://www.miit.gov.cn/jgsj/zbys/gzdt/art/2023/art_ d596e8def28647a09aac49b8f34ff412.html

5. Beijing Institute of Technology, Shenzhen Automotive Research Institute, National Engineering Laboratory for Electric Vehicles (Shenzhen Research Institute). Shenzhen Intelligent Connected New Energy Vehicle Industry Research Report, pp. 15–20 (2023)
6. Yu, Z., Jiang, K., Huang, Z., Zhang, P., Feng, Z.: Will I start an automated driving system? Report on the emotions, cognition, and intention of drivers who experienced real-world conditional automated driving. Cogn. Technol. Work **24**(4), 641–666 (2022)
7. Korber, M., Eichinger, A., Bengler, K., Olaverri-Monreal, C.: User experience evaluation in an automotive context. In: 2013 IEEE Intelligent Vehicles Symposium Workshops (IV Workshops), Gold Coast, QLD, Australia (2013)
8. Sonderegger, A., Sauer, J.: The influence of design aesthetics in usability testing: effects on user performance and perceived usability. Appl. Ergon. **41**(3), 403–410 (2010)
9. Tractinsky, N., Katz, A.S., Ikar, D.: What is beautiful is usable. Interact. Comput. **13**(2), 127–145 (2000)
10. Hassenzahl, M., Burmester, M., Koller, F.: AttrakDiff: Ein Fragebogen zur Messung wahrgenommener hedonischer und pragmatischer Qualität. In: Szwillus, G., Ziegler, J. (Eds.) Berichte des German Chapter of the ACM, vol. 57, pp. 187–196 (2003)
11. Hassenzahl, M., Monk, A.: The inference of perceived usability from beauty. Human-Comput. Interact. **25**(3), 235–260 (2010)
12. Tasoudis, S.: Mediated participatory design for contextually aware in-vehicle user-experiences with autonomous vehicles, Brunel University London (2019)
13. Jetter, H.-C., Reiterer, H., Geyer, F.: Blended Interaction: understanding natural human–computer interaction in post-WIMP interactive spaces. Pers. Ubiquit. Comput. **18**, 1139–1158 (2014)
14. Eriksson, A., Petermeijer, S.M., Zimmermann, M., de Winter, J.C.F., Bengler, K.J., Stanton, N.A.: Rolling out the red (and green) carpet: supporting driver decision making in automation-to-manual Transitions. IEEE Trans. Human-Mach. Syst. **49**(1), 20–31 (2019)
15. Zeng, F., Wang, M., Li, L., Cai, S.: Survey on the acceptance of smart cars amongst middle-aged and elderly in China. Technol. Soc. **73**, 102234 (2023)
16. Desmet, P., Hekkert, P.: Framework of product experience. Int. J. Des. **1**(1), 57–66 (2007)
17. Burnett, G.E., Ditsikas, D.: Personality as a criterion for selecting usability testing participants. In: Proceedings of IEEE 4th International conference on Information and Communications Technologies, Cairo, Egypt (2006)
18. Bernotat, J., Eyssel, F.: A robot at home—How affect, technology commitment, and personality traits influence user experience in an intelligent robotics apartment. In: 2017 26th IEEE International Symposium on Robot and Human Interactive Communication (RO-MAN), Lisbon, Portugal (2017)
19. Hecht, T., Weng, S., Kick, L.F., Bengler, K.: How users of automated vehicles benefit from predictive ambient light displays. Appl. Ergon. **103**, 103762 (2022)
20. Flanagan, J.C.: The critical incident technique. Psychol. Bull. **51**(4), 327–358 (1954). https://doi.org/10.1037/h0061470

Lesson Learned: Design and Perception of Single Controller Operations Support Tools

Robert Hunger[✉] [ID], Lothar Christoffels, Maik Friedrich[ID], Mohsan Jameel[ID],
Andreas Pick, Ingrid Gerdes, Peter Michael von der Nahmer[ID], and Fabio Sobotzki

German Aerospace Center (DLR), Braunschweig, Germany
{robert.hunger,lothar.christoffels,maik.friedrich,mohsan.jameel,
andreas.pick,ingrid.gerdes,peter.vondernahmer,
fabio.sobotzki}@dlr.de

Abstract. Skilled labour shortage is a well-known current issue throughout western hemisphere. It affects air navigation service providers as well in recruitment of future air traffic controllers. One promising solution is a highly-automated enhanced support system enabling a deployment of one single air traffic controller per sector instead of two for a standard layout. However, automation can be problematic if it is impossible to establish trust for humans into technology.

This paper presents design and interaction methods of validated support tools and functions during a validation campaign of single controller operations, the conduct of the validation itself and mainly the results regarding design and perception of air traffic controllers for support tools.

A validation was carried out with a total of seven air traffic controllers with twenty-one human-in-the-loop real-time simulation validation runs in 2023 to assess design, perception and usability of the tools proposed for single controller operations and to provide a proof of concept for the feasibility of the SCO concept and the system as a whole. A selection of seven support tools were evaluated under different traffic loads and defined frame conditions including a variety of typical controller tasks and events in air traffic control.

The results presented in this paper helped to rank and select support tools and functions, to detect possible improvements in design, interaction methods, human-machine information exchange and distribution of tasks in order to empower a human single controller to perform safe, efficient and sustainable operations in a team with a digital supporting environment.

Keywords: Single Controller Operations · Trust in Automation · Human Machine Teaming · Sonification

1 Introduction

1.1 Motivation

Air traffic levels are predicted to continuing increase worldwide [1]. At some crowded airspaces though, already today the maximum capacity cannot be made available at all times, in particular due to a lack of air traffic controllers [2–4].

D. Harris and W.-C. Li (Eds.): HCII 2024, LNAI 14693, pp. 15–33, 2024.
https://doi.org/10.1007/978-3-031-60731-8_2

The skills required of an air traffic controller are manifold, so it cannot be assumed that this deficit can be compensated by hiring and training additional. Demographic change in western hemisphere [5] and other countries will impair this even further. One possible solution is to reduce the number of planed controllers per control sector from two at present to one in future (single controller operation, SCO). The main research question addressed in this paper is which conditions and support tools are sufficient to enable SCO and how their interfaces to team up with humans should be designed.

1.2   Theoretical Background

Within the German Aerospace Center (DLR)-project *The Individual and Automated Air Traffic* (DIAL) the development of a concept and the construction of a prototype to demonstrate a single controller workstation for upper airspace was conducted [6, 7]. This involves a transition from the current system with one Radar Controller (Executive Controller) and one Planning Controller (Coordinator) to a single controller (SC) working together with a digital controller (DC). The results of a validation campaign of an intermediate step with one SC and enhanced support tools regarding subjective feedback from Air Traffic Controllers (ATCOs) collected through standard questionnaires and individual responses on design and perception are presented in this paper.

The underlying concept is presented in [6] and [7]. As expounded there SCO in en-route air traffic control (ATC) is still not widely researched except considering the more comprehensive concept of flight-centric ATC, which includes a single controller to be responsible for several aircraft throughout the flight time and is more comparable to the role of a pure Radar Controller [8–10]. Therefore, the focus of support tools is different (e.g. no consideration of coordination) and additional requirements relating to situational awareness must also be considered.

The SCO concept assumes a task shift in a way that the SC will take over task from Radar Controller (e.g. conflict solution) and from Planning Controller (e.g. coordination) whereas other tasks are automated (e.g. initial call). A major assumption is a higher coverage of Controller-Pilot-Data-Link-Communication (CPDLC) equipped aircraft [6] A wide range of different support tools in terms of design and functionality were proposed to support air traffic controllers as SC in the SCO concept presented in [6] and [7]. Support tools used in the validation campaign are summarised in Table 1. A short overview of each tool is given below. A detailed description can be found in [6, 7] and [11].

Attention Guidance Attention Guidance (AG) is a support tool that is supposed to enhances the situation awareness of ATCOs by promptly alerting them to critical flight events on the radar display. The tool is designed to provide three levels of visual alerts that communicate the urgency of events. Level 1 is indicated by a rectangular box around the flight label, Level 2 by a filled circle without a border, and Level 3, the highest alert, by a filled circle with a border. The activation of AG is sequential, starting with Level 1 and progressing to Level 2 and eventually Level 3 as the intensity of the identified event increases. For instance, if there is a conflict between two aircraft with a time to resolution less than five minutes, Level 1 is triggered on both aircraft labels. As the time to resolution decreases, the alert level progresses to Level 2 and eventually Level 3. The tool provides timely attention to important events and even recognizes ATCO interventions

Table 1. Overview of support tools and characteristics

Tool	can be switched on/off	configurable
Attention Guidance (AG)	No	No
Auto-Coordination	No	No
Boundary Arrival Task Manager (BATMAN)	No	Yes
Dynamic Heatmap (DHM)	Yes	Yes
Sonification	Yes	No
Trajectory Generation and Advisory Tool (TraGAT)	works on request only	No

by acknowledging through disabling AG. In essence, AG seamlessly integrates into the operational workflow with enhanced situation awareness and effective decision-making in fast-paced ATC environment. [7].

BATMAN The Boundary Arrival Task Manager should support ATCOs when handling aircraft to fulfil handover conditions. The GUI shows the flights listed on a timeline by their handover time to the adjacent sectors, and is intended to be an additional tool for the radar display. If handover constraints like flight levels or time separations are not met, BATMAN can give advisories and can check for possible conflicts and effect of these changes. [7] If all handover constraints are fulfilled it can initiate automatic sendover.

Sonification Sonification stands out as a transformative support tool in air traffic control, converting complex data into non-speech audio. This allows ATCOs to interpret and interact with critical information through auditory cues. As defined by Hermann [12], sonification is "the use of non-speech audio to convey information or perceptualize data," enabling ATCOs to process intricate information and patterns intuitively and efficiently.

Auto-Coordination The communication between Planning Controllers of adjacent sectors is automated to reduce workload. The requesting Planning Controller starts a coordination regarding a subject, e.g. like a flight level or a direct-to a certain waypoint, and sends it. The request is automatically checked for conflicts if it would be implemented. If so, the coordination is shown to the responsible controller to be responds with a rejection or an alternative value. If the request causes no issues, it is accepted by the controller working position (CWP) and all controllers are informed about.

Dynamic Heatmap Dynamic HeatMaps is an on-demand tool with the primary objective of highlighting the development of congestion or hotspots within the ATCOs area of responsibility. The tool conducts predictions of the traffic to construct a comprehensive outlook of future air traffic, leveraging flight plan information and forecasted aircraft positions within a specified time horizon adjustable by the ATCO. It results in specific aircraft positions in the future. However, as the future is uncertain, the exact location is not very useful for assessing which area of the airspace is occupied. To overcome this limitation, we implement a transformation of predicted future locations into density plots, which is achieved by extrapolating predicted future locations of aircraft to capture a broader influence of aircraft in neighbouring regions. DHMs are visualized as colour-coded maps and employ a spectrum of high to low-intensity colours. The high-intensity colour indicates areas of heightened congestion or hotspots, providing ATCOs with an intuitive representation of potential areas that require attention. Conversely, low-intensity colours signify open spaces within the airspace. As an on-demand tool, DHMs offer ATCOs to activate when needed with flexibility in choosing a time horizon. The colour coding and horizon options are configurable, allowing it to be integrated with various radar displays. [7].

TraGAT The main focus of Trajectory Generation and Advisory Tool lies on the generation of conflict free trajectories in dependence of a set of parameters describing the preferred trajectory type. These given specifications include sticking to a route network or generating short trajectories. For the automatic generation of a trajectory other flights and airspace restrictions can be considered when they are included in the trajectory request. As method for the trajectory generation Evolutionary Algorithms [13] in combination with Simulated Annealing are used.

The solution type is then defined by a set of weighted evaluation parameter describing criteria's like.

- avoiding conflicts
- prefer short trajectories,
- vertical structure and speeds of trajectory close to standard values,
- try to turn on official waypoints (beacons),
- similarity to original trajectory,
- usage of route network, punctuality and / or
- low number of speed changes.

Some of these evaluation functions do not work well together like preferring short trajectories in combination with using waypoints for turns. Those combinations should be avoided. The conflict avoidance is not only carried out for other flights but for restricted areas as well, as long as they are included in the trajectory request.

Restricted areas have restriction levels like avoid at all costs, avoid, prefer to avoid. As a result, only one trajectory is given back at the moment. For a fast solution the optimization can be restricted to a one-point solution created by a Simulated Annealing algorithm. This is a typical solution created by controllers supported by CWP's like ICAS of DFS.

1.3 Validation Aim and Hypotheses

The aim of the presented validation was divided into two parts. On the one hand the feasibility of the SCO concept and system as validated should be assessed with the following hypotheses:

1. The controller's workload remains the same when using the support tools and a maximum of 80% of the declared capacity.
2. The SC's situational awareness is comparable to that of an ATCO in an ATCO team
3. The SC's trust in the system is comparable to that of an ATCO in an ATCO team

On the other hand, the aim was to assess most suitable support tools to enable the SCO concept. Therefore, this exploratory research proposed a set of different support tools to the participating ATCOs to gather their feedback regarding design, perception and usability.

– Design as used in this paper describes the interface design including presentation of information and interaction with as well as the selection of addressed ATCO tasks and of presented information.
– Perception in the sense of this paper refers to the appearance and feeling that ATCOs convey to or through the tools.

2 Method

2.1 Sample

The sample consists of a total of seven Air Traffic Controller Officers (ATCOs). All of the seven participants were male with an average age of 30.86 years and an average experience of 8.57 years.

2.2 Experimental Design

The validation campaign took place in the DLR Institute of Flight Guidance's Air Traffic Validation Center in Braunschweig in autumn 2023. The simulation tool NARSIM was used within the Air Traffic Management and Operations Simulator (ATMOS) enabling real-time human-in-the-loop simulations.

The validation campaign was conducted with a 2×2 within subject design with the factor's workload (high and low) and workplace (normal vs. single). Furthermore, the normal working condition is named baseline and the single controller position is describes as solution scenario. Baseline scenarios are reference scenarios with two air traffic controllers (Radar Controller and Planning Controller) working together on the sector without additional means. Six ATCOs conducted the validation in teams of two executing the baseline scenarios together and the solution scenarios sequentially. One ATCO was supported by an additional domain expert not involved as participant. Therefore, this ATCO conducted the baseline scenarios always as Radar Controller. The baseline high scenarios were conducted twice by the three ATCO pairs with switched roles (Radar and Planning Controller), whereas the baseline low scenario was conducted once per team with one allocation to roles. Scenarios are summarised in Table 2.

The scenarios were based on a real traffic sample that were adjusted based on expert judgement in terms of sequence and amount of aircraft. Air traffic controllers for participation were acquired throughout Europe leading to the situation that they were asked to perform the validation runs on a foreign sector they have no endorsement for. This was considered by reducing the traffic amount of high and low scenarios to 80% respectively 40%, simplifying vertical boundaries of adjacent sectors and conducting a sector briefing prior to the validation runs (see Table 4).

The validation focused on the upper airspace (here: Flight Level 245 and above) and the Celle sector from the airspace above north-west Germany was chosen. A Reduced

Table 2. Scenarios of the validation

Scenario #	Scenario name	Number of ATCOs per run	Traffic amount
1	Baseline low	2	40% declared capacity (27 aircraft/hour)
2	Solution low	1	40% declared capacity (27 aircraft/hour)
3	Baseline high	2	80% declared capacity (55 aircraft/hour)
4	Solution high	1	80% declared capacity (55 aircraft/hour)

Vertical Separation Minimum (RVSM) equipment coverage of 100% was assumed resulting in a standard vertical separation minimum of 1000ft (no aircraft above FL 410). Lateral minima of 5 NM between aircraft and 2,5 NM to sector boundaries were applied. Furthermore, the scenarios were restricted to non-military traffic and without the influence of wind and weather to ensure a standard situation. As operational frame conditions no releases and agreements to adjacent sectors were assumed.

The validation runs were supported by one or two pseudo pilots handling aircraft inputs and one pseudo air traffic controller for all adjacent sectors handling coordination tasks. Each scenario included a predefined set of events as listed in Table 3. Since the development of traffic in the simulated scenarios is impossible to predict due to participants handling of the traffic some events were linked to a time-frame (5 min) rather than to individual aircraft.

Table 3. Amount and trigger of scenario events

Event	Time or aircraft related	Number of events (low/high scenarios)
R/F failure or wrong readback (Baseline) / CPDLC failure (Solution)	time	3/3
Pilot requests (RFL)	time	2/2
Sick passenger on board	aircraft	1/1
Differing exit flight level	aircraft	15/20
Release request	aircraft	2/2
Request from downstream sector (differing entry flight level or direct)	aircraft	4/3

(continued)

Table 3. (*continued*)

Event	Time or aircraft related	Number of events (low/high scenarios)
Request from upstream sector (differing exit flight level or direct (from upstream sector)	aircraft	3/3
Missing initial call	aircraft	1/1
Rate deviation	time	0/2
New aircraft	aircraft	0/1
(planned) Conflicts	aircraft	4/7

2.3 Set-Up

As CWP a radar display based on the ICAS CWP of the German air navigation service provider (DFS) with respect to user interface and functionality was used for all validation runs and working positions. However, for several parameters influencing the visual appearance of the CWP different settings were offered to the controller to allow a better personal experience and familiarity. For example, two colour-sets were offered which represents the two philosophies in presentation of radar display: negative presentation (bright head symbols and labels and dark background) and positive presentation (bright background and dark head symbols and labels). The baseline system included colour-coded flight status (incoming, in sector, leaving, passing by), adjustable velocity vector, optional trail dots, a flight-label resolution, a minimum distance measuring tool, a mouse-over trajectory indication and a conflict detection tool with a lead time of 7 min indicating separations of less than 10 NM. System inputs are done by mouse.

Any system inputs were conducted via mouse directly to the radar display. No (electronic) flight strip display was available (substituted by label functions) in any scenario. For the coordination process no telephone communication was possible, instead an electronic coordination interface within the radar display operated with mouse was provided for selected/required coordinations (exit/entry flight level, directs, release requests, request aircraft on frequency, new aircraft) for all scenarios.

2.4 Procedure

The validation per ATCO team last two and half days starting with a half day of introduction and training on the system. The following two days the validation runs and questionnaires were conducted. Table 4 summarizes the validation process applied to all participants. The sequence within baseline scenario (high, low) and within solution scenarios during day 2 and 3 varied between participant pairs to exclude trainings effects within results. The Baseline high scenario was validated twice with inverted roles of the both ATCOs and changed callsigns of the simulated aircrafts (not necessarily the third Baseline run).

Table 4. Validation procedure

Day	Validation process
1	• general briefing (project, validation aim, scenarios, pre-validation questionnaire) • sector briefing • introduction Baseline System • training Baseline System • introduction Single Controller Operation System • training Single Controller Operation System
2	• first Baseline run • first Solution run ATCO 1 • first Solution run ATCO 2 • second Baseline run
3	• second Solution run ATCO 1 • second Solution run ATCO 2 • third Baseline run • post-validation questionnaire

The duration of each validation run was one hour with 13 min for the ATCOs to set up radar display and get into the scenario and 47 min for actual validation run time.

During the validation the participants answered questionnaires prior the validation runs, after each validation run and at the end including standardized questionnaires as NASA-TLX, SATI and SASHA as well as tailor-made questions.

2.5   Tools in the Solution Scenarios

The system demonstrator used for solution scenarios was based upon baseline system including support tools described in Sect. 1.2 and elements of the proposed Single Controller Operations concept. For solution scenarios, a CPDLC coverage of 100% for single basic instructions (level, heading, turn, direct, rate, speed, frequency) was assumed. The participants were asked to use CPDLC as far as possible in solution scenarios, but had the possibility to use radio communication via headset. CPDLC-instructions were conducted via mouse input directly on the radar display. An impression of the SCO system is shown in Fig. 1

Attention Guidance AG is used in the validation for detected conflicts, aircraft approaching sector, CPDLC-Failure and sick passenger. Precondition is always that AG is triggered for considered events externally, e.g. a conflict detection tool or an CPDLC-initial call.

BATMAN The Boundary Arrival Task Manager is used in the validation as described in Sect. 1.2 and positioned on the right side of the radar display.

Sonification Sonification's implementation in ATC is intended to be both practical and adaptive, addressing a range of scenarios in the present validation with distinct auditory cues:

Fig. 1 Impression of SCO system with visible AG, BATMAN and DHM

1. CPDLC Login
2. BATMAN - Necessary Flight Level (FL) Change with Blocking Traffic
3. BATMAN - Necessary FL Change, Blocking Traffic Has Occurred
4. BATMAN - Necessary FL Change Without Blocking Traffic
5. Deviation from Assigned Rates
6. Notification of a Sick Passenger via CPDLC

Blocking traffic referring to a situation where one aircraft does not have a current conflict (infringement of minimal separation if ATCO does not intervene), but has to change the FL to comply with handover constraints with simultaneous crossing traffic between current FL and intended FL.

Auto-Coordination This tool can be interpreted as an enhanced functionality of electronic coordination used in baseline scenarios. There was no direct interaction with BATMAN, but if new handover conditions are set BATMANadapted to it.

Dynamic Heatmap Dynamic HeatMaps was used in the validation as described in Sect. 1.2 and positioned on the right side of the radar display.

TraGAT For the described validation two different possibilities were provided to apply the trajectory generation to a flight but only one predefined solution type (stick as close as possible to the original trajectory) was offered.

2.6 Data Gathering and Analysis

For the data analysis, standard questionnaires were used in the validation. For the measurement of workload, the Nasa-TLX [14] was selected. It is a well-known and established multidimensional assessment tool that rates perceived workload in order to assess a task, system, or team's effectiveness or other aspects of performance. It uses as 6-item scale and results in a combined NASA-TLX score from 0 to 100 (0 = workload insignificant; 100 = unable to perform) [14]. For measuring situation awareness, the SASHA-s questionnaire was selected. The SASHA-s assesses the level of situational awareness during the previous working period(s). In its short version it also uses 6 items rated on a scale from 0 to 6 (0 = "Never"; 6 = "Always"). The resulting score also ranges between 0 and 6 with an average of 3 [15]. In addition to workload and situation awareness the solution scenario system provided additional assistant systems to the participant that also needed to be evaluated in terms of trust. Therefore, the SHAPE Automation Trust Index (SATI) was applied. The SATI also contains 6 items on a score from 0 to 6 (0 = No Trust in the System; 6 = Trust in the System). The resulting score is also a value between 0 and 6 [15]. NASA-TLX, SASHA, and SATI provide detailed procedure to calculate their result scores.

In addition to the standard questionnaires, tailored questionnaires consisting of statements that had to be rated on a 5-point or 7-point rating scale were used. The tailor-made items are described in the result section. With regard to the proposed support tools, the ATCOs were asked to comment on their usability, understandability, usefulness, trustworthiness, simplicity and influence on safety.

Furthermore, during the debriefing individual feedback and comments were collected. They were allocated to a topic (scenario, frame condition, system (part)), to concerned support tools or baseline and to a type (bugs, questions, relevant for analysis, suggestions for improvements, notes for improved validation procedure). All feedback allocationed toone support tool were grouped to identify same or equal comments.

3 Results

3.1 General Results Regarding SCO Concept

Participants were asked to assess their average experienced traffic during their last operating month. Results are shown in Fig. 2. The validated scenarios can be allocated to the two bars indicating 21–30 and 41–50 aircraft per hour.

Results shown in the following are focused on participants feedback regarding design and perception. The focus is divided into two parts: the overall SCO concept on the one hand and the individual support tools on the other hand. Furthermore, the gathered individual feedback during debriefings sometimes points towards single functionalities of one support tool.

As all described support tools and frame conditions were validated together, the overall assessment of ATCOs regarding workload (see Fig. 3), system trust (see Fig. 4) and situational awareness (see Fig. 5) was crucial to determine system perception and feasibility of the overall SCO concept.

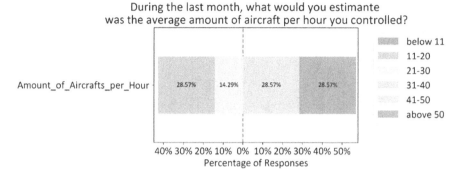

Fig. 2 Subjective assessment of average traffic experienced during last (operating) month

In both traffic conditions the participants rated their workload higher in the solution scenarios than in the baseline scenarios. However, the mean value deviation is small (5.54 and 6.81). Furthermore, as per concept and validation setup, in the solution scenarios the same traffic amount was worked by one ATCO instead of two in the baseline scenarios.

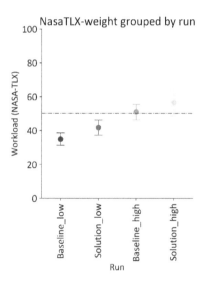

Fig. 3 NASA-TLX per scenario

For automation trust (see Fig. 4) and situational awareness (see Fig. 5) the highest value is given for baseline low scenario (3.43 respectively 5.57) with a distinct distance to all other scenarios. This indicates a decrease in situational awareness and trust with increasing traffic, but also in comparison with SCO system. Again, it has to be considered that solution scenarios were conducted by one single ATCO. Besides, the difference between baseline high and solution high scenarios is marginal. Therefore, a positive

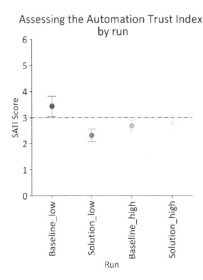

Fig. 4 SATI per scenario

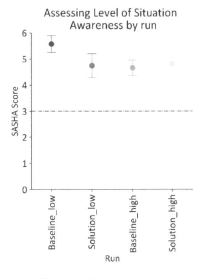

Fig. 5 SASHA per scenario

impact of the system (resulting from support tools) can be concluded for these two parameters for high traffic amount.

Individual feedback confirmed "generally good support from the tools", especially for low traffic scenarios. But participants consider them not yet conceivable for SCO. All ATCOs mentioned CPDLC frame condition as main enabler for SCO although only basic instructions were possible. Another feedback expressed the solution system to be too extensive and some support tools should be rejected.

3.2 Tools

For a more detailed analysis a closer look to the assessment of the support tools is required. Therefore, six tailored questions were asked after each solution scenario run.

In the following subsections, only the results of validation runs with high traffic amount are depicted in figures, as the results do not deviate substantially between high and low scenario. The scale presented to the participants to rate the tools with respect to the question is shown in Fig. 6 to enhance readability of the following figures.

The results presented in Figs. 7, 8, 9, 10, 11 and 12 are summarised subjective answers of all participants to the tailored questions per support tool following the rating scale. In the following subsection they will be described first. Thereafter, if applicable, summaries from individual feedback are given followed by a short conclusion.

Attention Guidance AG tools was used extensively by ATCOs (see Fig. 7). Green bars on right side of the dotted line indicate positive perception with increasing agreement related to the respective question, orange bars on the left side negative perception. This applies to all of the following figures. User also express high levels of trust in the functionality as well as usefulness in the information provided by the system. Majoritarian,

Fig. 6. Rating Scale

they deemed AG to work as expected, support them to work safely and provide the information in an easy to understand manner.

Individual feedback confirmed participants liked the visualization of information on the main radar screen and deemed it useful for highlighting events. They propose additional events to use AG for.

Overall, the AG tool was perceived useful in supporting ATCO tasks as it helped situation awareness and build trust in the tool.

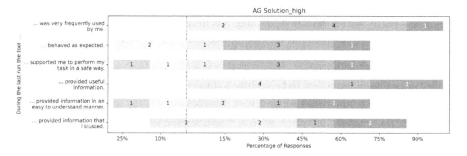

Fig. 7. Results tailormade questions Attention Guidance

BATMAN This tool was less used by the ATCOs in the runs, which can be traced back partly to missing trust, unexpected behaviour and/or difficult to understand presentation (see Fig. 8). The latter might be a result of the presentation on an additional screen beside the radar screen, moved the tool out of the visual focus.

One core functionality of BATMAN is based on conflict detection, which did not always work properly (based on additional ATCO feedback) for the use to detect potential conflicts when applying changes to follow sendover conditions. This can serve as an explanation for less trust. Nevertheless, ATCO highlighted the two BATMAN functionalities to automatic sendover aircraft to next sector and to check for potential conflicts if intending to climb or descent an aircraft to its exit flight level positively. The first mentioned were assessed to be implemented well ("Auto-Sendover is good, takes a lot of work off your hands").

To conclude, main drawbacks of BATMAN are the presentation of information and that crucial detection of possible conflicts did not work properly. In addition, the summarising of different functionalities in one tool might be unnecessary or even obstructive.

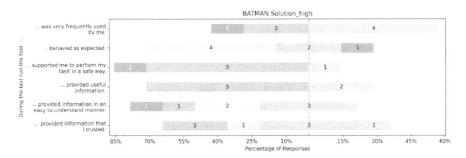

Fig. 8. Results tailormade questions Boundary Arrival Task Manager

Sonification The tool was assessed to behave as expected, but to be neither supportive, nor easy to understand (see Fig. 9).

Based on ATCOs' individual feedback both aspects can be traced back to missing training and partly wrong selection of situations to use Sonification for, which in turn increased workload ("Sonification very disruptive and generates additional workload").

Furthermore, the additional ATCO feedback provided a nuanced understanding of the operational application of Sonification, highlighting the delicate balance between auditory information provision and cognitive load management.

Sonification is a non-visual support tool. Besides the use for alerts this is the first time an auditory support tools were used in an air traffic control validation. Therefore, it was implemented to a wide variety of situations (see Sect. 2.5). Only the selected situation CPDLC-Login in combination with AG was assessed to be supportive.

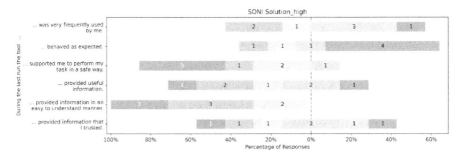

Fig. 9. Results tailormade questions Sonification

Auto-coordination Auto-Coordination was widely used by participants and assessed to behave as expected. Feedback regarding, the way of presentation, trust and support to work safe was divers (see Fig. 10).

According to individual feedback, the controllers had less workload, due to the automatic response of the system in non-conflict-requests. But, due to the quick response and the visualization only in a dialog window, the initiator of the coordination could miss the response.

The information provided by Auto-Coordination tool was difficult to grasp leading to additional workload although the functionality was assessed useful This can be identified as a design issue to be solved.

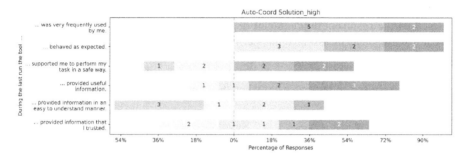

Fig. 10. Results tailormade questions Auto-Coordination

Dynamic Heatmap The participants feedback from the questionnaires for the DHM tool can be categorized into two parts. The first part represented the intended features and functioning of the tool. For this part, the user deemed the information provided by DHM as expected, which they can trust (Fig. 11). Additionally, the information visualization is also considered easy to understand and intuitive. The second part of the feedback corresponds to the intended use in performing ATCO tasks. In this part, users could not correlate the information, resulting in the tool not being used frequently and information needed to be more supportive of ATCO tasks.

Individual feedback confirmed that the selection of presented information did not support participants, whereas they liked the presentation itself.

A direct use of the DHM by ATCOs based on sector occupation should be discarded for SCO.

TraGAT Participants were not convinced that this tool would be helpful and did not use it (see Fig. 12).

Individual feedback confirms that partly participants did not use the tool at all as it is "difficult to access". Feedback from participants using TraGAT shows that they lack an understanding of how the tool works ("does the system knows why I like to calculate a new trajectory?")

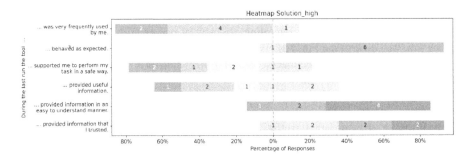

Fig. 11. Results tailormade questions Dynamic Heatmap

Based on the relatively high amount of neutral responses to all questions but the frequency of use, it can be assumed that partly it was not intuitive enough or not clear at all to the ATCOs how to activate or use the tool. Furthermore, the solution type "stick as close as possible to the original trajectory" was predefined for TraGAT. In turn, the controllers did not see an improvement when they applied this functionality tentatively to a conflict-free trajectory.

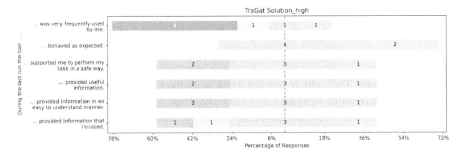

Fig. 12. Results tailormade questions Trajectory Generation and Advisory Tool

4   Discussion

Main aim of the presented validation was a proof-of-concept and an identification of most-promising support tools and functions to enable SCO. The results are sufficient to use for improvements and refinement of the concept and the system. Especially the diverse use of tools showed which design concepts support ATCOs in an SCO environment. One major result of this validation is that workload is increased due to an oversize of support tools. Debriefing feedback partly referred to single functionalities of tools.

Therefore, rejection of some support tools (e.g. Heatmap) and focus of smaller functionalities (e.g. auto-sendover from BATMAN) should be considered for future research in support tools for SCO.

Most promising support tools is Attention Guidance which showed required support for an SC to quickly identify important tasks and to be guided to essential information. Improvements should be strived for Auto-Coordination, Sonification and TraGAT.

The design of the presentation for Auto-Coordination was too difficult to grasp. As coordination will stay an important task for SC this led to higher workload.

In retrospect, the decision to offer only the solution type "stick as close as possible to the original trajectory" for TraGAT was not the best selection for the introduction of such a tool. An automatic solution proposal should be show upon conflict detection.

The cognitive capacity of ATCOs, especially in high-stress, high-stakes environments, is a premium resource. Sonification cues that are overly protracted or complex not only risk cognitive overload but also dilute the urgency and clarity of the information conveyed. The operational environment of ATC is a mosaic of auditory and visual stimuli. In such a context, the clarity and distinctiveness of Sonification cues are paramount to ensure that they cut through the ambient noise and deliver clear, unambiguous signals. The Sonification system must be finely attuned to the operational tempo and context of ATC. Sounds that induce undue stress or alarm can be counterproductive, distorting the situational awareness that Sonification seeks to enhance. The synergy between auditory and visual information streams is a cornerstone of effective ATC operations. Sonification cues must complement, not compete with, visual cues, ensuring a harmonious sensory interplay. Participants highlighted the positive effect of the concurrence of Attention Guidance and Sonification.

The questionnaires used for assessment are capable to measure subjective perception, what was intended to gather ATCOs feedback which tools fits best for enabling SCO. The comparison between tools allows conclusions about which design approaches works best for SCO support tools, even if the presented information is assessed as not required or not trustworthy. The overarching standard questionnaires ensure reproduction of the influence of the complete proposed SCO system on core parameters for ATC (workload, situational awareness and trust), which needs to be within acceptable range to judge the concept and system feasible.

The influence of trainings effects was minimized as far as possible by introducing baseline and solution system to the participants at the first day and change of sequence of low and high runs between participants.

As the main interface system is based on one operational system of the German ANSP DFS, the sector used for validation from EUROCONTROL and ATCOs participated from Austria and Germany (different operational system, no endorsement for the validated sector) the results can be seen as transferable to other ANSPs (sectors, ATCOs, systems). The validation took place in an en-route sector of upper airspace (here: FL > 245). Accordingly, the results cannot necessarily be transferred to other air traffic control sectors.

5 Conclusion and Next Steps

The present validation results show that the SCO concept is basically usable and that situational awareness and system trust of ATCOs in SCO is comparable to that of ATCOs in teams of Radar and Planning Controller with same traffic load (80 percent declared capacity). However, the workload is assessed to increase slightly. This can be traced back to the concrete support tools and their design as used in the validation.

The tailored questionnaires showed feasibility to identify diverse causes for non-acceptance or non-usability of ATCO support tools for the use in an SCO environment. From the questionnaires and the debriefing feedback it can be concluded that to be supportive a support tool for SCO requires:

1. an easy access design,
2. an understandable behaviour,
3. a suitable selection of supported task/situation,
4. a suitable selection of information presented,
5. a suitable design of the presentation of the information,
6. a proof of its functionality in operation

Except the last point these are all design related parameters. If one of the above conditions is not met the support tool is used less and trusted less. For example, TraGAT lacks an easy access design and Heatmap a suitable selection of supported task. In the overall view the design for SCO support tools should at best be such that information are presented directly on main radar display with as less text as possible. Furthermore, design of the presentation of the information which leads to a highlighting of new information were assessed as the most supportive and were even requested for support tools which did not had a comparable feature.

Future validation (and possible operational implementation) should put more emphasis on training of the new system. In general, the number of new support tools and functionalities made available to ATCOs must be reduced. As there is no use case for Heatmap it should be rejected for a future validation for direct use by the ATCO. The design of BATMAN would have to be revisited and a selection of the most supportive functionalities should be conducted. For Auto-Coordination a requirement was identified to better visualise and include it on main radar display the presented information. The Attention Guidance tool was assessed as best support tool for SCO. There are possibilities for improvements via connection with an eye tracking system or extension to more situations. The scientific development and integration of support tools for SCO within ATC systems are profoundly intricate endeavours. The feedback from ATCOs underscores the necessity for a user-centric design philosophy. For Sonification this philosophy advocates for sound cues that are clear, concise, contextually relevant, and cognitively considerate. Future research should pivot towards the development of personalized soundscapes, exploring the potential of spatial audio to enrich situational awareness without contributing to sensory overload. Main drawback of TraGAT was the access and restricted usability. Meanwhile, a set of solution types is offered which can be easily tested by controllers to familiarize with the tool. Furthermore, an automatic solution possibility presentation is in development.

Acknowledgments. This work is funded by DLR's internal project DIAL [16]. First versions of the herein presented tools BATMAN and Heatmap were developed under SESAR project PJ.33 FALCO. The PJ.33 FALCO Project has received funding from the SESAR Joint Undertaking under the European Union's Horizon 2020 research and innovation program under grant agreement No 101017479.

Disclosure of Interests. The authors have no competing interests to declare that are relevant to the content of this article.

References

1. EUROCONTROL Homepage: PRR 2022 Performance Review Reporthttps://www.eurocontrol.int/sites/default/files/2023-06/eurocontrol-prr-2022.pdf. Accessed 20 Jan 2024
2. EUROCONTROL Homepage: ATM Cost-Effectiveness (ACE) 2019 Benchmarking Report with Special Focus on COVID-19 Impacts in 2020, eurocontrol-ace-2019-benchmarking-report-special-focus-covid-19-impact-2020.pdf. Accessed 20 Jan 2024
3. EUROCONTROL, Network Manager: Annual Report 2021, p. 6, (2022). https://www.eurocontrol.int/publication/network-manager-annual-report-2021
4. DFS Deutsche Flugsicherung GmbH, Luftverkehr in Deutschland. Mobilitaetsbericht 2022, p. 17, (2023). https://www.dfs.de/homepage/de/medien/publikationen/
5. Fihel, A., Okolski, M.: Demographic change and challenge. In: Social and economic development in central and Eastern Europe, pp. 101–132 (2019)
6. Gerdes, I., Jameel, M., Hunger, R., Christoffels, L., Gürlük, H.: The automation evolves: Concept for a highly automated controller working position. In: 33nd Congress of the International Council of the Aeronautical Sciences (ICAS), Stockholm (2022)
7. Jameel, M., Tyburzy, L., Gerdes, I., Pick, A., Hunger, R., Christoffels, L.: Enabling digital air traffic controller assistant through human-autonomy teaming design. In: IEEE/AIAA 42nd Digital Avionics Systems Conference (DASC), pp. 1–9, Barcelona, Spain (2023). https://doi.org/10.1109/DASC58513.2023.10311220
8. Duong, V., Gawinowski, G., Nicolaon, J., Smith, D.: Sector-less Air Traffic Management. In: Proceedings of the 4 USA/Europe Air Traffic Management R & D Seminar (2001)
9. Volf, P.:Comparison of the flight centric and conventional air traffic control. In: 2019 Integrated Communications, Navigation and Surveillance Conference (ICNS), pp. 1–10. Herndon, VA, USA, (2019). https://doi.org/10.1109/ICNSURV.2019.8735109
10. Finck, T., Kluenker, C.S., Martins, A.: Validation of the flight centric ATC concept using Hungarian airspace as an example. In: AIAA AVIATION 2023 Forum (2023)
11. Abdellaoui, R., Finke, M., Pick, A., Ahrenhold, N.: Supporting air traffic controllers in handling sector specific tasks, enabled by the use of the Boundary Arrival Task Manager. In: 42nd IEEE/AIAA Digital Avionics Systems Conference, DASC, Barcelona (2023). ISBN 979–835033357–2. ISSN 2155–7195
12. Hermann, T., Hunt, A., Neuhoff, J.G.: The Sonification Handbook. Logos Verlag, Berlin (2011)
13. Gerdes, I., Klawonn, F., Kruse, R.: Evolutionäre Algorithmen. Vieweg, Wiesbaden (2004)
14. Hart, S.G., Staveland, L.E.: Development of NASA-TLX (Task Load Index): Results of empirical and theoretical research. Human mental workload 1, 139–183 (1988)
15. Skybrary Homepage, EUROCONTROL, FAA.: A Human Performance Standard of Excellence (2015). www.skybrary.aero
16. DIAL (Individual and Automated Air Transport) Homepage. http://dial.dlr.de. Accessed 23 Jan 2024

Gaze Distribution of an Observer While Imagining Wearing Clothing Portrayed in an Advertisement and Predicting the Impression on Others

Fuyuko Iwasaki, Michiko Inoue, and Masashi Nishiyama[✉][ORCID]

Graduate School of Engineering, Tottori University, 101 Minami 4-chome, Koyama-cho, Tottori 680-8550, Japan
nishiyama@tottori-u.ac.jp

Abstract. Observers using image-sharing social networking services often imagine wearing the clothing portrayed in advertising images and predict the impression on others. It is likely that an observer's gaze is drawn to specific body parts of the person shown wearing the clothes, and as such, the specific body parts that are focused on by the observer could provide cues regarding impression prediction. Although previous analytical studies have investigated the role of gaze distribution in evaluating the subject attractiveness, no studies have examined the gaze of observers while they imagined wearing clothes and predicted the impression on others. In this paper, we measured the gaze distribution while observers imagined wearing a portrayed subject's clothing and predicted the impression on others. We further investigated the degree to which an observer's gaze was focused on each subject's body part according to the characteristics of the gaze distribution. The experimental results showed that, in the case of an image taken from head to toe, the observer's gaze tended to be focused most on the subject's chest, followed by the head. In the case of images taken with the head occluded, the observer's gaze tended to focus most on the subject's chest, followed by the stomach.

Keywords: Gaze distribution · Impression prediction · Imagining wearing clothing · Advertising images

1 Introduction

In recent years, image-sharing social networking services (SNSs) have become a common platform for advertising and purchasing clothing [12,13]. As a result, SNS feeds often show many images of people wearing fashionably coordinated clothing. Here, we refer to the people in the images as subjects. The subjects in SNS images are often photographed from head to toe, or their heads are hidden. Here, a 'whole-body image' refers to an image in which a subject is visible from head to toe, while a 'head-occluded image' shows a subject with their head hidden.

D. Harris and W.-C. Li (Eds.): HCII 2024, LNAI 14693, pp. 34–47, 2024.
https://doi.org/10.1007/978-3-031-60731-8_3

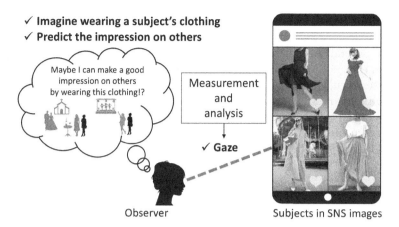

Fig. 1. We investigated gaze distribution by measuring and analyzing the female observer's gaze. The observer looks at the subject in the image, imagines wearing the subject's clothing, and predicts whether she would make a good impression on others.

People using image-sharing SNSs subjectively predict whether they would make a good impression on others in a certain outfit by imagining themselves wearing the portrayed subject's clothing [3,5,9]. This is the case for both whole-body and head-occluded images. In the following, we refer to people who use image-sharing SNSs as observers. When observers who are using SNSs make a prediction about the impression on others that a certain outfit would produce, they look directly at the subject's body, as shown in Fig. 1. While imagining wearing the subject's clothing, it is likely that the observer's gaze is drawn to the subject's body parts, which could provide cues about the impression on others. If we could identify the body parts that are the focus of the observer's gaze, we might be able to determine which body parts provide helpful information when making decisions about purchasing clothing. This information could be applied to the field of clothing marketing.

In this study, we investigated the gaze of female observers who were asked to imagine wearing a subject's clothing and to predict the impression on others. Although the analysis conditions differed from those in our present research, several previous studies investigated the subject body parts that were most frequently gazed at by observers who were asked to predict the degree to which others would find the subject attractive. For example, Gervais et al. [6] analyzed gaze characteristics for subjects with different body shapes in a whole-body image. Furthermore, Cornelissen et al. [4] examined gaze characteristics for naked subjects in a head-occluded image. However, these studies [4,6] did not consider the gaze of observers asked to imagine wearing a subject's clothing and to predict the impression on others.

In this paper, we attempted to determine which body parts in a whole-body image or a head-occluded image were the focus of a female observer who was asked to imagine wearing the portrayed subject's clothing and to predict the impression on others. First, we measured the gaze distribution while observers imagined wearing a portrayed subject's clothing and predicted the impression on others. Second, we investigated the degree to which an observer's gaze was focused on each subject's body part. We confirmed the following results in subjective assessments involving 24 female observers. The female observer's gaze tended to be focused most on the subject's chest, followed by the head, in the case of an image taken from head to toe. In contrast, the female observer's gaze tended to focus most on the subject's chest, followed by the stomach, in the case of images taken with the head occluded.

2   Hypothesis

In our subjective assessments, to investigate the degree to which the observer's gaze was focused on each subject's body part, we asked the female observer to imagine wearing the portrayed subject's clothing and to predict the impression on others. No existing analytical studies have conducted subjective assessments for this purpose, as described in Sect. 1. In our subjective assessments, we generated the following hypotheses based on the previous studies [4, 6].

H1: When a female observer imagines wearing a subject's clothing in a *whole-body* image and predicts the impression on others, the observer's gaze will be most focused on the subject's *head*.

H2: When a female observer imagines wearing a subject's clothing in a *head-occluded* image and predicts the impression on others, the observer's gaze will be most focused on the subject's *stomach*.

We explain the detail of the previous study [6] that we referred to when generating hypothesis H1. This previous study analyzed the observer's gaze when predicting the appearance attractiveness of the subject's body shape in a whole-body image. They used whole-body images of women wearing the same white tank top and blue jeans and conducted subjective assessments with male and female observers in this previous study. They reported that the observer's gaze was more focused on the chest and waist than the face when the observers were asked an appearance-focused question (compared to a personality-focused question). However, through the experimental results in [6], they also reported that the dwell time on the face is longer than that on the chest and waist. From these results, we generated hypothesis H1, that the gaze is drawn to the head.

Next, we explain the detail of the previous study [4] that we referred to when generating hypothesis H2. This previous study analyzed the observer's gaze when predicting the physical attractiveness of a naked subject in a head-occluded image. They used head-occluded images of naked women with mosaicing faces and conducted subjective assessments with male and female observers in this previous study. They reported that the observer's gaze was more focused on the upper abdomen and chest than the pelvic and hip when the observers were asked an attractiveness question. Furthermore, the experimental results in [4] demonstrated that female observers did not focus their gaze on the chest as much as male observers. From these results, we generated hypothesis H2, that the gaze focuses on the stomach.

3   Gaze Measurement from Observers

3.1   Stimulus Image

Figure 2 shows a part of the stimulus images used in our experiment. In the following, we denote a set of whole-body images as $\mathcal{S}_w$ and a set of head-occluded images as $\mathcal{S}_h$. The number of subjects in each stimulus image was set to 1. The total number of stimulus images per observer was 104, with 52 whole-body images and 52 head-occluded images. All subjects in stimulus images were female. To generate a head-occluded image, an area above the tip line of a chin was cropped from a whole-body image. We used only the subject's standing posture, where her clothes and face were visible. No restrictions were placed on the position and orientation of the limbs of subjects to ensure that the postures of subjects were aligned. We selected the subject's facial expressions that did not give a negative impression but gave a positive or neutral impression. The size of whole body images was resized to 900 pixels in height and 382±82 pixels in width while maintaining the aspect ratio. The size of head-occluded images was 757±9 pixels in height and 382±82 pixels in width. These stimulus images were downloaded from the photo material site[1].

Next, we describe how to select stimulus images for our experiments. We assumed a formal setting, such as a wedding or a concert, and a casual setting, such as an outdoor festival or a theme park, as scenes in which observers predict impressions on others. To consider these scenes, we prepared the same number of stimulus images for both formal and casual clothing. We also prepared the same number of stimulus images with backgrounds taken outdoors and indoors.

3.2   Observers

We recruited 24 observers (21.5±1.3 years old, university students, Japanese ethnicity). All observers were female. In the following, the female observer is denoted as o, and a set of the observers is denoted as $\mathcal{O}$.

We asked a female observer $o \in \mathcal{O}$ the following question when she viewed the subject in the stimulus image.

Q: When you imagine yourself wearing the subject's clothes, do you feel that the people around you will have a good impression of you?

Each observer responded on a 4-point scale (4: yes, 3: likely yes, 2: likely no, 1: no). Before performing our subjective assessments, we asked an observer to imagine a situation in which they would use image-sharing SNSs to purchase clothing that would make a good impression on others. We thoroughly explained the disadvantages of gaze measurement to the participants and obtained their consent on a form.

---

[1] https://www.photo-ac.com/.

(a) Whole-body images

(b) Head-occluded images

Fig. 2. A part of the stimulus images of $\mathcal{S}_w, \mathcal{S}_h$ used in our experiment.

3.3 Setting

Figure 3 shows our experimental setting. A 24-inch display (AOC G2460PF, 1920 × 1080 pixel resolution) was used to show the stimulus images. A gazepoint GP3 HD, a stationary eye-tracker, was used to measure the gaze of female observers. This eye-tracker was placed in front of the display. An observer was seated with her face facing the display screen. The distance from her face to the display screen was kept at 65 cm. The height of the observer's eyes varied among individuals, ranging from 110 cm to 120 cm from the floor. Observers were instructed to keep their faces as still as possible when measuring gaze. The sampling rate of the eye-tracker was set to 150 Hz. We performed resampling using linear interpolation at 50 Hz to ensure that the time intervals were equally aligned because the

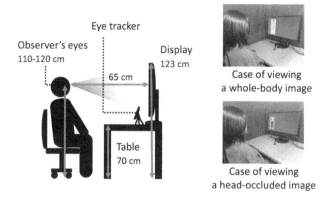

Fig. 3. Setting for gaze measurement.

time interval of the measured gaze was not constant due to the eye-tracker's specifications.

3.4 Procedure

We describe the procedure for measuring the female observer's gaze.

P_1: One observer o was randomly selected from a set of observers $\mathcal{O}$.

P_2: The question content and measurement procedure were explained to an observer o.

P_3: The start image was shown on the display for two seconds.

P_4: One stimulus image was randomly selected from a set of whole-body images $\mathcal{S}_w$ or a set of head-occluded images $\mathcal{S}_h$ and then shown on the display for three seconds without overlap. The observer's gaze was measured during this period.

P_5: The end image was shown on the display for two seconds. An observer answered the question Q described in Sect. 3.2.

P_6: The procedure from P_3 to P_5 was repeated until all stimulus images in $\mathcal{S}_w$ and $\mathcal{S}_h$ were selected.

P_7: The procedure from P_1 to P_6 was repeated until all observers in $\mathcal{O}$ were selected.

Examples of images shown on the display in procedures from P_3 to P_5 are shown in Fig. 4(a) for a whole-body image and Fig. 4(b) for a head-occluded image. When showing a stimulus image on the display, we need to be aware of center bias [1], which fixes the observer's gaze at the center of the display at the initial time. We asked an observer to look at the center of a randomly placed white cross in the start image of procedure P_3 to avoid center bias. In procedure P_4, a stimulus image was randomly placed to avoid overlapping the position of a white cross in the start image with the position of a subject in an image.

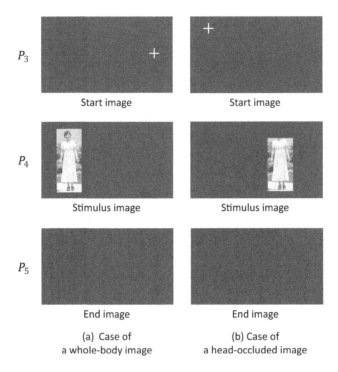

P_3 Start image   Start image

P_4 Stimulus image   Stimulus image

P_5 End image   End image

(a) Case of
a whole-body image

(b) Case of
a head-occluded image

Fig. 4. Examples of the images shown on the display when measuring gaze.

4 Gaze Analysis

4.1 Overview

When analyzing the observer's gaze, we need to notice that the pixels representing the body parts differ among the stimulus images. The subject's body parts
are not aligned in the stimulus images, as described in Sect. 3.1. For example, a
subject placed body parts with both hands downward, one hand on the waist,
both feet shoulder-width apart, or both knees crossed. When using a heatmap
representation on stimulus images for gaze analysis, such as [7,10,11], it is not
easy to compare the measured gaze pixels among stimulus images directly.

For gaze analysis, we used the body-part attention probability analysis [8],
which indicates how likely it was that the observer's gaze was focused on each
subject body part. This probability was calculated based on the distance between
a pixel representing each subject body part and a pixel where the observer's gaze
was measured. We describe the body parts used in gaze analysis in Sect. 4.2, and
the method for calculating the body-part attention probability in Sect. 4.3.

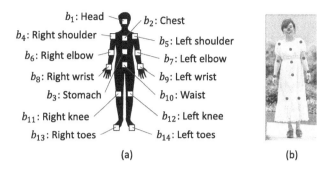

Fig. 5. Body parts for gaze analysis.

4.2 Body Parts for Gaze Analysis

Figure 5 shows the body parts used in gaze analysis. The body parts are defined as head b_1, chest b_2, stomach b_3, right shoulder b_4, left shoulder b_5, right elbow b_6, left elbow b_7, right wrist b_8, left wrist b_9, waist b_{10}, right knee b_{11}, left knee b_{12}, right toes b_{13}, and left toes b_{14}. When selecting the body parts for gaze analysis, we did not use those close to other body parts, such as fingers. Instead, we used the body parts that were distant from each other among the body parts. In the case of a whole-body image, we denote a body part b_w, and a set $\mathcal{B}_w = \{b_1, b_2, \cdots, b_{14}\}$ consisting of 14 body parts. In the case of a head-occluded image, we denote a body part b_h, and a set $\mathcal{B}_h = \{b_2, \cdots, b_{14}\}$ consisting of 13 body parts excluding the head b_1.

When perfoming gaze analysis, we detected the head position (b_1) and the 12 body part positions ($b_4, \cdots, b_{14}$) using OpenPose [2]. The head b_1 is indicated by the nose position of OpenPose. Note that this detector do not define body parts for chest b_2 and stomach b_3. Let b_2 be the 1:4 endpoint of the line segment connecting the midpoint of the line segment connecting the right shoulder b_4 and the left shoulder b_5 to the waist b_{10}. Let b_3 be the midpoint of the line segment connecting the chest b_2 and the waist b_{10}. In the following, we denote a pixel i_{b_w} representing a body part b_w detected in a whole-body image, and a pixel i_{b_h} representing a body part b_h detected in a head-occluded image.

4.3 Body-Part Attention Probability

In the case of a whole-body image, we calculate the body-part attention probability using [8] for body part b_w of Sect. 4.2. In the following, one whole-body image is denoted as $\mathcal{I}_w$ that is an element of a set of whole-body images $\mathcal{S}_w$. Suppose a pixel i_w is an element of $\mathcal{I}_w$. When a female observer $o \in \mathcal{O}$ views a whole-body image $\mathcal{I}_w$, the body-part attention probability $p(b_w | o, \mathcal{I}_w)$ represents that her gaze is focused on a body part b_w in the image. This probability is calculated as follows:

$$p(b_w|o, \mathcal{I}_w) = \sum_{i_w \in \mathcal{I}_w} \mathcal{N}(i_w|i_{b_w}, \Sigma)p(i_w|o, \mathcal{I}_w). \tag{1}$$

Note that this equation satisfies as follows:

$$\sum_{b_w \in \mathcal{B}_w} p(b_w|o, \mathcal{I}_w) = 1. \tag{2}$$

The first term $\mathcal{N}(i_w|i_{b_w}, \Sigma)$ of Equation (1) is a bivariate normal distribution, where a mean is i_{b_w} and a covariance matrix is $\Sigma = \text{diag}(\sigma^2, \sigma^2)$. The closer the distance from a pixel i_w to a pixel i_{b_w} of a body part b_w, the higher the value of $\mathcal{N}(i_w|i_{b_w}, \Sigma)$ is recorded. The second term $p(i_w|o, \mathcal{I}_w)$ of Equation (1) refers to the probability that the gaze of an observer o is focused at a pixel i_w that consists of a whole body image $\mathcal{I}_w$. The probability $p(i_w|o, \mathcal{I}_w)$ is calculated as follows:

$$p(i_w|o, \mathcal{I}_w) = \frac{1}{n(\mathcal{T})} \sum_{t \in \mathcal{T}} \mathcal{N}(i_w|i_g(t), \Sigma), \tag{3}$$

where $i_g(t)$ is a pixel representing the gaze measured from an observer o at time t, $\mathcal{T}$ is a set of times when the gaze was measured, and $n(\ )$ is a function that returns the number of elements in a set.

Next, in the case of a head-occluded image, we calculate the body-part attention probability using [8] for body part b_h of Sect. 4.2. In the following, one head-occluded image is denoted as $\mathcal{I}_h$ that is an element of a set of head-occluded images $\mathcal{S}_w$. Suppose a pixel i_h is an element of $\mathcal{I}_h$. The body-part attention probability for a head-occluded image is calculated as follows:

$$p(b_h|o, \mathcal{I}_h) = \sum_{i_h \in \mathcal{I}_h} \mathcal{N}(i_h|i_{b_h}, \Sigma)p(i_h|o, \mathcal{I}_h), \tag{4}$$

where the first and second terms of this equation are calculated in the same way as for a whole-body image.

5   Experiments

5.1   Subjective Assessments on Hypothesis H1 and Hypothesis H2

Protocol We explain the case of a whole-body image for the experiment on hypothesis H1 described in Sect. 2. Using a set of observers $\mathcal{O}$ and a set of whole-body images $\mathcal{S}_w$, we marginalized the body-part attention probability $p(b_w|o, \mathcal{I}_w)$ defined in Equation (1), and calculated the marginalized probability $p(b_w)$ for whole-body images as follows:

$$p(b_w) = \frac{1}{n(\mathcal{O})n(\mathcal{S}_w)} \sum_{o \in \mathcal{O}} \sum_{\mathcal{I}_w \in \mathcal{S}_w} p(b_w|o, \mathcal{I}_w), \tag{5}$$

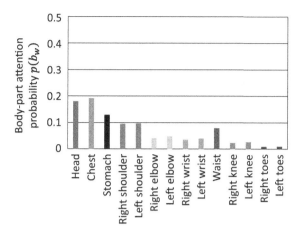

Fig. 6. Body-part attention probability $p(b_w)$ for a set of whole-body images $\mathcal{S}_w$.

where we set $n(\mathcal{O}) = 24$, $n(\mathcal{S}_w) = 52$.

Next, we explain the case of a head-occluded image for the experiment on hypothesis H2. Using a set of head-occluded images $\mathcal{S}_h$, we marginalized the body-part attention probability $p(b_h|o, \mathcal{I}_h)$ defined in Equation (4), and calculated the marginalized probability $p(b_h)$ for head-occluded images as follows:

$$p(b_h) = \frac{1}{n(\mathcal{O})n(\mathcal{S}_h)} \sum_{o \in \mathcal{O}} \sum_{\mathcal{I}_h \in \mathcal{S}_h} p(b_h|o, \mathcal{I}_h), \qquad (6)$$

where we set $n(\mathcal{O}) = 24$, $n(\mathcal{S}_h) = 52$.

Results for Hypothesis H1 Figure 6 shows a bar graph representation of the body-part attention probability $p(b_w)$ of Equation (5) for the case of a whole-body image. The horizontal axis shows the body part indicated in Fig. 5, and the vertical axis indicates the value of $p(b_w)$. The higher the probability of a certain body part, the more the gaze tended to be focused on that body part. The experimental results showed that the chest was the body part with the highest $p(b_w)$, and the head was the body part with the next highest $p(b_w)$. The difference between these probabilities was 0.01, indicating that the gaze probability was similar between the head and the chest. Hypothesis H1 stated that the female observer's gaze would be most focused on the subject's head, but this did not hold. Instead, in the case of full-body images, the female observer's gaze tended to focus most on the chest, followed by the head.

Results for Hypothesis H2 Figure 7 shows a bar graph representation of the body-part attention probability $p(b_h)$ of Equation (6) for the case of a head-occluded image. The experimental results showed that the chest was the body part with the highest $p(b_h)$, and the stomach was the body part with the next

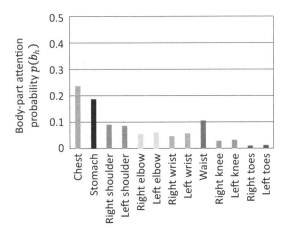

Fig. 7. Body-part attention probability $p(b_h)$ for a set of head-occluded images $\mathcal{S}_h$.

highest $p(b_h)$. The difference between these probabilities was 0.05, indicating a slightly different trend between the chest and stomach. Hypothesis H2 stated that the female observer's gaze would be most focused on the subject's stomach, but this did not hold. Instead, in the case of head-occluded images, the female observer's gaze tended to be focused most on the chest, followed by the stomach.

5.2 Visualization of Gaze Distribution for Each Stimulus Image

Protocol We visualized how the gaze was focused on body parts for each stimulus image. In the case of a whole-body image, we used the second term $p(i_w|o, \mathcal{I}_w)$ of Equation (1). This term refers to the probability that the gaze of a female observer o is focused on a pixel i_w consisting of a whole-body image $\mathcal{I}_w$, as described in Sect. 4.3. Using a set of observers $\mathcal{O}$, we marginalized $p(i_w|o, \mathcal{I}_w)$, and calculated the marginalized probability $p(i_w|\mathcal{I}_w)$ for each whole-body image as follows:

$$p(i_w|\mathcal{I}_w) = \frac{1}{n(\mathcal{O})} \sum_{o \in \mathcal{O}} p(i_w|o, \mathcal{I}_w). \tag{7}$$

In the case of a head-occluded image, we used the second term $p(i_h|o, \mathcal{I}_h)$ of Equation (4). Using a set of observers $\mathcal{O}$, we marginalized $p(i_h|o, \mathcal{I}_h)$, and calculated the marginalized probability $p(i_h|\mathcal{I}_h)$ for each head-occluded image as follows:

$$p(i_h|\mathcal{I}_h) = \frac{1}{n(\mathcal{O})} \sum_{o \in \mathcal{O}} p(i_h|o, \mathcal{I}_h). \tag{8}$$

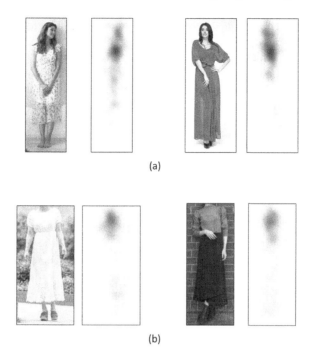

(a)

(b)

Fig. 8. Visualization of gaze distribution for each stimulus image. In (a), $p(i_w|\mathcal{I}_w)$ is for a whole-body image. In (b), $p(i_h|\mathcal{I}_h)$ is for a head-occluded image.

Results Figure 8(a) shows the visualization of $p(i_w|\mathcal{I}_w)$ of Equation (7) for each whole-body image. In this figure, the black area indicates that the observer's gaze is focused. In contrast, a white area indicates that the observer's gaze is not focused. In the subject on the left in Fig. 8(a), the observer's gaze was focused mainly on the chest, followed by the head. For the subject on the right, the observer's gaze was focused mainly on the chest, followed by the head. We believe that $p(i_w|\mathcal{I}_w)$ for each whole-body image indicates that the female observer's gaze tends to focus on the chest, followed by the head.

Next, Fig. 8(b) shows the visualization of $p(i_h|\mathcal{I}_h)$ of Equation (8) for each head-occluded image. In the subject on the left in Fig. 8(b), the observer's gaze was focused on the chest, followed by the stomach. For the subject on the right, the observer's gaze was focused mainly on the chest, followed by the stomach. We believe that $p(i_h|\mathcal{I}_h)$ for each head-occluded image indicates that the female observer's gaze tends to focus on the chest, followed by the stomach.

6   Conclusions

In this paper, we investigated which body parts in a whole-body image or a head-occluded image were the focus of a female observer who was asked to imagine wearing a subject's clothing and to predict the impression on others.

We confirmed that the female observer's gaze tended to be focused most on the subject's chest, followed by the head, in the case of whole-body images. We also confirmed that the female observer's gaze tended to focus most on the subject's chest, followed by the stomach, in the case of head-occluded images.

In future work, we will investigate the observer's gaze distribution by increasing the number of observers and measuring gaze diversity concerning the gender, age, and ethnicity of observers. We will also expand our analysis to various subjects' postures in stimulus images, such as sitting and side-facing standing postures.

Acknowledgment. This work was partially supported by JSPS KAKENHI Grant No. JP23K11145. We appreciate Professor Yoshio Iwai for his valuable advice and suggestions during this research.

References

1. Bindemann, M.: Scene and screen center bias early eye movements in scene viewing. Vision. Res. **50**(23), 2577–2587 (2010)
2. Cao, Z., Hidalgo, G., Simon, T., Wei, S., Sheikh, Y.: OpenPose: realtime multi-person 2d pose estimation using part affinity fields. IEEE Trans. Pattern Anal. Mach. Intell. **43**(1), 172–186 (2021)
3. Conner, B.H., Peters, K., Nagasawa, R.H.: Person and costume: effects on the formation of first impressions. Home Econ. Res. J. **4**(1), 32–41 (1975)
4. Cornelissen, P.L., Hancock, P.J., George, H.R., Tovée, M.J.: Patterns of eye movements when male and female observers judge female attractiveness, body fat and waist-to-hip ratio. Evol. Hum. Behav. **30**(6), 417–428 (2009)
5. Davis, F.: Fashion, Culture, and Identity. University of Chicago Press, Chicago (1994)
6. Gervais, S.J., Holland, A.M., Dodd, M.D.: My eyes are up here: the nature of the objectifying gaze toward women. Sex Roles **69**, 557–570 (2013)
7. Irvine, K.R., McCarty, K., Pollet, T.V., Cornelissen, K.K., Tovée, M.J., Cornelissen, P.L.: The visual cues that drive the self-assessment of body size: dissociation between fixation patterns and the key areas of the body for accurate judgement. Body Image **29**, 31–46 (2019)
8. Kinoshita, K., Inoue, M., Nishiyama, M., Iwai, Y.: Body-part attention probability for measuring gaze during impression word evaluation. In: Proceedings of 23rd International Conference on Human-Computer Interaction, pp. 105–112 (2021)
9. Naumann, L.P., Vazire, S., Rentfrow, P.J., Gosling, S.D.: Personality judgments based on physical appearance. Pers. Soc. Psychol. Bull. **35**(12), 1661–1671 (2009)
10. Nummenmaa, L., Jari, H., Santtila, P., Hyönä, J.: Gender and visibility of sexual cues influence eye movements while viewing faces and bodies. Arch. Sex. Behav. **41**(6), 1439–1451 (2012)
11. Piers, C., Peter, H., Kiviniemi, V., Hannah, G., Martin, T.: Patterns of eye movements when male and female observers judge female attractiveness, body fat and waist-to-hip ratio. Evol. Hum. Behav. **30**(6), 417–428 (2009)

12. Pujadas-Hostench, J., Palau-Saumell, R., Forgas-Coll, S., Matute, J.: Integrating theories to predict clothing purchase on SNS. Indus. Manage. Data Syst. **119**(5), 1015–1030 (2019)
13. Pujadas-Hostench, J., Palau-Saumell, R., Forgas-Coll, S., Sánchez-García, J.: Clothing brand purchase intention through SNS. Online Inf. Rev. **43**(5), 867–892 (2019)

Feasibility Verification of Ergonomic Design Based on Alert Indicators

Jin Liang[1,2]([✉]), Yang Yu[1,2], Liang Zhang[1,2], Xin Wang[1,2], Ye Deng[1,2], Si Li[1,2], Cong Peng[1,2], Xiaofang Xun[1,2], and Yulin Zhang[1,2]

[1] China Institute of Marine Technology and Economy, Beijing 100081, China
`liangjinpsy@126.com`
[2] National Key Laboratory of Human Factors Engineering, Beijing 100081, China

Abstract. The designers usually expect to ensure the best alertness level of operators through ergonomic design, to ensure that operators obtain better performance. But it is unclear whether ergonomic design can be based on alertness and which dimensions of ergonomic design can be guided by alertness. As a result, cognitive indicators according to cognitive needs cannot be used to guide ergonomic design practice. This research explore the sensitivity index of alertness for ergonomics design through experiment. The results showed that the normalized PVT reaction time was significantly positively correlated with the normalized visual fatigue score, negative emotion score, and task completion time. The normalized KSS score is significantly positively correlated with the normalized visual fatigue score and positive emotional score, but not significantly correlated with task completion time and accuracy. If it is necessary to focus on improving the performance level of operators or avoiding negative emotions in ergonomic design, it is recommended to choose objective vigilance evaluation indicators. If the focus of ergonomic design is to reduce visual fatigue and improve positive emotional levels, subjective evaluation indicators of alertness can be used. If only reducing visual fatigue is considered, both subjective and objective alertness indicators can be used. If ergonomic design comprehensively consider improving performance and positive emotions, and reducing negative emotions, it is recommended to use both subjective and objective vigilance evaluation indicators.

Keywords: Ergonomic Design · Alert Indicators · Feasibility Verification

1 Introduction

Ergonomic design needs to start from the perspective of humans and comprehensively consider human machine environmental factors, to achieve optimal human-machine adaptation. When conducting ergonomic design, it is often necessary to consider different aspects of human cognition, psychology, performance, and other aspects in conjunction with design requirements [1, 2]. The existing researches mainly focus on the influence of design elements on ergonomics, and the quantitative relationship between ergonomics design and personnel cognitive ergonomics needs is lacking. Alert is one of the important factors in maintaining normal work and life [3, 4]. The level of alert can

© The Author(s), under exclusive license to Springer Nature Switzerland AG 2024
D. Harris and W.-C. Li (Eds.): HCII 2024, LNAI 14693, pp. 48–56, 2024.
https://doi.org/10.1007/978-3-031-60731-8_4

significantly affect a person's performance, especially in flying, driving and other occupations that require high alertness [3, 5]. The designers usually expect to ensure the best alertness level of operators through ergonomic design, to ensure that operators obtain better performance. But it is unclear whether ergonomic design can be based on alertness and which dimensions of ergonomic design can be guided by alertness. As a result, cognitive indicators according to cognitive needs cannot be used to guide ergonomic design practice. The research on sensitivity index of alertness for ergonomics design and the relationship between alertness index and different dimensions of ergonomics design are of great significance for the realization of cognitive ergonomics maintenance through ergonomics design. So this research explore the sensitivity index of alertness for ergonomics design through experiment.

2 Methods

2.1 Participants

10 male participants were recruited through the society in this experiment. The participants had completed high school or college education, who were physically and mentally healthy. They all have no drug, alcohol, smoking, internet dependence and addiction, no history of inherited diseases, hepatitis b, hepatitis c, AIDS or other infectious diseases, and no history of severe allergies. They had no mental disorders, no psychological diseases, no organic and functional mental and neurological lesions, no sleep disorders or abnormalities in the two and three generations. All participants possessed normal visual acuity (or corrected visual acuity), hearing, smell and language expression ability, without color blindness, color weakness. All participants passed the interview, systematically physical examination and psychological evaluation.

2.2 Procedure

The participants were required to fully implement work and life schedule of the actual seafarer during the simulated long voyage, and carry out the ship simulation task during working time. Before and after their working time, we evaluated the alertness of workers using the Karolinska Sleepiness Scale(KSS), the objective alertness of workers using the psychomotor vigilance task (PVT task), the psychological ergonomic using the positive and negative affect score of positive and negative affect schedule(PANAS), the visual work efficiency using the visual fatigue scale(subjective visual fatigue) and flash fusion frequency test(objective visual fatigue), the job performance using the completion time and accuracy rate. A validation experiment on the feasibility of using vigilance indicators to guide ergonomic design was conducted to collect the data of PVT task, KSS scale, PANAS, visual fatigue scale, flash fusion frequency test and monitoring task of workers. After the experiment, PVT average reaction time and KSS scale score for the alert evaluation indicators, positive and negative emotion scores for psychological ergonomics evaluation indicators, visual fatigue scale score for visual ergonomics indicators, and the monitoring task completion time and accuracy for task performance indicators were extracted.

2.3   Test Tasks

Psychomotor Vigilance Task (PVT Task). Psychomotor vigilance task (PVT task) is a common task used to assess alertness ability and has a high sensitivity to changes in alertness level [6–8]. The participants were asked to sit in front of a computer, focus on the fixation point in the center of the screen when the psychomotor vigilance task (PVT task) start. The fixation time is random between 2000 and 10000 ms. The participants need press the "J" button immediately when the countdown began. The countdown would be continuing until the participant pressed the right key. The maximum response time allowed is 5 s. If the participant fails to respond on more than 5 s, the experiment will proceed to the next trial and a lapse would be recorded. The participant's response time and type was recorded by the computer. Participants were asked to respond as soon as possible, but not before the number appears, otherwise an error message would appear on the screen and an early response would be recorded. The duration of a PVT task is 5 min. Due to individual differences in response ability, the number of trials completed by each participant in a 5-min period may vary. The experimental process is shown in Fig. 1.

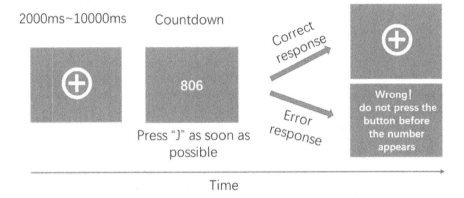

Fig. 1. Psychomotor vigilance task (PVT task)

Karolinska Sleepiness Scale (KSS). Karolinska Sleepiness Scale (KSS) commonly used for alertness and fatigue assessment, and has a high agreement with the PVT task in terms of alertness assessment [9, 10]. It only had one item asking participants represent their current awake status using 1–9 Figures. 1 represented extremely sober. 9 represented sleepiness. The scores among 1–9 expressed the participants' state from extremely sober to sleepiness. The smaller KSS score was, the higher alert participant was. The larger KSS score was, the higher sleepy participant was.

Positive and Negative Affect Scale (PANAS). Positive and Negative Affect Scale(PANAS) often used to assess emotional state [11, 12]. It consists of 20 adjectives, each representing an emotion, including 10 positive emotion words and 10 negative emotion words. When using the PANAS, participants need to rate their subjective emotional experience on a scale of 1–5. 1 indicates almost no emotion represented by the adjective, 2 indicates that the emotion represented by the adjective is relatively small, 3 indicates that there is a moderate degree of emotion represented by the adjective, 4 indicates that the emotion represented by the adjective is relatively large, and 5 indicates that the emotion represented by the adjective is extremely large. The score of positive emotion was calculated by the sum of positive emotion adjectives scores and the score of negative emotion was calculated by the sum of negative emotion adjectives scores after the test [13]. The smaller positive/negative emotion score was, the less positive/negative emotion the participant had. The larger positive/negative emotion score was, the more positive/negative emotion the participant had.

Visual Fatigue Scale (VFS). Visual fatigue scale(VFS) consists of 19 questions, each of which describes a symptom of visual fatigue. During the test, the participants were asked to assess the frequency and degree of visual fatigue symptoms according to their actual physical feelings. Frequency includes none, occasionally, often, and always. Intensity includes mild, moderate, and severe. The higher the score was, the higher fatigue degree participants had.

Critical Fusion Frequency (CFF). When the light stimulation continues to act on the human eye, it will cause the sensation of flickering. As the sustained frequency increases, a fusion sensation of light is created. The minimum intermittent frequency that can cause continuous fusion sensation is called the critical fusion frequency (CFF) [14]. There are great individual differences in the frequency of human eye fusion. CFF reflects the ability of the eye to distinguish the change of light stimulus in time, and the higher the CFF, the higher the visual acuity of time [15, 16]. In this experiment, the critical fusion frequency was measured by the minimum change method. The instantaneous transition point or threshold from one response to another is determined by increasing ($\uparrow$) or decreasing ($\downarrow$) changes in the stimulus in equally spaced small steps. In the incremental series, subjects saw the bright spot flickering when they began to observe, stopped when it did not seem to flicker by increasing the flicker frequency, and recorded critical frequency value. In the descending series, the subjects could not see the bright spot flashing at the beginning of observation, and stopped the flicker immediately when they saw it by reducing the flicker frequency, and recorded it.

Monitoring Task (MT). The monitoring task(MT) requires the participants to perform the sailing support task. The participants need to keep paying attention to whether the fault alarm occurs on the guarantee task interface. After the fault alarm occurs, the participants need to quickly handle the fault according to the plan of the threshold training, and the completion time and accuracy rate of the fault processing was recorded.

2.4 Analysis

This study collected the data of PVT task, KSS scale, PANAS, visual fatigue scale, flash fusion frequency test and monitoring task of workers. The reaction time of PVT task and the completion time of monitoring task were time data. PVT task response time is hundred-bit data, the unit is milliseconds. The monitoring task completion time ranges from units digit to tens digit (unit: second). KSS, VFS, PNAS are scale scores. KSS scores are units digit data, VFS, PNAS scores are tens digit data. The flash fusion frequency data is tens digit, and the unit is frequency. Due to significant differences in the names and categories of test data, the extracted test indicators were normalized after the experiment. A correlation analysis was conducted on normalized alertness and ergonomic evaluation indicators.

Extract Test Indicators. The average reaction time of PVT task was extracted as the cognitive behavior index of alertness, and the KSS score was used as the subjective evaluation index of alertness in this study. Visual fatigue score, positive emotion score, negative emotion score, the critical fusion frequency, and monitoring task completion time were calculated as ergonomic design indexes.

Normalize the Extracted Test Indicators. For indicators that change positively, normalization is done by 1- (maximum minus index value) /(maximum minus minimum value). The calculation formula is as follows:

$$N = 1 - \frac{Max - X}{Max - Min} \tag{1}$$

Max represent maximum, Min represent minimum, N represent normalized the Extracted Test Indicators. X represent Extract Test Indicators. The abbreviations below have the same meaning.

For indicators that change negatively, normalization is performed by (maximum minus index value) /(maximum minus minimum value). The calculation formula is as follows:

$$\frac{Max - X}{Max - Min} \tag{2}$$

Correlation Analysis of Normalized Alertness and Ergonomic Evaluation Indicators. In order to explore whether ergonomic design can be based on alertness and which dimensions of ergonomic design can be guided by alertness, the Pearson correlation coefficient between normalized alertness and ergonomic evaluation indicators was calculated in this study.

3   Results

Normalize Results of the Extracted Test Indicators. The normalize results of the extracted test indicators is shown in Fig. 2.

Correlation Analysis Results of Normalized Alertness and Ergonomic Evaluation Indicators. The results showed that the normalized PVT reaction time was significantly positively correlated with the normalized visual fatigue score, negative emotion score, and task completion time. The normalized KSS score is significantly positively correlated with the normalized visual fatigue score and positive emotional score, but not significantly correlated with task completion time and accuracy. The scatter diagram

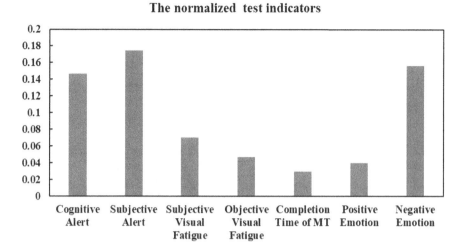

Fig. 2. Psychomotor vigilance task (PVT task)

of cognitive alert (normalized PVT reaction time) with subjective visual fatigue (normalized visual fatigue scale score), objective visual fatigue (normalized critical fusion frequency), completion time of monitoring task (normalized completion time of monitoring task), positive emotion (normalized positive emotion score) and negative emotion (normalized negative emotion score) were shown at the left of Figs. 3, 4, 5, 6, 7. The scatter diagram of cognitive alert (normalized PVT reaction time) with subjective visual fatigue, objective visual fatigue, completion time of monitoring task, positive emotion and negative emotion were shown at the right of Figs. 3, 4, 5, 6, 7.

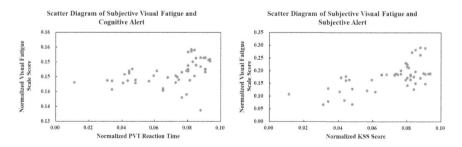

Fig. 3. The subjective visual fatigue has significantly correlated with subjective and cognitive alert

The results of correlation analysis between normalized alertness and ergonomic evaluation indicators is shown in Table 1. CA represent Cognitive Alert, SA represent Subjective Alert, SVF represent Subjective Visual Fatigue, OVF represent Objective

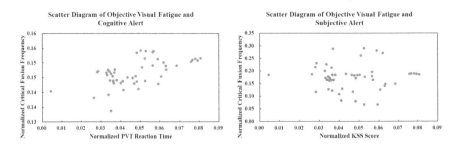

Fig. 4. The Objective visual fatigue only has significantly correlated with cognitive alert

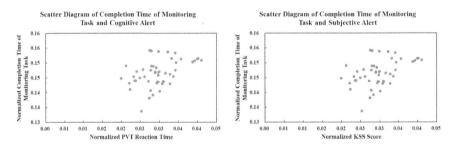

Fig. 5. The completion time of monitoring task only has significantly correlated with objective Alert

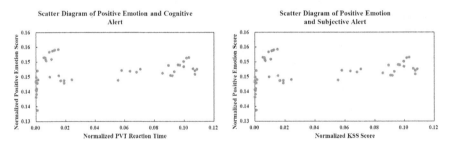

Fig. 6. The positive emotion has significantly correlated with subjective alert

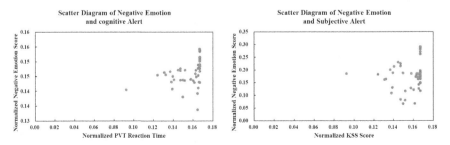

Fig. 7. The negative emotion only has significantly correlated with cognitive alert

Visual Fatigue, CTMT represent Completion Time of Monitoring Task, PE represent Positive Emotion, NE represent Negative Emotion in Table 1.

Table 1. The results of correlation analysis

	CA	SA	SVF	OVF	CTMT	PE	NE
CA	1	.35*	.44**	.57**	.45**	0.27	.40**
SA	.35*	1	.65**	0.02	0.17	.41**	0.13
SVF	.44**	.65**	1	.41**	0.21	0.14	.36**
OVF	.57**	0.02	.41**	1	.49**	0.024	.61**
CTMT	.45**	0.17	0.21	.49**	1	0.01	0.06
PE	0.27	.41**	0.14	0.02	0.01	1	0.13
NE	.40**	0.13	.36**	.61**	0.06	0.13	1

$* < 0.05$, $** < 0.01$, $*** < 0.001$.

4 Discussion

The results showed that the normalized PVT reaction time was significantly positively correlated with the normalized visual fatigue score, negative emotion score, and task completion time. This indicates that the faster PVT alertness reaction time, the lower visual fa-tigue experienced by operators, the less negative emotions, and the faster task com-pletion time. The objective level of alertness can reflect visual ergonomics, psychological ergonomics and job performance.

The normalized KSS score is significantly positively correlated with the normalized visual fatigue score and positive emotional score, but not significantly correlated with task completion time and accuracy. This indicates that the higher the KSS score, the lower the level of visual fatigue and the less negative emotion experienced by operators. The subjective alertness index can reflect the level of visual and psychological ergonomics, but cannot reflect the level of work performance.

In summary, vigilance indicators can be used to guide ergonomic design. If it is necessary to focus on improving the performance level of operators or avoiding negative emotions in ergonomic design, it is recommended to choose objective vigilance evaluation indicators.

If the focus of ergonomic design is to reduce visual fatigue and improve positive emotional levels, subjective evaluation indicators of alertness can be used. If only reducing visual fatigue is considered, both subjective and objective alertness indicators can be used.

If ergonomic design comprehensively consider improving performance and positive emotions, and reducing negative emotions, it is recommended to use both subjective and objective vigilance evaluation indicators.

The results of this study can be used to support ergonomic design for alertness maintenance, and have guiding significance for ergonomic design based on alertness index. Engineering application practice can be carried out to further verify the results of this study. The sample size can be increased, to collect more data, built the mapping relationship model between alertness and ergonomics, formulate relevant design standards. At the same time, the quantitative relationship between other cognitive indicators and ergonomic design factors, as well as between alertness indicators and other ergonomic factors, can be built with reference to this research method, so obtain a more comprehensive and systematic cognitive indicator system for ergonomic improvement.

References

1. Jun, Y., Yu, Z., Xiaofen, S., Jie, W., Hongwei, Z.: Rationality Evaluation of Ergonomic Simulation in Ship Cabin Design, Ship Engineering (2019)
2. Weide, R.V.D., Frieling, H., Malle, F., Miglianico, D.: Amsterdam Metro cab: ergonomics in the design, verification and validation process. Rail Human Factors (2013)
3. Liang, J., et al.: The Effect of a Long Simulated Voyage on Sailors' Alertness, pp. 454–462. Springer International Publishing, Cham (2020). https://doi.org/10.1007/978-3-030-49788-0_34
4. Viitasalo, K., Kuosma, E., Laitinen, J., Härmä, M.: Effects of shift rotation and the flexibility of a shift system on daytime alertness and cardiovascular risk factors. Scand. J. Work Environ. Health. **34**(3), 198–205 (2008)
5. Mahachandra, M., Yassierli, E.D.G.: The effectiveness of in-vehicle peppermint fragrance to maintain car driver's alertness. Procedia Manuf. **4**, 471–477 (2015)
6. Basner, M., Dinges, D.F.: Maximizing sensitivity of the psychomotor vigilance test (PVT) to sleep loss. Sleep **34**(5), 581–591 (2005)
7. Graw, P., Kr Uchi, K., Knoblauch, V., Wirz-Justice, A., Cajochen, C.: Circadian and wake-dependent modulation of fastest and slowest reaction times during the psychomotor vigilance task. Physiol. Behav. **80**(5), 695–701 (2004)
8. Butlewski, M., Hankiewicz, K.: Psychomotor performance monitoring system in the context of fatigue and accident prevention. Procedia Manuf. **3**, 4860–4867 (2015)
9. Freire, A.X., Freire, X.A.: Karolinska sleepiness scale pilot correlation with psycho-vigilance test and driving response failures - in a "Sleepy" Healthy Youth. Sleep **41**(suppl_1), 58–59 (2018)
10. Miley, A.A., Kecklund, G., Akerstedt, T.C.: Comparing two versions of the Karolinska Sleepiness Scale (KSS). Sleep Biol. Rhythms. **14**, 257–260 (2016)
11. Qiu, L., Zheng, X., Wang, Y.F.: Revision of the positive affect and negative affect scale. Chinese J. Appl. Psychol. **14**, 249–254 (2008)
12. Denollet, J., Vries, J.D.: Positive and negative affect within the realm of depression, stress and fatigue: The two-factor distress model of the Global Mood Scale (GMS). J. Affect. Disorders **91**(2–3), 171–180 (2006)
13. Yu, Y., et al.: The Influence of a Long Voyage on Mental Status: An Experimental Study, pp. 530–539. Springer International Publishing, Cham (2020)
14. Jenssen, T.A., Swenson, B.: An ecological correlate of critical flicker-fusion frequencies for some Anolis lizards. Vision. Res. **14**(10), 965–970 (1974)
15. Grandjean, P.B.E.: Effects of Repetitive Tasks with Different Degrees of Difficulty on Critical Fusion Frequency (CFF) and Subjective State, Ergonomics (1979)
16. Chen, C.M., Wang, H., Tang, Y., Zhang, X.: Visual fatigue caused by tablet PC based on critical fusion frequency and eye blink frequency. Appl. Mech. Mater. **401–403**, 544–547 (2013)

Evaluation Method and Capability Improvement Research Based on Controller Capability Characteristics

Jimin Liu[1], Ting-Ting Lu[2], and Ning Li[3(✉)]

[1] Strategic Development Department, East China Regional Air Traffic Management Bureau of Civil Aviation Administration of China, Shanghai 200335, China
[2] College of Air Traffic Management, Civil Aviation University of China, Tianjin 300300, China
[3] Air Traffic Control Industry Management Office, Civil Aviation Administration of China, Beijing 100010, China
13681830403@163.com

Abstract. First of all, this paper analyzed the status quo of domestic and foreign research on controller capability assessment and capability improvement. Then, based on 10 dimensions, such as professional character, language ability, reaction ability, mathematical application ability, spatial orientation ability, short-term memory ability, logical inference ability, situational awareness ability, attention switching ability, multitasking ability, the controller ability evaluation model was established. The rationality of the model was verified by selecting controllers at different stages for evaluation. Finally, based on 10 capability dimensions of controllers, a controller capability enhancement model was established. The research of this paper has important theoretical and practical significance, filling the theoretical gap in Chinese controller capability assessment and capability improvement research, and laying a good theoretical foundation for improving the overall capability of the controller team and ensuring flight safety.

Keywords: Evaluation Method · Capability Improvement · Controller Capability Characteristics · Evaluation Index System

1 Introduction

With the rapid development of the civil aviation industry, especially with the continuous expansion of the aviation market, the air traffic flow has increased sharply, and the task of air traffic control security has become increasingly serious. As the main body of air traffic control security, controller's ability plays an important role in ensuring aviation safety and improving air traffic flow. However, flight conflicts and even flight accidents still occur frequently in recent years due to the controller's own ability or training problems. Therefore, countries all over the world, especially aviation developed countries, pay more and more attention to controller capacity assessment and capability improvement training.

D. Harris and W.-C. Li (Eds.): HCII 2024, LNAI 14693, pp. 57–69, 2024.
https://doi.org/10.1007/978-3-031-60731-8_5

In foreign countries, Keye verified the effectiveness of the controller selection procedure, which included multiple predictive factors such as cognitive ability test and interview score. According to the training success rate of the selected controllers, it was confirmed that the selection procedure had a good predictive effect [1]. Yvonne analyzed the effectiveness of the selection procedure for control trainees based on the accuracy of predicting training success and the performance criteria of control trainees in the initial training [2]. Carretta studied the usability of the armed forces vocational aptitude test for the selection of controllers [3]. Oprins designed a capability based evaluation system and took the results of the system evaluation as an important basis for selecting controllers [4].

In China, the current research on the assessment and training of controller ability is still in the preliminary stage of exploration, there is no mature assessment and training system, only the preliminary research on the selection of controllers. It is still at the level of examining the theoretical knowledge and basic ability of students at present. Most of the domestic researches on the selection of controllers are based on the evaluation of the psychological selection index and the comprehensive quality evaluation of controllers. Xiang Heng designed the structural model of air traffic controller psychological selection index, and verified the correctness of the psychological selection index through fuzzy calculation of the psychological selection index of air traffic controller [5]. Miao Xuan et al. made a summary study and analysis on the selection and training of controllers [6–11]. Yang Changqi et al. studied the controller competency model [12–14].

The evaluation method and ability improvement research based on the capability characteristics of controllers in this paper can provide scientific basis and technical support for the evaluation of controllers majors in civil aviation colleges and universities before admission, the selection of controllers units in "3 + 1" and "4 + 1", and the ability evaluation of new students, so as to teach students according to their aptitude, make up for shortcomings and post allocation, and track and evaluate the ability of in-service controllers. It is of great significance to effectively improve the overall quality and ability of the controller team and ensure flight safety.

2 Research Thought

The research content of this thesis mainly includes two aspects of the controller's ability evaluation and improvement. The research idea of controller capability evaluation mainly includes the following three steps, as shown in Fig. 1.

Conduct investigation and analysis of the research status at home and abroad, visit civil aviation colleges and control units, interview experts and design questionnaires. 2. By analyzing the basic competence dimensions of controllers, selecting evaluation indicators, designing the weights of the index system, and testing the validity and reliability of the established evaluation index system. 3. Complete the development of the controller capability assessment system.

The research idea of controller capability improvement mainly also includes the following three steps, as shown in Fig. 2.

1. Based on the controller ability evaluation index system, the corresponding ability improvement training module is designed. 2. Carry out training system architecture

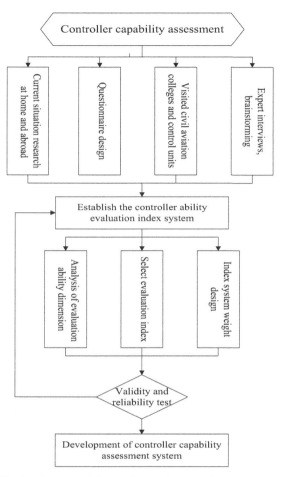

Fig. 1. The research ideas of controller capability evaluation

design, training system database construction, training system human-computer interface design. 3. Through the reliability and validity test, the controller ability improvement training system was developed.

3   Review of International Controller Selection

Air traffic control is an important part of the national transportation industry, and an important basis for ensuring the safety of national airspace and the development of aviation industry. The task of the air traffic control service is to prevent collisions between aircraft and aircraft, collisions between aircraft and obstacles in the maneuver area, and to maintain and accelerate the orderly flow of air traffic. The air traffic control work in China is uniformly organized and implemented by the Chinese People's Liberation Army Air Force, and the relevant flight control departments provide air traffic control services according to their respective responsibilities.

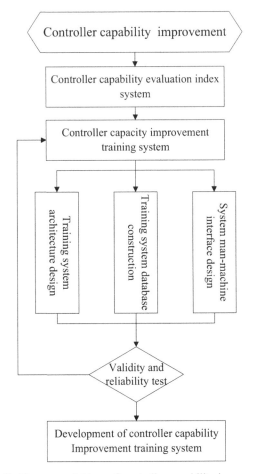

Fig. 2. The research ideas of controller capability improvement

The training of civil aviation air traffic control personnel includes two parts: cultivation training and post training. Cultivation and training is carried out by qualified institutions of higher learning. The source of civil aviation controllers in China are mainly three domestic universities: Civil Aviation University of China, Civil Aviation Flight College of China, Nanjing University of Aeronautics and Astronautics. The Air Traffic Control Office and the Air Traffic Management Bureau of the Civil Aviation Administration respectively provide industry leadership and business guidance for the professional teaching of air traffic control [15].

3.1 United States Controller Selection

The United States has the largest number of controllers in the world. FAA has experienced a long research and accumulated a lot of experience in the assessment of regulatory capability, and developed a set of assessment tools, including the assessment of arithmetic reasoning, spatial perception and abstract reasoning ability.

The current research on the selection system of controllers in the United States began in late 1996, mainly to address the problem that the number of controllers recruited due to the general strike would retire during the same period. After passing the system test, the trainees are hired by the FAA and sent to the aviation academy for approximately 15 weeks of training, and after passing the training performance evaluation, they are sent to the front-line control unit for on-the-job training. This selection system is the air traffic selection and training (AT-SAT), which is a set of computer-based tests that take six and a half hours and can be taken AT community testing centers in different places, which is very convenient. Therefore, it is officially used by the FAA as an official controller selection test. In the early stage, T-SAT was composed of 12 sub-tests, and after a lot of validity verification, 8 sub-tests were retained, namely the current AT-SAT (see Table 1). In the table, in addition to the experience questionnaire to test personality traits, the other seven are mainly cognitive ability tests. The air traffic scenario, angle, letter factory and scan tests are all dynamic and interactive, requiring a computer to complete, the rest are paper and pencil tests. Finally, the total score is weighted.

Table 1. FAA controllers select eight AT-SAT subtexts.

Test module	Test content description
Reading	Scan and understand readings from a bunch of similar instruments
Applied mathematics	Solve basic mathematical problems related to distance, speed and time
Scanning	Scan a dynamic digital display to detect frequently changing targets
Angle	Determine the Angle of the crossing lines
Alphabet factory	Participate in an interactive, dynamic activity that examines categorization skills, decision making, optimization, working memory, and situational awareness
Air traffic control scenario	Control aircraft for optimization in interactive, dynamic, low-fidelity air traffic scenario simulation
Analogy	Working memory and relational concepts are required for verbal and non-verbal analogies
Experience questionnaire	Answer the Ritter level questionnaire about your life experiences

3.2 European Controller Selection

Background of the Selection of European Controllers. At the end of the 1970s, European air transportation developed rapidly, but due to the particularity of its geographical distribution, most flights needed to cross multiple countries to complete, air traffic control became a problem, and because of the high elimination rate and instability of controller training, it caused difficulties in human resource planning and waste of social resources.

The fact also proves that through the scientific controller selection system, the elimination rate and stability have been greatly improved. In Sweden, for example, after its controllers adopted the selection system in 1993, the elimination rate of training was reduced from 46% in the 1970s and 34% in the 1980s to 27%, and the change range of the elimination rate was reduced from 73% to 29%, 47% to 14% to 37% to 10%. Other countries that have adopted specially developed selection systems have also seen a significant reduction in the elimination rate of subsequent training for controllers. Through a series of selection procedures and tests. European countries are basically able to recruit the most suitable control students, and the final admission ratio is about 10%. It can be said that those who remain are very rare. In the follow-up training and post work, very few have been eliminated, and basically they are competent for the control post work. Effectively ensure the overall quality of its controller team.

The European controller selection system can be basically divided into two categories: one is the selection system with equal emphasis on intelligence and psychology represented by Germany, Britain and Sweden, and the other is the selection system with emphasis on intelligence elements based on France. The two systems are quite different. The following takes Britain and France as examples to introduce these two selection systems.

Model of Working Ability of British Controllers. The development of the controller selection system in the United Kingdom began in 1983, when the British National Air Traffic Service (NATS) commissioned the occupational psychological testing company SHL to complete. The design of the selection procedure is mainly based on the analysis of the control task, through which the ability required by the controller is obtained (sec Table 2), and the corresponding test system is developed to measure it.

Model of Working Ability of France Controllers. In most European countries, the selection of controllers focuses on various cognitive abilities and personality traits in addition to intelligence or ability factors, and focuses on the assessment of candidates' knowledge, skills and techniques, with the aim of improving the probability of predicting candidates' success. In France, however, the concept is quite different, and the selection of controllers is mainly based on the academic performance of the candidates, with an emphasis on the evaluation of the candidates' academic and educational knowledge, skills and techniques. Candidates are admitted to aviation schools by passing a series of written and oral examinations in science, foreign languages and elective subjects. Although different from other countries, with additional safeguards, 95 per cent of the control trainees recruited through this method eventually became qualified controllers.

French controllers are mainly divided into two categories, one is ICNA, mainly including approach and route controllers, currently about 5,000 people, and the other is TSEEAC, mainly tower controllers, about 1,500 people, are trained by the French Civil Aviation University (ENAC).The French controller selection examination is very strict, the examination is divided into two kinds of written and oral, and only those who pass the written test can participate in the oral examination. First of all, the written test, in

Table 2. Model of working ability of British controllers.

Test module	Test content	Test content description
Preliminary selection	Basic information	It is mainly for the applicant's age, education experience, physical conditions, work experience and other standards to review
Ability test	Basic check test	Tests the candidate's ability to perceive speed and accuracy
	Mathematical calculation	Test the candidate's basic arithmetic ability
	Spatial reasoning	Test spatial imagination and mental description ability
	Image	Tests for short-term memory, convergent thinking, and complex command sending and receiving
	Learning style	Test the candidate's ability to adapt to the learning environment
	Air traffic control motivation	Test the candidate's knowledge of basic air traffic control knowledge
Personality test	Occupational personality questionnaire	The test measures a total of 32 personality traits in three areas of relevance, thinking and emotion
Interactive computer testing	Supplementary test (After the above test, it cannot reflect the relevant important abilities of the applicant)	The program mainly includes task classification, relative direction identification and moving target recognition, and mainly examines the above-mentioned abilities that are important to the work of controllers
Interview	Technical interview and personnel interview	It mainly examines the career motivation and achievement motivation of the candidate, such as reasoning ability, communication skills, team ability and so on

which mathematics, physics, French and English are required to take the written test, in addition, students have to choose one of the mathematics, physics and technology as the required written test. Aviation knowledge, computer science and a second foreign language are selected for the written examination. After passing the written examination, you are eligible for the next round of oral examination (see Table 3).

Table 3. Model of working ability of France controllers.

Written part			Speaking Part
Required examination	Written test (1 of 3)	Additional written test (1 of 2)	Take the written test after passing (required)
Math (4 h)	Math (4 h)	Aviation Knowledge (2 h)	Math (30 min)
Physics (4 h)	Physics (4 h)	Second foreign language (2 h)	Physics (30 min)
French (4 h)	Technology (4 h)		French (30 min)
English (2 h)			English (30 min)

Model of Working Ability of Chinese Controllers. In 2009, on the basis of comprehensive foreign selection methods and testing requirements, Civil Aviation University of China independently developed an initial controller selection system suitable for Chinese controller selection. This system has been approved by the Civil Aviation Administration of China and is used as the test standard for the selection of initial controllers in the Civil Aviation of China. This system has been approved by the Civil Aviation Administration of China, and combined with the theoretical test and interview as the test standard for the selection of initial controllers in the Civil aviation of China. Some test units can simultaneously test multiple elements of job quality requirements (see Table 4).

Table 4. Model of working ability of Chinese controllers.

Test module	Test content	Test content description
Preliminary test	Theoretical test	Test candidates' knowledge of civil aviation and knowledge of English (in addition to spoken English)

(*continued*)

Table 4. (*continued*)

Test module	Test content	Test content description
Human-computer interactive testing	Cognitive test	Attention focusing, global attention, short-term memory
	Scenario test	Priority ordering, high strength tolerance, emotional stability, accurate perceptual speed, situational awareness, advances thinking, short-term memory, dynamic visual ability
	Mathematics application ability test	Numeracy
	Dynamic visual	Attention focusing, global attention, dynamic visual ability, short-term memory
	Alphabet factory	Priority ordering, high strength tolerance, attention focusing, accurate perceptual speed, situational awareness, advance thinking, short-term memory, dynamic visual ability
	Azimuth test	Spatial imagination ability
	Bees collect honey	Accurate perceptual speed, situational awareness, advances thinking, short-term memory, dynamic visual ability
	Angle test	Thinking ahead, calculating ability, angle perception
Interview	Technical interview and personnel interview	It mainly examines the career motivation and achievement motivation of the candidate, such as reasoning ability, communication skills, and team ability and so on

4 Evaluation Model of Controller Capability

4.1 Evaluation Index System

Based on the author's many years of experience in air traffic control teaching and practice, this paper proposes that controllers should have the following ten basic qualities. The evaluation and capability improvement methods of each ability are given. It should be noted here that the applicant should first meet the IIIA medical examination standards stipulated by the Civil Aviation Administration of China (Fig. 3).

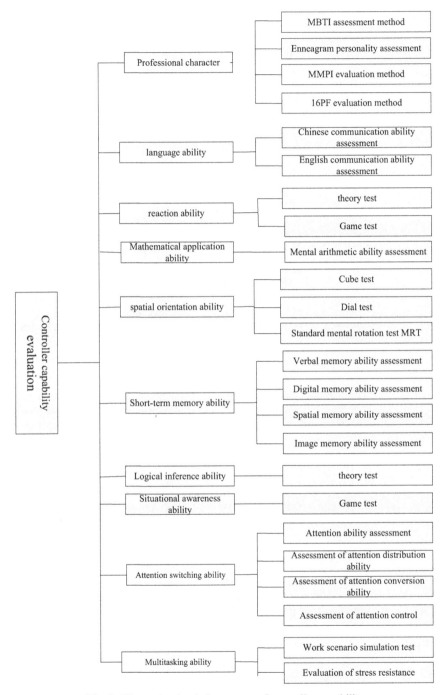

Fig. 3. The evaluation index system of controller capability

4.2   Evaluation Index Weight

The weights of evaluation indicators can be dynamically allocated among the ten modules according to the actual situation. The weight design of evaluation indicators is not immutable, and can be dynamically adjusted according to different units, different positions and different stages. Therefore, will not go into details here.

5   Example Evaluation

This paper selects controllers at different stages to evaluate their abilities in 10 dimensions. The following figure shows the evaluation results of a certain controller between initial selection and improved post-training (Figs. 4 and 5).

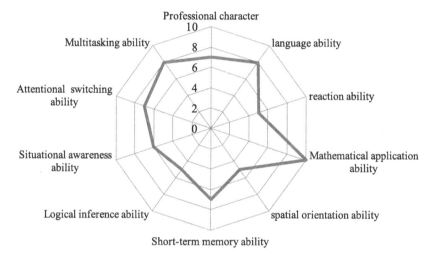

Fig. 4. Evaluation of the initial selection ability of a controller

Through the comparison before and after the test, it can be seen that the ability of controllers can be divided into two types: acquired and innate. The so-called acquired condition is the condition that can be cultivated and easily changed, such as language ability, mathematical application ability, logical inference ability, etc. The so-called innate condition is a condition that is born and difficult to change, such as professional character, situational awareness, attention switching ability and so on. Because the innate conditions have the characteristics of being difficult to change, this makes these become the necessary content of the selection of some special industries.

According to the evaluation index system of controller ability established above, the evaluation results can be used as an important reference for the assignment of controller posts [16]. Such allocation does not only refer to the strength of their achievements, but also needs to match the positions by integrating the ability and adaptability of all people, so as to form the optimal allocation plan.

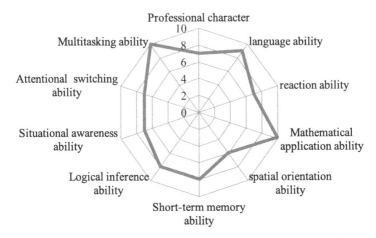

Fig. 5. Improved post-training competency evaluation of a controller

6   Conclusions

The paper establishes a controller capability enhancement model based on 10 capability dimensions of controllers. But there are limitations to any selection test. Not all those who pass the selection test are qualified for control. There are two main reasons for this phenomenon: first, there are defects in the test project, so that some congenital unqualified people are not tested. Due to the limitation of test conditions and test time, the selection test of the controller can only carry out the content that is easy to measure and the test time is short. Although some content is necessary to test, such as psychological characteristics, but due to technical means, testing environment, testing time and even testing funds, it cannot be tested or tested accurately. In addition, due to the subjective reasons such as fatigue or negligence of the examiners, the test error will also lead to the phenomenon. Second, the gap between ideal and reality makes some qualified people disheartened. When the working environment, work pressure, labor compensation and so on and the expectation gap is large, especially the internship progress is not smooth, produce a large anxiety, the phenomenon of giving up is easy to occur. This situation is not necessarily a problem with the innate conditions of trainees, and it may be more appropriate to explain it as "emotional fluctuations". Therefore, neither pilot selection, which started earlier, nor controller selection, which started later, can avoid elimination in actual work.

In this sense, the selection of controllers is not only a test for recruitment, but should run through several links including recruitment, learning and internship. Compared with the relatively mature pilot selection, the selection of controllers is still in the stage of exploration and research in China. In foreign aviation developed countries, there is no broad consensus. Therefore, while being brave in practice and innovation, we should pay attention to tracking the situation of the personnel who have been selected into the control positions, especially those who have poor performance in their work, compare their performance in the selection test, make corresponding analysis, and adjust and modify the test questions when necessary. In addition, particular attention should be paid to maintaining the stability of the selection team of controllers and not easily changing the examiners for each test item. Only in this way can the examiners accumulate experience in practice and gradually form an accurate grasp of the quality of the controllers.

Acknowledgments. This work was supported in part by National Social Science Foundation (No. 22XGL001); Key Project of Civil Aviation Joint Fund of National Natural Science Foundation (No. 2233209); Civil Aviation Safety Capacity Building Fund (No. [2022]156).

Disclosure of Interests. All authors disclosed no relevant relationships.

References

1. Keye, D., Conzelmann, K., Grasshoff, D., et al.: Validity of the selection procedure for air traffic controllers. Personal. Individ. Differ. **60**(1), S46 (2014)
2. Yvonne, P., Doris, K., Kristin, C., et al.: Predictive validity of a selection procedure for air traffic controller trainees. Aviat. Psychol. Appl. Human Factors **3**(1), 19–27 (2013)
3. Carretta, T.R., King, R.E.: Improved military air traffic controller selection methods as measured by subsequent training performance. Acrosp. Mcd. Human Pcrform. **79**(1), 36–43 (2008)
4. Oprins, E., Burggraaff, E., Weerdenburg, H.V.: Design of a competence-based assessment system for air traffic control training. Int. J. Aviat. Psychol. **16**(3), 297–320 (2006)
5. Heng, X.: Fuzzy comprehensive evaluation on psychological selection indices of air traffic controller. Space Med. Med. Eng. **22**(6), 422–426 (2009)
6. Xuan, M., Yonggang, L.: An international view of air traffic controller selection and its significance for China. Civil Aviat. China **12**, 18–21 (2008)
7. Hao Xueqin, W., Guocheng, L.P.: The progress of air traffic controller psychological selection. Chinese J. Aerosp. Med. **04**, 59–63 (2001)
8. Xiangning, D.: Research on the selection and training of air traffic control students based on quality. J. Nanjing Univ. Aeronaut. Astronaut. (Soc. Sci. Edn.) **14**(02), 42–45 (2012)
9. Man, L.: The training system of civil aviation controllers in France and its enlightenment. Vocat. Techn. Educ. **29**(02), 85–86+89 (2008)
10. Yuan, L.: Exploration on the selection of air traffic controllers. Civil Aviat. China **09**, 50–52 (2007)
11. Yanhua, L., Xiao, X., Yongning, H.: Discussion on air traffic controller evaluation system. J. Civil Aviat. Univ. China **01**, 32–36 (2004)
12. Lai, G.: Research on comprehensive evaluation system of controller training based on competency model. Civil Aviation Flight Academy of China (2020)
13. Li, J., Li, H., Zhao, N., et al.: Air traffic controller competency model and its influence relationship analysis. China Work Saf. Sci. Technol. **12**(02), 175–180 (2016)
14. Ruishan, S., Ning, Z., Jingqiang, L., et al.: Structure analysis of air traffic controller competency model. China Saf. Sci. J. **24**(10), 8–14 (2014)
15. Civil Aviation Administration of China. CCAR-93TM-R6–2022, Air traffic management rules of civil aviation of China. Beijing: Civil Aviation Administration of China (2022)
16. Yang, C., Wang, X., Guo, H.: Job allocation method based on controller competency model. Gen. Transp. **43**(06), 61–65+75 (2021)

A Small Icon and Its Effect on User Perception - How the Design of the Passenger Call Button Shapes Passengers Communication with Cabin Crew

Elizabeth Manikath[1,2]([✉]) [ID], Wen-Chin Li[1] [ID], Graham R. Braithwaite[1] [ID], and Pawel Piotrowski[2] [ID]

[1] Safety and Accident Investigation Centre, Cranfield University, Cranfield, UK
elizabeth.manikath@cranfield.ac.uk
[2] Lufthansa Technik AG, Hamburg, Germany

Abstract. "Learn how to see. Realize that everything connects to everything else" - Leonardo da Vinci. Flight attendants are usually perceived as service workers although their main responsibility is to ensure safety and security on board. This picture has been manifested due to historic developments such as the deregulation of commercial air travel and resultingly the focus on service as a mean for airlines to differentiate their offerings in the market. However, some of the relics of these times, such as the icon for the Passenger Call Button, do not seem to fit into the modern world where gender-equality is a strong value. **Research question.** This paper assess different icon configurations on an IFE screen to assess passenger's preference. **Methodology.** A video containing sample IFE screens with alternating icons were shown to participants to firstly identify whether the changes will be noticed and secondly to asses their preference on the design. **Results.** Passengers preferred the gender-neutral icons over feminized symbols mainly due to gender-neutrality. There was a significant relation between education and the preference of the icon which indicate that the higher the education level the more attention is paid to gender-equality. **Discussion.** The overall positive responses for the spot the difference test result from prolonged display times which could be shortened to induce change blindness. Further research e.g. using eye-tracking technology could provide more insights into the visual scanning process. **Conclusion.** This study provides insights into how an optimal icon design can change the perception of passenger's on how cabin attendants work shall be done. Detailed cross-cultural studies need to be carried out in order to understand whether gender-equality is equally important in all parts of the world.

Keywords: gender-equality · WAD vs. WAI · Flight attendants · Passenger Call Button · visual attention · user-centered design

© The Author(s), under exclusive license to Springer Nature Switzerland AG 2024
D. Harris and W.-C. Li (Eds.): HCII 2024, LNAI 14693, pp. 70–86, 2024.
https://doi.org/10.1007/978-3-031-60731-8_6

1 Introduction

Flight attendants are expected to have "effective" communication skills [14] [6]. In the initial stages of commercial air transport air travel was only accessible to a small passenger group [24]. Travelling these days should have recreated an intimate feeling of "being home" [24]. Therefore, the task of the so-called "sky girls" was to relieve the flight anxiety of predominantly wealthy business men [24]. Service offerings have been one of the major differentiation factors for airlines after the deregulation [19]. One aspect for perceived good service quality is responsiveness and communication according to [26]. Responsiveness refers to the service provider being able to provide the service in a timely manner (e. g. arranging meetings with the customer, quick call-backs and service) [26]. Communication means that the customer is informed in an understandable manner. Further examples for good communication routines are explanations of the provided service and re-assuring that occurring problems will be handled [26]. In an aircraft cabin the only mean for passengers to discreetly inform the cabin crew is to use the Passenger Call Button (PCB) [22]. According to Manikath et al., 2024 [21] the PCB is mainly used for service requests . Further, cabin crew use the button too as part of their own communication routine which makes it difficult to distinguish who has initiated the call [39]. Since the PCB is predominantly used for service requests, flight attendants usually do not attend the call immediately, assuming it is not an emergency [21]. This could have a negative effect on the perceived service quality but more importantly on task response in case of emergencies. Currently there is no mean to discreetly alert the cabin crew in case of emergencies [20]. The importance of efficient and clear communication can be seen in the accident of Japan Airlines Flight JAL516 at Tokyo Haneda Airport. According to Aviation Herald the landing initially seemed to be normal, however fires could be seen outside the windows [16]. The cabin crew made an announcement stating that everyone should remain calm and no one should take their luggage and stand up [16]. The cabin crew of flight JAL516 has been internationally praised for the efficiency of evacuation. All of the 379 passengers onboard were able to calmly evacuate the aircraft. No one was seen to be carrying their luggage, obstructing the evacuation by filming or panicking. This can be seen as the result of a well trained crew, as flight safety expert Prof. Dr. Graham Braithwaite stated in Business Insider [27] and their communication skills. The purpose of this study is to understand how the design of the PCB, specifically the icon is perceived by passengers and which implication it might have for future designs. Following research questions will be assessed in this paper:

RQ1: How can the design of the Passenger Call Button be improved to increase passenger's visual attention?
RQ2: What are passenger's requirements on the design of a Passenger Call Button?

Historical Development of the Passenger Call Button

In the following section some peculiar designs of the Passenger Call Button over the past decade of aviation history will be described. After researching in online archives and contacting archivist at aviation museums, there is evidence of an early design of a Passenger Call Button in the Vickers Viscount 724/757 series delivered to Trans Canada Airlines in 1954. The aircraft had approximately 48 to 53 (depending on the configuration) passengers in a two-abreast seating [38]. The picture taken from the Operations Manual shows the "Stewardess Call Button" located in between the two light switches [35]. The button needed to be pulled out and it then lit up (Figs. 1 and 2).

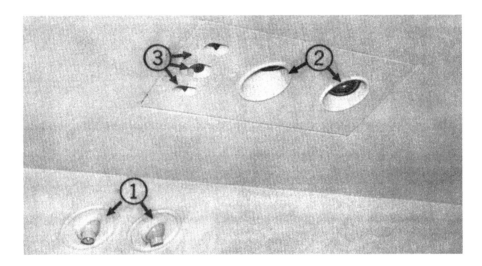

Fig. 1. Passenger Call Button in the Vickers Viscount 724 [35]

It was pushed back when the flight attendant reached the seat. The British de Havilland DH.106 Comet was the world's first turbojet engine aircraft [37]. The Comet 4 (first flight in 1958) had typically 56 seats to a maximum of 106 seats [37]. The "call switch" is located on the passenger's individual lamp panel, forward of the two light switches [12]. This could be the first attempt to separate the light switches from the reading lights, which in later cabin designs often lead to confusions for the passengers pressing accidentally the call button instead of the light switches. The call switch itself is a "three-position push-pull switch" [12]. The knob is pushed in and an amber lights illuminates. The flight attendants need to pull out the switch to reset the call.

The design of the Passenger Call System for both supersonic jets Tupolev Tu-144 and Concorde is similar (Fig 3). Bold rectangular push-buttons located in between the light switches with either an icon or a labelling could be found in pictures of the cabin interior of these aircraft [1,34].

Fig. 2. Passenger Call Button in the de Havilland DH.106 Comet 4 [23]

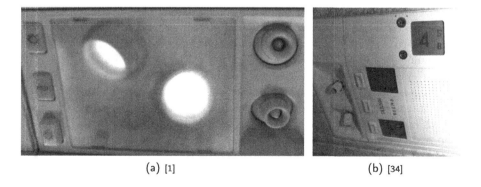

(a) [1]   (b) [34]

Fig. 3. PCB design in a Concorde (a) and a Tu-144 (b).

It can only be assumed why the aircraft designers chose to place the PCB close to the light switch which according to Boeing is a faulty design and lead to misuse of the PCB instead of the light switch [11]. The higher seat density and reduced space in the overhead passenger service channel could be reasons for this faulty design. Over the years designers tried to highlight the call button by marking it either with an eye-catching colour (e. g. red, blue, amber), striking icon or a different size/location of the button (cf. Fig. 4) [36].

Fig. 4. Detailed icon of Passenger Call Button in a Soviet aircraft [36]

Boeing claimed with their improved "Sky Interior" on the Boeing 737 Max that they "came up with a really good improvement" by positioning the PCB away from the reading lights and differentiating it [11]. However, looking back at the Comet 4 or even the Boeing 737-CL (depending on the individual configuration) the innovation is not as "radical" as it has been proclaimed by Boeing. The technological advancement can be seen in the button size, evolving from an initial mushroom shaped (Comet 4) to rectangular blocks (e. g. Concorde, Boeing 747) to a smaller, semi-spherical round shaped button.

In modern aircraft like the Airbus A350 or the Boeing 787 there is a virtual button embedded in the IFE screen in addition to the physical button. This is a true novelty and can be seen as the next technological advancement. The reason for having a virtual PCB could be due to the more spacious cabin design [2] with high ceiling heights which make it simply difficult to reach the physical PCB while being seated. Usually there is an additional button in the handset of the seat, if available. The new Panasonic IFE system called Panasonic eX3 offers motion control: whenever the passenger is waving his hand the menu for reading lights and flight attendant call will open on the IFE screen.

2   Methodology

Passenger Call Buttons exist in various designs and are constantly developed further to fit the requirements of the modern passenger. One prominent aspect which deserves a deeper look for instance is different icons are used as a symbol for the flight attendant. The objective of this study is to evaluate passenger's preference on the design of the Passenger Call Button.

2.1   Participants

In total 155 people participated in the online survey. It was required to be over 18 years old to complete the survey. The link to the survey was shared with the participants and granted anonymous participation. Participants could terminate the study at any time by closing the window of the survey. Ethics approval (CURES/21010/2023) was granted by the institutional research ethics committee.

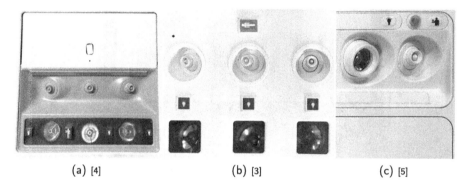

(a) [4]   (b) [3]   (c) [5]

Fig. 5. Different evolutions of the PCB in a Boeing 737 Classic (a), Boeing 737-200 (b), and Boeing 737 NG (c).

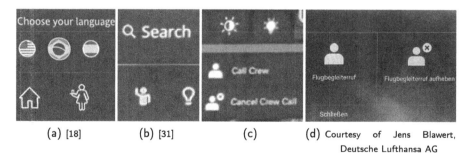

(a) [18]   (b) [31]   (c)   (d) Courtesy of Jens Blawert, Deutsche Lufthansa AG

Fig. 6. Virtual PCBs in Airbus A330-900 (a), (b), Boeing 747-400 (c), and Boeing 787 (d).

2.2 Material

A qualitative survey study was distributed to passengers online to assess the preference on the design of the Passenger Call Button. The questionnaire started with basic demographic questions to categorize the participants according to their travel experience. Secondly, a one-minute video was shown to assess perception and directed visual attention. The video contained slight differences in the IFE screen designs (as shown in Fig. 7).

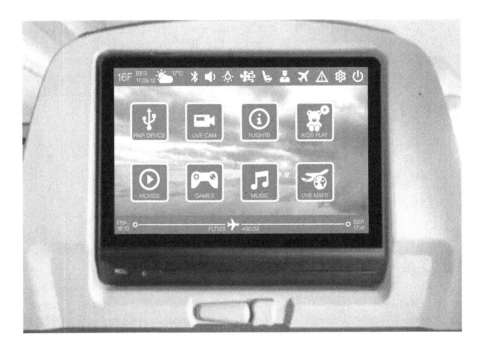

Fig. 7. Sample of an IFE screen

Six different screen samples were shown for five seconds with a white screen in between. Participants needed to watch the entire video and afterwards to detect the differences between the designs. The differences were only in the background objects (the icon for the Passenger Call Button). The icons shown are commonly found as the symbol for the flight attendant call in various aircraft types (see Fig. 8) and one novel symbol for service (hotel bell) which is not related to a depiction of a human. Icons A to D symbolize the desired final state (in this case having someone to come and provide support), Icon E symbolizes the action which is needed to create the final state (such as creating attention by waving or shouting), whereas Icon F stands exemplarily for the impending initial step which is needed to reach the final state (such as pressing the button). Based on this fundamental concept, most icons can be categorized into these three groups.

In case of the Passenger Call Button and also the Emergency Call Button it is desired to understand which category is most intuitive and favoured by the passenger and hence represents the fastest and easiest trigger.

A) Female wearing scarf and cap   B) Gender neutral torso   C) Gender neutral torso holding a cup   D) Female wearing skirt and holding traytable with glass   E) Gender neutral torso holding up arm   F) Hotel Bell

Fig. 8. Detailed icons of the Passenger Call Button

Afterwards, the passengers were asked open-ended questions of the identified differences and for their preferred design. Additionally, three different icons were shown to understand passenger's preference on the service call. A female icon, gender neutral icon and the symbol for a hotel bell were used to understand whether there is an incline towards gender associated service or the action of actively calling someone represented by the hotel bell (see Fig. 9). The first two icons are commonly found in the aircraft, whereas the last one is found as a symbol for pure service in hotels.

Fig. 9. Detailed icons of the Service Call Button

2.3   Research Design

The questionnaire was generated using the online survey software Qualtrics (www.qualtrics.com). The short video for the visual search task was embedded in the questionnaire. It took around 15 min to complete the survey. Participants were advised to use a laptop or desktop computer to complete the study since the screen resolution for the "spot-the-difference" video were best on a bigger screen.

2.4   Hypotheses

There are five alternate hypotheses which will be tested as follows:

Table 1. Basic demographics passengers

Category		Count	Percent
Gender	Male	117	75%
	Female	35	23%
	other	3	2%
Ethnicity	European	139	89%
	African	3	2%
	North American	3	2%
	South American	2	1%
	Asian	7	5%
	Oceanic	1	1%
Age	<30	42	27%
	31-40	55	35%
	41-50	36	23%
	>50	22	14%

H1: There is an association between familiarity and detection of change of the cabin crew icon

H2: There is an association between gender and the preferred icon for cabin attendant call

H3: There is an association between gender and the preferred icon for service

H4: There is an association between travel class and preference of cabin crew icon

H5: There is an association between travel class and preference on the service icon

H6: There is an association between educational background and the preference on the cabin crew icon

H7: There is an association between educational background and the preference on the service icon

Statistical analysis was conducted using IBM SPSS (Version 28.0).

3 Results

3.1 Basic Demographics

The average age of the participants was 37.8 ($SD = 10.6$). The majority of the participants were male (75%, $n = 117$) and of European descent (89%, $n = 139$). For details refer to Table 1 for a summary of the demographic information. Differences in participants' preferences of the Passenger Call Button were collected and quantified by Chi-Square Analysis.

Table 2. Results Spot-the-difference test

Category	Count	Percent
correct answer	117	77%
no difference spotted	21	14%
watched multiple times	10	7%
wrong answer	4	3%

3.2 Results of the "Spot-the-difference" Test

152 of the 155 participants answered the open-ended question on the "Spot-the-difference" test. The majority of the participants identified the changes in the icons for the Flight Attendant Call Button correctly. 14% ($n = 21$) did not notice any difference, whereas 7% ($n = 10$) specifically mentioned that they only noticed the changes after watching the video multiple times (which was against the instructions of the experiment). Only a minority provided a wrong answer. All the above mentioned, in total 23% ($n = 35$) did not provide a correct answer on the first spot. For further details refer to 2.

The overall high number of positive responses could result from the fact that the participants were able to memorize the images and the changes correctly. According to Potter, 1976 approximately 400 ms are needed to memorize an image [28]. In the experiment participants looked 5000 ms at the picture sequence with an interstimulus interval (ISI) of the same length (5000 ms). According to Rensink, 2001 change blindness can be induced with an ISI of 80 ms or more. However, since in this experiment the ISI had the same length as the picture sequence and six alternating pictures were shown it can be assumed that for the majority of participants change blindness was not induced and the change could be detected. Furthermore, participants were given a cue to actively look for changes in the shown video. To assess whether familiarity (how many times per year is the participant taking air travel?) had an influence on the detection of change a Chi-Square Analysis has been performed. The results for the Chi-Square Test ($\chi^2(2, n = 152) = 2.7, p = 0.259$) indicate that there is no association between familiarity and the detection of change in the shown video.

3.3 Preference on the Cabin Crew Icon

Following the "Spot-the-difference" test participants needed to choose their preferred icon for the cabin attendant call out of the six shown. 150 participants answered this question. The most preferred icon is the "gender-neutral torso holding up an arm" with 38% ($n = 57$), which belongs to the category of icons that focusses on the action. 25% ($n = 38$) preferred the icon showing a "gender-neutral torso holding a cup", whereas 23% ($n = 34$) chose the "female wearing a scarf and cap". Surprisingly, the icon showing a "female wearing a skirt and holding a tray-table with a glass" was the least preferred with only 5% ($n = 7$).

Table 3. Preferred icon for the cabin attendant call

Preference Cabin Crew Icon	Count	Percent
A	34	23%
B	14	9%
C	38	25%
D	7	5%
E	57	38%

Further, participants have been asked which icon would represent "Service" for them. Three different icons were shown: "gender-neutral torso holding a glass", "female wearing a skirt and holding a tray-table with a glass", and a "hotel bell". The majority (61%, $n = 91$) chose the gender neutral torso as the preferred symbol for service, which belongs to the category of icons that focusses on the desired final state. Additionally, surprisingly the feminized depiction was the least preferred (10%, $n = 15$).

Table 4. Preferred icon for the service

Preference Service Icon	Count	Percent
A	91	61%
B	15	10%
C	44	29%

To understand passenger's preference on the icon design hypotheses H2 - H6 have been tested. A Chi-Square Test for independence has been performed to assess the association between gender and preference on the symbol for the cabin attendant call (H2). The results of the Chi-Square Analysis are as follows: $\chi^2(10, n = 150) = 9.46$, $p = 0.45$. The calculated p value is greater than the chosen significance level of $\alpha = 0.005$. Therefore, the null hypothesis cannot be rejected.

Regarding the symbol for service hypothesis H3 (association between gender and icon for service) has been tested. The results for the Chi-Square Analysis ($\chi^2(6, n = 150) = 9.67$, $p = 0.13$) indicate that the null hypothesis cannot be rejected.

Additionally, the association between travel class and preference on the cabin attendant (H4) and service icon (H5) have been assessed. The results for the Chi-Square Analysis (relation between travel class and preference on the cabin crew icon) are as follows: $\chi^2(5, n = 150) = 7.95$, $p = 0.15$. Since the calculated p value is greater than the chosen significance level the null hypothesis cannot be rejected.

The results for the service call are similar: $\chi^2(3, n = 150) = 5.43$, $p = 0.13$. Therefore, the null hypothesis ("There is no association between travel class and preference on the service icon") cannot be rejected.

Lastly, the association between educational background and preference on the cabin crew (H6) and service icon (H7) have been analyzed using Chi-Square Test. The calculated values for the Chi-Square Test on the cabin crew icon are as follows: $\chi^2(15, n = 150) = 27.29$, $p = 0.01$. Since the calculated p value is smaller than the significance level α, the null hypothesis can be rejected and there is an association between the educational background and the preference on the cabin crew icon. Similarly, the calculated values for calculations on the service icon are as follows: $\chi^2(9, n = 150) = 19.53$, $p = 0.01$. Consequently, the null hypothesis can be rejected since the p value is smaller than the significance level α. Therefore, there is an association between educational background and the preference on the service icon.

3.4   Results of Content Analysis

Participants were asked which icons they associate when they want to call a flight attendant. Interestingly, the majority ($n = 94$, 60%) related a gender neutral torso either holding a glass/tray-table, holding an arm up with a cabin crew call. Whereas the gender neutral torso holding up an arm was mainly associated with a passenger calling for help. The reasons stated by the passengers were familiarity with the existing PCB design depicting a gender neutral person, but also actively choosing to be gender-neutral. Around 28% ($n = 43$) associated a female depiction (either full body, wearing uniform or holding a glass/tray-table) with a flight attendant call. It is surprising, that the majority of the participants chose the gender neutral icon when thinking about flight attendant calls (cf. Fig. 10).

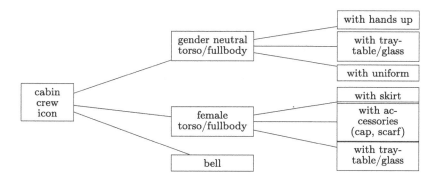

Fig. 10. Results of content analysis

4   Discussion

It might seem at the first glance that the current study focuses on a seemingly negligible topic, however, the historic development of the PCB design itself and the results of this study reveal the complex nature of the topic. The Passenger Call Button is an important feature for passengers to communicate with cabin crew [21]. The design of the button is a relict from the time when air travel developed as a form of mass transportation [22]. Unlike the mandatory warning signs such as Exit, No Smoking, and Fasten Seat Belt symbols (see EASA CS 25-811), the design of the Passenger Call Button is not standardized as it can be seen in the various designs as presented in Sect. 1 [13]. Further, the current design itself is "misleading" and can cause confusion [21]. Since the purpose of the PCB is not clearly defined and the button is mainly used for service requests ([21]), in some designs you will find a symbol of a person holding a tray-table and a glass (cf. Fig. 4, 5(a), 5(c), and 6(a)).

4.1   Visual Attention and Change Blindness

In this study two assessments have been conducted to understand passenger's visual attention and preference on the icon design. The "spot-the-difference" experiment revealed that 77% of the participants were able to note the change in the symbol for the flight attendant call, whereas 23% were either not able to note a change, noted the change after several trials or provided a wrong answer. The high number of positive responses could result from the fact that participants were able to memorize the picture and additionally they were given a cue to actively look for changes. In the introductory section of the questionnaire a note about the purpose of the study was given which could have been interpreted as a valid cue. The presence of a valid cue can speed up the detection of change [30], because attention might be more focused. The key factor to identify change is attention, without it change becomes unrecognizable (known as Coherence Theory) [30]. According to [30] change blindness can appear if for example the ISI were greater than 80 ms and according to Potter, 1976 400 ms are necessary to memorize a picture [28]. The video used for the "spot-the-difference" test consisted of scenes displayed for 5000 ms with an ISI of 5000 ms in between which is exceeds the conditions where change blindness typically occurs. Additionally, it is possible to detect only a few changes at any point in time [30]. The only change introduced in the video was the icon for the cabin crew call button. Further, according to [33] the search for presence of change is easier and faster than for the absence of a feature requiring a more thorough visual scan of the display [33]. Once the change is spotted it can be easily seen [29]. All these factors could be an explanation for the positive outcome of the "spot-the-difference" test. In case the display and the ISI times were shorter as suggested by Rensink, 1997, it can be assumed that change blindness can be observed and the ratio for non-detection would be higher. In cognitive psychology research revolves whether familiarity has an effect on the allocation of visuospatial attention [7]. The findings in [7] prove that a familiar item in a visual display might attract attention

faster than an unfamiliar item. At the same time there are also findings from
other researchers e. g. Johnston and Schwarting, 1997 which state that novel
items draw attention in searches quicker [17]. In the present study it could not
be clearly identified whether the novel or familiar items created the attention
for a change. The first three icons presented were familiar ones typically used on
Airbus A320, Boeing 737 aircraft. Icon D and E are only found in newer aircraft
types such as the Airbus A330-900 (e. g. Icon D: Azul Airlines Airbus A330-900;
Delta Airlines Airbus A330-900). Icon F is unfamiliar as a symbol for the Passenger Call Button. The Chi-Square Analysis results of hypothesis H1 indicate that
there is no association between familiarity and correct detection of the change
of the crew call icon. However, six participants (4%) specifically mentioned the
bell icon which seemed to draw their visual attention to the change. To assess
whether familiarity or novel icons created the attention detection rates need to
be measured which were not the focus of the current study [7].

4.2 Preferences on Icon Design

Surprisingly, in this study the participants preferred gender-neutral symbols for
the cabin crew as well as service icon. Further, the majority associated the icon
which shows the action to reach the target state (gender-neutral torso holding up an arm) as the preferred symbol for the cabin crew icon. This finding
implies that designers should focus more on depicting actions which lead to a
target state (e. g. person waving the hand or shouting) than the target state
(e. g. depiction of a uniformed person) or the initial step needed to complete
the task (e. g. ringing a bell). This can also be found in ISO 7010 where indication signs are standardized. For example Exit signs show a person running
towards a symbolized door [25]. Usually, women work predominantly as flight
attendants and the job is perceived as a "service occupation" [8]. Further, service and care are usually seen as a "natural part of femininity" [32]. Therefore,
the job of a flight attendant can be seen as a classic example for the "Work-as-
imagined" (WAI) vs. "Work-as-done" (WAD) dichotomy. "Work-as-imagined"
as per definition deals with the perception and assumptions of how work should
be done whereas "Work-as-done" refers to the actual how the work is carried
out [15]. The main reasons stated by the participants for choosing the "gender
neutral torso holding a glass" and the "hotel bell" were gender neutralism ("And
I strongly advise against the skirt-version (it is nearly 2024!)" and "Icon B is
outdated") and the association of ringing a bell with actively calling for support ("Ringing the bell is synonymous to service call"). The participants which
specifically mentioned the gender neutralism in their comment were mainly of
European descent where gender equality is strongly rooted as a core value [9].
However, the Chi-Square Analysis does not provide enough evidence to reject
the null hypothesis of that there is no association between gender and preferred
icon type. It would be interesting to assess in future studies whether there is a
cross-cultural difference in the perception of the cabin attendant icon. The only
significance could be found for the association between education and the preferred type of the icon. An assumption for this finding could be that the higher

the educational level, the more concerned are these people about gender equality and female empowerment. Higher education institutions serve as a platform where women can express their ideas and be empowered [10].

5 Conclusion

Flight attendants are the flagship of every airline. Marketing campaigns usually depict smiling cabin attendants. Consequently, according to Chute and Wiener, 1995 flight attendants are typically organised in the "marketing department" [8]. Since the focus of these advertisements was on service, the public perception of flight attendants duty are reduced to serving food and drinks only [8]. The feminization of the role can be rooted back to the 1930 s, where "Stewardesses" are mentioned in Boeing Air Transports first Flight Attendant Manual according to Mahler, 1991 as cited in [8]. A relict of these times is the Passenger Call Button, initially called "Stewardess Call Button" ([38]), in the first years with just a depiction and later on with icons. The most prevalent icons which can be found nowadays are either gender-neutral (full-body or upper body) torsos or a feminized version, depending on the requirements of the airline. The first finding of this research is that the majority of participants were sensitive about gender issues and preferred icons which are gender-neutral. A possible explanation could be the cultural background of the participants (mainly European) where gender-equality is considered to be a strong value. A significant association between education and the preference on the icon could be found which indicates that higher education levels could result in being more aware about gender discrimination. Additionally, icons showing the actions which are needed to reach a target were preferred by the participants. The results of the visual attention test indicate that change blindness could be induced with much shorter screen times (display time t <400 ms with an ISI t >80 ms). Both of these conditions were not met in this study resulting in overall positive change detection rates. It could also not clearly be identified whether the new icons or the familiarity was the cause for attention. Further eye-tracking studies should be done to better understand the visual scan process and assess the effect of familiarity of icons in the visual display. To conclude the findings of this study provide important insights into the user-centered design of the Passenger Call Button. A clever choice on the icon shapes how passengers perceive the PCB, either as a Service Call Button to order meal and beverages or as a mean to communicate with cabin crew.

References

1. Aerospatial, British Aerospace Company Concorde: Explore the world of concorde with heritage concorde (2010). https://www.heritageconcorde.com/carpets-and-overhead-luggage-bins. Accessed 07 Feb 2024
2. aircraft commerce: The evolution of aircraft seating & cabin technologies (2019). https://www.aircraft-commerce.com/wp-content/uploads/aircraft-commerce-docs/General%20Articles/2019/122_REV.pdf. Accessed 11 Feb 2024

3. Boeing Commercial Aircraft 737: B737-200. https://airskystore.com/shop/aloha-airlines-boeing-737-200-passenger-service-unit-psu/. Accessed 07 Feb 2024

4. Boeing Commercial Aircraft 737: B737cl. https://airskystore.com/shop/boeing-737-classic-passenger-service-unit/. Accessed 07 Feb 2024

5. Boeing Commercial Aircraft 737: B737ng. https://airskystore.com/shop/boeing-737ng-passenger-service-unit-psu/. Accessed 07 Feb 2024

6. Chen, C.F., Chen, S.C.: Investigating the effects of job demands and job resources on cabin crew safety behaviours. Tourism Manage. **41**, 45–52 (2014)

7. Christie, J., Klein, R.: Familiarity and attention: does what we know affect what we notice? Mem. Cogn.**23**(5), 547–550 (1995). https://doi.org/10.3758/BF03197256

8. Chute, R., Wiener, E.: Cockpit-cabin communication: I. A tale of two cultures. Int. J. Aviat. Psychol. **5**(3), 257–276 (1995). https://doi.org/10.1207/s15327108ijap05032

9. Commission, E.: Gender equality strategy (2023). https://commission.europa.eu/strategy-and-policy/policies/justice-and-fundamental-rights/gender-equality/gender-equality-strategy_en. Accessed 02 Feb 2024

10. Council, B.: Report: Gender equality in higher education - maximising impacts (2022). https://www.britishcouncil.org/gender-equality-higher-education-maximising-impacts. Accessed 02 Feb 2024

11. De Clerq, G.: Boeing rights a wrong: the flight attendant button (2011). https://www.reuters.com/article/oukoe-uk-airshow-button-idUKTRE75K2IR20110621/. Accessed 31 Jan 2024

12. deHavilland: Comet 4 maintenance manual; passenger announcement equipment trixadio system. Comet 4 Maintenance Manual **23-5-0** (1961)

13. EASA: EASA CS-25 Amendment 28 Certification Specifications and Acceptable Means of Compliance for large aeroplanes (2023). https://www.easa.europa.eu/en/document-library/certification-specifications/cs-25-amendment-28. Accessed 01 Feb 2024

14. Helfrich, W.: Improving airline cabin safety. J. Aviat. Aerosp. Educ. Res. **12**(2), 6(2003). https://doi.org/10.58940/2329-258X.1583

15. Hollnagel, E.: Can we ever imagine how work is done? HindSight **25** (2017)

16. Hradecky, S.: Accident: Jal a359 at Tokyo on Jan 2nd 2024, collided with coast guard dh8c on runway and burst into flames (2024). https://avherald.com/h?article=5132b9fe&opt=0. Accessed 31 Jan 2024

17. Johnston, W., Schwarting, I.: Novel popout: an enigma for conventional theories of attention. J. Exp. Psychol. Hum. Percept. Perform. **23**(3), 622 (1997). https://doi.org/10.1037/0096-1523.23.3.622

18. Klint, M.: Azula330neo (2021). https://liveandletsfly.com/azul-airlines-a330-900neo-business-class-review/. Accessed 13 Feb 2024

19. Konieczny, G.: Die Messung und Steigerung der Qualität von Dienstleistungen in der Flugzeugkabine - Ein Beitrag zur kundenorientierten Flugzeugentwicklung (2001)

20. Manikath, E., Li, W.C.: Usability evaluation of a web interface for passengers' health monitoring system on detecting critical medical conditions. Engineering Psychology and Cognitive Ergonomics: 19th International Conference, EPCE 2022, Held as Part of the 24th HCI International Conference, HCII 2022, Lecture Notes in Computer Science **13307** (2022)

21. Manikath, E., Li, W.C., Piotrowski, P.: Usability assessment on existing alerting designs for emergency communication between passengers and cabin crews. conference paper DLRK 2023 in Deutsche Gesellschaft für Luft-und Raumfahrt. Lilienthal-Oberth.e.V. (2024). https://doi.org/10.25967/610019

22. Manikath, E., Li, W.C., Piotrowski, P., Zhang, J.Y.: Usability evaluation of an emergency alerting system to improve discreet communication during emergencies. In: Engineering Psychology and Cognitive Ergonomics: 20th International Conference, EPCE 2023, Held as Part of the 25th HCI International Conference, HCII 2023, Copenhagen, Denmark, July 23–28, 2023, Proceedings, Part II **14018** (2023). https://doi.org/10.1007/978-3-031-35389-5_9
23. Montagu-Pollock, G.: Comet 4 (2023)
24. Murphy, A.: The flight attendant dilemma: an analysis of communication and sensemaking during in-flight emergencies. J. Appl. Commun. Res. **29**, 1 (2001)
25. International Standards Organization: ISO7010 (2023). https://de.wikipedia.org/wiki/ISO_7010. Accessed 28 Aug 2023
26. Parasuraman, A., Zeithaml, V.A., Berry, L.L.: A conceptual model of service quality and its implications for future research. J. Mark. **49**(4), 41–50 (1985)
27. Porter, T., Musumeci, N.: How did nobody die on the burning japan airlines plane? modern safety features and great training. (2024). https://www.businessinsider.com/japan-airlines-fire-how-passengers-managed-to-escape-burning-plane-2024-1. Accessed 31 Jan 2024
28. Potter, M.: Short-term conceptual memory for pictures. J. Exp. Psychol. Hum. Learn. Mem.**2**(5), 509 (1976). https://doi.org/10.1037//0278-7393.2.5.509
29. Rensink, R.: Seeing, sensing and scrutinizing. Vis. Res. **40** 1469–1487 (2020). https://doi.org/10.1016/S0042-6989(00)00003-1
30. Rensink, R.A.: To see or not to see: the need for attention to perceive changes in scenes. Psychol. Sci. **8**, 5 (1997)
31. Rosen, E.: Deltaa330neo (2023). https://thepointsguy.com/reviews/delta-one-suites/. Accessed 13 Feb 2024
32. Simpson, R.: Gender, space and identity: male cabin crew and service work. Gend. Manage.**29**(5), 291–300 (2014). https://doi.org/10.1108/GM-12-2013-0141
33. Treisman, A., Gormican, S.: Feature analysis in early vision: evidence from search asymmetries. Psychol. Rev. **95**(1), 15 (1988). https://doi.org/10.1037/0033-295X.95.1.15
34. Tupolev Tu-144: Tu144sst (2003). http://www.tu144sst.com/detailedpics/004/pop62.html. Accessed 07 Feb 2024
35. Viscount, V.: Viscount 72 ramp operations (1966)
36. Wayan, V.: Soviet airline flight attendant call button (2011). https://www.flickr.com/photos/dcmetroblogger/5799918208/in/photostream/. Accessed 07 Feb 2024
37. Wikipedia: dehavilland comet (2023). https://en.wikipedia.org/wiki/De_Havilland_Comet. Accessed 07 Feb 2024
38. Wikipedia: Vickers viscount (2024). https://en.wikipedia.org/wiki/Vickers_Viscount. Accessed 31 Jan 2024
39. Wong, S., Neustaedter, C.: Collaboration and awareness amongst flight attendants. In Proceedings of the 2017 ACM Conference on Computer Supported Cooperative Work and Social Computing. Association for Computing Machinery, New York, NY, USA (2017). https://doi.org/10.1145/2998181.2998355

Behavioural Dynamics Towards Automation Based on Deconstructive Thinking of Sequences of Effects: 'As Is – To Be' Automation Effects Change Lifecycle

Naomi Y. Mbelekani[✉] and Klaus Bengler

Chair of Ergonomics, Technical University of Munich, School of Engineering and Design, Boltzmannstr. 15, 85748 Garching b. Munich, Germany
ny.mbelekani@tum.de

Abstract. There rapid resurgence of Vehicle automation systems (VAS), this may result in different types of effects over time. Thus, investigating the impact of long-term effects on users' Behaviour Adaptability/Changeability (BAC) is imperative. Besides volatile markets and shorter process life cycles, automation is one of the most important influences the vehicle industry has to deal with in the next years. Desirable adaptability and changeability based on user behavioural-based safety towards AVs is a quality requirement to stay successful in times of unpredictable transitions. This paper offers the reader knowledge on users' ability to adapt or change due to exposed effects, either safely or riskily. The focus is hinged on structural, cognitive and psychological aspects behaviour. The major extension refers to interaction issues, based on social system theory. This results may contribute and cultivation a safety-based culture on-road and in-traffic. Moreover, highlight the interdepended and interconnected issues to long-term automation exposure and sequences of effects, *as-is effects* and *to-be effects*. Thus, in short, the "*power law of learning*" and "*power law of practice*" in understating users' automation use, bridged on a systematic understanding of extended learnability, trustability, and acceptability. One of the core objectives of this paper is to promote an expert-based culture of advanced strategies and actual application practices. Thus, we aim to provide the reader with fundamental models of BAC based on a deconstructive thinking of sequences of effects.

Keywords: Automation · Behavioural Adaptability/Changeability (BAC) · Behavioural Morphology · 'As-Is and To-Be' Automation effects lifecycle models

1 Introduction

Vehicle automation systems (VAS) have changed over the years in response to the bid to smart mobility technologies. Due to the introduction of new VAS, there is, (1) increased emphasis on that type of automation's effects (short-term effects and long-term effects) being realised (on top of the already realised effects from its preceding automation

D. Harris and W.-C. Li (Eds.): HCII 2024, LNAI 14693, pp. 87–108, 2024.
https://doi.org/10.1007/978-3-031-60731-8_7

system), and (2) constant development of new user behaviours changes formed, as well as (3) the pressing need for constant behavioural adaptability as automation changes. The aim is to reduce risk, increase safety and competence with VAS. The change from established to new processes (such as learning, trusting and accepting automation) cannot be realised instantly, as this takes time to understand. We aim to understand short-term and long-term effects and behavioural adaptability/changeability (BAC) over time.

To profusely comprehend the translation of long-term effects research theory into practice, Mbelekani and Bengler (2023) considered the correlation between learning effects and behaviour modification. They considered the stimulus of the '*power law of learning*' and '*power law of practice*', influenced by bounded knowledge acquisition, rationality/irrationality, an architecture of choices, cognitive biases and mentality, etc. User behaviour in this context can be described as the expressed behavioural ability (mentally, physically, and socially) to respond to internal stimuli (subjective to in-vehicle factors and affordances) and external environmental stimuli (subjective to out-vehicle factors and affordances) in road stream of traffic that affect experience. Thus, it is vital to consider decision-making processes that influence behaviour, and why certain actions are chosen (a perception of choice), and the effect of belief bias towards the VAS. Group (1990) prefer to behavioural adaptation (BA), as: "the collection of behaviours that occurs following a change to the road traffic system that were not intended by the initiators of the change". Different scholars have consider BA research (Saad, 2006; Patten, 2013; Beggiato, et al., 2015; Large, et al., 2017; Large, et al., 2019; Metz, et al. 2020; Metz, et al. 2021) and mental models (Allen, 1997; Beggiato & Krems, 2013). In a sense, BA is associated with time, as it proposes that changes in behaviour are a result of repeated exposure and experiencing the system in different situations, as also argued by Patten (2013). Moreover, Metz, et al. (2021) described it as the phenomenon of behavioural changes with growing experience with an automation system, from the introduction of the system. In essence, behaviour modification can be described as follows, with adaptability and changeability as mutually exclusive processes.

- Behaviour *adaptability*: Adaptability is a user's ability to adjust to changes induced by repeated exposure to automation. It is further understood as the ability of a user to (consciously or unconsciously) modify themselves or their behaviour towards automation (efficiently/inefficiently or safely/riskily in a fast/slow pace) based on the changed driving conditions. When considering the affordances that VAS operation provides, these kind of changes have an indirect/direct effect on how flexible users are willing to misbehave or behave over time. This considers how easily it is to adjust one's behaviour based on changing circumstances. For example, long-term exposure to VAS. Thus, learning or practicing adaptability may include how users are able to respond quickly to changes.
- Behaviour *changeability*: Changeability is the quality of being changeable, thus a user's potential to change when confronted by a situation. It is the ability of a user to "adapt" beyond the intended interaction corridors, with an emphasis on structural and mental adaption processes.

In a sense, changeability can be seen as a sub-characteristic of adaptability, as 'to adapt is to change and to change is to adapt'. For instance, a user needs to adapt in order to change, and to change in order to adapt. Moreover, the element of flexibility and maintainability enables the user to handle the daily unpredictability or precariousness of the automated driving processes in an unpredictable environment on road traffic. For a clear description of adapt and change, the following example is given. Adaptation is "adjusting" one's behaviour to something different from what was the norm (for example, manual driving vs. automated driving, etc.), and change is a "transition" from one state of behaviour outcome to another (e.g., one decides to trust an VAS, and then after some time exposure, one decides to distrust the VAS, etc.).

The aim is not to only frame a theory, but also formulate practical strategies that handle behaviour changes while moulding safe adaptation. For this reason, fundamental knowledge processes on BAC are significant to consider. Therefore, making long-term research a necessity for modelling automation effects from short-term to long-term, in a comprehensive approach. Moreover, gaining knowledge of the 'change point', which is embedded in the existing development of effects and loosely related to use experience (UX) processes. The continuous change in UX (learning, trust, and acceptance process) has to be considered. VAS has been identified as a game-changer in the transport industry, promising substantial reductions in road-traffic fatalities while cultivating smart mobility. However, the process to integrate VAS in traffic has been neglectful of long-term automation effects. Also, how these effects impact users to behave or misbehave. It is vital to consider different factors that may contribute to how these VAS may be received and used by humans, as well as the overarching sequences of effects, especially as automation evolves and humans evolve with it. It is imperative to understand that, as automation changes, so as users' behaviour towards it. However, it is currently unknown to what degree do these changes occur. Forster, et al. (2019) considers understanding users' learning to use automation and behavioural changes as important to understand. What we see in literature, is that knowledge is stuck in a loop of re-counting the knowledge of archaic VAS effects and perpetuating them to fit to new VAS. We aim to develop a nuanced approach that grasps the key constructs of effects, thus help provide a clear understanding of change processes to afford fundamental models applicable to different user types. For instances, a chromatic model that considers a sequence of effects contrast considering short-term and long-term models. In this paper, the scope of BAC is defined, change point and enablers are outlined, and effects monitoring approaches are highlighted.

1.1 Theorising Behaviour and UX

The purpose of contrasting the models is that, we can graphically illustrate where BAC nuances and change points. Moreover, gain knowledge on how learning, trust and acceptance changes over time. Learnability considers the 'learning to use' process and is described as the quality of being easily learnable (Grossman, et al. 2009; Mbelekani & Bengler, 2023). According to Grossman, et al. (2009) it is a key aspect of usability, however, there is little consensus as how it should be defined, evaluated, verified and validated. Mbelekani & Bengler (2023) described it as a quality attribute that evaluates how ease of learning, as well as infers methods for improving ease-of-learning to use and misuse. Trustability/Reliability considers trust and reliance in the automation. Many scholars consider trust as an important element (e.g., Lee & See 2004; Kraus, et al., 2020; Körber et al., 2018; Wintersberger et al., 2017). Trust is described as, "the attitude that an agent will help achieve an individual's goals in a situation characterized by uncertainty and vulnerability" (Lee & See, 2004), with psychological predictor for behavioural variables like use of automation and reliance decision components (Kraus, et al., 2020). Acceptability considers *the adoption of automation process*. Similar to trust, there is a lot of emphasis on acceptance (e.g. Molnar, et al., 2018; Nordhoff, et al., 2019). The behaviour based description of learnability, trustability/reliability, and acceptability are important to consider, especially over long-term automation exposure. It is imperative to investigate the changes in learning, acceptance, and trust/reliance with long-term automation exposure.

Technology Diffusion Model (by Rogers, 1995) focuses on profiles of users and considers five stages integral to this theory. For example, awareness, interest, evaluation, trial, and adoption. The theory also argued that, a user might reject the system at any time during or after the adoption process. The Technology Acceptance Model (TAM) aims to explain usage behaviour leading to acceptance, and covers perceived usefulness (PU), perceived ease of use (PEOU), and user attitude. TAM borrows from social cognition theories such as the Theory of Planned Behaviour (TPB) and the Theory of Reasoned Action (TRA). In order to predict actual behaviour, Davis (1989) considered the strength of the belief-attitude-intention-behaviour relationship, and how PU is influenced by PEOU. TAM was enhanced to TAM2 (Venkatesh & Davis 2000), Unified Theory of Acceptance and Use of Technology (UTAUT) (Table 1).

Table 1. Theorising behaviour

Theory	Dependent factors	Independent factors
TAM (Davis, 1989; Bagozzi, Davis & Warshaw, 1992)	BI to use, System usage	Perceived usefulness, PEOU
TPB (Ajzen, 1985/1991)	Behaviour, BI	Attitude to behaviour, Subjective norm, Perceived behavioural control
TRA (Fishbein, 1967; Ajzen & Fishbein, 1973; 1975)	Behaviour, BI	Attitude toward behaviour, Subjective norm
UTAUT (Venkatesh, Morris, Davis, & Davis, 2003)	BI, Usage behaviour	Performance expectancy, Effort expectancy, Social influence, Facilitating conditions, Gender, Age, Experience, Voluntariness of use

Automation use, trust and acceptance is rooted in internal processes and external structures within which users repeatedly operate. A methodological weakness is that, these models usually consider short-term studies through surveys. Thus, are constrained and weakened by their lack of long-term repeated measures and observing behavioural changes over time. In addition, criticised for being one-dimensional and limiting based on 'rationalistic causal models'. Moreover, seen as unhelpful in understanding how automation is experienced daily and the meaning construction that users have over long-term exposure, essentially void of assessing long-term effects. Based on human-AV interaction (HAVI), little is known about the way in which VAS impact on mobility structures, particularly on road traffic domesticity which border on usage patterns and the process of behavioural negotiation. Thus, neglect to explain learning, trust and acceptance based on a long-term framework, which is problematic due to the pervasive concern on automation effects. A further criticism is that, most of these models have a tendency to rely on supposed rational decisions, rather than viewing the interaction as a negotiation process, and full of unpredictability over time.

1.2 Behavioural Morphology

The transport systems is experiencing dynamically changing mobility structures that presents users with formidable changes to adapt to the newness. Thus, are encouraged towards prolifically, ergonomically, cautiously high level of safety reaction, awareness, and competence. Advances in in-vehicle behaviour monitoring systems and in-vehicle artificial intelligent (AI) systems are helping manufacturers meet these challenges. Thus, understanding users' ability to change and adapt to change is a fundamental prerequisite for safety science in risk-based conditions. In a sense, changeability is presented as an umbrella concept that encompasses many change enablers at various levels of user behaviour throughout the UX life cycle. In addition, also considering short-term and long-term effects as well as short-term and long-term behaviour changes. These modifications include safe and risky situations such as execution of Non-Driving Related Tasks (NDRT) as well as automation abuse and misuse (intended/unintended) (Fig. 1).

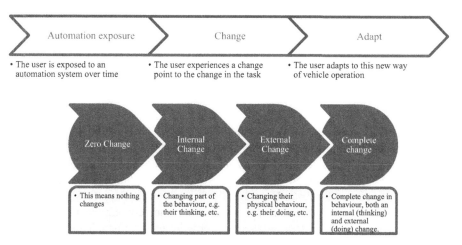

Fig. 1. Behaviour changes based on effects

Moreover, changes can occur in different forms, for instance,

- Change of driving tasks due to VAS. Changes behaviour performance over time.
- A shift in task priority to meet a social wants (NDRT). For example, the driving task (e.g. being attentive, vigilant, etc.) becomes secondary and the NDRTs (e.g. texting, emails, etc.) become primary due to expectations and belief biases, etc.

- Performance morph in response to unexpected changes, e.g. during high traffic flow. How to adjust behaviour to accommodate changes in driving becomes key.
- The evolution of VAS means a changed way of responding, action and reaction.

It is important to note that, both the process of adaptability and changeability are influenced by the power law of learning and practice. Also, vital to consider that, there is a difference between '*learning to use*' and '*learning to misuse*' automation.

Behavioural morphology considers structures of behaviours and how these behaviours are formed/changes over time based on long-term automation exposure and effects. There are different types of behavioural morphological. For instance, when an effect is induced, a new form of behaviour is produced with new meaning. The following are examples, see Fig. 2.

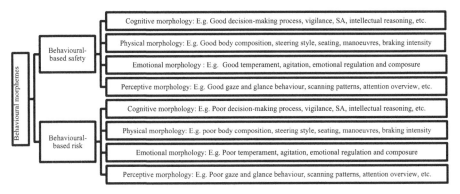

Fig. 2. Behavioural morphology

2 Method

In this industry expert-based interview study, $N = 20$ air and ground vehicle industry experts (automated farming 46%, flying 17%, trucking 8%, and driving 29%). With an understanding of the wider practice, environmental, economic, technical and social systems linked to AVs. Pseudonyms were used to respect confidentiality reasons. For example, *Car* Experts (CE), *Truck* Experts (TE), *Smart Farming* Experts (SFE), *Aircraft* Experts (AE). Each interview began with a verbal informed consent from experts, and information concerning to the task and their background, among others. This was used as an icebreaker, and to make sure the experts felt at ease to express themselves. A question list was used as a checklist to make sure that relevant questions are covered during the interviews. They were asked among other questions: what factors influence users' behaviour to change towards automation? To what extended does change occur and what factors influence it over time? Throughout the discussion, experts were encouraged to consider how plausible future events, allowing an improved understanding of key areas of concern and potentially important sources of exposure. The interviews covered topics related to the long-term effects and user behaviour, considering initial to long-term automation exposure. Furthermore, to support the information received, the experts were asked for sample materials (if need so) that they thought would be of value as supporting evidence, although this was optional. To close the interview, a concluding question was asked: Do you have any questions, or input that you felt were not addressed but important to consider.

The interviews were recorded, transcribed, and then analysed using qualitative content analysis in order to uncover nuances of understanding, resulting in anecdotal evidence of knowledge. The steps taken to analyse the data after transcription was done, were: data familiarisation, theme selection and coding, reviewing themes, categorising the themes for reporting, overall data comparison and integration, reporting the findings (irrespective of industry).

3   Integration of Findings

The link between Predictive Processing Theory and mental models was noted. Thus, stressed that mental models are always shifting due to different effects. Mental models are seen as a better way of understanding why users behave the way they do. CE5 studied first stages of learning a new system and how displayed messages had an effect on driver behaviour for the first phase of a new (e.g. a night-ITS [intelligent transportation system]) system's implementation in cars. For example, the user's phases of discovering functions and adapting behaviour to what is displayed.

Experts alluded that, some users do not phrase their 'thoughts' on whether they trust machines. In a sense, users should be judged more by '*what they do*' rather than '*what they say they do*'. Thus, questioning the notion of 'thinking' and 'doing', as well as considering trust 'as an action' rather than 'as a thought process'. Thus, it was seen as important to "differentiate between measures that make up things and things that are real" (CE2). Experts noted that, most users have a limited understanding of automated systems and are sometimes confused them. CE6 explained that, usually they see people falling asleep on the wheel after eight minutes due to an incompatibility of expectations, resulting in lower SA. The notion of over dramatizing designs was seen as affecting use patterns, and resulting in distractions and workload, which are considered negative HMI effects of user behaviour. Studies that verify the extent that in-vehicle infotainment systems are distracting users and causing cognitive workload were seen to be important. Moreover, experts noted importance in emphasising factors that impact UX, with regards to learnability/usability, trustability/reliability, and acceptability/adoptability. For instance, easy, easiness to discover, and easiness to use where UX measures used to understand users learning patterns. CE5 suggested that, "sometimes you discover it very slowly, but once you understand, you know how it works", thus reaching the plateau level. However, some experts had concerns about the aftermath of the plateau stage, and the decree of intentional misuses that may occur due to users' added knowledge about the system, especially for conditional VAS. Experts noted measures on how often they are reminded to touch the steering wheel. SFE4 mentioned difficulty in learning as a factor in whether people want to use it, as many users see technology as a way of making life easier and not an extracurricular activity. Thus, anything that falls outside the realm of easy learning, may result in rejection. For instance, "users are normally very emotional people, and they can be like, either I can understand it but if not, then I am not going to use it."

CE2 explained the importance of getting users to understand how and when they should takeover, as well as mitigating attentional issues that are associated with over trust. It was seen crucial to use a diagnosis list to measure trust, as it was seen as hard to describe or compute. CE5 advised that, it is hard to measure one metric, so the right approach is to aggregate many parameters and try to provide a model of how trust is built. Further explained that, "it is built differently depending on the driver state of mind, age, gender, etc. It is different from one person to another and experience" (CE5). For example, if automation drives really well for an hour, users tend to assume it can do anything. Considering diagnostic criteria to assess trust, CE2 suggested assessing trust as a time-based concept as it is not static. Experts stated that, users can always generate trust, as long as there is interest. CE1 saw trust as a continuous learning process, and considered the 'psychosomatic reinforcement' as an element in understanding trust. The different degree to which people trust systems are based on how well it performs, and the performance can vary quite widely depending on traffic and environment situations, and so forth. TE1 stated that, truck drivers tend to be conservative and prideful in their knowledge of driving, thus may have low trust in automation. For example, they say things like, "I know how to drive and this is my work domain. For them, driving is an art that they are fully knowledgeable about" (TE1). TE2 noted that, the discussion about automated gear shifting, "were they said no, I should not have it, because I know how to drive better." Further noted the effect of features that drivers see as useless. Thus, it is important to distinguish UX and trust based on personal VAS (where it is used for personal intentions) compared to work VAS (where it is used for work intentions) usages. Experts noted the correlation between UX and trust. SFE4 noted that, it depends on the character of the person, and SFE5 stated that "it has to be useful and good value for money". While, SFE6 stressed that "hardware and software should be easy to understand and use", and SFE7 saw system errors as an effect in user trust. AE2 mentioned that, even for the FMS (Flight Management System), the user should at least make a sanity check, because that can go wrong if the assumptions are mistaken or predictions are no longer true. For example, an Airbus aircraft that landed a couple of meters short of the runway, because the pilots over trusted the prediction of the FMS. Thus, it is essential to predict trust both under normal and abnormal conditions. Pilots are generally trained to monitor automation and FMS. The attitude is towards scepticism and to question automation rather than over relying on what the digital Marvel conveys. AE2 inferred that older pilots are much more wary of automation, because they have been working with unreliable systems of the first generation. Further, those who have flew an aircraft for decades have a decent understanding of the in-service reliability of the Autopilot, as they have encountered a issues in real life, thus have a realistic image of what to expect (AE2). AE2 noted that experience and knowledge can have either a negative or positive effect on trust. AE3 stated that, pilots who have experience on the more conventional aircrafts, do not trust automation that much, as they tend to say "I can trust less in automation because I trust in myself". Hence, case one is that the task is too complex, and case two is the system does not work as it should. The experts illustrated that, in a situation where the pilots over-trust the system, possibilities of ending up in a fatal situation are high. If trust declines, then interest to use declines.

Trust was seen as essential in archiving acceptance (CE2). The question of what induce humans to accept automation is vital to consider, as well as incentives that enforce or reinforce users to use or misuse. CE2 stressed that "unfortunately, technologies are not better than humans at the moment", and illustrated expectations as human paced versus automation paced. Thus argued that, "the better we understand what people expect, the better that we can design it" (CE2). However, this was seen as extremely abstract, as sometimes people's expectations are frictional based on something they saw on the internet. CE2 shared that expectations play an enormous role in crash causations and preventions. For example, drivers who let the car crash, as they said "I thought it would steer". Moreover, expectations can mean one thing and another to different user types, and designing for all is extremely challenging. CE5 stated that, there are intrinsic motivators, such as, using VAS to prove that they can use it or they are cool. TE1 noted that, "convenience to kind of relax from parts of the driving task" motivate users to accept VAS. Comfort and intelligence was considered, and CE5 stated that, they are continuously building more intelligence into ACC to negotiate up and down hills and curves, so it will adapt early to upcoming events. TE1 stated that, Cruise Control and ACC are seen as useful by truck drivers for different reasons. SFE1 noted that, automation should improve efficiency and reduce stress, "so you improve efficiency and improve human life." SFE3 stated that, the reputation of the system is a motivating factor. Further, there is increased acceptance over the years due to comfort and less stress. Automation has to create opportunity for the operator to complete other tasks, and SFE5 stated that, automation can work 24 h a day, seven days a week and that "normally it is easier to handle as we have a huge workers problems to get good drivers and workers into agriculture." SFE7 noted that, automation is very useful to everyday agronomic life, savings and better comfort, makes life easier, yields increase and altitudes decrease, and comfort. When it comes to disuse, CE6 noted annoying, erroneous, difficult to understand, complicated to use systems, and manual driving as a preference as factors. AE1 expressed that, the first motivation to switch off the autopilot is a pilot who likes manual flying and finds it pleasurable and exciting. And a major reason why they became pilots is flying. Another factor was the influence of system limitation, as pilots think that they can do it better. AE3 noted that, safety is the most important thing. AE4 emphasised on usefulness, and "when you look at the long distance flights that are 11 + hours, and you find that for 10 h the autopilot is controlling the plane." AE2 mentioned that, difference in short-range flights (short-haul flights) with long-range flights (long-haul flights, which are a standard of up to eight hours duration) as influential to consider when evaluating user behaviours. AE4 felt that, even though the Autopilot is great, it also has disadvantages. AE2 felt that any system that creates frequent malfunctions and nuisance alerts, the pilot will shut it down and not use it. Thus, things that work well, will be used more and those that don't, will be rejected.

When talking about misuses, CE2 explained that, people do things because they have to and because they want to. CE1 noted the significance of monitoring systems. CE4 noted different misuses by users. CE3 noted that, humans have a tendency to misuse things, and we have to differentiate between intended and unintended misuse. SFE6 noted the differences as direct or indirect misuse. SFE3 stated that, their systems are designed for farm work, however, some customers have a tendency to use on public roads. SFE1 noted that, "everything has its limits, but our rule is always do not underestimate Homo sapiens." SFE1 stressed that, there are "videos on the internet where people put their dogs on a machine and engage the system." People are always trying to check the limits of a system. According to AE4, there are many misuses, based on errors, caused by mishandling of the system, by a failure of the system and also many circumstances that causes complications. AE3 noted misunderstanding, workload, wrong decision-making, experience level, and experience with a different system as factors. According to AE2, there should be no severe misuse of the autopilot system, because the conditions and limitations are so clear. CE2 suggested the behaviourism's rewards and punishments to force users to behave. Experts noted that, it is vital to assume that everyone is going to misuse from the very beginning, and have a preventive strategy designed to mitigate that risk. The experts were in agreement that, it is still a challenge to calibrate trust, as system boundaries are sometimes not clear to users. CE4 noted that, there should be in-vehicle systems able to support the driver, thus, VAS should an extension of human skills (Table 2).

Table 2. Expert Views: Impacts of automation

Mental models	Expert
• "We are constantly building models of how everything works… and we trust some of our models more than others. We believe that some models have better predictions than others, because we have more or less experience with them" • "We often talk about the individual differences, just because it's easy for us to get a handle on, but the variation in people is much bigger than that, it's more a day by day variation"	CE2
• "There is a difference between what people say they do and what they actually do. You would ask them, do you speed a lot, they would say no, but the driving data says otherwise. Do you think ACC is a good system? They would say yes, it is fantastic. But looking at their data, they never have it on. Then they would answer by saying, but no, why should I use it"	CE1
• "We saw that some of their behaviours changed over time."	CE5
• "So in a way, it has to be intuitive as possible, but then the question becomes what does intuitive mean"	CE6
Learnability	
• "All systems for the first phase of their implementation, they will at the first step, display messages to drivers, and we studied how those messages had an impact on driver behaviour. We had phases of discovering the functions and adapting the behaviour to what is displayed. We saw that it changed over time. But we needed more data to be able to describe it in details, so the only thing we managed to have was the description of the first stages of learning a new system."	CE5
• "Learnability is actually safety critical. In that L3, if you don't understand what the takeover alert means and what you're supposed to do, you are in trouble That is safety critical." • "In their first minutes, hours, you know they learning it, are they behaving correctly though. You might not know what mental model they have, but are they taking over when they should"	CE2
• "If you are not educating the user to a broad extent, for example.., as a result we need to assume the worst that someone gets in the car and is really goofing around."	CE6

(continued)

Table 2. (*continued*)

• "Looking at the driving data, when you start using it, people might use it in less traffic, like low density traffic and then maybe on highways, and then suddenly you start using it while you're commuting, maybe in more urban environments, or ring roads, depending on traffic you might use it a bit more frequent, and then maybe you get scared, because it didn't respond as you were expecting at a curve or when it lost track of people or something. It needs to be safe to begin with."	TE3
• "Since we do not have L3, it feels like we can go with a less is more approach. There are like gamification, or something like that. But it depends on the use case and the system, there is no like one fits all when it comes to automation. The metrics depends on type of system."	TE2
• "There is a learning curve, they learn how to trust the system. In the beginning, they are sceptical but once they start using it, once they start seeing the outcome, then they fully rely on it"	SFE1
• "Because of different kinds of systems, it is kind of a huge grey zone for the user, thus this needs to be extremely clear, what responsibility does the driver have in different assistance"	CE3
Trustability	
• "That is why we have all these mode indicators and displays to help them build their mental model in greater detail, so they can develop trust and use it better" • "Trust and mental models are characteristic of the same thing. The mental model is all about prediction, and trust is just a measure of how well you think you could predict...If you predict that it is going to slow down for that car and it does, you have built a little trust; your model has been a little bit reinforced. And if sometime it drifts out of the lane without telling you, then you are like, Oh, I did not realize that could happen, now your mental model just grew an extra branch, and trust went down because apparently my whole model of this tree is weak" • "Kind of use trust as a subjective measure to see how people build their models and specific aspects of the models" • "If I have a driving automation system and I understand it, I have worked well with it, and I get comfort, convenience. Am I going to use it on the way to work? Sure, I will use it on that 3-h drive. Now, if it had some silent failure like drifted out of the lane, and I just happened to notice it one time, as I was using and I just happened to notice that it misread the lane line and drove out of lane. I am going to be like that is not trustworthy, and I am not going to use it, maybe for the rest of that drive. Well if it is a 3-h drive, maybe I will not use it for the next 1 h. Then after that, I will be like, I am tired, then put it back on, see if it is going to work. But my feelings about how trustworthy that system is are going to change based on which of the events I may have had. And because it's an optional comfort kind of system, I may or may not use it based on how much trust I have in it at the moment. So maybe if you look at trustworthy as sort of a criteria level on the trust scale, like a line in the sand saying, if I am above that level I will use it now, and if I am below that level, I will not use it now" • "Considering drowsiness or long haul truckers, not even a long haul trucker, anyone who has to drive night long distances... When referencing the notion of trustworthiness, sometimes people will still continue to use their cars even if they are not trustworthy, for example it left me stranded on the side of the road before. But I have to get to work, I don't have another car. So I am going to take this car, it is not trustworthy, but Im going to take it anyway, because I have to" • "Just because somebody maybe developed some level of trust in one system over here, does not necessarily mean now maybe there is a transfer. So, they're more likely to be a little higher trusting in some other because they had experience and the one you could maybe characterize that in a general way, the average over whatever, but it's very important to try and pin these subjective constructs to something that you can measure. And not to generalize and then make these sweeping statements, like in general people trust things that work more"	CE2

(*continued*)

Table 2. (*continued*)

• "They do trust people, but stuff is stuff to them, before it has a personality, its just stuff. We have learned more to judge people by what they do rather than what they say." • "So trust is almost like one of those diagnosis we use, some of those disorders where you get the diagnosis if you have enough of the symptoms, but the symptom list is very long. Then if you have 10 of those behaviours, we say you trust the system, and if you have five, we say you show some level of distrust. It is very hard to precisely describe or quantify trust, other than as a summary surrogates about what people actually do with stuff" • "We have two takes, one you can make anyone trust the system if the thing that you want to do or is asked to do is interesting enough. So if you put people in a self-driving car on a real road, and then we say the car is driving itself, do you want to play this game, they might be hesitant. Then you tell them, you are ranked – it is a competition, then they will play the game and not care a single thing about the car" • "Talking about driving support, where people risk falling into over reliance issues. It seems like we are talking about this concept of learned trust, where no matter what you know beforehand about what the car can or cannot do, you will extrapolate from how it behaves under a certain period of time, and some people seem completely immune to that, and others seem completely susceptible or completely inflexible" • "The problem in people is that they mentally switch to passengers and do something, you need to predict who will mentally checkout based on like general demographic attributes"	CE1
• "It is not a matter of if it is trustworthy, but it is a matter of if the people trust it appropriately, because over trust can be very dangerous and under trust can also be dangerous, and so the word trustworthy is kind of unspecific." • "Our goal, or any engineer who develops UI for automated driving generally, would focus on appropriate trust, and not over trust but appropriate trust. But I think that is a key challenge"	CE7
• "The history of the person certainly matters. If someone has had a bad experience with one of these systems, but also if someone has had a bad experience with driving in general. So when people were in a tragic accident, or near misses or something like this, they will have a very different perception of trust than someone who has not had this experience…When you are just starting to drive and you have not had these serious incident and experiences, and you do not have a mental concept for what can happen. People want to figure out what is their limit, can I do this, does it see this car in front of me, and can it drive without me even through this is a difficult construction zone, so can I do this and can I do that"	CE6
• "Users define a non-trustworthy system by shutting it off, they will not use it."	TE2
• "It is not designed at this point to be trusted fully, with the L2 system you need to be involved yourself."	TE1
• "Trust is tricky in the first phase of use. Then you are disappointed, because in some situations it does not work well and maybe, then the effect will be mistrust. Maybe you will start with over trust and then there is a phase of mistrust."	CE4
• "When people are overconfident on technology or automation they stop thinking what could go right and pay less attention to what could go wrong. So, when an accident happens, it's not only a root cause, but it's a cascade of root causes"	SFE1
• "If there is error, and users can detect it but the system does not communicate this, this triggers distrust"	SFE7
• "Experience has an effect of trust"	AE2
• "Transparency has to be established."	AE3

(*continued*)

Table 2. (*continued*)

• "Trustworthy automation is when it is technically doing what it is designed for and it is performing well." • "Users tend to understand that systems might fail, they mainly trust automation until it shows them it should not be trusted." • "There are various stages, and at the beginning, pilots are quite sceptical because they do not know how well it will work and they question it, and then they test the automated system in a critical situation, then they get overconfident if it works and then trust the automation too much, but then things might end up in a critical situation. Then they realize that it is not easy as they thought it may be, and then now they are getting more sceptical, and paying a closer look at what the system is doing" • "Pilots often express that I trust the automation, but I know that if the task is getting too complicated, automation might fail and it might be a situation where I have to take over manually"	AE4
Acceptability	
• "It has to be safe to be acceptable, and it has to be bling to the interesting"	CE1
• "Users' motivation is safety, they say, I want to use LDW because sometimes its hard for me to see the lines, I want it to tell me when I cannot see the lines, I want it to be better than me"	CE2
• "I am working with ADAS, so when I have an ACC system I use it, because to me it is easier however, someone who does not have that knowledge will not use it, because they do not know it. On the other hand, if someone explains to you how it works and then maybe you will use it later, because you know it, and you feel safe with it" • "Still it is not something for safety, the blind spot system does not make you prevent an accident, but still they like it and they feel reassured by this small light, which often shows a false alarm but they don't notice it. (…) I am not even sure whether they understand what it is there for, but they like the light, so they use it" • "To trust it, you have to use it, but to use it you, have to trust it, so it is a loop"	CE5
• "To use it, there is first curiosity, so they want to try it out, and see what it does"	CE6
• "For some people, the technical experience is fun, or they are curious and try to hit the buttons and see what happens, or enouranged by media or friends, those can be reasons to use it."	CE7
• "If they feel safer, if they feel more efficient, if they feel it reduces the fuel cost. Of course, it is much more important for trucks than for cars. If the company saves X percent of fuel costs every year, just because everyone drives with ACC, and if they reduce the cost for accident repair, that is a huge motivation. They are very much cost driven"	TE2
• "You know better over time that, what works well, what does not, and what the conditions are. So in large, you have a more realistic picture of what the automation does over time."	AE2
Confusion	
• "What you need to address first is the customer or the driver's understanding of the function, and this is really a hard thing to do… We already know today that people don't really know/understand how it works, and sometimes they just deactivate it because they don't understand, sometimes they rely on it, and they wait for some performances that we cannot provide actually, so this could be dangerous" • "Mode confusion, mixing up L3 with L2 hand-off. L2 hands-off is not L3, but it is sold as L3, that's really a problem."	CE5

(*continued*)

Table 2. (*continued*)

• "Many of the systems are event based, so you just need to make sure you get the correct response. It is not so much about higher levels of automation. So it's linked to crash events, and then you need to have the correct response and avoid incorrect response, and so you look at did the drivers dictate the potential crash object earlier. But for other types of system when it's not continuous support. For the event basis like milliseconds, let us look at L2, it needs to be there from the beginning, when you turn it on, you need to know, it should be part of the design. If they have a wrong mental model, when they turn it on for the first time, we need to change that mental model in 10 s"	TE2
Misuses	
• "Many of accidents most of the time are linked to human error or behaviour or use in unintended ways."	CE5
• "What do you think about texting? She said, I think it is very dangerous, but I have to do it sometimes. She said, if my boyfriend text me…, and also when my kids text me, I need to get back to them right away. She then said, I hate texting while driving, I never want to text, but I definitely do it, and I do it because I have to, but I do not want to do it. A person like that, who is actually most of us" • "That is the whole point of the DMS, is to mitigate misuse, and that is what it is for. The rewards have a much bigger effect, because people do not really care about the punishments"	CE2
• "How often they use the system and how much of this is within the intended use scope and what is outside, and also, how much of the intended use scope is covering, let's say if it's highway and low traffic situations, do they use it all the time within the scope or only a little?" • "Check biometrical data, like heart rate, transpiration, EEG, for example. Are they calmer, are they more relaxed using the system? Even to the extent, they fall asleep"	CE6
• "Have levels or nuances of misuse…Other types of are using what is there in a way that seems to work for you and then it's up to designers… Misuse is a bad term, because it is a retrospective analysis of something gone wrong, it is more useful to talk about affordances and what is possible or not possible to do, and then expect at least some portion of your drivers to do those things that are possible"	CE1
• "The type of misuse is different, at the beginning, it just a misunderstanding problem or an error or people do not know how it works, or the understanding is a different one." • "We observe such intended misuse behaviours, for example, like testing the limits, or let us try out, could I fake any situation and the system will not recognize it. Like so many YouTube clips where people try to find innovative solutions, working beyond system boundaries."	CE4
• "So, when you are developing automation systems, it's always part of the study to imagine misuses and to imagine its impact and to provide enough barrier modes, to be able to decrease the possibility that a crash happens."	CE5
• "If you have more time and know in 10 min you have to take over control, then you can misuse. As one reason people do not want to take over control immediately is that they are into something, I just need to finish this email or I just need to do this and that before I take over."	CE3
• "It is not direct misuse, but the problem can be that the settings are wrong. For example, when they do not understand how to put in the correct numbers from the width of the implement or the distance from the steering axle to the end of the implement, and when these measurements are not correct, then there are problems."	SFE6

(*continued*)

Table 2. (*continued*)

• "On such long segments, if you are flying just straight and level for quite a long time over water, with little interaction with air traffic control, then we are in a situation where vigilance, fatigue issue and complacency are an issue." • "Risk of misuse is bigger for assistance systems, you could get an over reliance on what you see on the screen, this is a bigger issue compared to let us say misuse of the autopilot."	AE2
• "There is a relationship between curiosity and ease-of-use"	AE4
• "You look at the situation awareness of the driver, like how he/she is able to detect things and ability to respond while driving in manual mode and compare with the system"	TE2
• "For the user it is all about feelings, so to always feel safe with it. That is also my personal experience when using new systems, it is always about how safe you feel with using it"	SFE2

4   General Discussion

The findings in this paper are based on experts' views on user behaviour based on automation effects. In a sense, aims to highlight the interdepended and interconnected issues of long-term automation exposure, and a description of '*as-is*' and '*to-be*' automation effects as users are exposed to automation over time. Thus, in short, we provide a chronicle of automation effects, user behaviour, using dynamics, bridged on a systematic understanding of learning, trust, and acceptance. This is shaped by an affiliation of factors: the human persona, automation, UX, sequence of time, effects and behaviour (misuse, etc.), and environment (weather, traffic density, road type, etc.). Based on data analysis, it was evident that the change in users' learning, trusting, accepting abilities has an effect on their behaviour to misuse or properly use vehicle automation. Out of the different vehicle industries, the automotive domain experts noted that users are more likely to experience rapid BAC in comparison to the others, with the aviation domain following route in second ranking. Most of the findings emphasised a key need for long-term research that investigate the interaction between humans and automation in real world scenarios (Fig. 3).

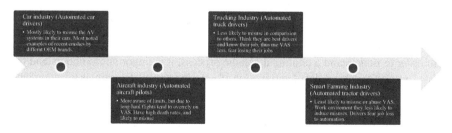

Fig. 3. Industry VAS misuses

4.1   '*As Is -To Be*' Automation Effects and the Perception of Change

As automation share spaces with humans over the sequence of time, there is a need to predict humans' behaviour towards these automation systems, especially as they evolve and change with time. Essentially, to derive safe adaptation processes. Such predictions can be particularly challenging when users exhibit sudden and impulsive shifts in behaviour towards automation. This may be linked to stress, belief biases, and time pressure, etc. For example, a driver can decide not to send an email or text while the VAS is activated (for SAE L2, for example), but then suddenly change their mind. Consequently, such impulsive choices and decision reversals may possibly have an effect on *in-the-loop* (behaviour-based safety situations) uses to then *out-the-loop* (behaviour-based risk situations) uses, and thus result in crashes. In a sense, it is important that researchers investigate the mechanisms of users' *changes-of-mind* in dynamic vehicle operation tasks under stress and time pressure. It's also crucial to consider change models of the 'stress factor' over long-term automation exposure. Therefore, derive models that describe *changes-of-mind* in dynamic tasks transfer and its interplay with long-term automation exposure, past consequences of risks, and knowledge acquisition. This will assist in deriving decision-making models of user behaviour towards automaton.

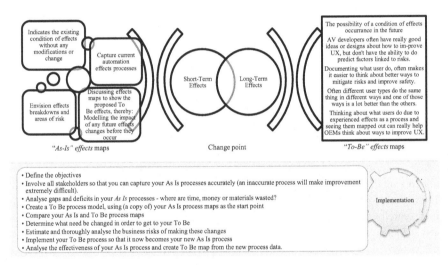

Fig. 4. Continuous '*As Is – To Be*' Automation Effects Change Lifecycle model

In order to understand a continual change process, it is important to understand the '*As Is – To Be*' lifecycle model of automation effects. In a sense, if the aim is to understand user behaviour as a result of automation-induced effects, it is imperative to model the current state of effects (*As Is*) and then the future state of effects (*To Be*) to either mitigate or improve users' behaviour. In short, we thus consider the *Effects Uncanny Valley* theory as a guideline in understanding and predicting automation effects as VAS evolves and changes. As VAS evolves, this will trigger uncanny short-term or long-term effects on user behaviours if not designed for. We discuss this concept in a more detailed approach in our forthcoming paper. It is important to bear in mind that, mapping sequences of effects may reveal behavioural changes. In a nutshell, it is important to understand '*As Is*' effects maps. The '*As Is*' effects maps shows the current experienced effects. Capturing the *As Is* effects may be helpful in understanding the *To Be* effects, for the following reasons (see Fig. 4). The '*To Be*' effects shows automation's proposed future effects. Implementing an '*As Is - To Be*' automation effects model and then continuously making improvements is time and resource taxing. However, by creating a process model of the '*To Be*' *effects,* researchers can consider the impact to behavioural changes and the outcome of the behavioural changes for future AV designs. The reason why '*As Is - To Be*' *automation effects* matters, is that, they can prevent behavioural-based risks before they occur, through an in-depth analysis of the '*As Is*' and '*To Be*'. When analysing *As Is* processes, effects could be streamlined across different user types. In order to capture the '*As Is*' effects and behavioural changes correctly and model the '*To Be*' effects and behavioural changes, a process mapping computation strategy could be used. For example, process mapping software that continuously document processes with understandable maps to support the assessment of change events.

4.2 Behavioural Change Processes

User behaviour can be unpredictable and the various effects that influence it are uncontainable and sometimes not considered nor designed for by developers. Essentially, trust-induced safety or safety-based trust is an important element in building collaborative interactions between humans and automation systems. Equally, trust-induced risks or risk-based trust (over-trust/distrust/mistrust) can be detrimental if not properly calibrated. In a situation of declining trust due to discontent/displeasure with an automation system's behaviour, users may want to reject the automation. Trust can also be seen as a discrete process of user engaging or disengaging automation, thus making it fluid and continuously changing. Therefore, users' learning, trusting, and acceptance of automation can be considered a process, and have the potential to influence each other over time. For example, a user might experience a situation where the automation's behaviour is unsatisfying to them, and this could result to deactivation and switching to manual mode (a form of automation rejection). While on the other hand, in situations where the user gets satisfied with the automation, this could result to activation and switching to automated mode (a form of automation acceptance). Poorly calibrated learning effects, trust and acceptance is often problematic. Thus, considering how to mitigate categorically destructive learning effects is a critical challenge with broad ramifications, particularly as automation becomes more complex and goes beyond a simple tool with clearly defined and easily comprehensible behaviours. Concerning disuse, in relation to misuse, we find that undesirable/destructive learning effects may introduce several confusing effects, such as continual takeover time delays, transfer negligence, poor SA, error, confusion, partial reactions, etc.

In situations where users might not comprehend how to respond to the automation's limitations, this could easily lead to overall undesirables, and thus open space for risk-taking behaviours. Even so, user behaviours are extremely complex to fit a *predict-and-provide* approach, because humans are often susceptible to changeability or unpredictability. As a result, we have to recognise the breadth of possible desirable safety-based behaviours, undesirable risk-based behaviours, and situations that might need to be demarcated by knowledge rules and then engraved in long-term automation exposure practices. The science behind '*rule-following*' (user following design rules) and '*rule-making*' (user making their own rules) over time (from initial to long-term use) should be considered. This loom larger on aspects at the adaptive lucidity of user behaviours, as human factor repertoires. Investigating the potential costs that users' might incur over time, and specific adaptive problems that must be solved.

It's important to discriminate on user behaviours selection towards automation based on their use etiquettes. We have categorised users into two types, as the misbehaved users (considering misbehavers [carelessness], fail to conduct oneself in a cautious manner) and behaved users (considering good behavers [carefulness], conduct oneself in a cautious manner) towards automation. If the aim is to model user behaviours based on their use manners, it's essential to diagnose them into categories. This considers behaviour selection as a theory and explores adaptation or change processes, in addition to investigate how *parental effects* (effects induced by the automation in connection with the user state and effects induced by the automation in connection with other factors such the environment, etc.) influences the components of behaviour selection. It also considers the multiple adaptive problems potentially by user types' preferences to act towards automation. This examines the lucidity of users' behavioural strategies and content of preferences. It is also important to understand that human behaviour is complex and interchanging, therefore, no one user can occupy one single category endlessly. In some cases, users are regarded as making calculated decisions based on contextual situation (family demands, work deadlines, etc.) as emotional beings who are influenced by social biases when making decisions.

Thus, the unruly with 'uncertainty' when it comes to user behaviour should be considered. However, can shapeshift based on deferring factors, such as user states (e.g. stress, fatigue, distractions, etc.), environmental factors (road type, weather conditions, traffic density, etc.), and automation boundaries (e.g. capabilities, limitations, errors, etc.) as well as the impact of users' preferences through vehicle brand expectations and patterns of competition. Furthermore, it's significant to understand that as much as it's important to emphasise the learning curve for users learning to use a new automated systems, it's also important to understand their learning curve for learning to misuse. The aim for research engineers, is to develop approaches able to detect these changes, and prevent any unsafe or risk-based behaviours as they occur, intended or unintended. Thus, consider cues to 'behaviour copying'. In short, evolution favours developers who consider safety and risk possessing attributes in understanding automation-induced effects that impose risk costs and those that safety benefits. These considers the rarely shown long-term adaptation/change process. User behaviour towards automation can be described based on two spectrums, as behaviour-based safety and behaviour-based risks. In essence, when assessing BAC, it's important to track these behaviour dynamics over time and understand which changes occur as a result of long-term use, contexts of use, and learning effects. These considers the change point in experience, from the experience perspectives of behavioural intention to use, disuse, and misuse. The route may not proceed in a linear order where each juncture is a prerequisite for entering the subsequent stage (Fig. 5).

The sequence can be dynamic and move in a non-linear, unsystematic or parallel mode, where user types shift between models (e.g., trusting and learning), jump between models (e.g., accept before learning or trust), or process each stage simultaneously (e.g., learning, trusting, and accepting). This process accounts for expert views on internal and

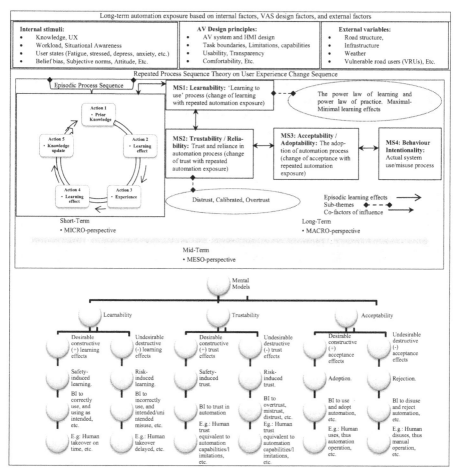

Fig. 5. Deconstructive thinking: learnability, trustability, and acceptability towards automation

external variables in understanding UX. Thus, we posit that user experiences are influenced by a variety of factors. From a methodological point of view, Metz, et al. (2020) suggest that, even though it is essential to consider a single usage of a system, however, sufficiently long exposure is highly important. For instance, repeated VAS exposure may induce knowledge that allows users to gain experience of the VAS's functionality, capabilities and limitations over time (the 'learning to use' process, for example). This knowledge helps build on trust and acceptance over time. Metz et al. (2020) also argues that, this learning process takes time and experiencing of the VAS in different states, situations and environments. Two phases in the learning process are suggested: in the "learning phase" the user learns how to operate the VAS, identifies system limits, and internalizes the system functionality. In effect, there are change points, which includes change enablers and impulses influencing behaviour over time. We believe it takes a phased process for experience to change, and this is influenced by external environmental variables, AV design, and internal stimuli (user state). The outcome of these factors can either be a refusal or an interest to explore the VAS. This moves to Model Stage (MS) 1, leading to a favourable (easiness of learning) or unfavourable (difficulty in learning) attitude towards VAS (learning effects). MS2, the decision process to trust (distrust – calibrated trust – over trust), and then MS3–4, the decision-making process to adopt/reject VAS (based on behaviour intention to accept) and finally the implementation of VAS into long-term practice. Therefore, elaborating on vehicle automation, we organise UX factors hierarchically. As shown in Fig. 4, the evaluation of fundamental external variables and domain-specific human factor aspects, precedes the symbolic-affective (MS1–2), moral-normative appraisal (MS2–3) towards VAS, and the behaviour intention appraisal (MS3–4). Thus, it is imperative to holistically investigate how these factors are shaped and influenced, based on developers' mental models of the VAS based on their experiences and expectation as well as users' mental models of the same VAS based on their experiences and expectations. This information helps with the process where humans simply just coexist with automation to where there is actual collaboration. The model integrates several impact factors, namely: expected risks, expected benefits, perceived cognitive effort in learning to use, perceived experiences and behaviours towards VAS over time. As a result, the aim is to consider implications in long-term automation exposure and the trade-off effects based on instrumental domain-specific, symbolic-affective and moral-normative characteristics of VAS.

5   Conclusion

In conclusion, based on the experts' levels of understanding, we proposed probable strategies that could account for conducting long-term research. Nonetheless, as these propositions are solely derived and pieced together based on industry experts' different views, they should be received as essentially a starting point to normalising long-term effects research. The finding from this study sets the tone for a theoretical foundation for investigating long-term effects on BAC, and cultivates the need for user behaviour models towards automation over time. In a sense, aims to highlight the interdepended and interconnected issues of long-term effects – "as-is" effects and "to-be" effects. Thus, in short, we provide a description of BAC bridged on a systematic understanding of learning effects, trust, and acceptance as intellectual foundations.

Acknowledgment. This project received support from the European Union's Horizon 2020 research and innovation program under Marie Skłodowska-Curie grant agreement No. 860410.

References

1. Grossman, T., Fitzmaurice, G., Attar, R.: A Survey of Software Learnability: Metrics, Methodologies and Guidelines. CHI 2009, 4–9 April 2009, Boston, Massachusetts, USA (2009)
2. Mbelekani, N.Y., Bengler, K.: Learnability in Automated Driving (LiAD): concepts for applying learnability engineering (CALE) based on long-term learning effects. Information **14**(10), 519 (2023). https://doi.org/10.3390/info14100519

3. Nordhoff, S., Kyriakidis, M., Van Arem, B., Happee, R.: A multi-level model on automated vehicle acceptance (MAVA): a review-based study. Theor. Issues Ergon. Sci. **20**(6), 682–710 (2019)

4. Group, O.S.E.: Behavioural adaptations to changes in the road transport system. Organisation for Economic Co-operation and Development (1990)

5. Körber, M., Baseler, E., Bengler, K.: Introduction matters: manipulating trust in automation and reliance in automated driving. Appl. Ergon. **66**, 18–31 (2018)

6. Forster, Y., Hergeth, S., Naujoks, F., Beggiato, M., Krems, J.F., Keinath, A.: Learning to use automation: behavioral changes in interaction with automated driving systems. Transport. Res. F: Traffic Psychol. Behav. **62**, 599–614 (2019)

7. Molnar, L.J., Ryan, L.H., Pradhan, A.K., Eby, D.W., Louis, R.M.S., Zakrajsek, J.S.: Understanding trust and acceptance of automated vehicles: an exploratory simulator study of transfer of control between automated and manual driving. Transport. Res. F: Traffic Psychol. Behav. **58**, 319–328 (2018)

8. Kraus, J., Scholz, D., Stiegemeier, D., Baumann, M.: The more you know: trust dynamics and calibration in highly automated driving and the effects of take-overs, system malfunction, and system transparency. Human Factors **62**(5), 718–736 (2010)

9. Lee, J.D., See, K.A.: Trust in automation: Designing for appropriate reliance. Hum. Factors **46**(1), 50–80 (2004). https://doi.org/10.1518/hfes.46.1.50_30392

10. Wintersberger, P., von Sawitzky, T., Frison, A.-K., Riener, A.: Traffic augmentation as a means to increase trust in automated driving systems. In: Proceedings of the 12th Biannual Conference on Italian SIGCHI Chapter (2017). https://doi.org/10.1145/3125571.3125600

11. Metz, B., Wörle, J., Hanig, M., Schmitt, M., Lutz, A., Neukum, A.: Repeated usage of a motorway automated driving function: automation level and behavioural adaption. Transport. Res. F: Traffic Psychol. Behav. **81**, 82–100 (2021). https://doi.org/10.1016/j.trf.2021.05.017

12. Metz, B., Wörle, J., Hanig, M., Schmitt, M., Lutz, A.: Change of acceptance with repeated usage of a L3-motorway chauffeur. In: 8th Proceedings of Transport Research Arena, Helsinki, Finland (2020)

13. Metz, B., Wörle, J., Hanig, M., Schmitt, M., Lutz, A.: Repeated usage of an L3 motorway chauffeur: change of evaluation and usage. Information **11**(2), 114 (2020). https://doi.org/10.3390/info11020114

14. Patten, C.J.: Behavioural adaptation to in-vehicle intelligent transport systems (Chapter 9). In: Rudin-Brown, C., Jamson, S. (eds.) Behavioural Adaptation and Road Safety: Theory, Evidence and Action, pp. 161–176 (2013)

15. Beggiato, M., Pereira, M., Petzoldt, T., Krems, J.: Learning and development of trust, acceptance and the mental model of ACC. A longitudinal on-road study. Transport. Res. F: Traffic Psychol. Behav. **35**, 75–84 (2015). https://doi.org/10.1016/j.trf.2015.10.005

16. Beggiato, M., Krems, J.F.: The evolution of mental model, trust, and acceptance of adaptive cruise control in relation to initial information. Transport. Res. F: Traffic Psychol. Behav. **18**, 47–57 (2013). https://doi.org/10.1016/j.trf.2012.12.006

17. Saad, F.: Some critical issues when studying behavioural adaptations to new driver support systems. Cogn. Technol. Work **8**(3), 175–181 (2006). https://doi.org/10.1007/s10111-006-0035-y

18. Large, D.R., Burnett, G., Salanitri, D., Lawson, A., Box, E.: A longitudinal simulator study to explore drivers' behaviour in level 3 automated vehicles. In: Proceedings of the 11th International Conference on Automotive User Interfaces and Interactive Vehicular Applications, pp. 222–232 (2019)

19. Large, D.R., Burnett, G., Morris, A., Muthumani, A., Matthias, R.: A longitudinal simulator study to explore drivers' behaviour during highly-automated driving. In: International Conference on Applied Human Factors and Ergonomics, pp. 583–594. Springer, Cham (2017). https://doi.org/10.1007/978-3-319-60441-1_57

20. Allen, R.B.: Mental models and user models. In: Helander, M., Landauer, T.K., Prabuh, P. (eds.) Handbook of Human-Computer Interaction, pp. 49–63. Elsevier, Amsterdam (1997)
21. Weinberger, M., Winner, H., Bubb, H.: Adaptive cruise control field operational test—the learning phase. JSAE Rev. **22**(4), 487–494 (2001)

Self-organising Maps for Comparing Flying Performance Using Different Inceptors

Arthur Nichanian⬤, Wen-Chin Li⁽✉⁾⬤, Wojciech Tomasz Korek⬤, Yifan Wang⬤,
and Wesley Tsz-Kin Chan⬤

SATM, Cranfield University, Cranfield, Bedford, UK
{a.nichanian,wenchin.li,W.T.Korek,Yf.Wang,
Wesley.Chan}@cranfield.ac.uk

Abstract. This paper addresses a new data analysis method which is suitable to cluster flight data and complement current exceedance-based flight data monitoring programmes within an airline. The data used for this study consists of 296 simulated approaches from 4.5 NM to 1 NM to the runway threshold, flown by 74 participants (both pilots and non-pilots) with either a conventional sidestick or a gamepad in the future flight simulator at Cranfield University. It was clustered and analysed with the use of Kohonen's Self-Organising Maps (SOM) algorithm. The results demonstrate that SOM can be a meaningful indicator for safety analysts to accurately cluster both optimal and less-optimal flying performance. This methodology can therefore complement current deviation-based flight data analyses by highlighting day-to-day as well as exceptionally good performance, bridging the cap of current analyses with safety-II principles.

Keywords: data analysis · human-machine interactions

1 Introduction

Flight data analysis has become an important part of each airline's safety management system (SMS) to the extent that establishing a flight data monitoring (FDM) programme is nowadays mandatory for aircraft operators over 27 tons as per ICAO regulations [1]. Airlines and regulators collect a vast amount of data, but only a small portion of it is typically analysed in depth [2]. This is due to the fact that only events which are considered "abnormal" are analysed, leaving most of the data to be stored without further use. This data about everyday performance can, however, contain useful safety information for airlines, both in terms of trend analyses and learning about exceptionally good performance [3]. Many studies have already been published about different algorithms and data analysis methods to derive new learning opportunities from existing data [4]. This study focuses on the use of self-organising maps (SOM) to cluster flight data collected during a simulated approach. Different performance metrics were then collected to assess the clustering performance and the possibilities of deriving new knowledge from the existing data.

2 Relative Work

This study focuses on applying self-organising maps, which is a machine learning algorithm, to flight data analysis methods. Many studies which focus on data analysis algorithms and techniques, especially about data clustering, have been published in the past. This study aims to contribute to the previous research in this field.

Airlines typically use FDM to analyse their daily safety performance. Various flight parameters (over 1000 different parameters for modern aircraft such as the Airbus A350 or Boeing 787) are recorded, downloaded, and processed by flight data analysts. Flight data analyses as of today mostly focus on capturing deviations from acceptable range of parameters, such as unusually high or low airspeeds for a specific flight phase, markers of an unstable approach (e.g. the aircraft not being fully configured for landing below a specific height) and dual pilot inputs. The data is usually also classified within a safety matrix to analyse trends both in terms of event frequency and severity [5, 6]. Some recent developments now also include performing big data analyses to monitor ongoing trends within an airline, consistent with a safety-II approach [3]. Deviations from an acceptable range of parameters can help airlines to monitor their pilots' proficiency and take mitigation measures such as specific training exercises if required [7]. As experts may accept minor deviations (that are within the acceptable range) in order to leave cognitive space for other objectives, an understanding of how these deviations interact with safety performance can prove very beneficial for airlines with pilots from diverse backgrounds featuring different piloting techniques, exposure to different equipment types, cultural values, and perspectives on individual safety objectives [8]. However, most analysis methods used in flight operations remain focused on identifying threshold exceedances, which leads to roughly only 3 to 5% of the data being analysed [9]. The 95% left could, however, lead to additional information about daily operations and normal occurrences, consistent with safety-II principles [10]. Furthermore, it heavily relies on the correct setting of the threshold for the exceedance event detection. If the detection threshold is too narrow, many events would be flagged, resulting in many false positives. Conversely, a too wide threshold would flag few events or no events at all, leading to many false negatives. Finally, it also relies on the supposition that a specific incident could occur. Unimagined potential incidents are hard to notice in the best case if no detection method has been designed previously [11]. Analysing flight data is not only done during everyday operation but also during the design stage of a new technology, such as using a touchscreen as means of flight control [12, 13].

Much previous research has demonstrated the benefits of adding machine learning to current flight data analyses. Machine learning can be defined as a programme's ability to increase its performance with experience, i.e. through learning from the data it is fed with [14]. Machine learning can be divided into two categories: supervised and unsupervised learning. Supervised learning involves knowing the correct solution for a given dataset, whereas unsupervised learning involves not knowing any solution for a specific dataset [9]. Previous research about machine learning in flight analysis comprises Bayesian networks [15], local outlier probability [11], Multiple Kernel Anomaly Detection (MKAD) [16] and clustering [17, 18] to cite a few.

Self-organising Maps (SOM), often used as a synonym for Kohonen's Self-Organising Map is a part of a broader type of machine learning techniques called artificial neural networks (ANN), which has not been researched extensively in conjunction with flight data analysis. ANNs are designed to simulate the sensory processing of the human brain. It simulates a network of model neurons, which can 'learn' many different types of problems, especially classifications [19]. The SOM algorithm specifically maps the data pattern from an input space (the original data patterns) into a n-dimensional space, known as the output space (Fig. 1). The mapping aims at preserving the topological relations between both spaces. In order to ease visualisation, the output space is usually one or two-dimensional. To map the output space, the SOM algorithm uses a neigh-bourhood function, which is responsible for the interactions between the different units. Therefore, SOM can be used effectively for clustering tasks and performs similarly to k-means clustering [20]. SOM are able to extract stabilised phases of flight as well as transient changes in flight parameters. Furthermore, SOM can handle large datasets, which makes them well-suited to analyse flight data and an interesting alternative to k-means clustering [21, 22].

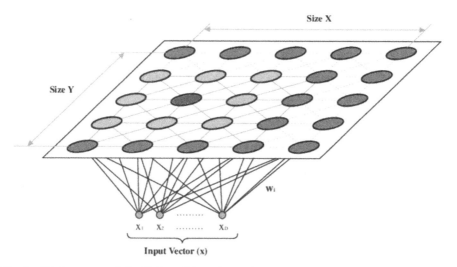

Fig. 1. SOM structure of size X times Y based on an input vector x. The winner neuron is in red, the neighboring neurons are in green and the other neurons in blue [23]

3 Methodology

3.1 Data Source

The dataset consists of 296 simulated approaches flown in an engineering flight simulator called the Future Systems Simulator at Cranfield University [24].

74 participants (55 males, 18 females, 1 preferred not to say) were asked to fly four approaches and landings. Table 1 displays the participants' demographical data. The first two approaches were performed with the use of a sidestick, the first one without any

turbulence and the second one with simulated turbulence. The following two approaches, again with and without turbulence, were performed this time with a gamepad. The participants were asked to follow a standard three-degree descent path while tracking the runway, assisted with the instrument landing system (ILS) through the use of the Flight Director (FD). Additionally, participants could follow the cues displayed to them by the precision approach path indicator (PAPI), while the auto throttle (ATHR) would control the engine thrust to maintain a constant approach speed. For the purpose of this study, the following parameters were considered: the anonymous participant ID, the altitude, calibrated airspeed (CAS), deviation in altitude from the three-degree glideslope, aircraft pitch, presence of a disturbance (turbulence) and the mean of controlling the aircraft (sidestick or gamepad).

Table 1. Participants' demographics

Age	$M = 31.7$ $(SD = 10.37)$
Number of active pilots	33
Number of non-pilots	41
Active pilots' number of flight hours	$M = 1034$ $(SD = 2483)$
Active pilots' simulator hours	$M = 114$ $(SD = 248)$

3.2 Research Procedure

The dataset was first cleaned to only keep the last 4.5 NM to 1 NM to the runway threshold. As most participants were not trained pilots, flying the last 1 NM to the runway threshold and landing the aircraft as per standard operating procedures (SOPs) turned out to be challenging and led to high data variability within the last section of the flight. Therefore, it was removed in addition to 22 different approaches, where the data featured too many inconsistencies. The data was also discretised and interpolated for every 0.05 NM by the distance to the threshold. A new variable called 'ΔGP' was created, which measures the participants' ability to track the three-degree glideslope given by the PAPI. It represents the difference in altitude from the aircraft's altitude compared to the reference altitude corresponding to an ideal 3-degree glide path. It has been determined as follows:

$$GP = \tan(3) \times x_{thr} \times 6076.12 + CH_{thr}$$
$$\Delta GP = Altitude - GP$$

The following parameters were used: x_{thr}, representing the aircraft distance to the runway threshold in NM and CH_{thr} – the crossing height, which is 50 ft above the runway threshold height.

The data was then divided into two sets: one for approaches flown with the sidestick and one for the approaches flown with the gamepad. The root mean square error was calculated for each ΔGP, both of the sidestick dataset (RMSES) and of the gamepad dataset (RMSEG). Each dataset was clustered by corresponding ΔGP variable using the self-organising map (SOM) algorithm to compare the participants' performance. Following the clustering, Welch ANOVAs, and subsequent Games Howell post-hoc tests were conducted on each cluster's RMSE to assess the clustering performance. Python 3.10.11 was used to conduct the analysis.

3.3 Statistical Tools Used

The SOM algorithm requiring the Python 'MiniSom' package was used. The SOM are a type of Artificial Neural Networks (ANN) which convert nonlinear statistical relationships on higher dimensions into a low-dimensional discretised representation map. The map consists of output neurons, usually arranged in a two-dimensional grid and trying to preserve topological relations. SOM and k-means algorithms are identical when the radius of the neighbourhood function in the SOM is equal to 0 [20]. The maximum number of clusters which can be obtained is equal to the number of output neurons. To obtain the optimal number of clusters, the Silhouette score was applied. It is equal to $S = \frac{b_i - a_i}{\max a_i, b_i}$, where a represents the mean cluster centroid distance and b the average nearest cluster distance for every sample i. The Silhouette score is a measure of how similar an object is to its own cluster versus the other clusters. It returns a value between -1 and 1, 1 being the best clustering. For each clustering, a variable optimisation algorithm was used, which calculated the SOM σ and learning rate for the best Silhouette score over $10'000$ iterations. The optimal grid dimension corresponds to $C = 5\sqrt{N}$, where C corresponds to the number of neurons and N the number of samples in the dataset [25]. For the size of the used dataset, it corresponds to a 3×3 grid. To analyse the SOM performance, several metrics were used: the normalised quantization error, the topographical error, the trustworthiness, and the neighbourhood preservation. The quantization error represents the mean difference between the input samples and the winning neurons. It is equal to $QE(M) = \frac{1}{n} \sum_{i=1}^{n} \|x_i - w_{c(x_i)}\|$, n representing the number of data points and w_{cxi} the weight vector of the best matching unit in the map for the data point x_i. The quantization error was then normalized by calculating the average quantization error for each node as follows: $NQE = \begin{cases} \frac{1}{N} \sum_{j=1}^{N} \left(\frac{\frac{1}{n} \sum_{i=1}^{n} \|\emptyset(x_i) - x_i\|}{norm(w_j)} \right), k \\ 1 \text{ if no data point matches the unit} \end{cases}$

corresponding to the number of vectors mapped of each unit. The topographical error is equal to $TE = \frac{1}{n} \sum_{i=1}^{n} d_i$ where n is the number of input vectors and d_i the distance between the best matching and second-best matching units. The trustworthiness is equal to $M_1(k) = 1 - \frac{2}{Nk(2N-3k-1)} \sum_{i=1}^{N} \sum_{x_j \in U_k(x_i)} (r(x_i, x_j) - k)$. The neighbourhood preservation is equal to $M_2(k) = 1 - \frac{2}{Nk(2N-3k-1)} \sum_{i=1}^{N} \sum_{x_j \in V_k(x_i)} (r^{\wedge}(x_i, x_j) - k)$. In both formulas, N represents the data set. $U_k(x_i)$ represents the data points which are k closest to the input space x_i and $V_k(x_i)$ the data points which are the k closest to x_i in the output space. $r(x_i, x_j)$ represents the rank of x_j when the data points are ordered by distance from x_i and $r^{\wedge}(x_i, x_j)$ represents the rank of x_j when ordered by distance in the projection. The elbow method was used to determine the optimal k value. As the data does not show variance homogeneity ($p_{Bartlett} < 0.05$ for both sidestick and gamepad clustering datasets), a Welch ANOVA and Games Howell post-hoc test were used to determine the clustering performance.

4   Results and Discussion

4.1   Sample Characteristics

A total of 278 approaches from 4.5 NM to 1 NM to the runway threshold were analysed through the SOM clustering methodology. Focus was set on analysing the participants' vertical performance, i.e. their ability to maintain a stable descent path according to a standard 3° descent. The clustering of the participants' tracking of the 3-degree glideslope making it possible to assess the participants' manual flying skills both in terms of good performance and common errors. The flight parameters look as displayed in Fig. 2.

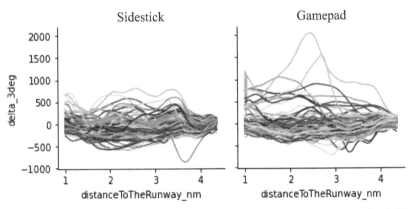

Fig. 2. Deviations from the glideslope expressed from the distance to the runway threshold with the sidestick and gamepad as means of control.

4.2   Clustering of the Deviation from the 3 Degrees Glideslope for Approaches Flown with a Gamepad

The variables shown in Table 2 were used to optimise the SOM algorithm to cluster the approaches flown with a gamepad. The Silhouette score indicates a moderately strong clustering performance with an optimised cluster number of four clusters [26]. The results from Table 3 demonstrate that SOM can be a meaningful tool to cluster the gamepad flight data. Although the NQE remains fairly high, indicating that some data points do not match the unit's weight vector [27], the topographic structure of the original data is well-preserved on the map [28, 29].

The approaches flown with a gamepad grouped by cluster are displayed in Fig. 3, which shows the CAS, deviation from the three degrees glideslope and pitch. The trials with disturbance appear to have been more difficult for some participants, as clusters

Table 2. Sigma, learning rate and corresponding silhouette score used as parameters for the SOM processing.

SOM parameters	Value
σ	0.62
Learning Rate	0.03
Resulting silhouette Score	0.34

Table 3. Clustering metrics obtained by the SOM algorithm.

SOM metrics	Value
Normalised quantization error	0.40
Topographic product	0.02
Trustworthiness	0.90
Neighbourhood preservation	0.94

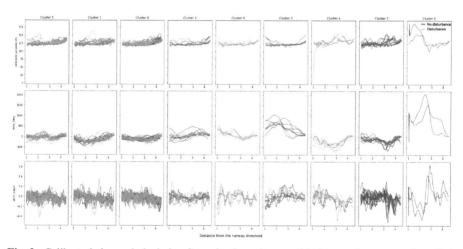

Fig. 3. Calibrated airspeed, deviation from the three-degree glideslope and corresponding pitch outputs for each cluster.

3, 6 and 7 are almost only composed of landings with disturbances and feature a comparatively higher RMSE (Fig. 3 and Table 4). The clusters are well-defined, the Welch ANOVA indicates significant differences between clusters ($F = 3015$, $p < 0.05$). The post hoc analysis shows significant differences in RMSE ($p < 0.05$) between the clusters (Table 5). Cluster 5 displays the least RMSE, and cluster 6 displays the highest RMSE (Table 4). The difference between experienced pilots and novices is less pronounced than within the sidestick dataset. A cause for this can be the smaller experience gap in using gamepads compared to flying with a sidestick.

Table 4. Average RMSE by cluster

Cluster	Average RMSE (ft)
1	159.86
2	118.35
3	416.70
4	272.86
5	73.89
6	794.47
7	169.14
8	103.91
9	130.37

Table 5. Summary of post-hoc results for the gamepad data

Cluster A	Cluster B	Mean RMSE difference (ft)	Standard error	P-value
1.0	2.0	41.51	1.38	<0.05
1.0	3.0	−256.84	3.82	<0.05
1.0	4.0	−113.0	2.81	<0.05
1.0	5.0	85.97	1.0	<0.05
1.0	6.0	−634.61	13.88	<0.05
1.0	7.0	−9.29	1.53	<0.05
1.0	8.0	55.95	0.91	<0.05
1.0	9.0	29.49	2.05	<0.05
2.0	3.0	−298.35	3.88	<0.05
2.0	4.0	−154.5	2.89	<0.05
2.0	5.0	44.46	1.19	<0.05
2.0	6.0	−676.11	13.9	<0.05
2.0	7.0	−50.79	1.66	<0.05
2.0	8.0	14.44	1.12	<0.05
2.0	9.0	−12.02	2.15	<0.05
3.0	4.0	143.85	4.59	<0.05
3.0	5.0	342.81	3.76	<0.05
3.0	6.0	−377.77	14.35	<0.05

(continued)

Table 5. (*continued*)

Cluster A	Cluster B	Mean RMSE difference (ft)	Standard error	P-value
3.0	7.0	247.56	3.93	<0.05
3.0	8.0	312.79	3.74	<0.05
3.0	9.0	286.33	4.16	<0.05
4.0	5.0	198.96	2.73	<0.05
4.0	6.0	−521.61	14.11	<0.05
4.0	7.0	103.71	2.96	<0.05
4.0	8.0	168.95	2.7	<0.05
4.0	9.0	142.49	3.26	<0.05
5.0	6.0	−720.57	13.86	<0.05
5.0	7.0	−95.25	1.36	<0.05
5.0	8.0	−30.02	0.58	<0.05
5.0	9.0	−56.48	1.92	<0.05
6.0	7.0	625.32	13.91	<0.05
6.0	8.0	690.56	13.86	<0.05
6.0	9.0	664.1	13.98	<0.05
7.0	8.0	65.24	1.3	<0.05
7.0	9.0	38.77	2.25	<0.05
8.0	9.0	−26.46	1.88	<0.05

4.3 Clustering of the Deviation from the 3 Degrees Glideslope for Approaches Flown with a Sidestick

The variables shown in Table 6 were used to optimise the SOM algorithm to cluster the approaches flown with a sidestick. The Silhouette score showed moderately strong clustering performance with an optimised cluster number of four clusters [26], although lower than the one corresponding to the gamepad flight data. The results from Table 7 demonstrate that SOM can be a meaningful tool to cluster the sidestick flight data. Although the NQE remains fairly high, indicating that some data points do not match the unit's weight vector [27], the topographic structure of the original data is well-preserved on the map [28, 29]. Overall, the clustering result metrics are very similar compared to the gamepad flight data, but the flying performance is better when participants flew with the sidestick. This can be due to the difference in experience, as qualified pilots would perform better than non-pilots with the sidestick whereas the overall flying performance is lower with the gamepad (Table 8).

The approaches flown with a sidestick grouped by cluster are displayed in Fig. 4, which shows the CAS, deviation from the three degrees glideslope and pitch. The trials with disturbance appear to have been more difficult for some participants, as clusters

Table 6. Sigma, learning rate and corresponding silhouette score used as parameters for the SOM processing.

SOM parameters	Value
σ	0.41
Learning Rate	0.63
Silhouette Score	0.35

Table 7. Clustering metrics obtained by the SOM algorithm.

SOM metrics	Value
Normalised quantization error	0.25
Topographic product	−0.003
Trustworthiness	0.90
Neighbourhood preservation	0.95

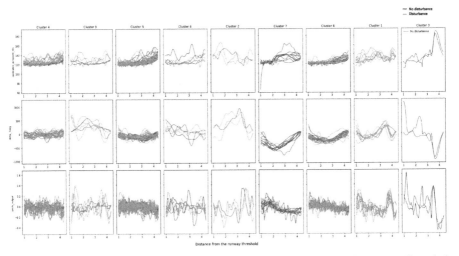

Fig. 4. Calibrated airspeed, deviation from the three-degree glideslope and corresponding pitch outputs for each cluster.

3 and 7 are almost only composed of landings with disturbances and feature a comparatively higher RMSE, similar to the results of the gamepad landings (Fig. 3 and Table 4). The clusters are well-defined, the Welch ANOVA indicates significant differences between clusters ($F = 5272$, $p < 0.05$). The post hoc analysis shows significant differences in RMSE ($p < 0.05$) between the clusters (Table 9). Cluster 4 displays the

least RMSE (Table 8) and cluster 2 displays the highest RMSE. The results are interesting with regards to the participants' experience, as both experienced pilots and novices are present in cluster 4.

Table 8. Average RMSE by cluster

Cluster	RMSE (ft)
1	148.56
2	382.99
3	278.28
4	66.92
5	105.20
6	132.85
7	336.90
8	190.00
9	274.14

Table 9. Summary of the post-hoc results for the sidestick data

Cluster A	Cluster B	Mean RMSE difference (ft)	Standard error	P-value
1.0	2.0	−234.43	5.27	<0.05
1.0	3.0	−129.72	8.1	<0.05
1.0	4.0	81.64	1.35	<0.05
1.0	5.0	43.36	1.32	<0.05
1.0	6.0	15.71	2.09	<0.05
1.0	7.0	188.34	2.5	<0.05
1.0	8.0	−41.44	1.5	<0.05
1.0	9.0	−125.58	2.75	<0.05
2.0	3.0	104.72	9.49	<0.05
2.0	4.0	316.07	5.13	<0.05
2.0	5.0	277.79	5.12	<0.05
2.0	6.0	250.14	5.37	<0.05
2.0	7.0	46.09	5.54	<0.05
2.0	8.0	193.0	5.17	<0.05
2.0	9.0	108.85	5.66	<0.05
3.0	4.0	211.36	8.01	<0.05

(*continued*)

Table 9. (*continued*)

Cluster A	Cluster B	Mean RMSE difference (ft)	Standard error	P-value
3.0	5.0	173.07	8.0	<0.05
3.0	6.0	145.43	8.16	<0.05
3.0	7.0	−58.62	8.28	<0.05
3.0	8.0	88.28	8.03	<0.05
3.0	9.0	4.14	8.36	1.0
4.0	5.0	−38.28	0.5	<0.05
4.0	6.0	−65.93	1.69	<0.05
4.0	7.0	−269.98	2.18	<0.05
4.0	8.0	−123.08	0.87	<0.05
4.0	9.0	−207.22	2.47	<0.05
5.0	6.0	−27.65	1.67	<0.05
5.0	7.0	−231.7	2.16	<0.05
5.0	8.0	−84.8	0.82	<0.05
5.0	9.0	−168.94	2.45	<0.05
6.0	7.0	−204.05	2.7	<0.05
6.0	8.0	−57.15	1.81	<0.05
6.0	9.0	−141.29	2.94	<0.05
7.0	8.0	146.9	2.28	<0.05
7.0	9.0	62.76	3.24	<0.05
8.0	9.0	−84.14	2.55	<0.05

4.4 Limitations

Several limitations are present in this study. Firstly, there is a high variance within the pilots' experience, ranging from novice to expert, which distorts the data, compared to an FDM dataset. Moreover, it can be difficult for non-pilots to follow the precision approach indicator (PAPI) and ILS guidance for the first time. The control forces on the sidestick are those of a generic aircraft which might also differ from some actual aircraft types. Finally, the SOM algorithm parameters could be optimised, and a stronger algorithm could be used for the clustering instead of the MiniSom package, which is an introductory package into SOM. This would provide a better overall clustering performance.

5 Conclusion

The clustering method through SOM provides useful information to analyse flight performance beyond exceedance events. For these datasets, it shows that, in overall, the flying performance is less susceptible to variability when flying with a sidestick compared to flying with a gamepad. This might indicate that for a novice, the use of a gamepad is easier than the sidestick. However, experienced pilots perform better when flying with the sidestick, as the average RMSEs for the sidestick data are lower than for the gamepad. Based on the deviation from the glidepath clusters, it is also possible to analyse the pilots' pitch inputs on the flight controls and determine the effects of the different flying techniques on the flight path. Furthermore, the results show that some participants had more difficulty handling approaches with disturbances, both with the sidestick and with the gamepad. A more detailed study could be accomplished with further tuning of the SOM parameter to increase the clustering performance. The use of SOM and clustering in general could prove beneficial for airlines to perform big data and trend analyses in addition to a purely exceedance-based analysis and so take a step further towards safety-II by considering the contexts behind detected exceedances which may be influenced by previous experience levels and familiarity.

References

1. ICAO: Annex 6 Part 1 (2010). Accessed 27 Aug 2021. https://store.icao.int/en/annex-6-ope ration-of-aircraft-part-i-international-commercial-air-transport-aeroplanes
2. Li, W.-C., Nichanian, A., Lin, J., Braithwaite, G.: Investigating the impacts of COVID-19 on aviation safety based on occurrences captured through Flight Data Monitoring. Ergonomics, 1–39 (2022). https://doi.org/10.1080/00140139.2022.2155317
3. Flight Safety Foundation: Learning From All Operations: Expanding the Field of Vision to Improve Aviation Safety, July 2021. Accessed 18 Nov 2021. https://flightsafety.org/wp-con tent/uploads/2021/07/Learning-from-All-Operations-FINAL.pdf
4. Alreshidi, I., Moulitsas, I., Jenkins, K.W.: Advancing aviation safety through machine learning and psychophysiological data: a systematic review. IEEE Access **12**, 5132–5150 (2024). https://doi.org/10.1109/ACCESS.2024.3349495
5. Walker, G.: Redefining the incidents to learn from: safety science insights acquired on the journey from black boxes to Flight Data Monitoring. Saf. Sci. **99**, 14–22 (2017). https://doi. org/10.1016/j.ssci.2017.05.010
6. Maille, N.: On the use of flight operating procedures for the analysis of FOQA data. In: 6th European Conference for Aeronautics and Space Sciences (EUCASS), Krakow: ONERA, July 2015. Accessed 9 Nov 2021. https://www.researchgate.net/publication/314973879
7. Bromfield, M.A., Landry, S.J.: Loss of control in flight – time to re-define? In: AIAA Aviation 2019 Forum, pp. 1–10 (2019). https://doi.org/10.2514/6.2019-3612
8. Chan, W., Li, W.-C.: Perception of causal factors in flight operations between Ab-Initio and expatriate pilots. In: 2023 7th International Conference on Transportation Information and Safety (ICTIS), pp. 1728–1732. IEEE, August 2023. https://doi.org/10.1109/ICTIS60134. 2023.10243970
9. Jasra, S.K., Valentino, G., Muscat, A., Camilleri, R.: Hybrid machine learning-statistical method for anomaly detection in flight data. Appl. Sci. **12**(20), 10261 (2022). https://doi.org/ 10.3390/app122010261
10. Hollnagel, E.: Safety–I and Safety–II, 1st edn. CRC Press, London (2018). https://doi.org/ 10.1201/9781315607511
11. Oehling, J., Barry, D.J.: Using machine learning methods in airline flight data monitoring to generate new operational safety knowledge from existing data. Saf. Sci. **114**, 89–104 (2019). https://doi.org/10.1016/j.ssci.2018.12.018
12. Li, W.-C., Wang, Y., Korek, W.T.: To be or not to be? Assessment on using touchscreen as inceptor in flight operation. Transp. Res. Procedia **66**, 117–124 (2022). https://doi.org/10. 1016/j.trpro.2022.12.013

13. Korek, W.T., Li, W.C., Lu, L., Lone, M.: Investigating pilots' operational behaviours while interacting with different types of inceptors. In: Harris, D., Li, WC. (eds.) HCII 2022, vol. 13307. LNAI, pp. 314–325. Springer, Cham (2022). https://doi.org/10.1007/978-3-031-06086-1_24

14. Mitchell, T.M.: Machine Learning. McGraw-Hill Science/Engineering/Math (1997)

15. Barry, D.J.: Estimating runway veer-off risk using a Bayesian network with flight data. Transp. Res. Part C Emerg. Technol. **128** (2021). https://doi.org/10.1016/j.trc.2021.103180

16. Das, S., Li, L., Srivastava, A.N., John Hansman, R.: Comparison of algorithms for anomaly detection in flight recorder data of airline operations. In: 12th AIAA Aviation Technology, Integration and Operations (ATIO) Conference and 14th AIAA/ISSMO Multidisciplinary Analysis and Optimization Conference. American Institute of Aeronautics and Astronautics Inc. (2012). https://doi.org/10.2514/6.2012-5593

17. Li, L., Das, S., Hansman, R.J., Palacios, R., Srivastava, A.N.: Analysis of flight data using clustering techniques for detecting abnormal operations. J. Aerosp. Inf. Syst., 587–598 (2015). https://doi.org/10.2514/1.I010329

18. Fernández, A., et al.: Flight Data Monitoring (FDM) unknown hazards detection during approach phase using clustering techniques and AutoEncoders. In: 9th SESAR Innovation Days. SESAR (2019)

19. Krogh, A.: What are artificial neural networks? Nat. Biotechnol. **26**(2), 195–197 (2008). https://doi.org/10.1038/nbt1386

20. Bação, F., Lobo, V., Painho, M.: Self-organizing maps as substitutes for K-means clustering. In: Sunderam, V.S., van Albada, GDick, Sloot, P.M.A., Dongarra, J. (eds.) Computational Science – ICCS 2005. LNCS, vol. 3516, pp. 476–483. Springer, Heidelberg (2005). https://doi.org/10.1007/11428862_65

21. Bardet, J.-M., Faure, C., Lacaille, J., Olteanu, M.: Design aircraft engine bi-variate data phases using change-point detection method and self-organizing maps. In: Grenada: ITISE, September 2017. Accessed 18 Jan 2024. https://www.safran-aircraft-engines.com

22. Bektas, O.: Visualising flight regimes using self-organising maps. Aeronaut. J. **127**(1316), 1817–1831 (2023). https://doi.org/10.1017/AER.2023.71

23. Andrades, I.S., Castillo Aguilar, J.J., García, J.M.V., Carrillo, J.A.C., Lozano, M.S.: Low-cost road-surface classification system based on self-organizing maps. Sensors **20**(21), 6009 (2020). https://doi.org/10.3390/s20216009

24. Flight simulator at Cranfield University wins international award. Accessed 31 Jan 2024. https://www.cranfield.ac.uk/press/news-2021/flight-simulator-at-cranfield-university-wins-international-award

25. Vesanto, J., Alhoniemi, E.: Clustering of the self-organizing map. IEEE Trans. Neural Netw. **11**(3), 586–600 (2000). https://doi.org/10.1109/72.846731

26. Shahapure, K.R., Nicholas, C.: Cluster quality analysis using silhouette score. In: 2020 IEEE 7th International Conference on Data Science and Advanced Analytics (DSAA), pp. 747–748. IEEE, October 2020. https://doi.org/10.1109/DSAA49011.2020.00096

27. Ayadi, T., Hamdani, T.M., Alimi, A.M.: A new data topology matching technique with multi-level interior growing self-organizing maps. In: 2010 IEEE International Conference on Systems, Man and Cybernetics, pp. 2479–2486. IEEE, October 2010. https://doi.org/10.1109/ICSMC.2010.5641936

28. Bauer, H.-U., Pawelzik, K.R.: Quantifying the neighborhood preservation of self-organizing feature maps. IEEE Trans. Neural Netw. **3**(4), 570–579 (1992). https://doi.org/10.1109/72.143371

29. De Bodt, E., Cottrell, M., Verleysen, M.: Statistical tools to assess the reliability of self-organizing maps. Neural Netw. **15**(8–9), 967–978 (2002). https://doi.org/10.1016/S0893-6080(02)00071-0

Trust Transfer in Autonomous Vehicles: The Role of Warm Brand Image Amid Automation Failure

Shaotian Qin[1,2], Chihao Li[1,2], and Yue Qi[1,2(✉)] (iD)

[1] The Department of Psychology, Renmin University of China, Beijing 100872, China
`qiy@ruc.edu.cn`
[2] The Laboratory of the Department of Psychology, Renmin University of China, Beijing 100872, China

Abstract. As automated driving technology becomes an integral part of daily life, the significance of consumer trust in autonomous systems grows. While existing research has explored human-machine trust, the role of brand image has been overlooked. Trust transfer theory posits that initial trust in new products often originates from existing brand trust. Given the limited awareness of self-driving products, this study investigates how attitudes toward current brands may transfer into trust in autonomous systems. This paper utilized CARLA for simulating autonomous driving scenarios and conducted three studies to explore the impact of brand image (warmth/competence) on human-machine trust and its influence on automation failure. Study 1 analyzed the brand images of 39 Chinese autonomous driving companies, revealing a predominant focus on competence. In Study 2, a one-way, three-level online experiment demonstrated that both competence-based and warmth-based brand images significantly enhance initial human-machine trust. Study 3 explored the impact of automation failure on trust and the moderating effect of brand image, using a 2 (automation failure: high vs. low) × 2 (brand image: competence vs. warmth) × 2 (measurement time: pretest vs. post-test) experimental design. The findings expand current understanding of human-machine trust and provide empirical support for the integrated model of human trust in AI. The research also offers strategic insights for self-driving brands, suggesting that adopting a warmth-based brand image could help maintain human-machine trust despite potential automation failures.

Keywords: brand image · automation failure · trust in automation · human-AI trust · warmth

1 Introduction

With the rapid development of autonomous driving technology, autonomous driving systems have become a prominent selling point for an increasing number of vehicles. Autonomous vehicles not only offer enhanced safety compared to manual driving [1], but also reduce the workload for drivers [2, 3], lower vehicle emissions, achieve higher

D. Harris and W.-C. Li (Eds.): HCII 2024, LNAI 14693, pp. 123–140, 2024.
https://doi.org/10.1007/978-3-031-60731-8_9

fuel efficiency, and save travel time for passengers. According to U.S. researchers' estimates, the annual economic benefits in the United States could reach up to $27 billion, when the penetration rate of autonomous driving vehicles among vehicle owners reaches 10% [4]. Considering the broader future benefits and higher penetration rates of autonomous driving, it is expected that the annual savings could exceed $450 billion with the widespread adoption of autonomous driving technology. Despite the vast prospects of this technology, there remains a significant obstacle to public acceptance and adoption of autonomous vehicles: distrust in autonomous driving cars [5]. Previous studies in aerospace, automotive, and other fields have shown that increasing the adoption rate of new technology depends on improving trust in that technology [6, 7]. Therefore, human-machine trust is crucial for the widespread promotion of autonomous driving.

Traditionally, most research on human-machine interaction has focused on factors influencing trust from the perspectives of operator characteristics, system features, and situational aspects [8, 9], with limited exploration into brand-related factors [10]. However, brands play a pivotal role in human-machine interaction. Trust transfer theory suggests that initial trust in new products often stems from existing brand trust, especially in the absence of relevant knowledge [11]. Some studies suggest that as the level of automation in autonomous driving systems increases, blame towards manufacturers escalates in the event of accidents [12], highlighting the growing importance of developer factors with advancing automation. Consumers' perceptions of autonomous driving system developers are primarily shaped by brand image. Furthermore, research indicates that brand image significantly influences the purchasing behavior of the majority when it comes to autonomous vehicles [13]. Lewis and Marsh [14] introduced the Integrated Model of Human Trust in AI, which, for the first time, proposes that Proxy Trust can impact people's levels of trust. Specifically, due to the lack of consumer awareness of self-driving products, their attitudes toward current brands would transfer into trust in self-driving products. Thus, this paper employs CARLA to simulate autonomous driving scenarios, and conduct three studies to examine the impact of brand image (warmth/competence) on human-machine trust and its influence on automation failure.

2 Related Work

2.1 Human-Machine Trust

The definition of human-machine trust proposed by Lee and See [15] has garnered wide acceptance among researchers [16, 17]. This definition suggests that human-machine trust is reflected in an individual's attitude when in a vulnerable situation, where they believe that the system can assist them in achieving a specific goal. Based on the development process of human-machine interaction, human-machine trust can be divided into three stages: initial trust, real-time trust, and post-event trust [8]. Initial trust, refers to the state of trust that the operator holds before using the automatic system. Studies have shown that the higher the brand reputation of an autonomous driving system, the higher the level of trust of the driver [10]. Real-time trust is developed on the basis of initial trust during human-machine interaction, and is the state of trust in individual interaction with automated systems. Studies have shown that situational factors (e.g., weather conditions and traffic density) and system factors (e.g., automation failure, transparency, and interaction design) will significantly affect the driver's real-time human-machine trust [18–24]. Post-event trust is the state of trust that arises after using an autonomous driving system, and it has a high degree of consistency with the influencing factors of real-time trust [8].

Automation failure is one of the most important factors affecting human-machine trust. Although the reliability of automated systems is increasingly strong, a completely perfect automated system does not exist [25]. Automation malfunctions refer to mechanical or software-level errors that are unexpected by the driver [26]. Previous research on the impact of automation failure has relatively consistent conclusions, and empirical research results show that automation failure significantly reduces the operator's trust in the system [27–29]. Based on this, this study proposes the following hypotheses:

H1: Automation failure significantly diminishes human-machine trust.

H1a: Systems with high automation failure rates will significantly reduce real-time human-machine trust compared to those with low automation failure rates.

H1b: Systems with high automation failure rates will significantly reduce post-event human-machine trust compared to systems with low automation failure rates.

2.2 The Impact of Brand Image on Human-Machine Trust

As consumers' perceptions of a specific brand, brand image is the associations and attributes linked with the brand name in consumers' minds, reflecting their impressions of the brand [30]. Aaker et al. [31] suggest that brand image can be categorized into warmth and competence dimensions. Warmth-based brand image mainly shows consumers the brand's honesty, sincerity, generosity, helpfulness, trustworthiness, and other traits, while competence-based brand image shows consumers competitive and intellectual traits. Brand image has been found to have a positive impact on brand trust [32, 33], and both perceived warmth and perceived competence in brand image can significantly predict consumer trust [34]. However, scholars have arrived at divergent conclusions regarding the influence of warmth-based brands on consumer trust. Aaker et al. [31] found that merely perceiving a brand as having high warmth does not increase consumers' trust in its products and their purchase intentions.

McKnight and Chervany [35] believe that there are three ways to establish trust, namely institution-based trust, knowledge-based trust, and trust transfer. For unfamiliar things to an individual, due to the lack of corresponding knowledge, the initial trust in them generally comes from trust transfer [11]. The integrated model of human trust in AI proposed by Lewis and Marsh [14] also expresses similar meanings, pointing out the importance of proxy trust, which refers to the degree of trust people have in other factors related to the system. For example, even if an individual knows nothing about the doctor treating them, they still trust him because of the medical training system. Lewis and Marsh [14] point out that the use of this model is very wide and can be applied to any trust decision scenario, but this theoretical model still lacks empirical support. In summary, we speculate brand image, as a source of proxy trust, can influence people's trust in an automation system, particularly in the context of initial trust. Therefore, this study proposes the following hypotheses:

H2: Brand image has a significant impact on human-machine trust.

H2a: Competence-based brand image has a significant positive impact on initial human-machine trust.

H2b: Warmth-based brand image has a significant positive impact on initial human-machine trust.

H2c: Compared to warmth-based brand image, competence-based brand image has a stronger positive impact on initial human-machine trust.

When a company's system encounters an automation failure, consumers' attribution of the failure may also be influenced by brand image. According to attribution theory [36], people tend to judge the cause and responsibility of the matter from three aspects: control point, stability, and controllability. If the cause of a negative accident is perceived as internal and controllable, consumers are likely to express more resentment and assign blame, significantly impacting consumer attitudes and customer loyalty [37]. For competence-based brands, consumers believe in their ability to produce superior products, often attributing negative marketing events to internal factors that are controllable. In contrast, for warmth-based brands, consumers are inclined to attribute automation failure to uncontrollable factors, resulting in a lesser impact on them. According to the psychological expectation violation theory, disparate cognitive states lead to pronounced violation emotional reactions [38]. Since consumers' expectations for warmth-based brands are inherently lower than those for competence-based brands, the emotional reaction is not as intense. Therefore, the researchers propose the following hypotheses:

H3: There is an interaction effect between brand image and automation failure on human-machine trust.

H3a: Following exposure to a high-failure-rate system developed by a warmth-based brand, the decrease in real-time human-machine trust is significantly less than that for a competence-based brand.

H3b: Following exposure to a high-failure-rate system developed by a warmth-based brand, the decrease in post-event human-machine trust is significantly less than that for a competence-based brand.

3 Study 1: Exploring Brand Image Distribution in Chinese Autonomous Driving Companies

Study 1 was designed to investigate the distribution of brand images, specifically warmth and competence, among current Chinese autonomous driving companies.

3.1 Data Source

Employing web crawlers, we extracted and analyzed the "About Us" text content from the official websites of 39 prominent Chinese autonomous driving companies. To ensure the authenticity of the brand image positioning, we relied solely on information from the brand's official website as the primary information source. If a company's website did not have an "About Us" page, we gathered the information from its homepage. For websites with anti-crawling mechanisms, we manually collected the relevant information.

3.2 Data Analysis

Five trained psychology graduate students served as raters, individually scoring the ability and warmth dimensions among the 101 features provided by the TextMind Chinese-Text Psychological Analysis System [39]. The mean scores of the five raters were used for further testing, with a Kendall's coefficient of concordance of 0.78, $p < 0.001$, indicating consistent reliability among the raters. Based on their ratings, two features were selected as evaluation indicators for competence and warmth brand images, respectively. The competence brand image is represented by work words and achievement words (e.g., work and jobs); the larger the eigenvalue, the more the brand leans towards a competence brand image. The warmth brand image is represented by the eigenvalues of family words (e.g., home and family) and affect words (e.g., care and love); the larger the eigenvalue, the more words of this category appear in the official website information, and the more the brand leans towards a warmth brand image. Eigenvalues are equivalent to word frequencies, which represent the proportion of each type of vocabulary appearing in the overall text.

3.3 Results

The competence brand image was determined by averaging the eigenvalues of work words and achievement words, while the warmth brand image was computed by averaging the eigenvalues of family words and affect words. T-test results showed that the mean of the competence brand image ($M = 0.112$, $SD = 0.06$) was significantly higher than the mean of warmth brand image ($M = 0.003$, $SD = 0.01$), $t(39) = 14.86$, $p < 0.001$, Cohen's $d = 2.53$. The findings indicate a notable emphasis on competence over warmth in the brand images of Chinese autonomous driving companies, highlighting a distinctive focus within the industry.

4 Study 2: The Impact of Brand Image on Human-Machine Trust

The results of Study 1 indicated that the predominant brand positioning for autonomous driving companies in China is competence-based. Building on this finding, Study 2 aims to investigate the influence of brand image on human-machine trust, specifically examining whether competence-based and warmth-based brands can significantly enhance individuals' trust in autonomous driving systems.

4.1 Method

Participants. To ensure the statistical power of the experiment, GPower3 software was employed to pre-estimate the required sample size prior to the experiment [40]. Taking into account the expected small effect size ($f = 0.15$) and setting α at .05, the minimum recommended sample size to achieve a statistical power of 0.8 is 73 participants. In this study, a total of 85 participants were recruited through the Credemo platform, with 12 being excluded due to failing the attention check questions. Ultimately, 73 valid participant data (31 males, 42 females) were retained, with ages ranging from 19 to 59 years old and an average age of 26.92 ± 7.88 years.

Experimental Design, Materials, and Measurements

Experimental Design. The experiment adopted a single-factor three-level within-subjects design, varying the brand image conditions (warmth, competence, generic), with human-machine trust as the dependent variable.

Experimental Materials. The manipulation method for brand image followed the approach by Liao et al. [41]. Based on the definitions of competence-based and warmth-based brand images and considering the actual situation of autonomous driving companies, brand introductions were compiled. Competence-based brand image was manipulated by highlighting the company's technical strength, R&D investment, and elite employees. For example: "Brand X is a company focused on autonomous driving technology, with its technology consistently leading the industry. To enhance product competitiveness, Brand X invested 28.4% of its net profit last year into the R&D of autonomous driving algorithms and artificial intelligence. To date, Brand X has 35 R&D centers and 25 collaborative laboratories worldwide, with 2,500 + employees from top universities globally. Brand X's vision: technology first, science supreme. Brand X's values: dare to know the future (lofty ambitions, innovation, inclusiveness, and pragmatism)."

Warmth-based brand image was manipulated by showcasing the company's focus on vulnerable groups and charitable donations. For example: "Brand Y is a diverse brand, dedicated to developing autonomous driving systems that can be used by people with disabilities and committed to charitable causes. The company has always conveyed a caring and friendly philosophy. To implement its brand values, Brand Y regularly recruits people with disabilities as product experience officers and even formal employees. The company offers comprehensive benefits, a sound employee assistance program, and special benefits such as family leave and family day. Brand Y's vision: by 2030, we will achieve our dreams together. Brand Y's values: technology makes life more convenient."

To eliminate the influence of participants' past experiences and inherent attitudes towards the brands, the stimulus materials used "X" and "Y" to represent the brand names. The generic brand image introduction was designed as a control condition. For example: "Brand Z is an autonomous driving company established in Hefei in 2017. In 2020, Brand Z changed its logo, which is composed of a symbol representing the vast sky and the road symbolizing action and progress. Brand Z's executive team: Founder and Chairman: Qin Bin, President: Liu Lihong, Vice Presidents: Shen Xin, Huang Yong."

Brand Image Scale. This six-item scale developed by Aaker [31] et al. consists two dimensions: warmth-based brand image and competence-based brand image. Each dimension contains three items. For instance, competence-based brand image includes items such as "I believe the brand can indeed fulfill the role mentioned in the advertisement," while warmth-based brand image features items like "I think the brand emphasizes friendliness between people." The scale employs a 7-point Likert scoring system, where 1 represents strongly disagree and 7 represents strongly agree. Higher scores indicate a closer alignment with the respective brand image. In this study, the Cronbach's alpha coefficient for the competence-based brand image questionnaire was 0.75, and for the warmth-based brand image questionnaire, it was 0.79.

Human-Machine Trust Scale. The scale developed by Jian [42] et al. comprises 12 self-assessment items such as "The system's behavior will produce harmful results" and "I have great confidence in this system." The scale uses a 7-point Likert scoring system, where 1 represents strongly disagree and 7 represents strongly agree. In this study, the Cronbach's alpha coefficient for the human-machine trust questionnaire was 0.95.

Procedure. The experiment was conducted online. Participants first saw the introductions of Companies X, Y, and Z, which were presented to different participants in a balanced manner using a Latin square design. After that, participants completed the two scales. The purpose of the brand image scale was to re-validate the manipulation of brand image from the pre-test, while the human-machine trust scale measured the dependent variable of the experiment.

4.2 Results

Brand Image. In the measurement of competence, the score of competence-based brand image, was significantly higher than that of warmth-based and generic brand images, $F(2, 144) = 92.16, p < 0.001, \eta_p^2 = 0.56$. Moreover, the score of warmth-based brand image was also significantly higher than that generic, $p < 0.001$. In the measurement of warmth, the score of warmth-based brand image, was significantly higher than that of competence-based and generic brand images, $F(2, 144) = 148.07, p < 0.001, \eta_p^2 = 0.67$. Therefore, the manipulation of brand images in this study was successful (Table 1).

Table 1. Brand Image Scale Scores of different brand images (Mean ± SD).

Brand image	Competence rating	Warmth rating
Competence	17.72 ± 1.89	12.49 ± 3.27
Warmth	16.60 ± 2.09	19.00 ± 2.02
Generic	12.82 ± 3.06	12.30 ± 3.14

Human-Machine Trust. A one-way repeated measures analysis of variance (ANOVA) showed that brand image significantly influenced the level of human-machine trust, $F(2, 144) = 94.05, p < 0.001, \eta_p^2 = 0.57$. Post-hoc test results revealed that the competence-based brand image had a significantly greater effect on the initial human-machine trust ($M \pm SD = 61.21 \pm 8.71$) than the warmth-based brand image ($M \pm SD = 56.30 \pm 10.14, p < 0.001$) and the generic brand image ($M \pm SD = 45.10 \pm 12.24, p < 0.001$). Additionally, the warmth-based brand image had a significantly greater effect on the initial human-machine trust than the generic brand image ($p < 0.001$).

4.3 Discussion

These results indicated that, in comparison to the generic brand image, both competence-based and warmth-based brand images significantly enhanced consumers' initial human-machine trust levels. Specifically, the competence-based brand image had a considerably more significant impact on the initial human-machine trust level than the warmth-based brand image. Study 2 validated hypotheses H2a, H2b, and H2c, aligning with previous research findings that both competence and warmth dimensions of brand image can influence consumers' purchase intentions [43]. Researchers have noted that most people prefer technology-based autonomous driving brands over neutral and new brands [13]. This suggests that for autonomous vehicles, competence-based brands may have a more substantial impact than warmth-based brands, with the positive effect on initial human-machine trust being significantly higher for competence-based brands.

5   Study 3: Brand Image Moderation: Mitigating Automation Failure's Impact on Human-Machine Trust

While current autonomous driving technology has advanced considerably, it remains unable to entirely eliminate automation failures. These failures have the potential to affect both real-time human-machine trust and post-event human-machine trust. In Study 3, automation failure was introduced to replicate the findings from Study 2, and concurrently explore the potential moderating role of brand image on the impact of automation failure on human-machine trust.

5.1   Method

Participants. To ensure the statistical power of the experiment, GPower3 software was used to pre-estimate the required sample size before the experiment [40]. It was expected to achieve a medium effect size ($f = 0.25$), and with α set at .05, a sample size of 52 participants was recommended to achieve a statistical power of 0.8. Therefore, 53 participants (18 males, 20 ± 1.91 years old) were recruited for this experiment, with ages ranging from 17 to 25 years old.

Experimental Design, Materials and Measurements
Experimental Design. The experiment conducted a 2 (automation failure rate: high/low) × 2 (brand image: competence/warmth) × 2 (measurement time: pre-/post-test) mixed design. Brand image and measurement time were within-subjects independent variables, and automation failure rate was the between-subjects independent variable. The dependent variables were initial human-machine trust, real-time human-machine trust, and post-event human-machine trust.

Experimental Materials. Independent variable manipulation: The manipulation of brand image followed the method of Liao et al. [41], using the warmth and competence brand image materials validated in Study 2.

Automation failure manipulation was conducted through the CARLA software. Based on data from the California Department of Motor Vehicles in 2019, Toyota's autonomous driving system exhibited subpar performance, registering 0.4 miles per disengagement. Baidu and Waymo's autonomous vehicle demonstrated commendable performance, requiring the intervention every 18,050 miles, and 13,219 miles, respectively [44]. Referring to the research of Khastgir [6] et al., this experiment set the high failure rate as 80% probability of autonomous driving errors, and the low failure rate as 1% probability of errors when encountering traffic lights, pedestrians, and ground markers.

Driving Simulation Platform. The driving simulation platform used in this experiment was CARLA version 0.9.13, with the rendering engine being UE4.22, deployed on a 64-bit Windows system. CARLA is an open-source simulator developed under the guidance of the Computer Vision Center of the Autonomous University of Barcelona, Spain, for various stages of autonomous driving system development, training, and validation [45–47]. This study used the default CARLA map 10 as the experimental map. Map 10 features a downtown urban environment with skyscrapers, residential buildings, and a waterfront promenade. In addition, map 10 has various types of intersection arrangements, various lane markings, crossroads, and signal types, which can satisfy the majority of traffic conditions that may be encountered in reality. All participants started driving at a fixed location, which was in front of an intersection on map 10. All participants drove a black Audi sedan, and the driving perspective was set to the first-person view (see Fig. 1).

This study used CARLA to develop the experimental program, which was presented on a 14-inch Windows laptop with a 3070Ti graphics card model for displaying experimental materials and collecting data. The automated failure rate control was managed by a pre-written CARLA program.

Brand Image. Same as the scale [31] used in Study 2. In this study, the Cronbach's alpha coefficient for the competence-based brand image questionnaire was 0.79, and for the warmth-based brand image questionnaire, it was 0.86.

Human-Machine Trust. Initial human-machine trust and post-event human-machine trust were measured using the Human-Machine Trust Scale [42]. In this study, the Cronbach's alpha coefficient for the human-machine trust questionnaire was 0.88. Real-time trust was measured by the time participants used the autonomous driving system during the experiment [48]. Specifically, the longer the participants used the autonomous driving system, the higher the real-time human-machine trust; conversely, the lower the trust.

Procedure. The experiment created a scenario where two companies developed autonomous driving car algorithms, asking users to test their performances for future promotion. Participants sequentially experienced two distinct algorithms. Initially, they viewed competence or warmth brand image introduction materials, with the order determined by a Latin square design. Following this, participants evaluated the brand image and completed an initial human-machine trust questionnaire. Subsequently, in a behavioral experiment, participants were randomly assigned to groups with high or low automation failure rate. Using CARLA's default map 10, the experiment simulated driving conditions with 10 pedestrians and 30 cars randomly generated within the map. Participants drove safely for three minutes, adhering to traffic regulations, to familiarize themselves with the driving simulator system and the transition between autonomous and manual driving. Safety precautions included reporting symptoms of simulator adaptation syndrome (SAS) and pausing the experiment if needed. After completing the driving task, participants filled out a post-event human-machine trust questionnaire.

Fig. 1. Example of an experimental scenario in Study 3

5.2 Results

Brand Image. In the measurement of competence, the score of competence-based brand image was significantly higher than that of warmth-based brand images, $t = 4.65$, $p < 0.001$. Conversely, the warmth brand scored significantly higher on the warmth dimension compared to the competence brand ($t = 4.62, p < 0.001$), demonstrating the successful manipulation of brand image.

Human-Machine Trust. The results of a 2 (automation failure: high failure rate vs. low failure rate) $\times$ 2 (brand image: competence vs. warmth) mixed-design analysis of variance (ANOVA) on human-machine trust at three different stages revealed the following:

Initial Human-Machine Trust. The main effect of brand image was not significant, $F(1, 51) = 1.61, p = 0.21, \eta_p^2 = 0.03$, indicating no significant difference in the impact of warmth and competence brands on human-machine trust, which is inconsistent with research hypothesis H2c.

Real-time Human-Machine Trust. Due to the large standard deviation and extreme values ranging from 0 to 172 s, a logarithmic transformation was applied to reduce kurtosis and skewness, following the study by Richard et al. [49]. The results showed that the main effect of brand image was not significant, $F(1, 51) = 0.13, p = 0.72, \eta_p^2 = 0.002$, indicating no significant difference in the overall impact of warmth and competence brands on human-machine trust, which is inconsistent with research hypothesis H2c. The main effect of automation failure was significant, $F(1, 51) = 16.46, p < 0.001$, $\eta_p^2 = 0.24$, with the real-time human-machine trust level in the high automation failure group ($0.71 \pm .13$) being significantly lower than that in the low automation failure group ($1.41 \pm .12$), which is consistent with hypothesis H1a. The interaction between brand image and automation failure was significant, $F(1, 51) = 4.19, p = 0.46, \eta_p^2 =$

0.08. Simple effect analysis results showed that the main effect of automation failure on warmth brand image was not significant, $F(1, 51) = 3.69$, $p = 0.06$, $\eta_p{}^2 = 0.07$; however, the main effect on competence brand image was significant, $F(1, 51) = 21.78$, $p < 0.001$, $\eta_p{}^2 = 0.30$, supporting H3a (see Fig. 2).

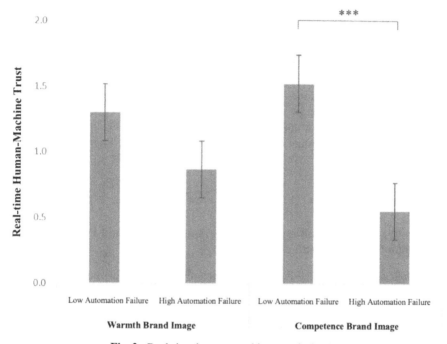

Fig. 2. Real-time human-machine trust in Study 3

Post-event Human-Machine Trust. The main effect of brand image was not significant, $F(1, 51) = 0.49$, $p = 0.49$, $\eta_p{}^2 = 0.01$, indicating no significant difference in the impact of warmth and competence brands on human-machine trust, which is inconsistent with research hypothesis H2c. The main effect of automation failure was significant, $F(1, 51) = 14.83$, $p < 0.001$, $\eta_p{}^2 = 0.23$, with the mean value of the high automation failure group ($M \pm SD = 42.85 \pm 1.92$) being significantly lower than that of the low automation failure group ($M \pm SD = 52.93 \pm 1.78$), which is consistent with hypothesis H1b. The interaction between brand image and automation failure was not significant, $F(1, 51) = 0.28$, $p = 0.60$, $\eta_p{}^2 = 0.005$, which is inconsistent with experimental hypothesis H3b.

5.3 Discussion

The results of Study 3 indicated that for both initial and post-event human-machine trust, the main effect of brand image is not significant, meaning that there is no significant difference in the impact of competence-based and warmth-based brand images on human-machine trust, which is inconsistent with hypothesis H1c. This is consistent with previous research findings in the field of brand trust. Studies have shown that both warmth-based and competence-based brand images can significantly and positively influence brand trust [50]. For real-time and post-event human-machine trust, the main effect of automation failure is significant, high automation failure rate decreases human-machine trust, which is consistent with previous research findings [28, 29, 51] and supports hypothesis H1.

For real-time human-machine trust, the interaction between brand image and automation failure is significant. Simple effect analysis results show that when using an autonomous driving system with a high error rate, compared to competence-based brands, warmth-based brand images can significantly slow down the decline of drivers' trust. For warmth-based brands, consumers have lower expectations compared to competence-based brands and are more likely to think that errors are uncontrollable. Therefore, compared to warmth-based brands, real-time trust declines more when the autonomous driving system produced by competence-based brands experiences automation failure.

6 General Discussion

6.1 Negative Impact of Automation Failures on Real-Time and Post-event Human-Machine Trust

Study 3 indicated that automation failure significantly and negatively impacts both real-time human-machine trust and post-event human-machine trust, which aligns with prior research [28, 29, 52]. Khastgir et al. [6] discovered that compared to high-capability systems, low-capability systems markedly diminish an operator's level of trust in human-machine interaction. Seet et al. [53] found that faults in self-driving cars have a more profound effect on ability trust within the context of human-machine trust. The dynamic trust model for autonomous driving stipulates that a driver's trust in the autonomous driving process is influenced in real-time by system performance [8]. Automation errors are a negative system performance. When an automation failure occurs, individuals perceive the automation system as unreliable, leading to a negative system performance perception and consequently, a reduction in their reliance on and trust in the autonomous driving system.

6.2 The Role of Competence and Warmth Brand Images in Enhancing Initial Human-Machine Trust

Study 1 revealed that all 39 domestic autonomous driving firms involved in this research have adopted a competence-based brand image positioning strategy. This aligns with consumer preferences, as research indicates that when purchasing a vehicle, the majority of individuals prefer competence-based autonomous driving brands over neutral or new brands [13]. Study 2 demonstrated that both competence-based and warmth-based brands significantly enhance initial human-machine trust, and trust in competence-based brands is significantly higher than in warmth-based brands. Study 3 did not uncover a significant difference in the impact of competence-based brands and warmth-based brands on trust in human-machine interaction. Therefore, the research findings offer partial support for Hypothesis H1. These results align with previous studies that both warmth-based and competence-based brand images significantly and positively influence brand trust [50]. While Aaker et al. [31] contend that a purely warmth-based brand image cannot enhance trust in human-machine interaction, they also discovered that when warm non-profit organizations are associated with monetary aspects, the disparity in consumer purchasing tendencies vanishes. This suggests that consumers' trust in warm brands increases. As the subjects of this research were all for-profit companies tied to financial aspects, the findings indicate that both warm and competence-based brands can elevate consumers' initial human-machine trust. The lack of a significant difference between competence and warmth brand images could be attributed to the fact that their effects on enhancing trust do not significantly differ.

Theoretically, according to the trust transfer mechanism and the integrated model of human trust in AI, a customer's attitude towards a brand plays a crucial role in shaping their perception of extended products [14]. Thus, when an operator interacts with an unfamiliar automated system, their trust in the system may be influenced by the brand image. Gidakovi and Zabkar [34] illustrate that individuals perceive warmth by recognizing that the brand is customer-centric, socially responsible, and a commendable employer; they perceive competence through the company's capabilities and performance. Consequently, this provides a theoretical explanation for the significant positive effects of both competence-based and warmth-based brands on initial human-machine trust.

6.3 The Interaction of Brand Image and Automation Failure on Real-Time and Post-event Human-Machine Trust

In terms of real-time trust, Study 3 revealed that after utilizing an autonomous driving system with a high failure rate, the real-time trust in human-machine interaction diminishes less for warmth-based brand images compared to competence-based brand images, corroborating Hypothesis H3a. On one hand, for competence-based brands, consumers expect superior product quality and tend to attribute negative marketing events to the company's internal factors, i.e., controllable elements. As per attribution theory, when a negative event arises from internal causes, it exerts a greater negative impact on consumers [36]. While for warmth-based brands, consumers' expectations are naturally lower compared to competence-based brands, leading them to perceive errors as uncontrollable, thereby reducing the blame attributed to warmth-based brands. On the other hand, compared to warmth-based brands, an autonomous failure produced by competence-based brands triggers strong emotional reactions, which then more profoundly affect the driver's trust in the autonomous driving system [38]. Prior research shows that people trust automation described as an expert system more [54], so when automation fails, this inconsistency with the driver's expectations leads to a rapid decrease in trust [55, 56], which aligns with the results of real-time human-machine trust in this study.

Concerning post-event trust, Study 3 indicated that the interaction effect of brand image and automation failure rate is not significant, conflicting with Hypothesis H3b.

This discrepancy may stem from differences in measurement methods. In trust research, the variation in measurement methods has long been a focal point for scholars. Glaeser et al. [57] compared the consistency of trust levels measured by game method and questionnaire method, finding no significant positive correlation between the two. In autonomous driving research, some scholars have identified inconsistencies between driver subjective reports and behavior measurements. Previous research has suggested that the sensitivity of the scale by Jian et al. [42] is lower than other measurement methods [58] and exhibits a positive bias [59]. Moreover, the results of self-reports do not align with actual trust behavior [60, 61]. This discrepancy may be partly attributed to the fact that self-report and behavior measurement methods capture different components of trust, and both measurement methods may have biases and cannot perfectly measure their expected structure [62]. Therefore, the difference in measurement methods of real-time human-machine trust and post-event human-machine trust may have led to divergent results.

6.4 Implications

The study enhances understanding of human-machine trust and uncovers the influence of brand image on human-machine trust and the interaction between brand image and automation failure on real-time human-machine trust. The study augments understanding of the evolution of human-machine trust. According to the process of driving, trust in autonomous driving system can be segmented into initial, real-time, and post-event human-machine trust. The current research identified the main effect of brand image on different kinds of human-machine trust, demonstrate the variability of human-machine trust and underscore the necessity of researching different stages of human-machine trust.

The advancement of autonomous driving technology not only enhances users' driving and riding experiences but also mitigates traffic accidents, and even holds the potential to reshape the entire industry chain. Thus, a multitude of companies are engaged in this sector, and one of their primary focuses is on how to earn consumer trust in their products. Our study examines the impact of competence-oriented and warmth-oriented brand images on human-machine trust, and provides preliminary conclusions that can assist enterprises in better optimizing their brand image strategy.

Acknowledgments. This research is supported by the National Natural Science Foundation of China (32000771); the Fundamental Research Funds for the Central Universities, and the Research Funds of Renmin University of China (21XNLG13).

Disclosure of Interests. The authors have no competing interests to declare that are relevant to the content of this article.

References

1. Cicchino, J.B.: Effectiveness of forward collision warning and autonomous emergency braking systems in reducing front-to-rear crash rates. Accid. Anal. Prev. **99**, 142–152 (2017). https://doi.org/10.1016/j.aap.2016.11.009

2. Balfe, N., Sharples, S., Wilson, J.R.: Impact of automation: measurement of performance, workload and behaviour in a complex control environment. Appl. Ergon. **47**, 52–64 (2015). https://doi.org/10.1016/j.apergo.2014.08.002

3. Tomzcak, K., et al.: Let tesla park your tesla: driver trust in a semi-automated car. In: 2019 Systems and Information Engineering Design Symposium (SIEDS), pp. 1–6. IEEE, Charlottesville, VA, USA (2019)

4. Fagnant, D.J., Kockelman, K.: Preparing a nation for autonomous vehicles: opportunities, barriers and policy recommendations. Transp. Res. Part A Policy Pract. **77**, 167–181 (2015). https://doi.org/10.1016/j.tra.2015.04.003

5. Choi, J.K., Ji, Y.G.: Investigating the importance of trust on adopting an autonomous vehicle. Int. J. Hum.-Comput. Interact. **31**, 692–702 (2015). https://doi.org/10.1080/10447318.2015.1070549

6. Khastgir, S., Birrell, S., Dhadyalla, G., Jennings, P.: Calibrating trust through knowledge: introducing the concept of informed safety for automation in vehicles. Transp. Res. Part C Emerg. Technol. **96**, 290–303 (2018). https://doi.org/10.1016/j.trc.2018.07.001

7. Molesworth, B.R.C., Koo, T.T.R.: The influence of attitude towards individuals' choice for a remotely piloted commercial flight: a latent class logit approach. Transp. Res. Part C Emerg. Technol. **71**, 51–62 (2016). https://doi.org/10.1016/j.trc.2016.06.017

8. Gao, Z., Li, W., Liang, J., Pan, H., Xu, W., Shen, M.: Trust in automated vehicles. Adv. Psychol. Sci. **29**, 2172–2183 (2021). https://doi.org/10.3724/SP.J.1042.2021.02172

9. Hancock, P.A., Billings, D.R., Schaefer, K.E., Chen, J.Y.C., De Visser, E.J., Parasuraman, R.: A meta-analysis of factors affecting trust in human-robot interaction. Hum. Factors **53**, 517–527 (2011). https://doi.org/10.1177/0018720811417254

10. Celmer, N., Branaghan, R., Chiou, E.: Trust in branded autonomous vehicles & performance expectations: a theoretical framework. Proc. Hum. Factors Ergon. Soc. Ann. Meet. **62**, 1761–1765 (2018). https://doi.org/10.1177/1541931218621398

11. Stewart, K.J.: Transference as a means of building trust in world wide web sites. In: ICIS 1999 Proceedings, vol. 47 (1999). http://aisel.aisnet.org/icis1999/47

12. Bennett, J.M., Challinor, K.L., Modesto, O., Prabhakharan, P.: Attribution of blame of crash causation across varying levels of vehicle automation. Saf. Sci. **132**, 104968 (2020). https://doi.org/10.1016/j.ssci.2020.104968

13. Eggers, F., Eggers, F.: Drivers of autonomous vehicles—analyzing consumer preferences for self-driving car brand extensions. Mark. Lett. **33**, 89–112 (2022). https://doi.org/10.1007/s11002-021-09571-x

14. Lewis, P.R., Marsh, S.: What is it like to trust a rock? A functionalist perspective on trust and trustworthiness in artificial intelligence. Cogn. Syst. Res. **72**, 33–49 (2022). https://doi.org/10.1016/j.cogsys.2021.11.001

15. Lee, J.D., See, K.A.: Trust in automation: designing for appropriate reliance. Hum. Factors **46**(1), 50–8062 (2004)

16. Cheng, P., Meng, F., Yao, J., Wang, Y.: Driving with agents: investigating the influences of anthropomorphism level and physicality of agents on drivers' perceived control, trust, and driving performance. Front. Psychol. **13**, 883417 (2022). https://doi.org/10.3389/fpsyg.2022.883417

17. Hensch, A.-C., Kreißig, I., Beggiato, M., Krems, J.F.: The effect of eHMI malfunctions on younger and elderly pedestrians' trust and acceptance of automated vehicle communication signals. Front. Psychol. **13**, 866475 (2022). https://doi.org/10.3389/fpsyg.2022.866475

18. Haghzare, S., Campos, J.L., Bak, K., Mihailidis, A.: Older adults' acceptance of fully automated vehicles: effects of exposure, driving style, age, and driving conditions. Accid. Anal. Prev. **150**, 105919 (2021). https://doi.org/10.1016/j.aap.2020.105919

19. Hoffman, R.R., Johnson, M., Bradshaw, J.M., Underbrink, A.: Trust in automation. IEEE Intell. Syst. **28**, 84–88 (2013). https://doi.org/10.1109/MIS.2013.24

20. De Visser, E.J., Pak, R., Shaw, T.H.: From 'automation' to 'autonomy': the importance of trust repair in human–machine interaction. Ergonomics **61**, 1409–1427 (2018). https://doi.org/10.1080/00140139.2018.1457725

21. Hoff, K.A., Bashir, M.: Trust in automation: integrating empirical evidence on factors that influence trust. Hum. Factors **57**, 407–434 (2015). https://doi.org/10.1177/0018720814547570

22. Kraus, J.M., Forster, Y., Hergeth, S., Baumann, M.: Two routes to trust calibration: effects of reliability and brand information on trust in automation. IJMHCI **11**, 1–17 (2019). https://doi.org/10.4018/IJMHCI.2019070101

23. Endsley, M.R.: Situation awareness in future autonomous vehicles: beware of the unexpected. In: Bagnara, S., Tartaglia, R., Albolino, S., Alexander, T., Fujita, Y. (eds.) Proceedings of the 20th Congress of the International Ergonomics Association (IEA 2018). AISC, vol. 824, pp. 303–309. Springer, Cham (2019). https://doi.org/10.1007/978-3-319-96071-5_32

24. Oliveira, L., Burns, C., Luton, J., Iyer, S., Birrell, S.: The influence of system transparency on trust: evaluating interfaces in a highly automated vehicle. Transp. Res. F Traffic Psychol. Behav. **72**, 280–296 (2020). https://doi.org/10.1016/j.trf.2020.06.001

25. Parasuraman, R., Riley, V.: Humans and automation: use, misuse, disuse. Abuse. Hum Factors **39**, 230–253 (1997). https://doi.org/10.1518/001872097778543886

26. Lee, J., Abe, G., Sato, K., Itoh, M.: Developing human-machine trust: impacts of prior instruction and automation failure on driver trust in partially automated vehicles. Transp. Res. F Traffic Psychol. Behav. **81**, 384–395 (2021). https://doi.org/10.1016/j.trf.2021.06.013

27. Ma, Y., Li, S., Qin, S., Qi, Y.: Factors affecting trust in the autonomous vehicle: a survey of primary school students and parent perceptions. In: 2020 IEEE 19th International Conference on Trust, Security and Privacy in Computing and Communications (TrustCom), pp. 2020–2027 (2020)

28. Mishler, S., Chen, J.: Effect of automation failure type on trust development in driving automation systems. Appl. Ergon. **106**, 103913 (2023). https://doi.org/10.1016/j.apergo.2022.103913

29. Wang, K., Lu, J., Ruan, S., Qi, Y.: Continuous error timing in automation: the peak-end effect on human-automation trust. Int. J. Hum.–Comput. Interact., 1–13 (2023). https://doi.org/10.1080/10447318.2023.2223954

30. Keller, K.L.: Conceptualizing, measuring, and managing customer-based brand equity. J. Mark. **57**, 1–22 (1993). https://doi.org/10.1177/002224299305700101

31. Aaker, J., Vohs, K.D., Mogilner, C.: Nonprofits are seen as warm and for-profits as competent: firm stereotypes matter. J. Consum. Res. **37**, 224–237 (2010). https://doi.org/10.1086/651566

32. Syed Alwi, S.F., Nguyen, B., Melewar, T., Loh, Y.H., Liu, M.: Explicating industrial brand equity: integrating brand trust, brand performance and industrial brand image. Ind. Manag. Data Syst. **116**, 858–882 (2016). https://doi.org/10.1108/IMDS-09-2015-0364

33. Huang, L., Wang, M., Chen, Z., Deng, B., Huang, W.: Brand image and customer loyalty: transmitting roles of cognitive and affective brand trust. Soc. Behav. Personal. Int. J. **48**, 1–12 (2020). https://doi.org/10.2224/sbp.9069

34. Gidaković, P., Zabkar, V.: The formation of consumers' warmth and competence impressions of corporate brands: the role of corporate associations. Eur. Manag. Rev. **19**, 639–653 (2022). https://doi.org/10.1111/emre.12509

35. McKnight, D.H., Chervany, N.L.: What trust means in E-commerce customer relationships: an interdisciplinary conceptual typology. Int. J. Electron. Commer. **6**, 35–59 (2001). https://doi.org/10.1080/10864415.2001.11044235

36. Weiner, B.: An attributional theory of achievement motivation and emotion. Psychol. Rev. **92**, 548–573 (1985). https://doi.org/10.1037/0033-295X.92.4.548

37. Jorgensen, B.K.: Components of consumer reaction to company-related mishaps: a structural equation model approach. Adv. Consum. Res. **23**(1), 346–351 (1996)

38. Lu, V.N., Capezio, A., Restubog, S.L.D., Garcia, P.R.J.M., Wang, L.: In pursuit of service excellence: investigating the role of psychological contracts and organizational identification of frontline hotel employees. Tour. Manage. **56**, 8–19 (2016). https://doi.org/10.1016/j.tou rman.2016.03.020

39. Zhao, N., Jiao, D., Bai, S., Zhu, T.: Evaluating the validity of simplified Chinese version of LIWC in detecting psychological expressions in short texts on social network services. PLoS ONE **11**, e0157947 (2016). https://doi.org/10.1371/journal.pone.0157947

40. Faul, F., Erdfelder, E., Lang, A.-G., Buchner, A.: G*Power 3: a flexible statistical power analysis program for the social, behavioral, and biomedical sciences. Behav. Res. Methods **39**, 175–191 (2007). https://doi.org/10.3758/BF03193146

41. Liao, Y., Xu, C., Gong, X.: Does nostalgic advertising contribute to the spread of a brand's word of mouth? An emotional two-dimensional perspective. Acta Psychol. Sin. **51**, 945–957 (2019). https://doi.org/10.3724/SP.J.1041.2019.00945

42. Jian, J.-Y., Bisantz, A.M., Drury, C.G.: Foundations for an empirically determined scale of trust in automated systems. Int. J. Cogn. Ergon. **4**, 53–71 (2000). https://doi.org/10.1207/S15 327566IJCE0401_04

43. Aaker, J.L., Garbinsky, E.N., Vohs, K.D.: Cultivating admiration in brands: warmth, competence, and landing in the "golden quadrant." J. Consum. Psychol. **22**, 191–194 (2012). https://doi.org/10.1016/j.jcps.2011.11.012

44. Disengagement Report 2019. https://thelastdriverlicenseholder.com/2020/02/26/disengage ment-report-2019/. Accessed 2 Feb 2024

45. Anzalone, L., Barra, P., Barra, S., Castiglione, A., Nappi, M.: An end-to-end curriculum learning approach for autonomous driving scenarios. IEEE Trans. Intell. Transp. Syst. **23**, 19817–19826 (2022). https://doi.org/10.1109/TITS.2022.3160673

46. Yao, J., Ge, Z.: Path-tracking control strategy of unmanned vehicle based on DDPG algorithm. Sensors **22**, 7881 (2022). https://doi.org/10.3390/s22207881

47. Yang, L., Lei, W., Zhang, W., Ye, T.: Dual-flow network with attention for autonomous driving. Front. Neurorobot. **16**, 978225 (2023). https://doi.org/10.3389/fnbot.2022.978225

48. Banks, V.A., Eriksson, A., O'Donoghue, J., Stanton, N.A.: Is partially automated driving a bad idea? Observations from an on-road study. Appl. Ergon. **68**, 138–145 (2018). https://doi.org/10.1016/j.apergo.2017.11.010

49. Richard, O.C., Barnett, T., Dwyer, S., Chadwick, K.: Cultural diversity in management, firm performance, and the moderating role of entrepreneurial orientation dimensions. Acad. Manag. J. **47**(2), 255–266 (2004). https://doi.org/10.2307/20159576

50. Sung, Y., Kim, J.: Effects of brand personality on brand trust and brand affect. Psychol. Mark. **27**, 639–661 (2010). https://doi.org/10.1002/mar.20349

51. Chavaillaz, A., Wastell, D., Sauer, J.: System reliability, performance and trust in adaptable automation. Appl. Ergon. **52**, 333–342 (2016). https://doi.org/10.1016/j.apergo.2015.07.012

52. Xu, Z., et al.: When the automated driving system fails: dynamics of public responses to automated vehicles. Transp. Res. Part C Emerg. Technol. **129**, 103271 (2021). https://doi.org/10.1016/j.trc.2021.103271

53. Seet, M.S., et al.: Subtype divergences of trust in autonomous vehicles: towards optimisation of driver–vehicle trust management. In: 2020 IEEE 23rd International Conference on Intelligent Transportation Systems (ITSC), pp. 1–6. IEEE, Rhodes, Greece (2020)

54. de Vries, P., Midden, C., Bouwhuis, D.: The effects of errors on system trust, self-confidence, and the allocation of control in route planning. Int. J. Hum. Comput. Stud. **58**, 719–735 (2003). https://doi.org/10.1016/S1071-5819(03)00039-9

55. Kraus, J., Scholz, D., Stiegemeier, D., Baumann, M.: The more you know: trust dynamics and calibration in highly automated driving and the effects of take-overs, system malfunction, and system transparency. Hum. Factors **62**, 718–736 (2020). https://doi.org/10.1177/001872 0819853686

56. Madhavan, P., Wiegmann, D.A.: Effects of information source, pedigree, and reliability on operator interaction with decision support systems. Hum. Factors **49**, 773–785 (2007). https://doi.org/10.1518/001872007X230154

57. Glaeser, E.L., Laibson, D.I., Scheinkman, J.A., Soutter, C.L.: Measuring trust*. Quart. J. Econ. **115**, 811–846 (2000). https://doi.org/10.1162/003355300554926

58. Schaefer, K.E.: Measuring trust in human robot interactions: development of the "trust perception scale-HRI." In: Mittu, R., Sofge, D., Wagner, A., Lawless, W.F. (eds.) Robust Intelligence and Trust in Autonomous Systems, pp. 191–218. Springer, US, Boston, MA (2016). https://doi.org/10.1007/978-1-4899-7668-0_10

59. Gutzwiller, R.S., Chiou, E.K., Craig, S.D., Lewis, C.M., Lematta, G.J., Hsiung, C.-P.: Positive bias in the 'Trust in Automated Systems Survey'? An examination of the Jian et al. (2000) scale. Proc. Hum. Fact. Ergon. Soc. Ann. Meet. **63**, 217–221 (2019). https://doi.org/10.1177/1071181319631201

60. Wiegmann, D.A., Rich, A., Zhang, H.: Automated diagnostic aids: the effects of aid reliability on users' trust and reliance. Theor. Issues Ergon. Sci. **2**, 352–367 (2001). https://doi.org/10.1080/14639220110110306

61. Satterfield, K., Baldwin, C., De Visser, E., Shaw, T.: The influence of risky conditions in trust in autonomous systems. Proc. Hum. Factors Ergon. Soc. Ann. Meet. **61**, 324–328 (2017). https://doi.org/10.1177/1541931213601562

62. Kohn, S.C., De Visser, E.J., Wiese, E., Lee, Y.-C., Shaw, T.H.: Measurement of trust in automation: a narrative review and reference guide. Front. Psychol. **12**, 604977 (2021). https://doi.org/10.3389/fpsyg.2021.604977

Ergonomic Analysis on the Effect of Background Music on Working Ability

Yuan Yao and Xiaozhou Zhou[✉]

Southeast University, Nanjing, China
zxz@seu.edu.cn

Abstract. This study investigates the impact of background music tempo on human work performance, specifically focusing on a finger dexterity task. Recognizing the acoustic environment's role in work efficiency, the study addresses sound distractions that can affect attention, stress levels, and overall performance. Despite interventions like soundproofing and background music, research has not reached a consistent conclusion on the effects of background music on human work performance. An experiment is designed to let participants complete a specified hand operation task under both fast and slow background music conditions. Results revealed a significant difference in task completion times, with participants demonstrating greater efficiency under slow-tempo music. This suggests that fast-paced background music may impede work efficiency in tasks requiring fine hand motor skills. The finding aligns with human factors theory, indicating that slow music better aligns with optimal arousal levels, minimizing sensory overload and stress, and enhancing focused task performance. The study contributes valuable insights into the nuanced relationship between background music tempo and human work performance, particularly in tasks involving precision and attention to detail.

Keywords: Ergonomic · Human Work Performance · Awareness

1 Introduction

Human work performance is influenced by numerous factors, which can be broadly categorized into personal, social, managerial, and environmental aspects. Indoor environment factors like thermal conditions, lighting, sound, and air quality, have been identified as critical determinants of work efficiency [1]. This study focuses on the acoustic environment, particularly the influence of background music rhythms on human work performance.

In modern society, human work across various professions usually involves hand manipulation, such as programmers, designers, surgeons, and assembly line workers. Typically, in these types of working spaces, colleagues in charge of different jobs gather around in a large opening area. Therefore, the acoustic environment becomes a significant working performance influencing factor. Sound such as background noise in the room, like air conditioning equipment, and the conversation between colleagues can easily distract the attention of the staffs and lead to stress, work performance decline, and other problems [2]. This is because the noisy environment will interfere with state regulation, cause the cognitive system to overreact, and even directly interfere with the task information processing. On the other hand, it can also lead to psychological complaints, thus diverting human's attention.

Many methods have been tried to reduce the negative impact of the acoustic environment in the working space and improve people's work performance, such as installing soundproof windows, wearing earplugs for staff, and playing background music. In regard of current research, there has yet to be a consistent conclusion on whether background music can have a positive effect on human work efficiency under the premise of isolating noise [3]. For example, Boghdady's study [4] found that background music can significantly enhance the surgical tasks of surgeons, and the medium volume of guitar music is the best. Timothy [5] also found that listening to motivational music improved performance in hot environments. However, studies have also found that music may have a negative impact on workers' productivity [6].

This study aims to explore the influence of the tempo of background music on work performance. An experiment is designed to test the work efficiency of completing a specified hand operation task under background music of both fast and slow rhythms in order to study the relationship between music tempo and human work performance by comparing the task completion time under the two conditions.

2 Related Works

2.1 Psychological and Physiological Regulation Mechanism of Human Work Performance

The human body perceives changes in the internal and external environment through sensory organs, and all senses originate from the activities of the nervous system. Different types of stimuli will stimulate different receptors and produce corresponding sensory signals. These signals are transmitted to the central nervous system after complex processing in the sensory pathway, and finally cause perception.

Memory can be divided into short-term memory and long-term memory. Short-term memory describes the characteristics of temporary retention of information, while working memory more comprehensively considers the short-term retention of information and is more deliberate. Working memory is a memory system for temporary storage and operation of information, and plays an essential role in complex tasks such as language, understanding, learning and reasoning [7]. The medial temporal lobe memory system, including the hippocampus structure and its adjacent cortical areas, is one of the key parts. Studies have shown that information storage is closely related to information processing, and all kinds of sensory information are processed and stored in the neural network composed of primary and secondary sensory areas, associative areas, the medial temporal lobe memory system and the frontal associative cortex.

When hearing a sound, the central nervous system initiates a series of reactions by comparing the intensity and frequency of the sound and combining it with previous experiences, so as to determine whether the sound is noise (negative environmental factors) or normal and acceptable sound. Auditory pathway includes direct pathway (from inner ear to auditory cortex) and indirect pathway. Through indirect pathway, sound is transmitted to reticular activating system connecting limbic system and other parts of the brain, and enters the autonomic nervous system and neuroendocrine system. Therefore, noise may stimulate the release of steroids from hypothalamic-adrenal axon, and affect the release of norepinephrine, epinephrine and other substances from sympathetic-adrenal axon, and then affect individual vigilance, cognitive ability and operational ability [8].

2.2 Sound Environment and Its Influence on Human Work Performance

Currently, there is extensive research on the acoustic environment's impact on work performance within office spaces. The acoustic environment of indoor spaces is primarily investigated through three dimensions: sound source type, sound pressure level, and reverberation time. Jikke proposed a comprehensive conceptual model outlining the role of room acoustics in influencing human performance [9].

In the realm of sound's impact on human performance, studies have shown that noise affects behavioral cognition. Xinyao et al. discovered that instrumental music can enhance creativity through various factors such as emotional arousal, cognitive interference, music preference, and psychological restoration [10]. Gonzalez's findings indicated that music generally impairs complex task performance, while complex music can facilitate simple task performance [11].

Arboleda et al. conducted a between-group experiment with three conditions: slow-tempo music, fast-tempo music, or no music. They suggested that turning off music during stressful activities is favorable for performance [12]. Cheah et al. emphasized the necessity of task-specific, music-specific, and population-specific analyses when studying the effects of background music on cognitive task performance [13].

3   Methods

The purpose of this work is to find out the effect of background music tempo on human work performance. In this experiment, the task is designed to focus on works where manual operation is primarily needed, which need subjects to manipulate using their fingers. The independent variable is the tempo of the background music. The dependent variable is the dexterity of the finger, which is revealed by the observed variable: time to complete the task.

3.1 Participants

A total of 7 participants were recruited for this study, including 4 males and 3 females. None of the participants reported any visual impairment or abnormal operating ability. Before participating in the experiment, participants were asked to get plenty of rest and engage in activities that can reduce cognitive load. To ensure the accuracy of the results, each participant completed three repetitions of the experiment. All participants know and consent that their operational data is being used in this study and that these data will be protected for privacy.

3.2 Materials

In the experiment, two songs with fast tempo and slow tempo were chosen, and their tempo was quantified into BPM for comparison, as shown in Table 1. Subjects were asked to wear a pair of noise-cancelling earphones Sony WF-SP700N which plays the songs with disturbing outside noise eliminated.

Table 1. Experimental material: Background music with two types of rhythms.

Tempo	Music	BPM
Fast	Getting High on the Down Low	117.45
Slow	A Gallant Gentleman	107.67

To identify the tempo in the music, we computed the onset strength of the audio. Onset strength is a measure of the energy or intensity of the audio signal over time. It presents abrupt changes in the audio, such as the beginning of musical notes, which correspond to the beats. Then we analyzed the onset envelope and represented the tempo in beats per minute (BPM). The onset envelope represents the intensity of abrupt changes in audio over time. Peaks in the onset envelope correspond to the beginnings of musical events, such as beats. The timing of beats in the music is determined by identifying the peaks in the onset envelope, which is the average inter-onset interval (IOI). Finally, the BPM is estimated by converting the average IOI through the following formula.

$$BPM = 60/Average\ IOI \tag{1}$$

Here, "60" is used to convert the average IOI to BPM, as there are 60 s in a minute.

In order to measure finger flexibility, BD-II-601 finger flexibility tester was used in this experiment. The experimental platform can record the time taken by a pair of tweezers to insert the needle into all the holes, so as to reflect the work performance of the subject. The instrument consists of four parts (Fig. 1):

1. 10 * 10 small hole lattice;
2. Several needles;
3. 1 pair of tweezers;
4. 1 timer.

3.3 Process

Participants were instructed to pick up a plunger with their dominant hand and insert it into the first row of holes from left to right while wearing noise-canceling earphones which is playing the designated background music. Timing began as the participant inserted the first plunger into the leftmost hole and stopped when they completed inserting the last plunger into the rightmost spot. Each participant completed three tests, with a 10-min break between each set. The order of testing, using fast or slow music, was randomized.

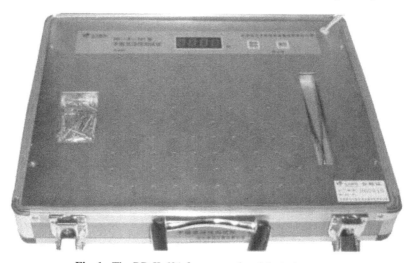

Fig. 1. The BD-II-601 finger speed and dexterity tester

In order to control unrelated variables, there are the following requirements during the testing process.

1. There were two types of background music, a fast tempo song and a slow tempo song. Both songs did not change in individual tests. Participants use noise-cancelling headphones to ensure the environment is not disturbed.
2. Participants have 30 s to adjust the background music.
3. Participants were given a 10-min break between each test to avoid fatigue and adaptability (Fig. 2).

Fig. 2. Subject manipulating on the BD-II-601 tester

4   Results

Experiment data were processed as follows (Figs. 3 and 4):

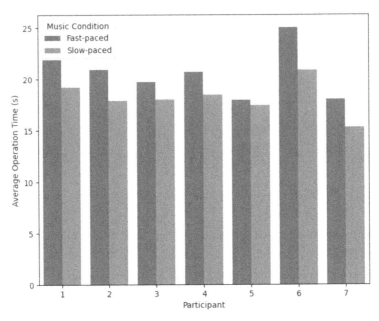

Fig. 3. Average Operation time by Participants

We analyzed the operation time at two musical rhythms (Fast paced and Slow paced), and the data set consisted of multiple observations of seven subjects at different musical rhythms. Here are the main findings of the analysis (Table 2):

Descriptive Statistics. First, we performed descriptive statistics on the operating time for each musical rhythm. The results show that the average operation time seems to be slightly higher with the tempo of the Fast paced music than with the tempo of the Slow paced music, but we need to conduct a statistical test to confirm whether the difference is significant.

Box Diagram. By drawing a box plot, we can more intuitively compare the distribution of operating time under two musical rhythms. The box plot shows the median, upper and lower quartiles, and possible outliers. Looking at the boxplot helps to understand the overall distribution of the data.

Statistical Test. We used a paired T-test and a Wilcoxon signed rank test to compare the operating time at two musical rhythms. The results showed that the operation time under Fast paced music was significantly higher than that under Slow paced music ($p < 0.05$). This means that, in our dataset, musical rhythm has a significant effect on operation time.

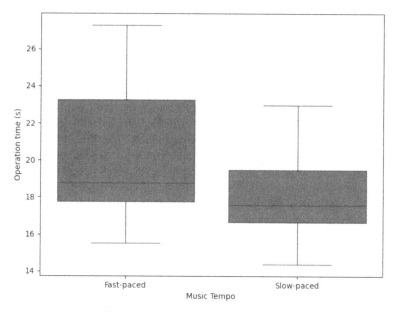

Fig. 4. Operation time by Music Tempo

Table 2. Operation time of music rhythm distribution statistics

Tempo	count	mean	std	min	25%	50%	75%	max
Fast	21.0	20.603333	3.671669	15.54	17.78	18.77	23.26	27.28
Slow	21.0	18.176667	2.373481	14.39	16.66	17.57	19.48	22.97

5   Discussion

The phenomenon that people work more efficiently under slow-paced music than under fast-paced music can be analyzed from the perspective of human factor theory, taking into account all aspects of sensation, central nervous system, attention, cognition, etc.

Central Nervous System. Human factor theory recognizes the Yerkes-Dodson law, which shows that the relationship between arousal levels and performance follows an inverted U-shaped curve. Too little or too much excitement can hinder performance, and performing tasks effectively requires an optimal level of excitement. For tasks that require focus and precision, slower music is more likely to keep arousal levels within the optimal range. Slow music has a calming effect on the central nervous system, potentially reducing stress and anxiety. In contrast, fast-paced music may raise stress levels due to increased physiological arousal, which can negatively affect performance.

Attention. Fast-paced music requires more attention due to its rapid changes, making it challenging to maintain selective attention to the task. In this regard, slow music is less demanding, allowing individuals to allocate their attention to work more effectively.

Fast-paced music may cause distraction, as people may involuntarily stomp their feet, nod their heads, or experience other rhythmic movements. This distraction reduces the cognitive resources needed to complete the task.

Awareness. Cognitive load theory suggests that the capacity of working memory is limited. While the brain processes fast auditory information, fast-paced music may increase cognitive load. In contrast, slower music reduces cognitive load and frees up mental resources for the task at hand. Cognitive performance often benefits from a calm and focused mental state, and slow music can promote this. It allows for better attention and cognitive efficiency, especially on tasks that require attention to detail and precision.

In conclusion, slow music is generally more consistent with optimal arousal levels, minimizes sensory overload, reduces stress, promotes selective attention, and reduces cognitive load. All of these factors contribute to a relaxed state of focus that promotes efficient task performance, especially for tasks that require precision and attention to detail. However, personal preferences and specific task requirements may also play a role in determining the effect of music on productivity.

6 Conclusion

The results of this study reveal a significant difference in human work performance particularly in the time taken to complete the finger dexterity task between the two background music conditions. Participants completed the task more quickly when exposed to slow-tempo music compared to fast-tempo music. This suggests that fast-paced background music reduces work efficiency in tasks requiring fine hand motor skills.

The phenomenon that people work more efficiently under slow music can be explained through the perspective of human factors theory. Slow music generally aligns better with optimal arousal levels. It can effectively minimize sensory overload and simultaneously alleviate stress. This aids in promoting selective attention and reducing cognitive load, contributing to a relaxed focus that enhances efficient task performance, especially for tasks requiring precision and attention to detail.

The research finding of this article aligns with previous speculations that the rhythm of background music can influence human performance, and it builds upon earlier studies to draw further conclusions. However, it is worth noting that more working scenarios and music types should be tried and validated in order to apply the conclusions of this paper to practice, due to the small sample size of this study.

References

1. Roelofsen, P.: The impact of office environments on employee performance: the design of the workplace as a strategy for productivity enhancement. J. Facil. Manag. **1**(3), 247–264 (2002)
2. Kaarlela-Tuomaala, A., Helenius, R., Keskinen, E., et al.: Effects of acoustic environment on work in private office rooms and open-plan offices – longitudinal study during relocation. Ergonomics **52**(11), 1423–1444 (2009)
3. Dalton, B.H., Behm, D.G.: Effects of noise and music on human and task performance: a systematic review. Occup. Ergon. **7**(3), 143–152 (2008)

4. El Boghdady, M., Ewalds-Kvist, B.M.: The influence of music on the surgical task performance: a systematic review. Int. J. Surg. **73**, 101–112 (2020)

5. English, T., Mavros, Y., Jay, O.: Listening to motivational music mitigates heat-related reductions in exercise performance. Physiol. Behav. **208**, 112567 (2019)

6. Furnham, A., Bradley, A.: Music while you work: the differential distraction of background music on the cognitive test performance of introverts and extraverts (1997)

7. Baddeley, A.: Working memory: the interface between memory and cognition. J. Cogn. Neurosci. **4**(3), 281–288 (1992)

8. Rylander, R.: Physiological aspects of noise-induced stress and annoyance. J. Sound Vib. **277**(3), 471–478 (2004)

9. Reinten, J., Braat-Eggen, P.E., Hornikx, M., et al.: The indoor sound environment and human task performance: a literature review on the role of room acoustics. Build. Environ. **123**, 315–332 (2017)

10. Xiao, X., Tan, J., Liu, X., et al.: The dual effect of background music on creativity: perspectives of music preference and cognitive interference. Front. Psychol. **14**, 1247133 (2023)

11. Gonzalez, M.F., Aiello, J.R.: More than meets the ear: investigating how music affects cognitive task performance. J. Exp. Psychol. Appl. **25**(3), 431–444 (2019)

12. Arboleda, A., Arroyo, C., Rodriguez, B., et al.: A stressful task is when to turn off the music: effect of music on task performance mediated by cognitive effort. Psychol. Music **50**(1), 298–311 (2022)

13. Cheah, Y., Wong, H.K., Spitzer, M., et al.: Background music and cognitive task performance: a systematic review of task, music, and population impact. Music. Sci. **5**, 205920432211343 (2022)

How to Present Paired Information on the HUD Interface: The Effects of Horizontal and Vertical Angles on Object Discrimination

Ying Zhou[1,2], Ying Wen[1], Liu Tang[3], and Yan Ge[1,2(✉)]

[1] CAS Key Laboratory of Behavioural Science, Institute of Psychology,
Chinese Academy of Sciences, Beijing, China
gey@psych.ac.cn
[2] Department of Psychology, University of Chinese Academy of Sciences, Beijing, China
[3] Chongqing Changan Automobile Co, Ltd., Chongqing, China

Abstract. Many studies have explored the influence of the position of a single piece of information in a head-up display (HUD) system on driving performance. However, few studies have evaluated the range of multiple visual angles. This study aimed to examine the positions and visual aspects of driving information presentation that enhance drivers' driving performance. Considering the horizontal and vertical directions, we designed two experiments to identify an appropriate area to present driving information. Experiment A was designed as a 4 (horizontal angles: 10°, 20°, 30°, 40°) × 3 (vertical positions: −5°, 10°, 20°) within-subject experiment to evaluate the effects of the horizontal angle and vertical position of information on the reaction time and difficulty rating. The results showed that when the vertical position was −5° or 10° and the horizontal angle was 10°, the driver's reaction time was faster and the driver felt easier. Experiment B was designed as a 3 (vertical angles: 5°, 15°, 25°) × 3 (horizontal positions: −15°, 10°, 25°) within-subject experiment to explore the effect of the vertical angle and horizontal position of the information on the reaction time and difficulty rating. The results showed that when the horizontal position was 10° and the vertical angle was 5°, the driver's reaction time was faster and felt that the task was easier. The two experimental results showed that participants responded faster and rated the task as easier when information was placed near the center visual field. The results may be useful for designers to present multiple pieces of driving information on HUDs and provide theoretical guidance for HUD interface design.

Keywords: Head-up display · Horizontal angle of view · Vertical angle of view · Field of view

1 Introduction

With rapid technological advancements, the functionality of automotive head-up displays (HUDs) is expanding significantly [1]. HUDs project driving-related information onto drivers' forward field of vision, allowing them to maintain focus on the road while

D. Harris and W.-C. Li (Eds.): HCII 2024, LNAI 14693, pp. 150–162, 2024.
https://doi.org/10.1007/978-3-031-60731-8_11

simultaneously receiving crucial data [2–4]. This approach contrasts with traditional head-down displays (HDDs), which require drivers to look downward, thus diverting their attention. HUDs not only alleviate mental strain but also enhance driving safety by reducing the amount of time that drivers' spend not looking at the road [5–15].

As in-vehicle information increases, so does the need for intuitive HUD system interface designs that correspond with drivers' behavioural patterns. According to cognitive load theory, a cluttered HUD interface can significantly increase cognitive load, leading to reduced focus on driving tasks [7, 16]. Therefore, optimizing the useful field of view (UFOV) within the HUD is critical for minimizing cognitive load and enhancing driver safety and performance [17]. The UFOV is defined as the region of the visual field from which the driver can extract information at any time [18]. The current HUD system adopts a field of view in the range of $8° \times 3°$ [19]. We further distinguished horizontal and vertical UFOVs, as shown in Fig. 1. Park and Im (2020) and Wolfe et al. (2019) reported that central HUD displays improve individuals' response times more than peripheral displays, which can cause delays and missed information [20, 21]. Haeuslschmid et al. (2015) determined that hazards presented at horizontal angles up to $14°$ were recognized more swiftly than at $21°$ and recommended placing such information within a $20°$ horizontal angle for improved effectiveness [22]. Similar results were found in cognitive training tasks using smartphones. Redlinger et al. (2021) asked subjects to perform an adaptive training task at three separate horizontal visual angles ($10°/20°/30°$) and found that their performance was best when the horizontal visual angle was $20°$ [23].

However, despite its importance, the vertical positioning of HUD elements has received less attention. Pioneering studies have revealed that vertical placement is a crucial factor for effective HUD design. Inuzuka et al. (1991) were among the first to suggest that HUD imagery placed between $6°$ and $10°$ below the centre line improves visibility [24]. Watanabe et al. (1999) designed 15 locations where warning triangles were presented (3 rows of 5 columns). They found that responses to warnings in the middle row were significantly faster than those in the $\pm5°$ rows, and responses to warnings in the $0°$ and $\pm5°$ columns were significantly faster than other columns [25]. Similarly, Tsimhoni (2001) reported that optimal HUD performance is achieved when information is displayed within $\pm5°$ of the centre, both vertically and horizontally [26]. Morita (2007) designed 4 degrees in the vertical direction ($-6°$, $-3°$, $0°$, $3°$) and found that improved safety when the display range was between $-4°$ and $7°$ in the vertical direction [27]. These insights underscore the necessity of integrating vertical considerations into HUD interface design to enhance drivers' safety and performance.

Continuing research has expanded our understanding of the optimal horizontal and vertical positions for HUD elements. Haeuslschmid et al. (2017) explored response times across 17 positions within a wide visual angle of $35° \times 15°$ and discovered that responses tended to slow as eccentricity increased. In particular, the most efficient reaction times were less than $5°$ at horizontal angles and vertical angles [28]. They found that response times generally increased with eccentricity. Topliss et al. (2019) segmented a full windshield display into nine areas and found that drivers exhibited improved performance and preference for HUD imagery positioned closer to their direct line of sight [14]. Building on this, Topliss et al. (2020) examined 48 different windshield positions to determine the onset of unsafe driving behaviours and found that lower central positions delayed the time before lane departure compared to higher positions [29]. Zhou et al. (2023) enlarged the FOV range of a stimulus to 50° × 50° and designed 77 different positions where the stimulus appeared. Their results showed that drivers' recognition response was better in the range of −10° to 20° horizontally and −5° to 15° vertically [30]. These studies collectively suggest that drivers exhibit better performance when HUD stimuli are displayed with lower eccentricity, ideally within 20° horizontally and 15° vertically of their natural line of sight [22, 23, 30, 31].

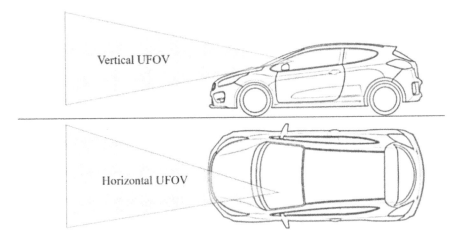

Fig. 1. The useful field of view of drivers

Previous studies have examined the information access effort (IAE) and analysed how the separation of visual angles affects the cognitive and physical effort required to shift attention between different sources of information [27, 33]. IAE is influenced by the visual angle that separates two pieces of information [32], with less effort needed when they are within 0° to 4° of each other, close to the foveal area of the eye. Beyond this 4° threshold, there is a marked increase in the information access time (IAT), which stabilizes between 4° and 30°, necessitating eye movement for information recognition. As separation progresses, requiring head and body movement, the IAT correspondingly increases [32–34]. Notably, most research indicating a trend of performance improvement based on the IAE has focused on vertical displacement [33, 35]. In contrast, Warden et al. (2022) reported that this IAE-related performance trend is not consistent across a horizontal visual angle range of 2° to 50° [32]. Therefore, our research questions have not yet been answered: except for the position of 0°, which positions may be safer for presenting information, and in what range is it safe to display multiple pieces of driving information at a location?

To determine the most effective positions and angles for presenting multiple driving-related information, this study conducted two experiments. In Experiment A, we presented paired information at various vertical levels from the same horizontal angle, as illustrated in Fig. 2 (A), to assess how different vertical placements affected reaction time and perceived difficulty. Experiment B varied the horizontal placement of paired information from different vertical angles, as depicted in Fig. 2 (B), to evaluate the impact on drivers' responses in unilateral visual fields. By comparing the reaction times and difficulty ratings across varying angles and positions, these experiments aimed to provide suggestions for HUD interfaces with paired driving information.

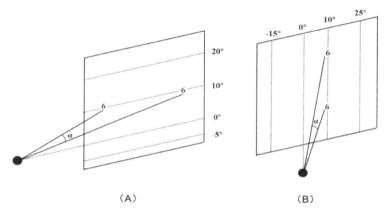

Fig. 2. Information presented at different angles at different locations in two experiments. (A) Schematic illustrations of information presentation in Experiment A; (B) Schematic illustrations of information presentation in Experiment B

2   Method

2.1   Participants

Thirty-three drivers aged 18 to 50 years (mean = 32.04, SD = 4.56) were recruited to participate in this study. The participants included 3 women. All participants had at least one year of driving experience (mean = 6.89, SD = 3.96). All of them had normal or corrected-to-normal vision and no 3D vertigo.

2.2   Experimental Design and Tasks

- **Experiment Design.** Two experiments were designed to explore the effect of different levels of horizontal/vertical angles at different positions on object discrimination. A 4 (horizontal angles: 10°, 20°, 30°, 40°) × 3 (vertical positions: −5°, 10°, 20°) within-subject design was used in Experiment A, while Experiment B was designed as a 3 (vertical angles: 5°, 15°, 25°) × 3 (horizontal positions: −15°, 10°, 25°) within-subject experiment. The tasks of these two experiments were the same.
- **Driving task.** The subjects were required to drive on a two-way 4-lane country road and maintain a speed of 80 km/h in the same lane. If their speed exceeded ±10 km/h, they heard a reminder beep.

- **Number discrimination task**. During the driving task, two numbers (6/9) were displayed on the screen in each condition according to the experimental design. The participants were asked to determine whether the two numbers were the same. They pressed the right button when the two numbers were the same and pressed the left button when the two numbers were different. The proportion of trials with the same number to trials with different numbers was 1:1. The reaction time and percentage of correct responses were recorded.
- **Subjective rating task**. After the driving task, all conditions of both experiments were shown on the driving scenes. The participants rated the difficulty of the number discrimination task in each condition on a 5-point Likert scale, where 1 indicated that it was very difficult, while 5 indicated that it was very easy to distinguish these two numbers.

2.3 Equipment and Materials

The experiments were conducted in the laboratory of the R&D Centre of Changan Automobile Company in Chongqing, China. Visual Test Drive (VTD) software was used to simulate the actual road environment (see Fig. 3). In the experiment, the simulated driving road we designed was 50 kms long, including three left turns and four right turns, and all corners had the same curvature. It was designed as a two-way 4-lane road with a side width of 3.5 m. The simulated scene was projected on a circular screen of 6.15 m × 5.5 m. A Logitech G29 steering wheel set was fixed on a 0.8 m high table for driving control. Its distance from the screen was 3 m, which was aligned with the centre line.

Fig. 3. Experimental driving environment (a subject is performing an experimental task)

2.4 Procedure

When the participants arrived at the laboratory, the researchers introduced the study to them and adjusted the seat height to ensure that the centre of their vision was at zero in both the vertical and horizontal directions. The participants subsequently practised the driving simulator for 5 min to ensure familiarity with the driving task and the number discrimination task. In the formal experiment, the participants needed to drive at 80 km/h and complete the number discrimination task at the same time. In one trial, two numbers were presented for 2 s, while the next numbers appeared at random intervals of 5 to 12 s. Each condition had four trials. The order of Experiment A and Experiment B was balanced between subjects. The time required to complete the procedure was approximately 8 min for Experiment A and 6 min for Experiment B. After the driving task, the participants were asked to rate the difficulty of the number discrimination task in each condition. This study was approved by the Institutional Review Board of the Institute of Psychology, Chinese Academy of Sciences.

3   Results

3.1   Reaction Time at Different Horizontal Angles and Vertical Positions (Experiment *A*)

The means (M) and standard deviations (SD) for the reaction time and difficulty rating from the number discrimination task are shown in Table 1. Repeated-measures ANOVA with the horizontal angle (10°/20°/30°/40°) and vertical position (−5°/10°/20°) as within-subject factors was used to compare the reaction times under different conditions. The main effects of the horizontal angles were significant. Pair-wise comparisons revealed that the reaction time at a horizontal angle of 40° was significantly longer than that at 10° ($p < 0.001$), 20° ($p = 0.003$) or 30° ($p = 0.021$). In addition, the reaction time at a horizontal angle of 30° was significantly longer than at a horizontal angle of 10° ($p = 0.001$). The main effects of the vertical position were not significant.

The two-way interaction effect on the average reaction time was significant (see Fig. 4(A)). Bonferroni post hoc analysis confirmed that at a vertical position of −5°, the reaction times at horizontal angles of 40° ($p < 0.001$) and 30° ($p = 0.017$) were significantly longer than at a vertical position of 10°. At a vertical position of 10°, the reaction time at a horizontal angle of 40° was significantly longer than at 10° ($p < 0.001$), 20° ($p < 0.001$) and 30° ($p = 0.021$). At a vertical position of 20°, the reaction times at horizontal angles of 40° ($p = 0.023$) and 30° ($p < 0.001$) were significantly longer than at a horizontal angle of 20°.

3.2   Subjective Ratings at Different Horizontal Angles and Vertical Positions (Experiment A)

For the difficulty rating, the main effects of both the horizontal angle and the vertical position were significant (see Fig. 4 (B)). The results showed that the difficulty of horizontal angles of 10° was significantly easier than 20° ($p < 0.001$), 30°($p < 0.001$) and 40° ($p < 0.001$). The difficulty of obtaining a horizontal angle of 20° was significantly greater than that of obtaining a horizontal angle of 30° ($p < 0.001$) and 40° ($p < 0.001$). The difficulty of obtaining a horizontal angle of 30° was significantly greater than that of obtaining a horizontal angle of 40° ($p < 0.001$). In the vertical positions, we found that only the ratings at 10° were significantly easier than those at 20° ($p = 0.036$).

The interaction effect on the average difficulty ratings was also significant. The results of the post hoc analysis indicated that at a vertical position of −5°, the difficulty at a horizontal angle of 10° was significantly greater than at 20° (p < 0.001), 30° (p < 0.001) or 40° (p < 0.001). In addition, the difficulty of obtaining a horizontal angle of 20° was significantly greater than the difficulty of obtaining a horizontal angle of 30° (p < 0.001) or 40° (p < 0.001). The difficulty of obtaining a horizontal angle of 30° was significantly greater than the difficulty of obtaining a horizontal angle of 40° (p < 0.001). At a vertical position of 10°, the difficulty at a horizontal angle of 10° was significantly greater than at 20° (p < 0.001), 30° (p < 0.001) or 40° (p < 0.001). The difficulty at a horizontal angle of 20° was significantly greater than at 30° (p < 0.001) or 40° (p < 0.001). The difficulty of obtaining a horizontal angle of 30° was significantly greater than the difficulty of obtaining a horizontal angle of 40° (p < 0.001). At a vertical position of 20°, the difficulty at a horizontal angle of 10° was significantly greater than at 20° (p = 0.002), 30° (p < 0.001) and 40° (p < 0.001). In addition, the difficulty of obtaining a horizontal angle of 20° was significantly greater than the difficulty of obtaining a horizontal angle of 30° (p = 0.008) or 40° (p < 0.001). The difficulty of obtaining a horizontal angle of 30° was significantly greater than the difficulty of obtaining a horizontal angle of 40° (p < 0.001).

Table 1. Results of ANOVAs at different horizontal angles and vertical positions.

Indices		10°	20°	30°	40°	Total	Horizontal Angles	Vertical Positions	Interaction
Reaction time(s)	-5°	1.26 (0.23)	1.43 (0.49)	1.37 (0.25)	1.48 (0.27)	1.38 (0.05)	$F(3,93)=$ 16.51*** $\eta_p^2=0.35$	$F(2,62)=$ 0.53 $\eta_p^2=0.02$	$F(6,186)=$ 2.57* $\eta_p^2=0.08$
	10°	1.29 (0.28)	1.30 (0.30)	1.36 (0.27)	1.50 (0.33)	1.36 (0.05)			
	20°	1.31 (0.33)	1.29 (0.33)	1.50 (0.34)	1.46 (0.27)	1.39 (0.04)			
	Total	1.28 (0.04)	1.34 (0.06)	1.41 (0.05)	1.48 (0.04)				
Diffculty Rating	-5°	4.64 (0.49)	3.50 (0.96)	2.54 (1.14)	2.04 (1.07)	3.18 (0.14)	$F(3,81)=$ 119.71*** $\eta_p^2=0.82$	$F(2,54)=$ 4.75* $\eta_p^2=0.15$	$F(6,162)=$ 6.56*** $\eta_p^2=0.20$
	10°	4.57 (0.63)	3.79 (0.88)	2.50 (1.26)	1.86 (1.01)	3.18 (0.14)			
	20°	3.86 (1.08)	3.25 (1.35)	2.71 (1.27)	1.82 (0.98)	2.91 (0.20)			
	Total	4.36 (0.11)	3.51 (0.18)	2.58 (0.21)	1.91 (0.19)				

Notes: *p<0.05; ***p<0.001.

3.3 Reaction Times at Different Vertical Angles and Horizontal Positions (Experiment *B)*

The mean reaction time and difficulty ratings in all conditions are shown in Table 2. First, a repeated measure ANOVA with factors of vertical angle (5°/15°/25°) and horizontal position (−15°/10°/25°) was performed to assess the effects of vertical angle, horizontal position, or the interaction between the vertical angle and horizontal position. The analysis revealed a significant main effect of the vertical angle and horizontal position, but no interaction effect was found between the vertical angle and horizontal position. Pairwise

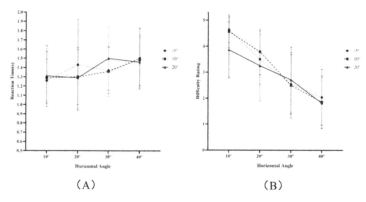

Fig. 4. Mean reaction time (A) and difficulty rating (B) for each horizontal angle at different vertical positions. Error bars denote the 95% confidence intervals.

comparisons revealed that the reaction time at a vertical angle of 25° was significantly longer than at a vertical angle of 5° ($p = 0.012$). In addition, we found that the reaction times at horizontal positions of −15° ($p < 0.001$) and 25° ($p < 0.001$) were significantly longer than at 10°.

3.4 Subjective Ratings at Different Vertical Angles and Horizontal Positions (Experiment B)

The same repeated-measures ANOVA was conducted on the difficulty ratings. Overall, there was a significant main effect of horizontal position but not of vertical angle or the interaction between vertical angle and horizontal position. Specifically, the difficulty of

Table 2. Results of ANOVAs at different vertical angles and horizontal positions.

Indices		5°	15°	25°	Total	Vertical Angles	Horizontal Positions	Interaction
Reaction time(s)	-15°	1.39 (0.24)	1.49 (0.32)	1.54 (0.36)	1.47 (0.05)	$F(2,64)=$ 4.48* $\eta_p^2=0.12$	$F(2,64)=$ 26.69*** $\eta_p^2=0.46$	$F(4,128)=$ 1.86 $\eta_p^2=0.06$
	10°	1.27 (0.34)	1.28 (0.28)	1.32 (0.23)	1.29 (0.04)			
	25°	1.38 (0.30)	1.48 (0.33)	1.41 (0.25)	1.42 (0.04)			
	Total	1.35 (0.04)	1.42 (0.05)	1.42 (0.04)				
Difficulty Rating	-15°	3.83 (1.14)	3.86 (0.95)	3.45 (1.21)	3.71 (0.14)	$F(2,56)=$ 2.72 $\eta_p^2=0.09$	$F(2,56)=$ 59.06*** $\eta_p^2=0.68$	$F(4,112)=$ 1.61 $\eta_p^2=0.05$
	10°	4.48 (0.83)	4.28 (0.80)	4.07 (1.19)	4.28 (0.14)			
	25°	3.07 (1.10)	2.55 (1.01)	2.59 (1.18)	2.74 (0.17)			
	Total	3.79 (0.16)	3.56 (0.14)	3.37 (0.19)				

Notes: *$p<0.05$; ***$p<0.001$.

accessing a vertical angle of 10° was significantly greater than the difficulty of measuring a vertical angle of $-15°$ ($p = 0.001$) or 25° ($p < 0.001$). The difficulty at a vertical angle of $-15°$ was significantly greater than at 25° ($p < 0.001$).

4 Discussion

This study aimed to investigate the role of the position and angle of paired driving information and eyes in an HUD system in simulated scenes. Experiment A focused on the effect of paired information on horizontal angles and vertical positions, and Experiment B focused on the effect of paired information on vertical angles and horizontal positions. The experimental results showed that drivers reacted faster and had a lower difficulty rating when paired information was presented at a lower eccentricity (closer to the central visual field). Previous studies have reported similar findings [14, 36].

For the average reaction time, the results of Experiment A showed that the main effect of horizontal angle was significant. As the horizontal angle increased, the average response time also gradually increased. When the horizontal angle was 40°, the response time was the longest. This may have occurred because when the horizontal angle increased, the paired stimuli were farther from the central visual field. The results were also confirmed by difficulty rating. Participants reported that task difficulty was lowest when the horizontal angle was 10°, while task difficulty was highest when the horizontal angle was 40°. The results also revealed that it is important for paired stimulus designs to appear in the central field of view to ensure driving safety. The difficulty rating results demonstrated that participants considered the task in which the driving information appeared in the vertical position of 20° to be significantly more difficult than the vertical position of 10°. Previous studies have compared response times at vertical positions of 0° and $\pm5°$ and found that the response to warnings in the middle row is significantly greater than in the other rows [25]. In other words, there are also eccentricity effects in the vertical direction on the HUD layout. For the $-5°$ vertical position, there was no significant difference from the 10° difficulty rating. This finding is similar to previous results comparing ratings of difficulty and eye movement data [27]. These studies found higher levels of safety when the display range was between $-4°$ and 7° in the vertical direction.

In addition, the results revealed a significant interaction effect between the horizontal angle and the vertical position on the average reaction time and difficulty rating. On average, the participants reacted more slowly and rated the task as more difficult at a vertical position of 20° and a horizontal angle of 40°. Therefore, designers should consider drivers' visual processing physiology and design driving information at positions that require a low workload. Specifically, an area under 20° above the horizontal line is safer in the vertical direction, and the horizontal angle between the paired information and the eyes should be set to 10° or 20°.

Experiment B explored the effect of the vertical angle and horizontal position. First, as shown for the reaction time data, compared with a vertical angle of 5°, participants responded more slowly when the vertical angle was 25°. Second, reaction times at vertical angles of $-15°$ ($p < 0.001$) and 25° ($p < 0.001$) were significantly longer than at 10°. Third, in terms of difficulty ratings, among the three horizontal positions, the task involving paired stimuli at a horizontal position of 10° was considered easiest, while the task involving a horizontal position of 20° was considered most difficult. Previous studies have compared 5 different horizontal locations ($-7°$, $0°$, $7°$, $14°$, $21°$) and suggested placing hazard information closer than 20° [22]. One possible explanation for the eccentricity effect may be connected with visual processing physiology. The macular area contains a large number of cone cells that can quickly and clearly identify visual stimuli. Several studies have shown that the corresponding angle of view of the macular area is approximately 18° [37]. Therefore, paired driving information should be placed close to the central visual field, not more than 20°. Furthermore, based on the results of the study, the vertical angle of paired driving information may be 10°.

This study has several limitations. First, to achieve a balance between task aim and time assumption, the independent variables used in the two experiments were designed at only three or four levels. Future research could consider using different experimental paradigms to systematically identify areas suitable for presenting multiple pieces of driving information. Second, this study adopted the number matching task. However, there are diverse driving information signs that have different shapes, colours, and information available from the HUD system. In the future, we can use information that is closer to real driving scenarios. Finally, the study asked participants to simulate driving on a two-way 4-lane country road. We did not investigate the interaction between road conditions and the HUD layout design. Previous studies have shown that different real-road conditions influence drivers' performance [38, 39]. Future research can include driving scenarios such as city roads to ensure that the experimental results are universal across situations with HUD layouts.

5 Conclusion

This study preliminarily explored the influence of the angle and position of paired stimuli on driving performance. The results indicated that the position and angle between pairs of driving information clearly and significantly impacted driving performance. When the paired stimuli were closer to the central visual field, the subjects responded faster and the task evaluation was easier. In this study, we mainly addressed the issue of presenting paired information signs. Overall, this study provides support for the design of paired stimuli in HUD layouts.

Acknowledgement. This study was supported by the National Natural Science Foundation of China (Grant No. 32071066) and the Key Project of Chongqing Technology Innovation and Application Development (Grant no. cstc2021jscx-dxwtBX0020).

References

1. Park, J., Park, W.: Functional requirements of automotive head-up displays: a systematic review of literature from 1994 to present. Appl. Ergon. **76**, 130–146 (2019). https://doi.org/10.1016/j.apergo.2018.12.017

2. Guo, H., Zhao, F., Wang, W., Jiang, X.: Analyzing drivers' attitude towards HUD system using a stated preference survey. Adv. Mech. Eng. **6**, 380647 (2014). https://doi.org/10.1155/2014/380647

3. Li, X., Rong, J., Li, Z., Zhao, X., Zhang, Y.: Modeling drivers' acceptance of augmented reality head-up display in connected environment. Displays **75**, 102307 (2022). https://doi.org/10.1016/j.displa.2022.102307

4. Ward, N.J., Parkes, A.: Head-up displays and their automotive application: an overview of human factors issues affecting safety. Accid. Anal. Prev. **26**, 703–717 (1994). https://doi.org/10.1016/0001-4575(94)90049-3

5. Ablassmeier, M., Poitschke, T., Wallhoff, F., Bengler, K., Rigoll, G.: Eye gaze studies comparing head-up and head-down displays in vehicles. In: 2007 IEEE International Conference on Multimedia and Expo, pp. 2250–2252 (2007). https://doi.org/10.1109/ICME.2007.4285134

6. Barbotin, N., Baumeister, J., Cunningham, A., Duval, T., Grisvard, O., Thomas, B.H.: Evaluating visual cues for future airborne surveillance using simulated augmented reality displays. In: 2022 IEEE Conference on Virtual Reality and 3D User Interfaces (VR), pp. 213–221 (2022). https://doi.org/10.1109/VR51125.2022.00040

7. Charissis, V., et al.: Employing emerging technologies to develop and evaluate in-vehicle intelligent systems for driver support: infotainment AR HUD case study. Appl. Sci. **11**, 1397 (2021). https://doi.org/10.3390/app11041397

8. Charissis, V., Papanastasiou, S.: Human–machine collaboration through vehicle head up display interface. Cogn. Tech. Work. **12**, 41–50 (2010). https://doi.org/10.1007/s10111-008-0117-0

9. Harkin, D., Cartwright, W., Black, M.: Descomposing the map: using head-up display for vehicle navigation (2005)

10. Liu, Y.-C.: Effects of using head-up display in automobile context on attention demand and driving performance. Displays **24**, 157–165 (2003). https://doi.org/10.1016/j.displa.2004.01.001

11. Liu, Y.-C., Wen, M.-H.: Comparison of head-up display (HUD) vs. head-down display (HDD): driving performance of commercial vehicle operators in Taiwan. Int. J. Hum.-Comput. Stud. **61**, 679–697 (2004). https://doi.org/10.1016/j.ijhcs.2004.06.002

12. Medenica, Z., Kun, A.L., Paek, T., Palinko, O.: Augmented reality vs. street views: a driving simulator study comparing two emerging navigation aids. In: Proceedings of the 13th International Conference on Human Computer Interaction with Mobile Devices and Services, pp. 265–274. Association for Computing Machinery, New York, NY, USA (2011). https://doi.org/10.1145/2037373.2037414

13. Smith, M.I.: Informing design of in-vehicle augmented reality head-up displays and methods for assessment (2018)

14. Topliss, B.H., Pampel, S.M., Burnett, G., Gabbard, J.L.: Evaluating head-up displays across windshield locations. In: Proceedings of the 11th International Conference on Automotive User Interfaces and Interactive Vehicular Applications, pp. 244–253. Association for Computing Machinery, New York, NY, USA (2019). https://doi.org/10.1145/3342197.3344524

15. Weinberg, G., Harsham, B., Medenica, Z.: Evaluating the usability of a head-up display for selection from choice lists in cars. In: Proceedings of the 3rd International Conference on Automotive User Interfaces and Interactive Vehicular Applications, pp. 39–46. Association for Computing Machinery, New York, NY, USA (2011). https://doi.org/10.1145/2381416.2381423

16. Paas, F., Renkl, A., Sweller, J.: Cognitive load theory and instructional design: recent developments. Educ. Psychol. **38**, 1–4 (2003). https://doi.org/10.1207/S15326985EP3801_1

17. Gish, K.W., Staplin, L.: Human factors aspects of using head up displays in automobiles: a review of the literature (1995)

18. Sekuler, B., Bennett, P.J., Mamelak, M.: A effects of aging on the useful field of view. Exp. Aging Res. **26**, 103–120 (2000). https://doi.org/10.1080/036107300243588

19. Blankenbach, K.: Requirements and system aspects of AR-head-up displays. IEEE Consum. Electron. Mag. **8**, 62–67 (2019). https://doi.org/10.1109/MCE.2019.2923936

20. Park, K., Im, Y.: Ergonomic guidelines of head-up display user interface during semi-automated driving. Electronics **9**, 611 (2020). https://doi.org/10.3390/electronics9040611

21. Wolfe, B., Sawyer, B.D., Kosovicheva, A., Reimer, B., Rosenholtz, R.: Detection of brake lights while distracted: separating peripheral vision from cognitive load. Atten. Percept. Psychophys. **81**, 2798–2813 (2019). https://doi.org/10.3758/s13414-019-01795-4

22. Haeuslschmid, R., Schnurr, L., Wagner, J., Butz, A.: Contact-analog warnings on windshield displays promote monitoring the road scene. In: Proceedings of the 7th International Conference on Automotive User Interfaces and Interactive Vehicular Applications, pp. 64–71. Association for Computing Machinery, New York, NY, USA (2015). https://doi.org/10.1145/2799250.2799274

23. Redlinger, E., Glas, B., Rong, Y.: Impact of screen size on cognitive training task performance: an HMD study. Int. J. Psychophysiol. **166**, 166–173 (2021). https://doi.org/10.1016/j.ijpsycho.2021.06.003

24. Inuzuka, Y., Osumi, Y., Shinkai, H.: Visibility of head up display (HUD) for automobiles. Proc. Hum. Factors Soc. Ann. Meet. **35**, 1574–1578 (1991). https://doi.org/10.1177/154193129103502033

25. Watanabe, H., Yoo, H., Tsimhoni, O., Green, P.: The effect of HUD warning location on driver responses. Presented at the Proceedings of 6th World Congress on Intelligent Transport Systems (ITS), Toronto (1999)

26. Tsimhoni, O., Green, P., Watanabe, H.: Detecting and reading text on HUDs: effects of driving workload and message location. Presented at the 11th Annual ITS America Meeting (2001)

27. Morita, K., Sekine, M., Tsukada, Y., Okada, T., Toyofuku, Y.: Consideration on appropriate display area for head-up displays. In: Proceedings of 14th Asia Pacific Automotive Engineering Conference (2007)

28. Haeuslschmid, R., Forster, S., Vierheilig, K., Buschek, D., Butz, A.: Recognition of text and shapes on a large-sized head-up display. In: Proceedings of the 2017 Conference on Designing Interactive Systems, pp. 821–831. Association for Computing Machinery, New York, NY, USA (2017). https://doi.org/10.1145/3064663.3064736

29. Hannah Topliss, B., Harvey, C., Burnett, G.: How long can a driver look? Exploring time thresholds to evaluate head-up display imagery. In: 12th International Conference on Automotive User Interfaces and Interactive Vehicular Applications, pp. 9–18. Association for Computing Machinery, New York, NY, USA (2020). https://doi.org/10.1145/3409120.3410663

30. Zhou, Y., Tang, L., Huang, J., Xiang, Y., Ge, Y.: How the position distribution of HUD information influences the driver's recognition performance in different scenes. In: Harris, D., Li, W.-C. (eds.) Engineering Psychology and Cognitive Ergonomics. HCII 2023. LNCS, vol. 14017, pp. 383–395. Springer, Cham (2023). https://doi.org/10.1007/978-3-031-35392-5_30

31. Wilson, M., Chattington, M., Marple-Horvat, D.E.: Eye movements drive steering: reduced eye movement distribution impairs steering and driving performance. J. Mot. Behav. **40**, 190–202 (2008). https://doi.org/10.3200/JMBR.40.3.190-202

32. Warden, A.C., Wickens, C.D., Rehberg, D., Clegg, B.A., Ortega, F.R.: Information access effort: are head movements "cheap" or even "free"? Proc. Hum. Factors Ergon. Soc. Ann. Meet. **66**, 2203–2207 (2022). https://doi.org/10.1177/1071181322661127

33. Martin-Emerson, R., Wickens, C.D.: The vertical visual field and implications for the head-up display. Proc. Hum. Factors Soc. Ann. Meet. **36**, 1408–1412 (1992). https://doi.org/10.1177/154193129203601810

34. Wickens, C.D.: Computational Models of Human Performance in the Design and Layout of Controls (1997)
35. Warden, A.C., Wickens, C.D., Mifsud, D., Ourada, S., Clegg, B.A., Ortega, F.R.: Visual search in augmented reality: effect of target cue type and location. Proc. Hum. Fact. Ergon. Soc. Ann. Meet. **66**, 373–377 (2022). https://doi.org/10.1177/1071181322661260
36. Nabatilan, L.B., Aghazadeh, F., Nimbarte, A.D., Harvey, C.C., Chowdhury, S.K.: Effect of driving experience on visual behavior and driving performance under different driving conditions. Cogn. Tech. Work. **14**, 355–363 (2012). https://doi.org/10.1007/s10111-011-0184-5
37. Remington, L.A., Goodwin, D.: Clinical Anatomy and Physiology of the Visual System E-book: Clinical Anatomy and Physiology of the Visual System E-book. Elsevier Health Sciences (2021)
38. Li, R., Chen, Y.V., Zhang, L., Shen, Z., Qian, Z.C.: Effects of perception of head-up display on the driving safety of experienced and inexperienced drivers. Displays **64**, 101962 (2020). https://doi.org/10.1016/j.displa.2020.101962
39. Park, H.S., Park, M.W., Won, K.H., Kim, K.-H., Jung, S.K.: In-vehicle AR-HUD system to provide driving-safety information. ETRI J. **35**, 1038–1047 (2013). https://doi.org/10.4218/etrij.13.2013.0041

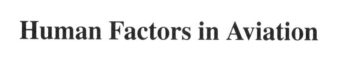

Human Factors in Aviation

Seeing with Touch: The Effect of Full-Body Positional Haptic Feedback During Low-Visibility Aviation Ground Operations

Christopher Bodsworth[1]([⊠]), Will Blewitt[2], and James Blundell[1]

[1] Centre for Future Transport and Cities, Coventry University, Coventry, UK
bodswor2@uni.coventry.ac.uk, James.Blundell@cranfield.ac.uk
[2] Faculty of Engineering, Environment and Computing, Coventry University, Coventry, UK
ac9550@coventry.ac.uk

Abstract. Objective: Through interaction between the Teslasuit and XPlane 11, we evaluate the impact of full-body positional haptic feedback during low-visibility aviation ground operations. This paper presents a working pipeline for Teslasuit-based flight simulator experiments and provides a preliminary human-in-the-loop evaluation of the system based on objective and subjective pilot performance and workload results.

Method: We interface between a Teslasuit and XPlane 11 via the Unity Game engine and an application specific dynamic linked library (DLL). Source files for the interface are provided as supplementary material within a GitHub repository. The preliminary study involved six non-pilot participants completing 8 simulated taxiing tasks in a light-aircraft between two locations at Munich airport (EDDM) in low-visibility conditions. Evaluation of the haptic human machine interface (HMI) on participant performance was based on stopping distance from a threat. Subjective workload data was collected via NASA TLX questionnaires that were administered after each trial.

Results: Raw TLX results were significantly lower during trials with the haptic HMI (M: 7.36, SD: 2.33) compared to trials without (M: 9.53, SD: 3.87) $- (t(5) = -2.01; p = .05)$. Conversely, participants stopping distance (metres) from threats was larger with the haptic HMI (M: 140.44, SD: 84.84) than without (M: 119.31, SD: 33.26).

Conclusions: Full-body haptic feedback warnings reduced mental workload when performing ground-based taxi operations but did not improve stopping distance. A larger sample size, with a representative pilot population, would be helpful for ascertaining a fuller understanding of full-body haptic feedback benefits within airport ground operations.

Keywords: Haptics · tactile · ground navigation · reaction time · mental workload

·

1 Introduction

In most modern interfaces, information is displayed via visual or auditory methods. With warning systems specifically, most people are accustomed to receiving either visual notifications or alert sounds to warn them of an incoming threat. Communicating information via these two senses is satisfactory in many day-to-day situations, such as when receiving navigational instructions while driving, but could be insufficient in high-arousal situations with high sensory demand, such as flying a plane in adverse weather conditions. Wickens' 4-D multiple resource model, a model describing how sensory modalities use distinct cognitive resources, highlights the limited nature of these audiovisual resources and the value that multimodal information presentation has in reducing potential cognitive interference (Wickens, 2008). The work performed in this paper will evaluate the use of the sense of touch as a warning channel that could provide an alternative feedback method when other senses are overloaded.

For this research, we will explore the impact of haptic feedback on reaction time and mental workload in the aviation ground operations context. Taxiing a plane, especially in low-visibility conditions, is a demanding task in high-arousal situations. As a pilot needs to be able to focus on complicated control interfaces while constantly monitoring cockpit navigational displays and responding to control tower auditory communications; both auditory and visual senses are commonly overloaded. Hence, this then becomes a valuable context for evaluating the benefits that haptic warnings could provide. Research has previously been performed on the benefits of force feedback haptic displays for low-visibility taxi operations (Blundell et al., 2023; Gauci et al., 2022; Tang et al., 2005) but limited research explores the use of tactile haptic displays that communicate directional information to users while piloting or driving.

In the current study, real-time positional information is provided via the tactile sensory channel using a cutting-edge piece of full-body haptic hardware: the Teslasuit™. This technology provides tactile haptic feedback via localised electro-muscle stimulations delivered across the body. This human-machine interface (HMI) allows the communication of positional haptic feedback, spatial information, and proximity of incoming simulated threats to participants.

Through the development of a pipeline to communicate between a flight simulator and the Teslasuit, we will evaluate the impact of haptic warning pulses on participant reaction times and mental workload in the context of threat detection during aviation ground operations. This research will aim to provide an answer to the following question: "Can the presence of upper-body Teslasuit positional haptic feedback decrease reaction time and mental workload when performing airport ground operations in low-visibility?".

This paper will have the following structure: we will briefly explore related works in the field of haptics and Teslasuit research, describe the created system and performed experiments, present experiment results, and then finish with a conclusion and discussion.

1.1 Definition of Terms

Below are terms that will be referred to in this paper:

- High-arousal situations: situations with a high level of arousal, level of arousal is defined by SKYbrary as a combination of factors including situational awareness, vigilance, distraction level, stress, and direction of attention (SKYbrary Aviation Safety, 2023).

- Haptic feedback: feedback communicated via the sense of touch and proprioception. Many properties of touch can be perceived on the skin via cutaneous receptors (Kappers and Tiest, 2013).
- Human-machine interfaces (HMI): pieces of software or hardware that allow humans to interact with computer systems (National Institute of Standards and Technology, 2023).
- Mental workload: we choose to define mental workload as the subjective experience of a user to the demands of a task. This term is particularly difficult to define as there is no formal definition that has been universally accepted (Castillo et al., 2020).

1.2 Related Works

Haptic Warnings. Chai et al. (2022) propose a meta-analysis of 71 papers dealing with vibro-tactile displays for human-computer interactions. The research indicates that haptic systems provide significant benefits for warning systems, especially when other senses are already overloaded, but are detrimental for conveying spatial information.

This value of haptics for warning systems is also highlighted by work performed by Sayer et al. (2005), who compared audio and haptic warning systems in a fleet of instrumented automotive vehicles via participant testing. The results suggest that haptic warnings via seat vibrations were able to provide more localised warnings and were deemed less distracting. Audio cues were preferred when providing different types of warnings with more complex information. The haptics being simple seat vibrations as opposed to full-body localised feedback could have led to this result.

Ma et al. (2022) found that no significant difference was found in participant performance between various warning modalities tested in a driving simulator. When comparing results with multimodal, auditory, visual, and haptic warnings, the researchers found that the chosen modality had insignificant results on driving performance, visual workload, and subjective evaluation. There was, however, significant improvement of reaction times when using multimodal warnings; all single-modality warning system reaction time results were equivalent.

Haptic Cueing. With regards to haptic cueing, Etzi et al. (2020) performed 35 participant experiments with a custom-made haptic harness to encourage participants into specific poses. This research is similar to the previously presented work by Caserman et al. Etzi et al.'s research findings indicate that haptic cueing led to more accurate poses but required more training time when compared to purely visual directions.

White and Hancock (2020) evaluated differences in reaction times and target accuracy in a military context with varying cue modalities (multimodal, auditory, visual, haptic). The findings suggest that infantry participants had better performance for target detection with multimodal cues involving haptic pulses.

This collection of haptic research, both for cues and warnings, is valuable for the work outlined in this report and will inform design choices going forward. This report's research is more focused on the role of haptics as a warning system but will follow findings sourced from all researched papers. The collection of both reaction time and subjective workload data is particularly relevant and analogous to research methods previously employed.

Teslasuit Research. The Teslasuit is a relatively new piece of equipment, only starting its Kickstarter campaign back in 2016 (Wirtz, 2023), hence the use of the equipment in academic work is still limited. However, some researchers have worked with the equipment over the last couple of years both for its motion capture capabilities as well as its haptic interface.

Caserman et al. (2021) explored the use of the suit as a way to recognise and correct exercise errors via haptic pulse cues. The researchers trained movement models to perform exercises and used localised haptic feedback to encourage participants to follow the exercise. After 15 participant experiments, the paper suggests that the motion capture of the suit was promising for movement assessment. The work also indicates that the haptic interface was successful in giving appropriate feedback to improve user movements.

Morcos et al. (2023) tested full-body haptic feedback to give cueing to pilots in low-visibility situations. This work is close to our research, differing mainly in the information being communicated to the user – in our case, warnings as opposed to control actions. In the work outlined in the paper, the researchers gave participants both tracking, roll and pitch compensatory tasks and were given feedback through the suit to adjust controls. Participants wore foggles to simulate degraded visual environments. Results suggest that the use of full-body haptics can lead to improved pilot vehicle system performance when primary visual cues are impaired.

Both of these pieces of research deal with haptic cueing and are valuable for the work performed in this report. They both suggest that full-body haptics via Teslasuit may help users to augment accuracy of movements and perception. In our case, we will be doing research to evaluate the impact of haptic cues on reaction time and workload. The second paper evaluates full-body haptics in low-visibility, which is a criterion that we will also be testing. The emergence of Teslasuit academic research over the last few years proves the importance of our research.

This review of related research helps us gain an understanding of current haptic human-machine interface research and Teslasuit academic use. Haptic warnings, designed to provide immediate and urgent information to users, are found to be particularly effective when other channels are overloaded, especially when communicating localised information or when used in combination with other modalities. Haptic cueing, designed to provide more continuous guiding directions to users, is found to provide more accurate training results with longer training time requirements. Preliminary research performed with the Teslasuit has revealed positive results for use as a haptic cueing system. These literature findings served as reference material in developing the positional haptic feedback used in the current study to enhance reaction times and reduce mental workload in low-visibility aviation ground operations. The next section of this paper will outline the methods employed and software developed for the simulator study.

2 Methods

2.1 System Overview

To evaluate the impact of the haptic suit on participant reaction time and mental workload, an experiment using XPlane™ 11 was conducted. Libraries written in C were created to interface between X-Plane Connect – a NASA-developed plugin to receive real-time aircraft and environment information from the XPlane simulation model via UDP - and Unity. Plane positions were received from XPlane and sent to Unity, allowing for proximity checks to be calculated, which subsequently drove the spatial mapping of Teslasuit electro-muscular stimulations (via the Teslasuit SDK). The full pipeline showcasing the interactions between XPlane, Unity and Teslasuit is illustrated in the following diagram:

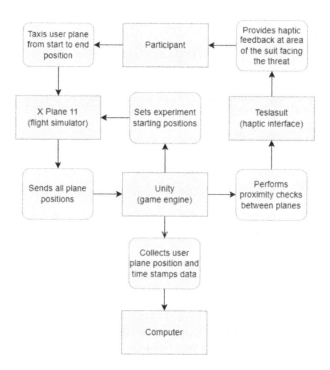

Fig. 1. System Diagram

Unity was also used to set up the placement of the aircraft within the different experimental trials, to display target plane paths to the participant and record participant performance data.

2.2 System Feature Details

The source code of the project is publicly available on GitHub at the following link: https://github.coventry.ac.uk/bodswor2/SeeingWithTouch. Below is a list of all features that have been scripted:

Experiments. Experiment protocol scripts which include: 1) the setting of aircraft starting locations, 2) the communication protocol between XPlane and Unity via UDP, 3) the Unity user interface display for participants during experiments, 4) logging of air-craft positions/time stamps in a JSON format, and 5) drawing of plane trajectories.

Map. A world map is displayed in Unity to help the user follow the desired path. The Mapbox SDK is used, and scripts have been created to control the map data and convert XPlane Latitude/Longitude/Altitude coordinates to Unity XYZ coordinates. Below is an annotated screenshot of the Unity view with plane location and trajectory (Fig. 2).

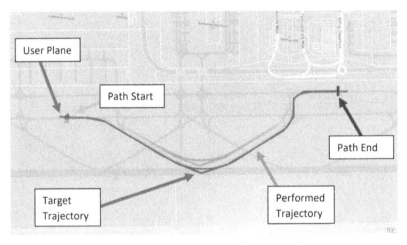

Fig. 2. Annotated Screenshot of the Unity view

Teslasuit. The Teslasuit SDK is used to determine the proximity check functionality that has been implemented. In the current study, each aircraft has an associated sphere collider which triggers haptic feedback whenever collisions are detected. For this, the collision point is equated and mapped onto an identical sphere surrounding the Teslasuit "rig" (see Fig. 3). Haptic "projectiles" are shot from the collision point (the other aircraft) to the centre of the "rig" (and centre of the participant's position) with increasing frequency as the distance between aircraft decreases. As the projectiles travel towards the centre of the "rig", they collide with the nearest virtual body part on the "rig" and communicate this information haptically to the participant on the respective location of the worn Teslasuit.

NASA XPlane Connect. We are using NASA's X-Plane Connect plugin to interface between XPlane and Unity. The plugin does not have native support for C# code, so we have written a DLL called "XPCUnity-Bridge-C" in C that is then used in Unity. The

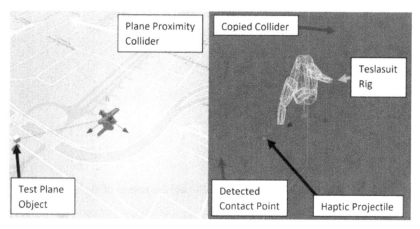

Fig. 3. Annotated Screenshot of the Teslasuit setup

visual studio project for this DLL is also available in the repository. The DLL provides functions to set and receive data references from XPlane. It has been set up to receive IP addresses in order to display planes from multiple systems running XPlane.

2.3 Experiment Design

The experiment involved 8 trials that required participants to taxi an aircraft in low-visibility conditions (see Fig. 4) between two locations in a simulation of Munich airport (EDDM). This airport was selected as it provides a satisfactory number of runways and paths. Two distinct taxi routes were prepared that were based on similar human-machine interaction research (Blundell et al., 2023). The two routes were presented on either side of the airport (see Fig. 5 and 6) and also presented in reverse, creating four total paths for the experiment. Routes are labelled 1 to 4.

Fig. 4. Screenshot of participant view

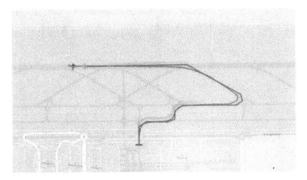

Fig. 5. Screenshot of Route 1 (route 2 is reverse of 1)

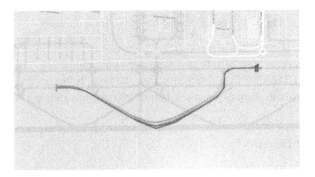

Fig. 6. Screenshot of Route 3 (route 4 is reverse of 3)

The 8 trials were divided into 2 blocks – a block with the Teslasuit's haptics active (Haptic On) and a block where the haptics were inactive (Haptic Off). The order of these blocks was counterbalanced between participants. Within each block, all four routes were completed in a randomised order with a random threat selection. In half of trials, participants encountered an incursion threat in the form of an external aircraft encroaching upon the participant's assigned taxi path. On the two devised routes, this threat could appear at one of two locations: A or B. External aircraft threats were controlled by a separate researcher. Figure 7 shows the position where external threats were placed (marked "X") and the direction that the threat travelled in. Threat positions and movement were manipulated so that the encroaching aircraft intersected the taxi way ahead of the participant.

2.4 Procedure

All participants signed forms stating that they had no adverse health conditions and had no problem with the suit or other equipment used. The Teslasuit was calibrated specifically for each participant to ensure that the delivered haptic stimulation was within a comfortable range for each participant. After familiarisation with the experiment and aircraft handling, participants were instructed to follow the Unity view of the taxi map,

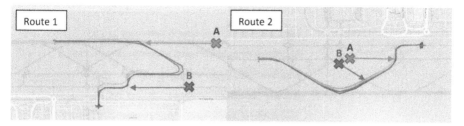

Fig. 7. Annotated Screenshot displaying experiment threats

which directed them from the start to the end of their assigned route. Participants were requested to keep their speed under 25 knots and reduce to 15 knots when turning. Participants controlled their aircraft using a Microsoft™ flight stick. The participant was asked to announce at what point they were aware of an encroaching aircraft, before stopping to let them pass. The time to complete the study took approximately 1 h 30.

2.5   Data Collection and Analysis

Participants' performance was measured as the distance (metres) between the point at which the participant had brought their aircraft to a stop and the encroaching threat. The decision to stop (i.e., awareness of the threat) was also recorded. This data was based on XPlane aircraft positions, which were tracked and exported to JSON.

To measure participant mental workload, a NASA-TLX questionnaire was completed after each block. Raw NASA-TLX scores were used in the analysis. Functional near-infrared spectroscopy data was collected but is not reported in this paper. Statistical analysis of mental workload results was completed using a related t-test to compare the effects of haptics. All statistical inference tests were performed using RStudio running R 4.3.2.

3   Results

3.1   Participant Demographics and Haptic Calibration

Six non-pilot participants volunteered to participate in trials conducted within a one week testing period. Though fewer than planned, this number of participants is nevertheless sufficient for a small-scale proof of concept. Across the participants, there is a 50/50 male-female split and ages ranging from 22 to 37. Figure 8 below displays the mean calibration settings that participants chose for each area of the suit jacket. For each body part that can be stimulated by the suit, each value equates to a percentage of the full stimulation that could be applied. Participants chose a minimum value (the point at which the stimulus was noticeable) and a maximum value (the maximum stimulation that they were comfortable with receiving). Full data participant calibration data is available in Appendix 1.

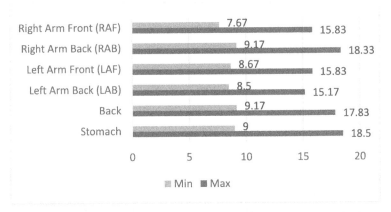

Fig. 8. Clustered Bar Chart of Mean Teslasuit Calibration Results (in %)

3.2 Mental Workload

The mean NASA TLX results for trials with haptics and non-haptic trials are shown in Fig. 9 (full participant TLX data is available in Appendix 1). The box plot shows that, compared to when Teslasuit haptics were absent ($M = 9.53$; $SD = 3.87$), self-reported workload was lower with the haptics ($M = 7.36$; $SD = 2.33$). In addition, there was less variance in results. A related samples one-tailed t-test revealed these improvements to be significant. A mean difference of 2.16 in TLX score between conditions without haptics and with haptics was significant ($t\,(5) = -2.01$; $p = .05$). This is associated with a large effect size (Cohen's $D = -.82$).

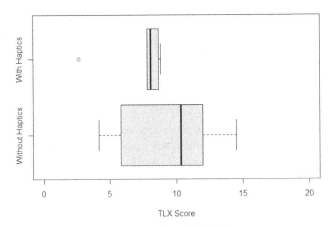

Fig. 9. Box Plot of NASA TLX scores

3.3 Performance

Data from 2 participants was lost due to a software technical issue. Consequently, only descriptive results are provided for the remaining 4 participants. Participants' awareness of the threats was evaluated by stopping distance from a detected threat. The box plot (Fig. 1) suggests that the presence of haptic feedback has a negligible effect on the stopping distance when encountering a threat. Compared to when the haptics were absent ($M = 119.31$; $SD = 33.26$), stopping distance was larger with the haptics ($M = 140.44$; $SD = 84.84$). Subject variance was larger with haptics (Fig. 10).

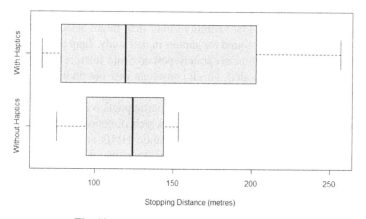

Fig. 10. Box Plot of Mean Stopping Distance

Finally, a difference in the frequency of correctly detecting an aircraft threat was found between conditions (i.e., participants stopped when they perceived a threat). An increase in error was found when participants used the haptic device (42% of threats missed) compared to when it was absent (25% of threats missed). Participants stopped correctly in the majority of cases. These errors could have been caused by haptic warnings not being noticed or technical errors (that were subsequently fixed in the provided project) causing haptic warnings not to be generated. The full data is available in Appendix 2.

4 Discussion and Conclusion

In summary, it was found that the presence of haptic feedback in the trials had a large effect on reducing mental workload, as reported by participant subjective workload via NASA TLX questionnaires. It was, however, found that the presence of haptics had a negligible effect on stopping distance when facing a threat, as reported by analysis of user plane positions and timings. The loss of data experienced for some participants may have lowered the accuracy of the stopping distance performance results and must be kept in mind to nuance the acquired data. These results are favourable to our initial aims; however, further participant experiments would be necessary to increase the accuracy of our data.

Throughout this project, we have developed a fully working XPlane to Teslasuit pipeline using the Unity Game Engine as an intermediary. We have written functionality to receive data from the flight simulator into the game engine to display aircraft models, experiment data, and have also written functionality to send data back to XPlane to control the simulation. Unity has been set up with all the necessary tools and functionalities to run effective experiments, and proximity checks between XPlane aircrafts have been implemented to directly provide positional feedback on the Teslasuit.

Analysis of the results presented findings that haptic feedback through the Teslasuit has a significant impact on subjective workload. These results are in-line with previous work. For example, Blundell et al. (2023) found that haptic feedback reduced workload on the effort specific dimension of NASA TLX, though that study investigated the use of haptics to aid navigation in low-visibility rather than threat detection. Similarly, no performance improvement was found for haptics in that study. Tang et al.'s (2005) paper showcases that users were able to accurately perceive and interpret haptic data while having their visual sense overloaded. This is consistent with our findings, as participants were able to sense and react to haptic pulses while focusing their vision on both the aircraft view and map directions. In our study, participants reported that they noticed haptic warnings but were not able to pinpoint which direction it came from. This is in-line with Chai et al.'s (2022) finding that haptic HMIs are valuable for warning systems, but not spatial information. We found that there was negligible effect of haptic warnings on reaction time. This is consistent with Ma et al. (2022), who found that all single-modality warnings systems have equivalent impact on driver reaction time. The success in development of our Teslasuit interface is in-line with both papers by Caserman et al. (2021) and Morcos et al. (2023) and provides further justification for use of this technology as an experimental haptic HMI.

However, given the already small sample that was further decreased by software technical issues, the performance data indicates that the effect of haptics on reaction time and stopping distance is negligible. Further experiments would be needed to increase result accuracy.

Various limitations exist within our work, specifically with regards to limited participant numbers and technical inconsistencies with the prototyped software. More participants would provide further insight into both the mental workload and reaction time results. Though the developed pipeline worked effectively, it required a long setup phase when running experiments and a more streamlined system that didn't rely on multiple computer systems would be beneficial. In addition, given the aviation focused context of the task, a more representative sample of pilot participants is required in future work.

Future work would benefit from evaluating the workload improvements of haptics from an objective perspective. For instance, functional near infrared spectroscopy (fNIRS) data were recorded during this evaluation but are not reported here. Possible future research could involve seeing how the Teslasuit may be used as a navigational system to help users taxi planes in the low-visibility conditions.

Appendix 1

See Tables 1 and 2.

Table 1. Full Teslasuit Participant Calibration Data (in %)

ID	RAF Min	RAF Max	RAB Min	RAB Max	LAF Min	LAF Max	LAB Min	LAB Max	Back Min	Back Max	Stomach Min	Stomach Max
1	11	18	13	18	14	19	13	19	9	14	9	14
2	8	19	12	20	9	20	9	20	9	20	12	24
3	11	21	7	30	10	20	11	18	15	28	10	28
4	4	9	5	10	4	8	5	10	7	12	7	12
5	5	10	6	12	8	14	6	10	7	16	6	15
6	7	18	12	20	7	14	7	14	8	17	10	18
Mean	7.67	15.83	9.17	18.33	8.67	15.83	8.50	15.17	8.17	17.83	9.00	18.50

Table 2. Full Participant NASA TLX Data

ID	With Haptic	Mental Demand (Very Low – Very High)	Physical Demand (Very Low – Very High)	Temporal Demand (Very Low – Very High)	Performance (Perfect – Failure)	Effort (Very Low – Very High)	Frustration (Very Low – Very High)	TLX Score
1	1	12	7	10	5	9	9	8.67
1	0	13	7	8	8	16	7	9.83
2	1	8	5	5	10	15	6	8.17
2	0	9	8	9	15	12	12	10.83
3	1	3	1	2	6	3	1	2.67
3	0	5	1	3	10	5	1	4.17
4	1	8	10	7	12	12	4	8.83
4	0	14	14	14	17	15	13	14.5
5	1	11	5	11	7	8	5	7.83
5	0	5	3	11	5	5	6	5.83
6	1	6	6	6	18	10	2	8
6	0	11	13	11	16	15	6	12
Mean	1	8.00	5.67	6.83	9.67	9.50	4.50	7.36
Mean	0	9.50	7.67	9.33	11.83	11.33	7.50	9.53

Appendix 2

See Table 3.

Table 3. Full Participant Performance Data

ID	Trial ID	With Haptic	Path	Threat	Stopped	Stopping Distance (m)	Responded Correctly
1	1	0	1	A	1	86.2053229	1
1	2	0	4	B	1	182.627302	1
1	3	0	3	None	0	-	1
1	4	0	2	None	0	-	1
1	5	1	3	None	0	-	1
1	6	1	4	A	0	-	0
1	7	1	2	None	0	-	1
1	8	1	1	B	1	66.15885262	1
2	1	1	3	None	0	-	1
2	2	1	1	None	0	-	1
2	3	1	4	A	1	90.2047727	1
2	4	1	2	B	0	-	0
2	5	0	2	None	0	-	1
2	6	0	4	None	0	-	1
2	7	0	1	B	1	179.0012352	1
2	8	0	3	A	1	127.5045437	1
3	1	0	1	None	0	-	1
3	2	0	2	None	0	-	1
3	3	0	3	B	0	-	0
3	4	0	4	A	1	93.68351731	1
3	5	1	4	None	0	-	1
3	6	1	1	B	0	-	0
3	7	1	2	A	0	-	0
3	8	1	3	None	0	-	1
4	1	1	1	None	0	-	1
4	2	1	4	A	1	18.66888728	1

(*continued*)

Table 3. (*continued*)

ID	Trial ID	With Haptic	Path	Threat	Stopped	Stopping Distance (m)	Responded Correctly
4	3	1	2	B	0	-	0
4	4	1	3	None	0	-	1
4	5	0	2	B	0	-	0
4	6	0	1	A	0	-	0
4	7	0	4	None	0	-	1
4	8	0	3	None	0	-	1
5	1	0	3	B	1	85.76401003	1
5	2	0	4	None	0	-	1
5	3	0	2	A	1	142.1379249	1
5	4	0	1	None	0	-	1
5	5	1	4	None	0	-	1
5	6	1	3	None	0	-	1
5	7	1	1	B	1	263.9148263	1
5	8	1	2	A	1	249.1592098	1
6	1	1	1	None	0	-	1
6	2	1	3	None	0	-	1
6	3	1	2	A	1	96.40453527	1
6	4	1	4	B	1	201.3290137	1
6	5	0	3	A	1	85.35876787	1
6	6	0	4	None	0	-	1
6	7	0	2	None	0	-	1
6	8	0	1	B	1	65.88222843	1

References

Blundell, J., et al.: Low-visibility commercial ground operations: an objective and subjective evaluation of a multimodal display. Aeronaut. J. **127**(1310), 581–603 (2023). https://doi.org/10.1017/aer.2022.81

Caserman, P., Krug, C., Göbel, S.: Recognizing full-body exercise execution errors using the Teslasuit. Sensors **21**(24), 8389 (2021). https://doi.org/10.3390/s21248389

Castillo, J.M., Galy, E., Thérouanne, P.: Mental workload and technostress at work. Which perspectives and theoretical frameworks can help us understand both phenomena together? In: Harris, D., Li, W.-C. (eds.) Engineering Psychology and Cognitive Ergonomics. Mental Workload, Human Physiology, and Human Energy. LNCS (LNAI), vol. 12186, pp. 14–30. Springer, Cham (2020). https://doi.org/10.1007/978-3-030-49044-7_2

Chai, C., Shi, J., Wu, C., Zhou, Y., Zhang, W., Liao, J.: When to use vibrotactile displays? A meta-analysis for the role of vibrotactile displays in human–computer interaction. Appl. Ergon. **103** (2022). https://doi.org/10.1016/j.apergo.2022.103802

Etzi, R., et al.: Conveying trunk orientation information through a wearable tactile interface. Appl. Ergon. **88** (2020). https://doi.org/10.1016/j.apergo.2020.103176

Gauci, J., Galea, M., Muscat, A.: Human-in-the-loop evaluation of an active sidestick control system for aircraft taxiing. In: AIAA Aviation 2022 Forum. American Institute of Aeronautics and Astronautics (2022). https://doi.org/10.2514/6.2022-4141

Kappers, A., Tiest, W.B.B.: Haptic perception. Wiley Interdisc. Rev. Cogn. Sci. (2013). https://doi.org/10.1002/WCS.1238

Ma, J., Li, J., Huang, H.: Evaluation of multimodal and multi-staged alerting strategies for forward collision warning systems. Sensors **22**(3), 1189 (2022). https://doi.org/10.3390/s2203118

Morcos M., et al.: Full-body haptic cueing algorithms for augmented pilot perception in degraded/denied visual environments. In: Proceedings of the 79th Annual Forum of Vertical Flight Society (2023). https://doi.org/10.4050/F-0079-2023-18072

National Institute of Standards and Technology: Guide to Operational Technology (OT) Security (2023). https://doi.org/10.6028/NIST.SP.800-82r3

Sayer, T., Sayer, J., Devonshire, J.: Assessment of a driver interface for lateral drift and curve speed warning systems: mixed results for auditory and haptic warnings. In: Driving Assessment Conference, vol. 3, pp. 218–224 (2005). https://doi.org/10.17077/drivingassessment.1164

SKYbrary Aviation Safety: Level of Arousal (2023). https://skybrary.aero/articles/level-arousal

Tang, A., McLachlan, P., Lowe, K., Saka, C.R., MacLean, K.: Perceiving ordinal data haptically under workload. In: Proceedings of the 7th International Conference on Multimodal Interfaces, pp. 317–324 (2005). https://doi.org/10.1145/1088463.1088517

Wickens, C.: Multiple resources and mental workload. Hum. Factors (2008). https://doi.org/10.1518/001872008X288394

Wirtz, B.: Tesla just added a TeslaSuit to add to your inventory of VR tech tools (2023). https://www.gamedesigning.org/gaming/teslasuit/

White, T.L., Hancock, P.A.: Specifying advantages of multi-modal cueing: quantifying improvements with augmented tactile information. Appl. Ergon. **88** (2020)

Research on Autonomy Control of Air Traffic Based on Accurate Awareness and Estimation of Wake Vortex

Yanyan Chen[1]([✉]) and Yuan Zhu[2]

[1] Civil Aviation Management Institute of China, Beijing 100102, China
Chenyanyan@Camic.cn
[2] Central South Air Traffic Management Bureau, CAAC, Guangzhou 510405, China

Abstract. This study examines the existing wake turbulence separation and operational modes in terminal airspace to address the challenges posed by the continuous increase in air traffic volume and the imperative of managing flight punctuality. It introduces and evaluates aircraft Self-Separation technology, which leverages wake vortex awareness, detailing its development status, existing challenges, benefits, and drawbacks. The paper concludes by identifying key technical and scientific challenges, offering insights for the strategic decision-making of relevant authorities.

Keywords: Performance-based operation · Wake turbulence separation · Aircraft self-separation · Visual separation · Airspace capacity

1 Introduction

Limited maneuverability, numerous flight path intersections, frequent altitude crossing activities, and significant operational safety pressures characterize the terminal control airspace. It represents a vulnerable and bottlenecked segment within the air traffic assurance framework [1, 2]. According to forecasts by institutions such as the ICAO, IATA, and ACI, the demand for air traffic flow is expected to double every 10 to 15 years before 2050 [3]. There is an urgent need to address the challenge of expanding capacity and enhancing efficiency within the constraints of limited airspace resources to meet the rapidly increasing requirements for transit capacity.

The current air traffic control operation model relies mainly on individual controllers to predict and avoid flight conflicts and interact with their intentions by radio communication with pilots. Then, the controller realizes their intentions by depending on the pilots' operations [4–6]. However, civil aviation management organizations have developed experience-based separation standards, which are relatively crude and conservative because of the limited experience and skills, the relatively low capacity of air-ground interaction, as well as the scientific community's limited under-standing of the evolution patterns of safety threats such as wake turbulence, hazardous weather, and the uncertainty of sudden deviations in flight paths.

With the advancement of CNS (Communication, Navigation, and Surveillance) technologies, the risk of collision has gradually decreased, and the separation intervals for collision avoidance have continuously been reduced, highlighting the increasing constraints that wake turbulence and its separation impose on terminal capacity. By thoroughly perceiving and accurately predicting the factors affecting control separation and constructing a control separation calculation method based on acceptable safety levels, it is possible to reduce separation minima dynamically based on favorable meteorological elements. Through measures such as visual operation based on airborne situational awareness, autonomous separation management based on coordination between pilots and onboard equipment, and intelligent onboard separation management, it is feasible to enhance the efficiency of flight separation provisioning and the quality of control operations. This enables the transformation of air traffic management operations from "human-centric" to "digital air traffic management" and "smart air traffic management," improving the overall transit capacity, direct flight ratio, and operational efficiency of busy airspace and meeting the green, sustainable development needs of the civil aviation industry.

2   Operation Status of Terminal Airspace

The wake turbulence separation standards, established in the late 1960s, are based on NASA flight experiments and empirical data. Aircraft were categorized into several classes according to their maximum takeoff weight, and then minimum safe separation distances for different category combinations were specified [7, 8]. Due to the lack of consideration for actual flight parameters, aircraft weight, atmospheric temperature, wind speed, and other influencing factors, these standards need to be updated, leading to over-separation in many instances. Limited by the scientific community's understanding of the mechanisms of aircraft wake turbulence evolution, as well as deficiencies in risk assessment and situational awareness capabilities, it is not yet possible to dynamically reduce wake separation minima based on actual parameters such as wind speed and direction, navigational precision, flight speed, and aircraft mass.

The ATC (Air Traffic Control) separation delivery procedures include acquiring aircraft positions, calculating flight trends, formulating ATC instructions, and exchanging intentions via voice communication. Due to the limited intelligence of the situation projection and decision-making capabilities of the ATC automation system, it becomes necessary to rely on the experience and skills of individual controllers to anticipate and resolve flight conflicts. Consequently, there is a certain degree of delay and uncertainty in understanding, response, operation, and monitoring, necessitating an increase in the safety margin to ensure flight safety. The current separation standards and operational modes cannot meet future demands for increased runway capacity and operational efficiencies in terminal airspace. This inadequacy is attributed to the limitations of a "relatively conservative separation standard," the "lengthy and excessive procedures for conflict resolution," and the "heavy reliance on voice communication for the exchange of intentions (Fig. 1)."

The contradiction between robust demand and limited airspace resources has made the proposition and study of new concepts, models, and technologies to enhance the operational efficiency of air traffic management (ATM) one of the significant challenges. In

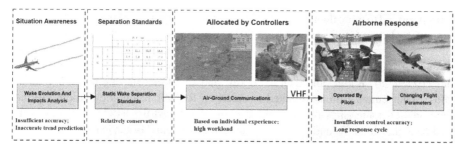

Fig. 1. Current ATC Separation Allocation

2018, the International Civil Aviation Organization (ICAO) outlined and forecasted the development prospects of new air traffic technologies in the fifth edition of the Global Air Navigation Plan. Similarly, the United States' NextGen and Europe's SESAR have undertaken comparable planning and analysis, identifying the focal points for ATM research and the industrial sector and accelerating the research, development, and application of new ATM technologies [9, 10].

To enhance the throughput capacity of terminal airspace, the FAA and Eurocontrol began implementing "visual separation and visual approach" operations in the 1990s. Similarly, the Civil Aviation Administration of China started promoting this technology at major airports from 2008. Under suitable meteorological conditions, pilots are authorized to rely on subjective judgment and experience to maintain separation, based on visual contact with the preceding aircraft and terrain. This approach, not constrained by existing separation standards and relying more on pilots for perception and management, has optimized the flight control chain, significantly increasing airport landing capacity. In operations involving visual separation and visual approach, the overall air traffic operation situation depends on the experience, skills, and preferences of individual pilots, resulting in lower predictability of traffic flow, more potential flight safety hazards, and poorer robustness of the traffic flow, making the system overall more fragile.

Moreover, visual separation and visual approach require pilots to maintain continuous visual contact with the preceding aircraft, demanding good meteorological conditions. The workload and pressure on pilots are also greater. In the absence of onboard situational awareness and auxiliary equipment, the actual implementation rate of "visual separation and visual approach" is not high.

3 Self-separation Technology Based on Wake Vortex Awareness

In terms of wake turbulence awareness and dynamic separation reduction, EUROCONTROL proposed the Reclassification of Aircraft's Wake Separation (RECAT) in 2007, aircraft were re-assigned to one of six new categories (A through F) which were derived by redefining the transition weight between the old categories. The FAA started to carry out the feasibility study of the RECAT technology jointly with Europe in 2009 and took the lead in carrying out RECAT operation in Memphis Airport in November 2012, which has been applied to more than twenty airports; Europe started to implement RECAT operation at Charles de Gaulle airport from 2015, which has been used to five airports so far.

Since 2010, China has gradually achieved a reduction in terminal radar separation from "10 km" to "8 km," and then to "6 km" and "5.6 km"; starting in 2015, the Air Traffic Management Bureau initiated research on RECAT technology tailored to the operational characteristics of domestic airports, developed the RECAT-CN standards based on domestic traffic and aircraft type characteristics, and began experimental operations at Guangzhou and Shenzhen airports from December 5, 2019. By the end of 2020, this was further expanded to fourteen airports in Beijing and Shanghai.

Regarding dynamic wake turbulence separation, near-ground wind fields significantly impact the dissipation of wake vortex strength, vortex movement, and evolution. Fully utilizing favorable meteorological elements to achieve dynamic wake turbulence separation according to weather changes can effectively enhance the operational efficiency of terminal airspace. NASA proposed a wake vortex separation system (AVOSS) in the late 1990s and researched related technologies. The FAA initiated the Wake Turbulence Mitigation for Departures (WTMD) and Wake Turbulence Mitigation for Arrivals (WTMA) projects in 2012, dynamically reducing wake turbulence separation for closely spaced parallel runways through accurate perception and pre-diction of near-ground wind field data at airports and has conducted technological validations at IAH and SFO airports.

Supported by the SESAR project, Germany's DFS developed The Wake Vortex Warning System (WVWS), which uses statistical methods to analyze and predict winds over airports, forecasting the dispersion and lateral transmission location of wake vortices generated by approaching aircraft and determining the "Hazard Time" of wake vortices. On this basis, DFS developed the Wake Vortex Prediction and Monitoring WSVBS system, which dynamically reduces wake turbulence separation un-der safe conditions based on meteorological conditions and wake vortex status, achieving tactical-level improvements in approach and landing capacity. The European Union launched the CROPS project (SESAR 1P1) in June 2010, which optimizes runway utilization by conditionally reducing the separation between arriving and departing aircraft under crosswind conditions. London Heathrow Airport initiated operations based on Time-Based Separation (TBS) in May 2015, dynamically adjusting current separation standards based on headwind data.

Since 2017, the Air Traffic Management Bureau of China has initiated the development of dynamic wake turbulence separation management and prototype systems. This effort has led to the creation of the wake turbulence separation reduction system, dynamic separation operational verification platform, and wake turbulence separation safety alert system, laying the technical foundation for the implementation of dynamic separation.

In the field of research on airborne autonomous separation management technology, the use of airborne ADS-B In technology for perceiving surrounding traffic situations allows Flight Interval Management (FIM) devices to predict flight conflicts, generate flight parameter adjustment instructions, and provide these to pilots for execution via the Mode Control Panel (MCP). Since this does not involve upgrading the aircraft's flight management system or flight control system, the technical difficulty is relatively low, and the current technology research in Europe and the United States belongs to this stage. NASA's Langley Research Center developed the Airborne Spacing for Terminal Arrival Routes (ASTAR) algorithm, which dynamically plans flight parameters based on the relative positions of leading and following aircraft. This was integrated and implemented on the Boeing 787 eco Demonstrator, with five flight validations conducted on December 12, 2014. To test the integration of airborne interval management with other NextGen technologies, a second phase of experiments was initiated in 2017 (Fig. 2).

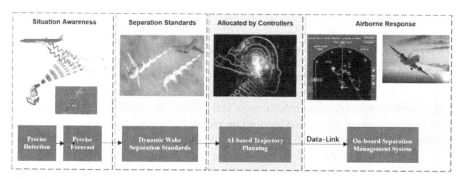

Fig. 2. Operation scenario of Self Separation technology based on wake vortex awareness

4 Critical Technologies to Be Solved

Achieving dynamic reduction in wake turbulence separation to enhance air traffic management quality, improve throughput capacity, direct flight ratio, and operational efficiency in congested airspace is crucial for meeting the civil aviation industry's green and sustainable development goals. This objective necessitates addressing critical technological challenges, including the development of advanced prediction and mitigation technologies for wake vortices, leveraging high-throughput satellite communications, artificial intelligence, and data analytics for navigational accuracy and situational awareness. Such innovations are essential for optimizing flight paths, reducing fuel consumption and environmental impact, and transforming air traffic management to accommodate increasing air travel demand while adhering to environmental stewardship principles.

4.1 Precision Perception Technology for Navigational Elements

The dynamic response of an aircraft to wake vortices, significantly impacted by variables such as aircraft type, pilot expertise, and prevailing atmospheric conditions, underscores the critical necessity for advancing precision perception technologies. These technologies are pivotal in accurately pinpointing aircraft location, delineating flight parameters, ensuring navigation precision, and assessing meteorological conditions with unparalleled accuracy. To fulfill this requirement, it is essential to harness the capabilities of cutting-edge systems like the Beidou navigation system, high-throughput satellites, and 5G ATG. Such integration aims to foster a holistic comprehension and anticipatory framework for near-ground wind fields and the spatiotemporal dynamics of navigational elements. By amalgamating data from diverse sources, this research trajectory promises to revolutionize the precision with which navigational elements are perceived, thereby significantly enhancing the safety, efficiency, and reliability of air traffic management in the face of wake turbulence challenges. This endeavor not only seeks to mitigate the risks associated with wake vortices but also aims to set a new benchmark in navigational accuracy, contributing to the broader objectives of air traffic safety and operational excellence.

4.2 Dynamic Reduction Technology for Wake Separation

The formation, dissipation, and movement of wake vortices are influenced by factors such as the local wind field, atmospheric turbulence, temperature stratification characteristics, and ground effects, with some mechanisms still unclear. Particularly, the mechanisms of wake vortex rupture dissipation induced by atmospheric conditions and multi-vortex coupling entanglement require further exploration. Additionally, wake detection equipment can only acquire data on wake vortices near runways or at specific flight positions, making real-time detection of wake vortices throughout the entire terminal area impossible. Therefore, research is needed into the evolution mechanism of aircraft wake vortex behavior characteristics under the coupled influence of near-ground wind fields. This encompasses breakthroughs in key technologies such as precise inversion of wake vortex characteristic parameters based on lidar, accurate prediction of the spatiotemporal evolution characteristics of wake vortices throughout their entire lifecycle, estimation of wake separation envelopes under uncertain conditions, and dynamic reduction of wake separation under precise perception conditions.

4.3 Autonomous Technology for Onboard Threats

In the realm of contemporary air traffic management, the reliance on pilots to passively receive and manually execute control instructions within the cockpit introduces significant delays and potential for misinterpretation, thereby compromising the aircraft's responsiveness and escalating pilot workload. This scenario underscores the imperative for integrating advanced air-ground high-speed interconnect technologies, including ADS-B In, satellite communications, and Air-to-Ground (ATG) systems, to revolutionize the cockpit's operational environment. By leveraging these technologies, it becomes feasible to provide pilots with an intuitive, real-time visualization of comprehensive flight scenarios directly on the Navigation Display (ND), significantly enhancing situational awareness and decision-making efficiency. The advancement of research in ADS-B In-based onboard situational awareness tools, coupled with the development of algorithms capable of predicting short-term flight adjustments in response to unforeseen meteorological conditions, represents a critical step forward. Furthermore, the implementation of autonomous self-separation strategies and the integration of systems for onboard wake turbulence risk assessment and alerting are pivotal in transitioning towards a more autonomous, reliable, and safe air traffic management system. These technological innovations aim to minimize the reliance on traditional voice communications, reduce the margin for human error, and streamline the execution of instructions, thereby marking a significant leap towards enhancing the overall resilience of air navigation services in the face of evolving airborne threats.

4.4 Collaborative Technology for 4D Trajectories

Trajectory-based operations (TBO) are widely recognized within the international civil aviation community as the core operational concept for the next generation of flight systems. TBO represents a revolutionary solution to accommodate the continuous and rapid growth of air transport capacity. It breaks away from the existing time-based, segment-based, and head-based management models, facilitating a fundamental shift in air traffic management. This shift moves from "control sectors" to "entire airspace" coverage, from "tactical" to "strategic" planning, from "control" to "management," and from micro-level collision avoidance to macro-level situational control. The challenge of accurately forecasting flight paths within controlled airspace is compounded by the limitations of aircraft Communication, Navigation, and Surveillance (CNS) systems, unpredictable weather patterns, and the inherent uncertainties in aircraft maneuvers and pilot intentions. The current reliance on air traffic controllers' expertise for devising conflict-free, efficient multi-aircraft trajectories and crafting appropriate control directives underscores the urgent need for advanced research in the domain of 4D trajectory management. This research should focus on developing sophisticated methods for predicting 4D trajectory envelopes under conditions of uncertainty, leveraging enhanced situational awareness for trajectory adjustments, and facilitating strategic negotiations to establish initial conflict-free paths for multiple aircraft. Additionally, it should aim at refining tactical planning and control processes for managing the precise timing and altitude of aircraft at specific waypoints. The ultimate goal of these endeavors is to empower pilots with the capability for autonomous control, sanctioned by air traffic controllers and informed by precise instrument alerts. This paradigm shift is expected to streamline the separation allocation process, markedly reduce the necessity for air-ground communication exchanges, diminish the operational burden on pilots and controllers alike, and significantly boost the overall efficiency and effectiveness of air-ground collaboration. Such advancements in collaborative technology for 4D trajectories are pivotal for the evolution of air traffic management, promising a future where airspace is utilized more optimally, safety margins are enhanced, and the aviation industry moves closer to realizing its vision for seamless, integrated, and more autonomous air navigation services.

Based on the research of key technologies, further development and implementation of near-ground wake detection and inversion equipment, dynamic interval reduction operational verification systems, conflict-free multi-aircraft trajectory prediction and negotiation systems, ADS-B In-based onboard situational awareness equipment, and onboard autonomous separation and wake turbulence alerting systems are needed. This includes the production of equipment systems and conducting three application technology demonstration verifications: Time-Based Separation (TBS) operations, Cockpit Assisted Visual Separation (CAVS) based on onboard perception, and Full-Domain

4D Trajectory-Based Operations (4D-TBO). This aims to dynamically reduce wake safety intervals, effectively enhance air-ground collaborative efficiency, and significantly reduce controller workload, thereby effectively increasing the throughput capacity under limited airspace resources. The specific technical roadmap is illustrated in the following diagram (Fig. 3):

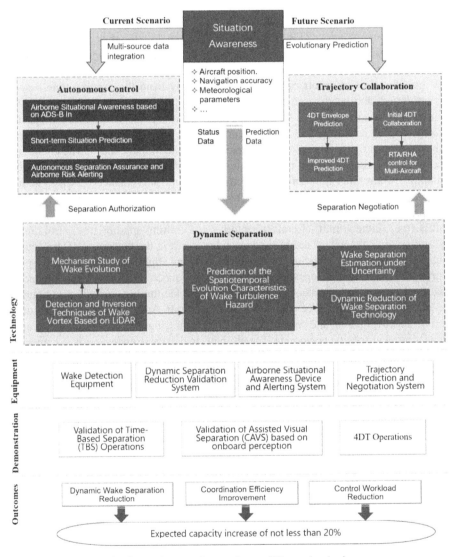

Fig. 3. Implementation roadmap of Key technologies

In addressing the pressing need to enhance throughput capacity within congested airspaces, the targeted breakthroughs in the four critical technological domains outlined previously offer a promising pathway to revolutionize air traffic management. By implementing dynamic reductions in wake turbulence separation, we anticipate a substantial improvement in air-ground collaborative efficiency and a significant reduction in controller workload. Such advancements are poised to markedly elevate the capacity of limited airspace resources, effectively tackling the challenges associated with airspace expansion. The integration of these technologies is expected to not only streamline operations but also ensure a safer, more efficient airspace management system. Consequently, this approach is projected to increase the overall capacity of constrained airspace resources by at least 20%, representing a significant leap forward in our ability to accommodate the rapid growth in air traffic demand while maintaining high safety and efficiency standards. This strategic enhancement in operational capacity and efficiency underscores the transformative potential of adopting a trajectory-based operation philosophy, marking a fundamental shift towards a more integrated, strategic, and management-focused air traffic system.

5 Conclusion

In conclusion, this research has thoroughly explored the domain of autonomous air traffic control, highlighting the indispensable role of precise wake vortex awareness and estimation in augmenting the efficiency and safety of air traffic management (ATM). Through the adoption of cutting-edge technologies such as ADS-B In, satellite communications, and high-speed air-to-ground connectivity, this study introduces groundbreaking approaches to dynamic wake turbulence management, accurate perception of navigational elements, and the autonomous mitigation of onboard threats. These technological advancements are crucial for enhancing the operational capacity of congested airspaces, safeguarding flight safety, and promoting environmentally sustainable practices within the civil aviation industry.

The findings of this study advocate for a paradigm shift from the conventional, conservative methods of ATM to more flexible, data-centric strategies that capitalize on the power of real-time data acquisition and predictive analytics. Such a transformation is anticipated not only to mitigate operational bottlenecks and expand airspace utilization but also to resonate with the overarching objectives of the global aviation community towards achieving greater operational efficiencies and minimizing the ecological footprint of aviation activities.

Looking ahead, it is imperative that future research endeavors concentrate on refining these innovative technologies, particularly aiming to improve the precision of wake vortex prediction models and the resilience of autonomous control frameworks. A collaborative effort spanning the entire aviation ecosystem, including regulatory authorities, technology developers, and air traffic management professionals, is vital for the standardization and worldwide adoption of these technological breakthroughs.

The successful amalgamation of autonomous control mechanisms and wake vortex detection technologies marks a pivotal advancement towards the realization of an air traffic management system that is not only more efficient and safer but also more aligned with the principles of sustainability. This research lays a solid groundwork for subsequent innovations in ATM, heralding a new epoch of air travel characterized by enhanced operational efficiency and a deep-rooted commitment to environmental stewardship.

References

1. Xu, X., Zhao, H., Wang, Z.: A review of wake turbulence separation reduction technology. J. Aeronaut. **31**(04), 655–662 (2010)
2. Roper, R.D., Koch, M.R., Johnson, W.C., Swieringa, K.A.: Airborne spacing for terminal arrival routes (ASTAR) proof-of-concept flight test. NASA/TM–2019-220404, September 2019
3. Tittsworth, J.A., Lang, S.R., Johnson, E.J., et al.: Federal aviation administration wake turbulence program- recent highlights. In: Air Traffic Control Association Conference & Exposition (2013)
4. Holzpfel, F., Dengler, K., Gerz, T., et al.: Prediction of dynamic pairwise wake vortex separations for approach and landing. DLR Deutsches Zentrum fur Luft- und Raumfahrt e.V. - Forschungsberichte **2012** (2012)
5. Wei, Z., Qu, Q., Liu, W., Xu, X.: A review of simulation calculation methods for aircraft wake vortex flow field parameters. J. Aerodyn. **37**(01), 33–42 (2019)
6. Tang, X., Zheng, P.: Autonomous interval control of aircraft under sequential flight conditions on air routes. J. Nanjing Univ. Aeronaut. Astronaut. **51**(06), 742–748 (2019)
7. Kibler, J.L., Wilson, S.R., Hubbs, C.E., et al.: Aiz1 (ATD) Interval Management for Near-Term Operations Validation of Acceptability (IM-NOVA) Experiment. NASA/TP–2015-218767, May 2015
8. Hallock, J.N., Greene, G.C., Burnham, D.C.: Wake vortex research - a retrospective look. Air Traffic Control Q. **6**(3), 161–178 (2016)
9. Abdelmoula, F., Holzaepfel, et al.: Performance of onboard wake-vortex prediction systems employing various meteorological data sources. J. Aircr. **53**(5), 1505–1516 (2016)
10. Kauertz, S., Holzäpfel, F., Kladetzke, J.: Wake vortex encounter risk assessment for crosswind departures. J. Aircr. **49**(1), 281–291 (2015)
11. Zuschlag, M., Burki-Cohen, J., Chandra, D.C.: An algorithm for generating data accessibility recommendations for flight deck automatic dependent surveillance-broadcast (ADS-B) applications. Aircraft Separation (2014)
12. Prinzel, L.J.,III, Shelton, K.J., Kramer, L.J., et al.: Flight deck-based delegated separation: evaluation of an on-board interval management system with synthetic and enhanced vision technology. Comptes Rendus Mecanique (2011)
13. Howell, D., Dean, R., Paull, G.: Benefits and costs of ADS-B in efficiency applications in US airspace. In: Thirteenth USA/Europe Air Traffic Management Research and Development Seminar (ATM 2019)
14. Penhallegon, W.J., Bone, R.S.: Field test of interval management-spacing during an optimized profile descent arrival and approach. MITRE Technical report, MTR110426R1, McLean, VA, April 2016
15. Barmore, B.E., et al.: Interval management: development and implementation of an airborne spacing concept. In: The Proceedings of the AIAA Guidance, Navigation, and Control Conference (2016)
16. de Gelder, N., Bussink, F., Westerveld, E., Janssen, C.: Interval management (IM) in a fixed route TMA environment. Presentation at the 2nd ICAO Global Air Navigation Industry Symposium (GANIS), Montreal, Canada, December 2017
17. Hercencia-Zapana, H., Herencia-Zapana, H., Hagen, G.E., et al.: A framework for probabilistic evaluation of interval management tolerence in the terminal radar control area. In: 2012 IEEE/AIAA 31st Digital Avionics Systems Conference (DASC). IEEE (2012)
18. Murdoch, J.L., Wilson, S.R., Hubbs, C., et al.: Acceptability of flight deck-based interval management crew procedures. In: AIAA Modeling and Simulation Technologies (MST) Conference (2013)

19. Author, F.: Article title. Journal **2**(5), 99–110 (2016)
20. Author, F., Author, S.: Title of a proceedings paper. In: Editor, F., Editor, S. (eds.) Conference 2016. LNCS, vol. 9999, pp. 1–13. Springer, Heidelberg (2016)
21. Author, F., Author, S., Author, T.: Book title, 2nd edn. Publisher, Location (1999)
22. Author, F.: Contribution title. In: 9th International Proceedings on Proceedings, pp. 1–2. Publisher, Location (2010)
23. LNCS Homepage. http://www.springer.com/lncs. Accessed 25 Oct 2023

An Analysis of Pilot's Eye Movement Metrics in Simulated Flight Scenarios

Shan Gao⬤, Yu Bai⬤, Yuanyuan Xian⬤, and Lei Wang$^{(\boxtimes)}$⬤

College of Safety Science and Engineering, Civil Aviation University of China, Tianjin, China
wanglei0564@hotmail.com

Abstract. Pilot's visual activities are closely related to flight safety in approaches with visual flight rules (VFR). The objective of this study is to investigate the differences in eye movement metrics among captains and first officers in simulated approaches with different visibility conditions. A total of twenty commercial airline pilots (ATP licensed, ten captains and ten first officers, all males) who qualified on B737-800 were recruited to participate in this study. They performed two 6 nautical mile approaches with high- (Ceiling and Visibility Okay) and low-visibility (VFR minimum) conditions with a balanced order in a high-fidelity fixed-based B737 flight training device, which can be used for flight training. Pilot's eye movements were recorded via a glasses-type eye-tracker, including fixation, saccade, blink, and pupil diameter. The results showed main effects of visibility on mean pupil diameter, saccade count, and mean fixation time. Compared to the high-visibility condition, pilots exhibited larger mean pupil diameter, less saccade counts, and shorter mean fixation time in the low-visibility condition. Meanwhile, pilot type exerted a main effect on mean pupil diameter. Compared to captains, first officers exhibited larger mean pupil diameter. As visibility deteriorates, pilots may adjust their attention allocation strategies to cope with environmental issues. Notably, compared to captains, first officers suffered a higher level of stress in approaches, which may further influence their visual performance. The integration of eye-tracking technology and flight training in the cockpit can be used in evidence-based training to provide better understanding about pilot's eye movements and visual performance.

Keywords: Attention Allocation · Eye Movement · Expertise

1 Introduction

Throughout a flight, pilots have to make numerous decisions based on substantial visual cues. The judicious attention allocation, a key cognitive faculty for pilots, closely correlates with flight safety. A considerable number of aviation accidents is intrinsically linked to deficiencies in pilots' attention allocation. For example, inefficient monitoring is recognized as a pivotal contributor to aviation accidents [1]. Such issue has garnered attention in academia and industry [2–4].

Pilot type, a crucial factor influencing eye movements, reveals notable individual differences in authority, responsibilities, and experiential depth [5]. Captains, in general,

D. Harris and W.-C. Li (Eds.): HCII 2024, LNAI 14693, pp. 192–201, 2024.
https://doi.org/10.1007/978-3-031-60731-8_14

have more flight experience than first officers, and their eye activities exhibit significant differences. For instance, Taber conducted a comparative analysis between captains and first officers in simulated emergency scenarios, showing first officers could benefit from the radial instrument scans implemented by captains [6]. Similarly, a study by Lounis and colleagues scrutinized the eye movements of neophytes and seasoned pilots during simulated manual landings [7]. The findings underscored that professional aviators exhibited more frequent and concise fixations, indicative of nuanced visual scanning patterns.

Nevertheless, the presumed safeguarding effect of experience on performance has been challenged by some empirical investigations and accident reports. As pilots accumulate a certain threshold of flight hours, the positive impact of experience tends to plateau and, in some instances, diminish [8]. According to an 11-year longitudinal study of commuter aviation pilots spanning from 1987 to 1997, the threshold for the protective effect of flight hours on accident prevention was at 10,000 h [9, 10]. Meanwhile, the influence of flight hours on mitigating incident involvement exhibited marginal significance among Chinese commercial airline pilots [11]. Additionally, Gao and Wang also ascertained that pilots with moderate levels of flight experience were more likely to be involved in aviation incidents [12].

Low-visibility condition is acknowledged as a determinant influencing pilots' proficiency in discerning and extracting pertinent visual information [13]. It may escalate stress levels, particularly among pilots with limited experience [14]. Consequently, in this exploratory study, we executed two 6-nautical-mile approaches under varying weather conditions (Ceiling and Visibility Okay vs. VFR minimum) utilizing a high-fidelity fixed-based flight simulator. Using a glasses-type eye-tracker, pilots' attention allocation can be investigated and analyzed by interpreting their eye movement metrics. Our primary emphasis encompassed fixation, saccade, blink, and pupil diameter, examining the impact of pilot type (captain vs. first officer) on eye movement metrics during simulated approaches with different visibility conditions. The findings of this research are expected to provide valuable insights to our comprehension of pilots' eye movement metrics within the domain of flight training, particularly during approach phases.

2 Method

2.1 Participants

To ensure the quality and reliability of data, sample selections were based on the following criteria: (a) first officers and above who qualified on B737-800; (b) at least 1 year of service time; (c) more than one flight in the last week; (d) 50 or more flight times per year in total. A total of twenty commercial airline pilots (ATP licensed, ten captains and ten first officers, all males) who qualified on B737-800 from a Chinese airline were recruited to participate in this study. Their ages ranged from 26 to 41 years ($M = 30.95$, $SD = 3.98$), and their flight experience varied between 2100 and 15,000 h ($M = 6296.55$, $SD = 3729.23$). This research was approved by the ethics committee of the author's university. Informed consent was obtained from each subject.

2.2 Apparatus

Experiment was conducted in a high-fidelity fixed-based B737-800 flight training device (FTD, Level five) that can be used for flight training (Fig. 1). In adherence to the China Civil Aviation Regulations, the visual system of the flight simulator (Level five) must satisfy specific criteria, encompassing: (a) a minimum pilot field of view of 18° vertical and 24° horizontal; (b) a maximum parallax error of 10° for each pilot; (c) a minimum resolution for computing and displaying pixel sizes at 5 arcminutes; and (d) a maximum lag or transmission delay not exceeding 300 ms. The simulator is integrated with high-definition databases sourced from Boeing's original data package, employs sophisticated image generation systems utilizing three 1920 × 1200 laser projectors, and features realistic physics-based equipment, ensuring fidelity in cockpit displays, operations, and settings for routine pilot training. Additionally, a dedicated console is utilized by the instructor for the installation of flight scenarios.

Fig. 1. The B737-800 flight simulator.

Throughout the experiment, pilot's eye movements were recorded via a glasses-type eye-tracker (Tobii Glasses 2, Tobii Inc., Sweden) (Fig. 2). This glasses-type eye-tracking system empowers pilots to articulate head movements without constraints. The incorporated accelerometer and gyroscope sensors facilitate the system in steadfastly maintaining the absolute fixation point, thereby ensuring data accuracy even in instances of glasses misalignment. The apparatus comprises eye-tracking glasses, a calibration card, and power equipment. Notably, the sampling frequency of this glasses-type eye-tracker is set at 100 Hz. Prior to the formal experiment, the eye-tracker undergoes calibration using Tobii's Controller software with the aid of a calibration card. This meticulous calibration procedure ensures the precision of subsequent eye-tracking measurements. The recorded video footage capturing eye movements and associated data can seamlessly and wirelessly be transferred to a computer for in-depth analysis and further scrutiny.

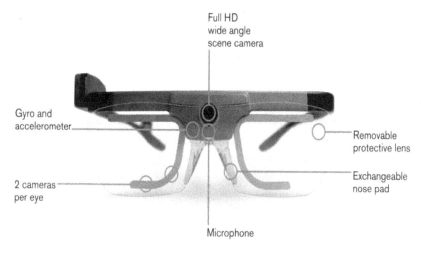

Fig. 2. The glasses-type eye-tracker.

2.3 Design

Two approach missions with different visibility conditions (low and high) were designed. In the high-visibility condition, pilots performed a VFR approach with clear vision. While in the low-visibility condition, the runway visual range (RVR) was limited to 500 m (the lowest visibility allowed for safe landing in China). Participants performed two 6 nautical mile approaches with high- (Ceiling and Visibility Okay) and low-visibility (VFR minimum) conditions with a balanced order.

2.4 Measures

Fixation constitutes an intrinsic statistical characterization of observed eye movement behaviors, denoting a collection of focal points or a sequence of data points representing eye gaze vectors concentrated on a stationary target within an individual's visual field. It stands as the temporal span during which an individual engages in visual acquisition and interpretation of information within their field of view, providing insights into the intricacy of information extraction.

Saccades, on the other hand, encompass rapid movements involving both eyes, signifying the exerted effort in visual exploration. An augmented frequency of saccades indicates a correspondingly heightened extent of visual searches being undertaken. Additionally, pupil size and blink count serve as pivotal metrics for assessing the visual attention and workload of operators. Typically, an escalation in workload corresponds with an increase in pupil diameter, coupled with a reduction in blink counts.

In this study, eight eye movement metrics, including mean pupil diameter, minimum pupil diameter, maximum pupil diameter, blink counts, saccade counts, fixation time, mean fixation time and fixation count were extracted.

2.5 Procedure

Prior to the experiment, the pilots were presented with an informed consent form, which they perused and signed as an indication of their voluntary participation in the study. Subsequently, they were presented with a concise description of the purpose of the study and were briefed about the approaching task. Following this, they were given an opportunity to practice as a captain (10–20 min) to familiarize themselves with the simulator. Lastly, the pilots completed the official experiment, and their eye movements were recorded by the eye-tracker. The whole experiment lasted about 45 min.

2.6 Data Analysis

In this study, we selected 30 s of eye-tracking data including the decision-making procedure for analysis. The process of eye movement data and fixation classification are similar with our previous study [14] (Table 1).

Table 1. Parameters and methods of gaze data processing and fixation classification [14].

Parameter	Method	Value and unit
Gaze data processing		
Interpolation	Max gap length	75 ms
Eye selection	Strict average	–
Noise reduction	Moving median filtering	–
	Window size	3 samples
Fixation classification		
Velocity calculator	Window length	20 ms
I-VT classifier	Velocity threshold	30°/s
Merge adjacent fixations	Max time between fixation	75 ms
	Max angle between fixation	0.5°
Discard short fixation	Minimum fixation duration	60 ms

We used SPSS 25.0 (IBM, Armonk, USA) for calculation and analysis. Firstly, we presented the characteristics of our sample, including the mean and standard deviation of the eye movement metrics among different pilot types and visibilities. Secondly, two-way repeated measure ANOVA was performed to examine the differences of eye movement metrics across different pilot types and visibilities in simulated flight scenarios. The Shapiro-Wilk's test was used to assess normality assumption violations. The effect sizes of samples were quantified by partial eta square (η_p^2), and the post hoc pairwise comparisons were performed by Bonferroni.

3 Results

3.1 Descriptive Statistics

The descriptive statistics of the eye movement are shown in Table 2. As an example, for the first officer, the mean pupil diameters in high visibility and low visibility are 4.49 ± 0.50 and 4.72 ± 0.52, respectively. And for the captain, the mean pupil diameters in high visibility and low visibility are 3.91 ± 0.59 and 4.91 ± 0.59, respectively.

Table 2. Description of the statistical eye movement metrics.

Eye movement metrics	High visibility condition		Low visibility condition	
	Captain	First officer	Captain	First officer
Mean pupil diameter	3.91 (0.59)	4.49 (0.50)	4.04 (0.59)	4.72 (0.52)
Minimum pupil diameter	2.90 (0.41)	3.06 (0.33)	2.91 (0.48)	3.20 (0.36)
Maximum pupil diameter	4.92 (0.80)	5.44 (0.72)	4.74 (0.49)	5.39 (0.67)
Blink count	12.90 (8.10)	15.20 (11.28)	14.50 (17.21)	7.90 (6.39)
Saccade count	256.90 (60.38)	223.80 (49.36)	203.70 (39.44)	195.20 (55.33)
Fixation time	6.02 (1.52)	5.75 (1.67)	4.06 (2.05)	5.42 (1.82)
Mean fixation time	0.27 (0.08)	0.32 (0.16)	0.20 (0.06)	0.25 (0.07)
Fixation count	14.30 (3.17)	11.93 (4.91)	12.15 (5.02)	14.30 (3.85)

3.2 ANOVA

The independent variables were visibility and pilot type. As visibility and pilot type were a within-subject factor and a between-subject factor respectively, two-way repeated measure ANOVA was performed to determine the effects of visibility and pilot type on eye movement metrics. Results are shown in Table 3.

Mean Pupil Diameter. The results of the two-way repeated measure ANOVA revealed the significant effects of visibility ($F_{(1, 18)} = 13.13$, $p = 0.002$, $\eta_p^2 = 0.422$) and pilot type ($F_{(1, 18)} = 6.68$, $p = 0.019$, $\eta_p^2 = 0.271$) on mean pupil diameter. According to the pairwise comparisons, compared to captains, first officers showed larger mean pupil diameter ($\triangle = 0.63$, $p = 0.001$); compared to high-visibility condition, participants in the low-visibility condition showed larger mean pupil diameter ($\triangle = 0.18$, $p = 0.002$). The interaction effect of the pilot type and visibility on mean pupil diameter was not significant ($p > 0.05$) (Fig. 3a).

Saccade Count. The results of the two-way repeated measure ANOVA revealed the significant effects of visibility on saccade count ($F_{(1, 18)} = 8.78$, $p = 0.008$, $\eta_p^2 = 0.328$). According to the pairwise comparisons, compared to high-visibility condition, participants in the low-visibility condition showed less saccade count ($\triangle = 40.90$, $p = 0.008$).

The main effect of pilot type and the interaction effect of the pilot type and visibility on saccade count were not significant (all $ps > 0.05$) (Fig. 3b).

Mean Fixation Time. The results of the two-way repeated measure ANOVA revealed the significant effects of visibility on saccade count ($F_{(1, 18)} = 4.75$, $p = 0.043$, $\eta_p^2 = 0.209$). According to the pairwise comparisons, compared to high-visibility condition, participants in the low-visibility condition showed less mean fixation time ($\triangle = 0.07$, $p = 0.043$). The main effect of pilot type and the interaction effect of the pilot type and visibility on mean fixation time were not significant (all $ps > 0.05$) (Fig. 3c).

Table 3. Analyses of variance testing for the effects of pilot type and visibility on pilots' eye movement metrics.

Eye movement metrics	Source of variation	F	p	η_p^2
Mean pupil diameter	Pilot type	**6.68**	**0.019**	**0.271**
	Visibility	**13.13**	**0.002**	**0.422**
	Pilot type × Visibility	0.74	0.402	0.039
Minimum pupil diameter	Pilot type	1.73	0.205	0.088
	Visibility	1.60	0.222	0.082
	Pilot type × Visibility	1.49	0.239	0.076
Maximum pupil diameter	Pilot type	3.98	0.061	0.181
	Visibility	1.75	0.203	0.088
	Pilot type × Visibility	0.55	0.468	0.030
Blink count	Pilot type	0.24	0.630	0.013
	Visibility	1.11	0.306	0.058
	Pilot type × Visibility	2.71	0.117	0.131
Saccade count	Pilot type	1.26	0.277	0.969
	Visibility	**8.78**	**0.008**	**0.328**
	Pilot type × Visibility	0.79	0.385	0.042
Fixation time	Pilot type	0.93	0.348	0.049
	Visibility	4.18	0.056	0.188
	Pilot type × Visibility	2.15	0.160	0.107
Mean fixation time	Pilot type	2.33	0.144	0.115
	Visibility	**4.75**	**0.043**	**0.209**
	Pilot type × Visibility	<0.001	0.975	<0.001
Fixation count	Pilot type	0.01	0.942	<0.001
	Visibility	0.01	0.926	<0.001
	Pilot type × Visibility	3.60	0.074	0.166

Other Eye Movement Metrics. The effects of visibility, pilot type, and the interaction effect between them on other eye movement metrics (minimum pupil diameter, maximum pupil diameter, blink count, fixation time, and fixation count) were not significant (all $ps > 0.05$).

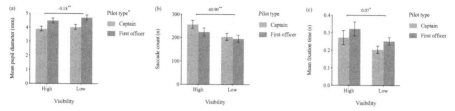

Fig. 3. The effects of pilot type and visibility on (a) mean pupil diameter, (b) saccade count, and (c) mean fixation time. Error bars = $\pm$ S.E. $^{*} = p < .05$, $^{**} = p < .01$.

4 Discussion

The principal aim of this study is to investigate the differences in pilots' eye movements between captains and first officers during simulated approaches under varying visibility conditions. Visibility is one of the important environmental factors influencing the acquisition and extraction of information during VFR approaches [15]. Notably, pivotal cues from both the internal cockpit and the external environment are imperative for pilots to ensure flight safety. Saccade is considered to be the act of shifting eye movements from one gaze point to the next gaze point. In accordance with our findings, participants exhibited noteworthy reductions in saccade counts and mean fixation time as visibility diminished. Poor visibility engenders challenges in information extraction, creating a stressful milieu for pilots and augmenting their visual workload [16]. In conditions of diminished visibility, the study by Dong and colleagues observed that pilots engaged in heightened visual searches to contend with marginal weather conditions [17], aligning with our observations of decreased saccade counts and shorter mean fixation time in low-visibility scenarios. This observation suggests that pilots may adapt their attention allocation strategy in response to varying visibility conditions [14].

Moreover, our results delineate that the pilot type and visibility independently exert a significant effect on the pilots' mean pupil diameter. Notably, previous relevant studies have established a correlation between pupil diameter responses and perceived stress, with an augmentation in response to heightened task difficulty [18, 19]. According to the ANOVA results, diminished visibility tends to correspond to an augmented mean pupil diameter. Concurrently, in comparison to captains, first officers exhibited larger mean pupil diameter, irrespective of prevailing visibility conditions. These revelations intimate that pilots experienced heightened stress as visibility diminishes during the approach, particularly manifesting as pronounced nervousness in first officers [14]. Such heightened stress has the potential to engender human errors [2]. This observation suggests that the risks associated with low-visibility conditions can be mitigated through accumulated flight experience, emphasizing the criticality of attention allocation training for less experienced first officers.

In conclusion, we undertook an examination of pilots' eye movement metrics among first officers and captains under different visibility conditions in a flight-simulation experiment. Our results demonstrated that poor visibility resulted in high visual demand in approaches, particularly for less experienced pilots. In subsequent investigations, we recommend two aspects facets. Firstly, the implementation of specialized visual training regimens, encompassing attention span and gaze-based training, to enhance the proficiency of inexperienced pilots. For instance, Ahmadi and colleagues introduced a gaze-based training for student pilots to mitigate the risks of loss of control under instrument meteorological conditions (IMC) [20]. Secondly, as pilots exhibited different visual strategies [2, 14], it would be considerable interest to further investigate the two crew members' eye movements in the flight deck for verifying the efficiency of their cross-checking processes and overall performance.

Acknowledgments. This study was funded by the Chinese Fundamental Research Funds for the Central Universities (grant number 3122024026).

References

1. Flight Safety Foundation: A practical guide for improving flight path monitoring (2014). Retrieved from flight safety.org/files/flightpath/EPMG.pdf
2. Dehais, F., Behrend, J., Peysakhovich, V., Causse, M., Wickens, C.D.: Pilot flying and pilot monitoring's aircraft state awareness during go-around execution in aviation: a behavioral and eye tracking study. Int. J. Aerosp. Psychol. **27**(1–2), 15–28 (2017)
3. Ziv, G.: Gaze behavior and visual attention: a review of eye tracking studies in aviation. Int. J. Aviat. Psychol. **26**(3–4), 75–104 (2016)
4. Federal Aviation Administration: Instrument Flying Handbook (FAA-H-8083-15b): U.S. Department of Transportation (2012). https://www.faa.gov/regulations_policies/handbooks_manuals/aviation/media/FAA-H-8083-15B.pdf
5. Palmer, M.T., Lack, A.M., Lynch, J.C.: Communication conflicts of status and authority in dyadic, task-based interactions: status generalization in airplane cockpits. J. Lang. Soc. Psychol. **14**(1–2), 85–101 (1995)
6. Taber, M.J.: Investigating offshore helicopter pilots' cognitive load and physiological responses during simulated in-flight emergencies. Int. J. Aerosp. Psychol. **31**(1), 56–69 (2021)
7. Lounis, C., Peysakhovich, V., Causse, M.: Visual scanning strategies in the cockpit are modulated by pilots' expertise: a flight simulator study. PLoS ONE **16**(2), e0247061 (2021)
8. You, X., Ji, M., Han, H.: The effects of risk perception and flight experience on airline pilots' locus of control with regard to safety operation behaviors. Accid. Anal. Prev. **57**, 131–139 (2013)
9. Li, G., Baker, S.P., Grabowski, J.G., et al.: Age, flight experience, and risk of crash involvement in a cohort of professional pilots. Am. J. Epidemiol. **157**(10), 874–880 (2003)
10. Rebok, G.W., Qiang, Y., Baker, S.P., et al.: Age, flight experience, and violation risk in mature commuter and air taxi pilots. Int. J. Aviat. Psychol. **15**(4), 363–374 (2005)
11. Ji, M., Yang, C., Li, Y., et al.: The influence of trait mindfulness on incident involvement among Chinese airline pilots: the role of risk perception and flight experience. J. Safety Res. **66**, 161–168 (2018)

12. Gao, S., Wang, L.: More experience might not bring more safety: negative moderating effect of pilots' flight experience on their safety performance. Int. J. Ind. Ergon. **95**, 103430 (2023)
13. Cheung, B., et al.: In-flight study of helmet-mounted symbology system concepts in degraded visual environments. Aerosp. Med. Hum. Perf. **86**(8), 714–722 (2015)
14. Gao, S., Wang, L.: How flight experience impacts pilots' decision-making and visual scanning pattern in low-visibility approaches: preliminary evidence from eye tracking. Ergon., 1–17 (2024)
15. Wang, Z., Zheng, L., Lu, Y., Fu, S.: Physiological indices of pilots' abilities under varying task demands. Aerosp. Med. Hum. Perf. **87**(4), 375–381 (2016)
16. Zhang, X., Qu, X., Xue, H., Liu, J.: Pilots' fixation patterns during taxiing and the effects of visibility. Aerosp. Med. Hum. Perf. **90**(6), 546–552 (2019)
17. Dong, W., Liao, H., Zhan, Z., Liu, B., Wang, S., Yang, T.: New research progress of eye tracking-based map cognition in cartography since 2008. Acta Geogr. Sin. **74**(3), 599–614 (2019)
18. Chen, S., Epps, J.: Using task-induced pupil diameter and blink rate to infer cognitive load. Hum.-Comput. Interact. **29**(4), 390–413 (2014)
19. Diaz-Piedra, C., Rieiro, H., Cherino, A., Fuentes, L.J., Catena, A., Di Stasi, L.L.: The effects of flight complexity on gaze entropy: an experimental study with fighter pilots. Appl. Ergon. **77**, 92–99 (2019)
20. Ahmadi, N., Romoser, M., Salmon, C.: Improving the tactical scanning of student pilots: a gaze-based training intervention for transition from visual flight into instrument meteorological conditions. Appl. Ergon. **100**, 103642 (2022)

Pre-shift State Assessment of Air Traffic Controllers Based on Improved Grey Correlation Theory

Qiuli Gu[1]([envelope]), Keren Wang[1], and Xiaofu Fan[2]

[1] Civil Aviation University of China, Tianjin 300300, China
qlgu@cauc.edu.cn
[2] Purdue University, West Lafayette, IN 47906, USA

Abstract. In order to accurately assess the pre-shift competence of controllers, the thesis formulates eight assessment indicators affecting the pre-shift status of controllers based on the actual working conditions of controllers, the contents of pre-shift questioning and the existing research results. According to the partial correlation analysis, the rationality of the selected indicators is proved. The weights of the eight assessment indicators were determined by the entropy weight-CRITIC combination method, and the relative relevance of the indicators affecting the pre-shift status was further determined by applying the improved gray correlation theory, and the pre-shift status of the controllers was sorted according to the size of the relative relevance, and differentiated into three grades. Grade 1 controllers had the highest pre-shift status correlation, which indicated that they had the best pre-shift status and were able to carry out control work smoothly; Grade 2 controllers had medium pre-shift status correlation, which was affected by their age and long posting, and had average pre-shift status; Grade 3 controllers had the smallest pre-shift status correlation, which indicated that they were young and had short posting, and had average control ability and higher psychological pressure.

Keywords: Controller Pre-shift Competence · Entropy Weight-CRITIC Combination Method · Improved Gray Correlation Theory · Correlation Analysis

1 Introduction

At present, China's civil aviation is in the opening stage of the "14th Five-Year Plan" period, and one of the main tasks of civil aviation in the "14th Five-Year Plan" period is to adhere to the bottom line of flight safety and to build a perfect, safe and efficient production and operation guarantee system [1]. Air traffic management is an important part of civil aviation safety, with the increasing reliability of air traffic control equipment, the level of control ability of air traffic controllers (hereinafter referred to as controllers) is particularly important for the safety of the air traffic control system. Controllers complete the relevant training, post experience, license theory examination and skills assessment in order to obtain the civil aviation air traffic controller license [2]. Therefore, under normal circumstances, the control ability of each controller is in line with the requirements of the position.

As the controller's work requires long-term day and night shifts, high mental concentration, and heavy workload, and at the same time, the 24/7 working conditions require that the controller may be on duty at any time [3], it is difficult to avoid the emergence of fatigue, nervousness, stress, impatience, negativity, and illness before going to work [4–6] and other undesirable conditions, these undesirable pre-shift states, which result in the lowering of the controller's work ability and performance, and bring the Therefore, it is very important to evaluate the pre-shift status of controllers.

In actual operation, the current ATC industry mainly relies on the pre-shift reporting system to determine whether the controller is now fit for duty, "whether he is physically unwell, whether he has invoked alcohol and drugs within the specified time [7]..." For the influencing factors of controllers' working ability, domestic and foreign scholars have conducted relatively in-depth studies. Sleep disorder [8, 9] is a common problem in the work of controllers, and little sleep and poor quality will lead to reduced alertness, cognitive decline, slow reaction, decision-making difficulties, and lack of concentration, resulting in giving instructions not fast enough and accurate enough, which induces control risks, and at the same time leads to controllers' moods of irritability and annoyance, which affects the communication between the shifts. Because the quality of sleep is closely related to the body's physiological age and biological clock. With the increase of age and the working mode of day and night shifts, the sleep quality of human body will gradually decrease [10], and there are individual differences in the duration of sleep demand. Therefore, adequate sleep duration and efficient sleep quality are prerequisites for ensuring the physical and mental health of controllers, as well as for achieving efficient work capacity [11].

In order to be able to minimize controller fatigue and maintain good working condition under the existing shift work pattern. Scholars have studied the effects of different shift systems on controller fatigue, and by comparing the shift systems of controllers working two on two off and one on two off, it is found that the shift pattern of working two on two off is more suitable for controllers [12], and the shift pattern of working two on two off is adopted by the majority of control units at present. In order to further verify the effect of shift system on controllers' pre-shift fatigue, scholars confirmed the significant effect of different shift systems on controllers' pre-shift fatigue by designing experimental protocols and conducting on-site surveys, and found that fatigue indirectly weakened controllers' basic reactive and judgmental decision-making abilities [13, 14]. In addition to the effects of sleep, shift system, psychological stress, physical health, and fatigue on controllers' work status, it was found that different ages and personality traits also had a greater effect on controllers' work performance [15], and younger controllers were found to be more prone to tension and anxiety and to have greater emotional fluctuations than their older counterparts. Older controllers were found to be more prone to fatigue and difficulty in recovering from it than younger controllers due to the gradual deterioration of their physical functions. Too high or too low a posting age also affects controllers' ability to control [16, 17].

In summary, most of the literature focuses on the fatigue of controllers and the impact of fatigue on controllers, but fatigue is only an important indicator, not the only one, for assessing pre-shift status. Therefore, this paper combines the content of the actual questioning of controllers' pre-shift status in frontline control units, and develops the assessment indexes of controllers' pre-shift status from the factors that diminish controllers' ability.

2 Model

Analysis of indicators for assessing the pre-shift status of controllers. Based on the current state of research on pre-shift status assessment indicators, the following eight assessment indicators were developed from the physiological and psychological perspectives of controllers, based on the nature of their work and the possible causes of their pre-shift maladies: fatigue [3, 4, 6–11], age [11, 15], length of shift [11, 15–17], quality of sleep [8, 10, 11], average duration of sleep [8. 10,11], number of shifts [10–14], psychological stress [3, 7, 10, 11, 15], and physical health [5, 6, 10, 11, 15], and the assessment indicators are explained in Table 1.

After reviewing the domestic and international literature and our regulations, we found that there is a mutual influence relationship between the controllers' pre-shift status assessment indicators, so we conducted a partial correlation analysis on the eight indicators, and the results of the analysis are shown in Table 2.

The closer the absolute value of the partial correlation coefficient is to 1, the greater the influence between the two, if the partial correlation coefficient is greater than 0, it means that there is a positive correlation between the two; if the partial correlation coefficient is less than 0, there is a negative correlation between the two. Combined with the results of partial correlation analysis in the above table, it can be seen that the older the age, the greater the fatigue, the worse the sleep quality, the shorter the average sleep time, and the more likely to have health problems. The relationship between shift age and psychological pressure is the closest, and controllers with longer shift age are more capable and experienced, and have less psychological pressure before going to work. The higher the number of shifts, the poorer the sleep quality and the greater the fatigue before the shift. The partial correlation analysis of the eight assessment indexes coincided with the conclusions of most of the related literatures, which proved that the results of the partial correlation analysis were accurate.

3 Method

3.1 Modeling Process Based on Improved Gray Correlation Theory

The basic idea of gray correlation theory is to determine the proximity of each indicator to the superior and inferior reference indicators from the similarity of the geometric shape of the sequence curves, i.e., the closer the shape, the closer the pattern of development and change, and the greater the degree of association [22]. Gray correlation analysis is suitable for measuring the degree of association between each evaluation object and the pre-existing state of the superior and inferior classes. In addition, gray correlation analysis can clearly show the specifics of the subjects themselves and the differences between them and other subjects.

Table 1. Explanation of controllers' pre-shift status assessment indicators

Controller pre-shift status assessment indicators	Descriptive
age	The physiological age of the controllers, the older they are, the more likely they are to be fatigued and difficult to recover from, indirectly leading to a poor pre-shift state [11, 15]
Length of experience in a job	The amount of time a controller has worked since being released from the order represents the controller's rank and work experience [11], with up to 10 years of service positively affecting pre-shift status, and more than 10 years of service negatively affecting pre-shift status [16]
Quality of sleep	The better the sleep quality, the better the pre-shift state of the controller achieved during the normal sleep time before work [11]. Larger values obtained from the Stanford Sleep Index Scale [18] indicate poorer sleep quality
Average sleep time	The shorter the average amount of time that controllers normally sleep during the week, the more severe the sleep deprivation and the more likely it is to cause a poor pre-shift state [19]
Number of shifts	The number of shifts a controller works during the week reflects circadian rhythmicity; the more shifts, the more disorganized the circadian rhythm is, the more likely it is to cause fatigue, indirectly leading to poor pre-shift status [9]
stress level	The extent to which controllers are in a state of physical and mental stress in the near future due to personal, family, and work problems that put the individual in a state of stress, the greater the psychological stress the more likely it is to stimulate undesirable emotions, which leads to a poorer pre-shift state [20]. The higher values measured by the Stress Perception Scale [21] indicate higher psychological stress

(continued)

Table 1. (*continued*)

Controller pre-shift status assessment indicators	Descriptive
fitness level	individual's physical health, the healthier the controller is the more beneficial the pre-shift status [19]. The physical fitness of the controllers who had taken drugs and alcohol during the pre-shift was recorded as 0, and those who had not were recorded as 1
fatigue	The more fatigued the controller is the worse the pre-shift condition is [19]. Larger values measured by the Samn-Perelli Crew Condition Check Scale [6] indicate more fatigued controllers

Table 2. Partial correlation analysis

relevant type		age	length of experience in a job	Quality of sleep	Average sleep time	Number of shifts	stress level	fitness level	fatigue
PCE	age	1.000	0.900	0.809	−0.468	0.084	−0.600	−0.624	0.801
	length of experience in a job	0.900	1.000	0.632	−0.410	−0.149	−0.893	−0.547	0.622
	Quality of sleep	0.809	0.632	1.000	−0.585	0.623	0.511	0.631	0.926
	Average sleep time	−0.468	−0.410	−0.585	1.000	0.273	0.045	0.191	−0.504
	Number of shifts	0.084	−0.149	0.623	0.273	1.000	−0.535	−0.582	0.740
	stress level	−0.600	−0.893	0.511	0.045	−0.535	1.000	0.076	0.552
	fitness level	−0.624	−0.547	0.631	0.191	−0.582	0.076	1.000	−0.390
	fatigue	0.801	0.622	0.926	−0.504	0.740	0.552	−0.390	1.000

There is no objective and scientific quantitative standard for the resolution coefficient of each indicator in the gray correlation theory, and the empirical value of 0.5 (when the number of indicators is 4) is mostly used, and many studies have shown that this method of assigning the value does not necessarily conform to the situation where the indicators have different degrees of influence on the whole at the same time and may lead to a low resolution of the results. Scholars such as Duan Zhisan [23] found that the value of the resolution coefficient should be dynamic rather than static. Therefore, it is necessary to redefine the assignment principle of the to improve the correlation resolving power, so that the correlation better reflects the wholeness of the system.

The value of the resolution coefficient determines the degree of influence of other series on the reference and comparison series, which in turn affects the size of the correlation distribution interval and ultimately affects the results of correlation analysis. The current methods of determining the resolution coefficient mainly include specifying its value according to whether the observed series is smooth or not [23], designing the dynamic resolution coefficient by using triangular fuzzy numbers [24], and assigning the value by using the information pairs of each indicator in the entropy weighting method [25], and so on.

In this chapter, the entropy weight-CRITIC combination method is used to assign values to the discrimination coefficients, and then the improved gray correlation theory is used to assess the controller's pre-shift status.

3.2   Weight Calculation Method Based on Entropy Weight-CRITIC Combination Method

The Basic Idea of Entropy Weight-CRITIC Combination Method. Entropy weight method is a kind of objective assignment that can be used for multiple evaluation programs and multiple evaluation indicators, and the weights are determined by the magnitude of the degree of change in the differences of the indicators [26]. The more useless the information provided by the indicators, the larger the entropy value and the smaller the entropy weight, and the smallest entropy weight is 0. However, when the entropy weights of all the indicators are close to 1, even small differences will affect the weight values to carry out exponential changes, which will lead to some unimportant indicators to be given mismatched weights.

The CRITIC weight method is an objective assignment method that integrates the weights of indicators based on the strength of the contrast of the evaluation indicators and the conflict between the indicators [27]. The more informative indicators provide a greater role in the whole evaluation index system, and the weight is correspondingly greater. Contrast strength is the size of the difference between the values provided by different evaluation objects for the same indicator, expressed in the form of standard deviation, the larger the standard deviation, the greater the variability, and consequently the greater the weight. Conflict between indicators is expressed in terms of correlation coefficient, if there is a strong positive correlation between two indicators, the smaller the conflict is, indicating that the information reflected by these two indicators in the evaluation of the strengths and weaknesses of the object has a greater similarity, and therefore the smaller the weight. However, this method cannot measure the degree of dispersion between indicators.

The combined weight coefficients are solved using the game theory aggregation model [27, 28], which is essentially a multi-player optimization problem that seeks consistency among different weights to minimize the gap between the combined weights and the weights obtained by the entropy weight method and the CRITIC weight method, respectively, as much as possible. The game theory aggregation model can determine the contribution rate of the above two assignment methods according to the nature of the indicator data, providing a more objective and accurate calculation method than the average distribution or artificial distribution of the contribution rate.

The evaluation object in this paper is the controller's pre-shift status data, so when calculating the weights of each indicator, in addition to the need to consider the degree of dispersion between the indicators, but also to take into account the comparative strength and conflict between the indicators, so the entropy weight-CRITIC combination method and the game theoretic aggregation model are chosen to calculate the combined weight coefficients, which more objectively reflect the weights of the indicators.

Entropy Weight-CRITIC Combination Method Calculation Steps. First of all, statistic raw data matrix. Assuming that there are m evaluation objects, each evaluation object has n indicators, construct the original data matrix R:

$$R = (r_{ij})_{m \times n} \tag{1}$$

Normalize the original matrix R to get a new matrix R':

$$R' = (r'_{ij})_{m \times n} \tag{2}$$

which $i = 1, 2, \cdots, m; j = 1, 2, \cdots, n$. When the indicator is positive, $r'_{ij} = \frac{r_{ij} - r_{\min}}{r_{\max} - r_{\min}}$; When the indicator is inverse, $r'_{ij} = \frac{r_{\max} - r_i}{r_{\max} - r_{\min}}$. The maximum $r_{\max}$ and minimum $r_{\min}$ values of the same indicator in different evaluation objects, respectively.

Define the entropy of evaluation indicators H_j.

$$H_j = -k \sum_{i=1}^{m} f_{ij} \times \ln f_{ij} \tag{3}$$

式中 $f_{ij} = \frac{r'_{ij}}{\sum\limits_{i=1}^{m} r'_{ij}}, k = \frac{1}{\ln m}$, 且当 $f_{ij} = 0$时, $f_{ij} \times \ln f_{ij} = 0$。

Define entropy weights for evaluation indicators ω_j^1.

$$\omega_j^1 = \frac{1 - H_j}{n - \sum\limits_{j=1}^{n} H_j} \tag{4}$$

where, $0 \le \omega_j^1 \le 1$, and it satisfies $\sum\limits_{j=1}^{n} \omega_j^1 = 1$。

Define indicator variability S_j, expressed as standard deviation.

$$S_j = \sqrt{\frac{\sum\limits_{i=1}^{n} (r'_{ij} - \overline{r'_j})^2}{n - 1}} \tag{5}$$

Where, $\overline{r'_j} = \frac{1}{m} \sum\limits_{i=1}^{m} r'_{ij}$。

Define indicator conflictivity δ_j, expressed as a correlation coefficient.

$$\delta_j = \sum_{i=1}^{m} (1 - r'_{ij}) \tag{6}$$

Defining the amount of information C_j.

$$C_j = S_j \times \delta_j \tag{7}$$

Defining objective weights ω_j^2.

$$\omega_j^2 = \frac{C_j}{\sum\limits_{j=1}^{n} C_j} \tag{8}$$

Denote the weight vector calculated by the entropy weight method as W_1^T, denote the weight vector computed by the CRITIC assignment method as W_2^T, W is defined as a linear combination of W_1^T and W_2^T.

3.3 Calculation Steps of the Improved Gray Correlation Theory

$$W = \sum_{p=1}^{2} \alpha_p \cdot W_p^T \tag{9}$$

where $p = 1, 2$, α_p is the portfolio weight coefficient, α_1 is the weight coefficient of the entropy weight method, and α_2 is the weight coefficient of the CRITIC weight method.

Define the objective function L based on the set modeling principle of game theory.

$$L : \min \left\| \sum_{p=1}^{2} \alpha_p \cdot W_p^T - W_i^T \right\| \tag{10}$$

where $i = 1, 2$.

Define the objective function based on the set modeling principle of game theory.

$$\sum_{p=1}^{2} \alpha_p \cdot W_i \cdot W_p^T = W_i \cdot W_i^T \tag{11}$$

Define the system of linear equations to be solved α_p after optimization of the objective function.

$$\begin{pmatrix} W_1 \cdot W_1^T & W_1 \cdot W_2^T & \cdots & W_1 \cdot W_p^T \\ W_2 \cdot W_1^T & W_2 \cdot W_2^T & \cdots & W_2 \cdot W_p^T \\ \vdots & \vdots & \vdots & \vdots \\ W_i \cdot W_1^T & W_i \cdot W_2^T & \cdots & W_i \cdot W_p^T \end{pmatrix} \begin{pmatrix} \alpha_1 \\ \alpha_2 \\ \vdots \\ \alpha_p \end{pmatrix} = \begin{pmatrix} W_1 \cdot W_1^T \\ W_2 \cdot W_2^T \\ \vdots \\ W_i \cdot W_i^T \end{pmatrix} \tag{12}$$

α_p is normalized to α_p' to obtain the final portfolio weights W'.

$$W' = \sum_{p=1}^{2} \alpha_p' W_p^T \tag{13}$$

3.4   Calculation Steps of the Improved Gray Correlation Theory

Let i be the serial number of the evaluation object, X_k be the kth assessment indicator, and $x_k(i)$ be the observed data of the factor in the ith object, then $\{X_k\} = (x_k(1), x_k(2), \cdots, x_k(i))$ is the behavioral sequence of the factor X_k. In this experimental scheme, 8 pre-shift status assessment indicators are identified as the behavioral characteristic data of the gray system, i.e., $k = 8$; 40 controllers are identified as the subject samples as the object sequence of the system, i.e., $i = 40$. Since each indicator has a different magnitude and order of magnitude, it is necessary to standardize the raw data according to Eq. (2).

Define the optimal reference sequence $\{Y_{sk}\}$ and the worst reference sequence $\{Y_{tk}\}$. The optimal reference sequence is the sequence composed of the maximum value of each evaluation index specification in all evaluation objects, which is the largest reference standard for measuring the pre-shift status of all subjects, and the closer the correlation coefficient of a subject is to the optimal reference sequence, the worse the pre-shift status of the subject is; while the worst reference sequence is the sequence composed of the minimum value of each evaluation index specification in all evaluation objects, which is the smallest reference standard for measuring the pre-shift status of all subjects, and the closer the correlation coefficient of a subject is to the worst reference sequence, the better the pre-shift status of the subject is.

$$\{Y_{sk}\} = \{\max(Y_1(i)), \max(Y_2(i)), \cdots, \max(Y_k(i))\} \tag{14}$$

$$\{Y_{tk}\} = \{\min(Y_1(i)), \min(Y_2(i)), \cdots, \min(Y_k(i))\} \tag{15}$$

Define the optimal difference sequence $\triangle Y_{sk}(i)$, the worst difference sequence $\triangle Y_{tk}(i)$. Calculate the difference between the comparison sequence $\{Y_k(i)\}$ and the optimal reference sequence and the worst reference sequence, respectively.

$$\triangle Y_{sk}(i) = (|Y_k(1) - Y_{sk}|, |Y_k(2) - Y_{sk}|, \cdots, |Y_k(i) - Y_{sk}|) \tag{16}$$

$$\triangle Y_{tk}(i) = (|Y_k(1) - Y_{tk}|, |Y_k(2) - Y_{tk}|, \cdots, |Y_k(i) - Y_{tk}|) \tag{17}$$

Define the correlation coefficient $\gamma^i_{k(s)}$ relative to the optimal reference sequence, i.e., the correlation coefficient of the points of the comparison series to the points of the optimal reference sequence.

$$\gamma^i_{k(s)} = \gamma(Y_{sk}, Y_k(i)) = \frac{\min\limits_k |\triangle Y_{sk}(i)| + \xi_k \max\limits_k |\triangle Y_{sk}(i)|}{|\triangle Y_{sk}(i)| + \xi_k \max\limits_k |\triangle Y_{sk}(i)|} \tag{18}$$

Where $\min\limits_k |\triangle Y_{sk}(i)|$ is the minimum value in the sequence of the optimal difference of each indicator in all evaluation objects, $\max\limits_k |\triangle Y_{sk}(i)|$ is the maximum value in the sequence of the optimal difference of each indicator in all evaluation objects, and ξ_k is the discrimination coefficient of the kth assessment indicator, defined by the combination weight ξ_k of each indicator to take the value.

Define the correlation coefficient $\gamma_{k(t)}^{i}$ relative to the worst reference sequence, i.e., the correlation coefficient of the points of the comparison series to the points of the worst reference sequence.

$$\gamma_{k(t)}^{i} = \gamma(Y_{tk}, Y_k(i)) = \frac{\min_{k}|\triangle Y_{tk}(i)| + \xi_k \max_{k}|\triangle Y_{tk}(i)|}{|\triangle Y_{tk}(i)| + \xi_k \max_{k}|\triangle Y_{tk}(i)|} \tag{19}$$

where $\min_{k}|\triangle Y_{tk}(i)|$ is the minimum value in the worst-case sequence for each indicator in all evaluation objects, and $\max_{k}|\triangle Y_{tk}(i)|$ is the maximum value in the worst-case sequence for each indicator in all evaluation objects.

Define the correlation $\gamma_{i(s)}$ relative to the optimal reference sequence, and the correlation $\gamma_{i(t)}$ relative to the worst reference sequence.

$$\gamma_{i(s)} = \frac{\sum_{k=1}^{n} \gamma_{k(s)}^{i}}{n} \tag{20}$$

$$\gamma_{i(t)} = \frac{\sum_{k=1}^{n} \gamma_{k(t)}^{i}}{n} \tag{21}$$

Define the relative relevance γ_i and rank the evaluation objects according to the magnitude of γ_i.

$$\gamma_i = \frac{\gamma_{i(s)}}{\gamma_{i(s)} + \gamma_{i(t)}} \tag{22}$$

4 Example Analysis

In order to truly evaluate the pre-shift status of the controllers, the subjects were all on-duty controllers in the approach control room of a terminal control center of an ATC unit, with a total of 40 subjects, all male and right-handed, aged 27–43 years old, with an average age of 32.7 years old. 40 subjects held a controller's license, and the age distribution of the subjects ranged from 3 to 21 years, with 4 of them ranging from 3 to 5 years old, and 36 ranging from 6 to 21 years old, as shown in Fig. 1. The age and post age distribution of the controllers is shown in Fig. 1.

In this experiment, the state of approach controllers was measured at the moment before the controllers went to work after a normal rest, and the physiological data of each controller were mainly obtained by subjective measurement, including age, post age, sleep quality of the previous night, the average sleep time of this week, the total number of shifts in this week, the psychological stress level of the recent period, the current fatigue level, and the health condition of the body. The sleep quality, psychological stress level and fatigue level were self-assessed by the Stanford Sleepiness Scale (Exhibit 1), the Stress Perception Scale (Exhibit 2), and the Samn-Perelli Crew State Examination Scale (Exhibit 3), respectively, and the results of the Stress Perception Scale are shown in Exhibit 4. A ten-point scale was also used to record the subject's overall evaluation of the current state, and the closer the score is to 10, the better the state the subject is in. The closer the score is to 10, the better the subject's state is.

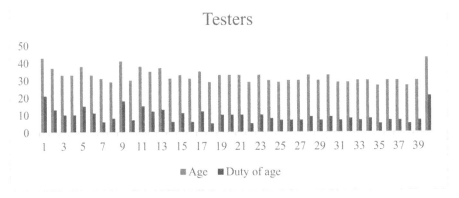

Fig. 1. Distribution of subjects' age and post age

4.1 Entropy Weight-CRITIC Combination Method to Calculate the Discrimination Coefficient

Based on the controller's pre-shift status research data, the original data matrix R is constructed as follows:

$$R = \begin{pmatrix} 43\ 21\ 2\ 7\ 2\ 1\ 3\ 1 \\ 37\ 13\ 3\ 4\ 4\ 2\ 3\ 0 \\ \vdots\ \ \vdots\ \ \vdots\ \ \vdots\vdots\vdots\ \vdots\vdots \\ 43\ 21\ 3\ 7\ 4\ 1\ 3\ 1 \end{pmatrix}$$

Normalization was performed according to Eq. (2) to obtain the data matrix:

$$R' = \begin{pmatrix} 0.000\ 0.000\ 0.667\ 1.000\ 1.000\ 1.000\ 0.000\ 0.000 \\ 0.375\ 0.800\ 0.333\ 0.000\ 0.333\ 0.500\ 0.000\ 1.000 \\ \vdots\ \ \ \ \ \vdots\ \ \ \ \ \vdots\ \ \ \ \ \ \ \ \ \ \ \ \ \ \ \vdots\vdots\vdots\ \vdots\vdots \\ 0.000\ 0.400\ 0.333\ 1.000\ 0.333\ 1.000\ 0.000\ 0.000 \end{pmatrix}$$

The entropy weight of each influencing factor is calculated according to Eqs. (3) and (4), as shown in Table 3.

Table 3. Entropy weights of each influencing factor of controllers' pre-shift state

entropy weight	age	length of experience in a job	Quality of sleep	Average sleep time	Number of shifts	stress level	fatigue	fitness level
ω_k^1	0.070	0.166	0.072	0.145	0.090	0.043	0.317	0.095

The correlation analysis of the influencing factors was performed using SPSS software and the results are shown in Table 4.

Table 4. Correlation matrix of factors influencing controllers' pre-shift status

	age	length of experience in a job	Quality of sleep	Average sleep time	Number of shifts	stress level	fatigue	fitness level
age	1.000	−0.234	0.070	0.010	−0.013	−0.326*	0.477**	0.420**
length of experience in a job	−0.234	1.000	0.372*	0.060	0.057	0.491**	0.131	0.354*
Quality of sleep	0.070	0.372*	1.000	0.656**	0.656**	0.738**	0.687**	0.493**
Average sleep time	0.010	0.060	0.656**	1.000	0.353*	0.568**	0.602**	0.176
Number of shifts	−0.013	0.057	0.656**	0.353*	1.000	0.454**	0.549**	0.226
stress level	−0.326*	0.491**	0.738**	0.568**	0.454**	1.000	0.479**	0.232
fatigue	0.477**	0.131	0.687**	0.602**	0.549**	0.479**	1.000	0.390
fitness level	0.420**	0.354*	0.493**	0.176	0.226	0.232	0.390*	1.000

Note: *Significantly correlated at the 0.05 level (bilateral); **Significantly correlated at the .01 level (bilateral)

The objective weights determined by the CRITIC method were then obtained according to Eqs. (5)–(8) and are shown in Table 5.

Table 5. Objective weights for each influencing factor of the controller's pre-shift status

entropy weight	age	length of experience in a job	Quality of sleep	Average sleep time	Number of shifts	stress level	fatigue	fitness level
ω_k^2	0.132	0.155	0.080	0.140	0.118	0.120	0.127	0.127

Since the weights calculated by entropy weighting method and CRITIC weighting method are inconsistent, the game set model is used to find the combination weights, and the final weights of each influencing factor are obtained according to Eqs. (9)–(13), which are shown in Table 6.

Table 6. Final weights for each influencing factor of the controller's pre-shift status

Portfolio weights	age	length of experience in a job	Quality of sleep	Average sleep time	Number of shifts	stress level	fatigue	fitness level
ω_k	0.072	0.166	0.073	0.145	0.091	0.046	0.311	0.096

This results in separate objective assignments of the discrimination coefficients ξ_k, where $\xi_1 = 0.072$, $\xi_2 = 0.166$, $\xi_3 = 0.073$, $\xi_4 = 0.145$, $\xi_5 = 0.091$, $\xi_6 = 0.046$, $\xi_7 = 0.311$, $\xi_8 = 0.096$。

4.2 Improvement of Gray Theory to Calculate the Correlation Coefficient

The correlation coefficient $\gamma_{k(s)}^i$ of each evaluation object relative to the optimal reference sequence is calculated according to Eqs. (14) (15) (16) and is shown in Table 7.

Table 7. Correlation coefficients of each evaluation object relative to the optimal reference sequence

	age	length of experience in a job	Quality of sleep	Average sleep time	Number of shifts	stress level	fatigue	fitness level
1	0.067	0.142	0.180	1.000	1.000	1.000	0.237	0.088
2	0.104	0.453	0.099	0.126	0.120	0.084	0.237	1.000
3	0.161	1.000	0.180	0.303	0.120	1.000	0.384	1.000
4	0.161	1.000	1.000	1.000	1.000	1.000	1.000	1.000
5	0.095	0.293	0.099	0.126	0.120	0.084	0.237	0.088
6	0.161	1.000	1.000	1.000	1.000	1.000	1.000	1.000
7	0.224	0.172	1.000	1.000	0.215	1.000	1.000	1.000
8	0.366	0.293	0.180	1.000	0.120	1.000	1.000	1.000
9	0.076	0.192	1.000	1.000	1.000	1.000	0.237	1.000
10	0.279	0.217	0.180	0.303	0.120	1.000	1.000	1.000
11	0.095	0.293	0.099	0.126	0.215	0.084	0.237	1.000

(*continued*)

Table 7. (*continued*)

	age	length of experience in a job	Quality of sleep	Average sleep time	Number of shifts	stress level	fatigue	fitness level
12	0.126	0.624	0.180	1.000	0.120	1.000	0.237	1.000
13	0.104	0.453	0.180	1.000	0.215	1.000	0.237	1.000
14	0.224	0.172	0.068	0.126	0.120	0.044	0.237	0.088
15	0.161	1.000	1.000	0.303	0.215	1.000	0.384	1.000
16	0.224	0.172	1.000	1.000	1.000	1.000	1.000	1.000
17	0.126	0.624	0.099	0.303	0.083	0.084	0.237	1.000
18	0.366	0.142	0.099	1.000	0.120	0.044	0.384	0.088
19	0.161	1.000	1.000	1.000	0.215	1.000	0.384	1.000
20	0.161	1.000	1.000	1.000	1.000	1.000	1.000	1.000
21	0.161	1.000	1.000	1.000	1.000	1.000	1.000	1.000
22	0.366	0.142	0.099	1.000	0.120	0.044	0.384	1.000
23	0.161	1.000	1.000	1.000	1.000	1.000	1.000	1.000
24	0.279	0.293	0.180	0.126	0.215	0.084	0.237	1.000
25	0.366	0.217	0.180	1.000	0.120	0.084	0.384	1.000
26	0.279	0.217	1.000	1.000	0.120	1.000	0.384	1.000
27	0.279	0.217	0.180	1.000	0.120	0.084	0.384	1.000
28	0.161	0.453	1.000	1.000	1.000	1.000	1.000	1.000
29	0.279	0.217	1.000	1.000	1.000	1.000	1.000	1.000
30	0.161	0.453	1.000	1.000	0.120	0.084	0.384	1.000
31	0.366	0.217	1.000	1.000	1.000	1.000	1.000	1.000
32	0.366	0.293	0.099	0.126	0.120	0.084	0.237	1.000
33	0.279	0.217	0.180	1.000	1.000	1.000	1.000	1.000
34	0.279	0.293	1.000	1.000	1.000	1.000	1.000	1.000
35	1.000	0.142	0.099	0.303	0.215	0.044	0.384	1.000
36	0.279	0.217	0.180	0.303	0.215	0.084	0.384	1.000
37	0.279	0.217	1.000	1.000	1.000	1.000	1.000	1.000
38	1.000	0.142	0.099	0.126	0.215	0.084	0.237	1.000
39	0.279	0.217	1.000	1.000	1.000	1.000	1.000	1.000
40	0.067	0.217	0.099	1.000	0.120	1.000	0.237	0.088

The correlation coefficient $\gamma^i_{k(t)}$ of each evaluation object relative to the worst reference sequence is calculated from Eqs. (15) (17) (19) and is shown in Table 8.

Table 8. Correlation coefficients of each evaluation object relative to the worst reference series

	age	length of experience in a job	Quality of sleep	Average sleep time	Number of shifts	stress level	fatigue	fitness level
1	1.000	1.000	0.099	0.126	0.083	0.044	1.000	1.000
2	0.161	0.172	0.180	1.000	0.215	0.084	1.000	0.088
3	0.104	0.142	0.099	0.178	0.215	0.044	0.384	0.088
4	0.104	0.142	0.068	0.126	0.083	0.044	0.237	0.088
5	0.187	0.217	0.180	1.000	0.215	0.084	1.000	1.000
6	0.104	0.142	0.068	0.126	0.083	0.044	0.237	0.088
7	0.088	0.453	0.068	0.126	0.120	0.044	0.237	0.088
8	0.076	0.217	0.099	0.126	0.215	0.044	0.237	0.088
9	0.366	0.356	0.068	0.126	0.083	0.044	1.000	0.088
10	0.082	0.293	0.099	0.178	0.215	0.044	0.237	0.088
11	0.187	0.217	0.180	1.000	0.120	0.084	1.000	0.088
12	0.126	0.156	0.099	0.126	0.215	0.044	1.000	0.088
13	0.161	0.172	0.099	0.126	0.120	0.044	1.000	0.088
14	0.088	0.453	1.000	1.000	0.215	1.000	1.000	1.000
15	0.104	0.142	0.068	0.178	0.120	0.044	0.384	0.088
16	0.088	0.453	0.068	0.126	0.083	0.044	0.237	0.088
17	0.126	0.156	0.180	0.178	1.000	0.084	1.000	0.088
18	0.076	1.000	0.180	0.126	0.215	1.000	0.384	1.000
19	0.104	0.142	0.068	0.126	0.120	0.044	0.384	0.088
20	0.104	0.142	0.068	0.126	0.083	0.044	0.237	0.088
21	0.104	0.142	0.068	0.126	0.083	0.044	0.237	0.088
22	0.076	1.000	0.180	0.126	0.215	1.000	0.384	0.088
23	0.104	0.142	0.068	0.126	0.083	0.044	0.237	0.088
24	0.082	0.217	0.099	1.000	0.120	0.084	1.000	0.088
25	0.076	0.293	0.099	0.126	0.215	0.084	0.384	0.088
26	0.082	0.293	0.068	0.126	0.215	0.044	0.384	0.088
27	0.082	0.293	0.099	0.126	0.215	0.084	0.384	0.088
28	0.104	0.172	0.068	0.126	0.083	0.044	0.237	0.088
29	0.082	0.293	0.068	0.126	0.083	0.044	0.237	0.088
30	0.104	0.172	0.068	0.126	0.215	0.084	0.384	0.088
31	0.076	0.293	0.068	0.126	0.083	0.044	0.237	0.088

(*continued*)

Table 8. (*continued*)

	age	length of experience in a job	Quality of sleep	Average sleep time	Number of shifts	stress level	fatigue	fitness level
32	0.076	0.217	0.180	1.000	0.215	0.084	1.000	0.088
33	0.082	0.293	0.099	0.126	0.083	0.044	0.237	0.088
34	0.082	0.217	0.068	0.126	0.083	0.044	0.237	0.088
35	0.067	1.000	0.180	0.178	0.120	1.000	0.384	0.088
36	0.082	0.293	0.099	0.178	0.120	0.084	0.384	0.088
37	0.082	0.293	0.068	0.126	0.083	0.044	0.237	0.088
38	0.067	1.000	0.180	1.000	0.120	0.084	1.000	0.088
39	0.082	0.293	0.068	0.126	0.083	0.044	0.237	0.088
40	1.000	0.293	0.180	0.126	0.215	0.044	1.000	1.000

The optimal correlation, the worst correlation and the relative correlation of each evaluating object are calculated by Eqs. (20)–(22) respectively, and the pre-shift status of each evaluating object is sorted according to the size of the relative correlation, and the results of the calculations and the sorting results are shown in Table 9.

Table 9. Relative relevance and pre-shift status ranking of each evaluation object

NO.	Best correlation	Worst correlation	Relative correlation	Sort	NO.	Best correlation	Worst correlation	Relative correlation	Sort
1	0.464	0.544	0.461	32	21	0.895	0.112	0.889	4
2	0.278	0.362	0.434	35	22	0.394	0.384	0.507	29
3	0.518	0.157	0.768	20	23	0.895	0.112	0.889	5
4	0.895	0.112	0.889	1	24	0.302	0.336	0.473	31
5	0.143	0.485	0.227	39	25	0.419	0.171	0.711	23
6	0.895	0.112	0.889	2	26	0.625	0.162	0.794	18
7	0.701	0.153	0.821	15	27	0.408	0.171	0.704	24
8	0.620	0.138	0.818	16	28	0.827	0.115	0.878	6
9	0.688	0.266	0.721	22	29	0.812	0.128	0.864	9
10	0.512	0.154	0.768	21	30	0.525	0.155	0.772	19
11	0.269	0.359	0.428	36	31	0.823	0.127	0.866	8

(*continued*)

Table 9. (*continued*)

NO.	Best correlation	Worst correlation	Relative correlation	Sort	NO.	Best correlation	Worst correlation	Relative correlation	Sort
12	0.536	0.232	0.698	25	32	0.291	0.357	0.449	34
13	0.524	0.226	0.698	26	33	0.709	0.132	0.844	12
14	0.135	0.719	0.158	40	34	0.821	0.118	0.874	7
15	0.633	0.141	0.818	17	35	0.398	0.377	0.514	28
16	0.799	0.149	0.843	13	36	0.332	0.166	0.667	27
17	0.320	0.351	0.476	30	37	0.812	0.128	0.864	10
18	0.280	0.498	0.360	38	38	0.363	0.442	0.451	33
19	0.720	0.134	0.843	14	39	0.812	0.128	0.864	11
20	0.895	0.112	0.889	3	40	0.354	0.482	0.423	37

4.3 Validation of Results

According to the relative correlation of each subject's pre-shift state in Table 9, correlation analysis was conducted with the subjects' self-measurement of the current overall state, and the results are shown in Table 10.

Table 10. Correlation matrix between subjects' pre-shift status correlations and self-assessment values

		Pre-shift state correlations	Subjects' self-assessed values
Pre-shift state correlations	Pearson correlation	1	0.740**
	Significance (bilateral)		0.000
	N	40	40
Subjects' self-assessed values	Pearson correlation	0.740**	1
	Significance (bilateral)	0.000	
	N	40	40

Note: ** indicates significant correlation at the 0.01 level (two-tailed)

The pre-shift status correlations calculated by the subjects through the modified gray correlation theory were significantly correlated with the subjects' self-rated pre-shift status values ($P < 0.01$), thus validating the feasibility of the present model.

5 Results and Discussion

1. In this study, the objective assignment of discriminant coefficient values based on the entropy weight-CRITIC combination method revealed that fatigue had the greatest weight, indicating that fatigue had the greatest influence on controllers' pre-shift status. Next in order of influence on controllers' pre-shift status are post age, average sleep time this week, physical health, number of shifts this week, sleep quality, age and psychological pressure.

2. A gray correlation theory pre-shift status assessment model was established to assess the controllers' pre-shift status. The relative correlation was comprehensively ranked by relative correlation, and it was found that the correlation of the controllers' pre-shift status relative to the optimal reference sequence ranged from 0.158 to 0.889, which indicated that there was a certain degree of difference in the pre-shift status among the controllers. The larger the relative correlation of the pre-shift status, the better the pre-shift status of the controller.

3. The relative correlation of the pre-shift status is categorized into three levels from large to small: 0.667–1 corresponds to the first level status, i.e., the controller's pre-shift status is good; 0.333–0.667 corresponds to the second level status, i.e., moderate; and 0–0.333 corresponds to the third level status, i.e., poor. The numbers and weights of controllers in different pre-shift status levels are shown in Fig. 2. It can be seen that the controllers under good pre-shift status account for a larger proportion, but there are still controllers with relatively poor pre-shift status.

4. Statistics on the distribution of personnel under each grade and the mean values of the eight assessment indicators are shown in Fig. 3, and the characteristics of each pre-shift status grade are described.

The age of controllers under the first level of status is mostly concentrated between 30–33 years old, which is the prime stage of control work. Sleep time generally satisfies 7 h, sleep quality is good, and they wake up full of vigor and vitality [18]. Low psychological pressure, low fatigue, good physical health, able to adapt to the shift work mode, able to meet the controller's pre-shift status requirements, and able to carry out the control and command work smoothly.

The age of the controllers in the secondary state is partly concentrated at 35 years old and above, with more than 10 years of posting experience. Due to their age, the decline in physical fitness is more likely to cause physiological fatigue and is not easy to recover, resulting in a higher fatigue level. However, because they have been engaged in control work for a long time, their psychological pressure is low, and they can still keep calm and not be nervous in the face of high-intensity work. This type of controller may have timely but not sensitive reaction ability, and is conscious but slightly slack.

The controllers in the third level are all 27 years old, with a lower posting age, which leads to higher psychological pressure due to the lack of control ability and experience. According to the interpretation of the Stress Perception Scale, it can be seen that the stress at this stage is persistent and cannot be calmed quickly, which has an impact on sleep and leads to insufficient sleep time and quality. However, the level of fatigue of the controllers in this state remained at a moderate level due to their young age, high energy level and good recovery ability.

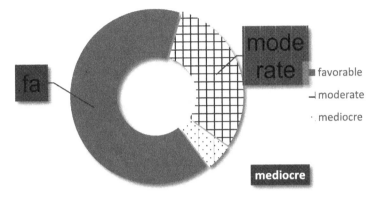

Fig. 2. Distribution of the number of people in different pre-shift status levels

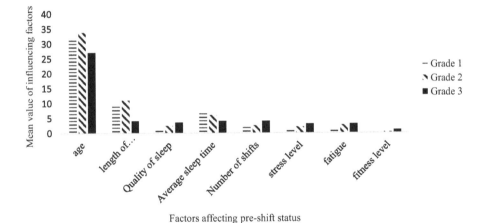

Fig. 3. Characteristic distribution of each influencing factor at different pre-shift status levels

6 Conclusion

1. In this thesis, eight indicators affecting the pre-shift status of controllers were formulated, and a gray correlation theory pre-shift status assessment model was established. And the entropy weight-CRITIC combination method was used to determine the influence weight of each factor of controller pre-shift state on controller pre-shift ability, and it was found that fatigue had the greatest influence on the control pre-shift state, followed by post age, the average sleep time of this week, and physical health.

2. The discriminating coefficient of the gray engineering theory was determined through the entropy weight-CRITIC combination method, which improved the reliability of the gray correlation theory. The relative correlation degree of each evaluation factor was determined through the gray correlation theory, and it was found that the correlation degree of the controller's pre-shift status relative to the optimal reference

sequence was in the range of 0.158–0.889, which indicated that there was a certain degree of difference in the pre-shift status among the controllers.

3. The controllers' pre-shift states were ranked according to the relative correlation of the pre-shift states, and three levels were distinguished. The greater the relative relevance of the pre-shift status, the better the controller's pre-shift status. Grade 1 controllers have the best pre-shift status and are able to carry out control work smoothly; Grade 2 controllers, due to their older age and longer years of service, have a greater impact on their pre-shift status; Grade 3 controllers, due to their younger age and shorter years of service, have higher psychological pressure and need regular psychological counseling and skill training to improve their control ability and reduce psychological pressure.

4. This thesis can provide a reference for ATC units to evaluate the pre-shift status of controllers, reduce the safety hazards arising from poor pre-shift status of controllers, and further improve the safety level of air traffic management work.

Acknowledgements. The cooperation of air traffic controllers in the study is greatly appreciated, and it is their support that enabled the authors to successfully complete the experimental content and conduct the controller competency assessment study.

Disclosure of Interests. The authors have no competing interests to declare that are relevant to the content of this article.

References

1. Feng, Z.: Promoting high-quality development of civil aviation industry. Large Airplanes (06), 12–14 (2021)
2. CCAR-93-R5: Civil Aviation Air Traffic Management Rules
3. Zhang, Y.: Research on controller pre-shift alertness metrics. Civil Aviation University of China (2020)
4. Zhang, X., Bai, P.: A survey study on the characteristics of controllers' poor working condition. J. Civil Aviat. Univ. China **36**(06), 21–26 (2018)
5. Giovanni, C.: Working and health conditions of Italian air traffic controllers. Int. J. Occup. Saf. Ergon. **6**(3), 365–382 (2015)
6. Putri, E.D., Nurmaida, H.A., Warsito, T., et al.: The effect fatigue levels of air traffic control (ATC) on work effectiveness in Soekarno-Hatta international airport. Adv. Transp. Logist. Res. **2**, 46–50 (2019)
7. Civil aviation controller fatigue management reference study material. Civil Aviation Administration of China Air Traffic Control Industry Management Office (2017)
8. Gao, Y., Li, H., Li, J.: Effects of wake-up time and sleep duration on alertness in control positions. Sci. Technol. Eng. **16**(36), 147–151 (2016)
9. Sun, R., Li, T.: Survey research on sleep quality and fatigue of air traffic controllers. Safety Environ. Eng. **24**(03), 164–169 (2017)
10. Rules for the qualification and validation of public air transportation carriers operating large aircraft. Bull. State Council People's Republic China (2017)
11. Wu, F.-G.: Quantitative research on comprehensive evaluation of air traffic controller fatigue. Civil Aviation Flight School of China (2016)

12. Zhang, J., Sun, R., Li, J.: A comparative study of controller shift system in various regions of China. Occup. Health **31**(24), 3510–3513 (2015)
13. Wang, N.: Research on key methods and system implementation of air traffic controller scheduling. Civil Aviation University of China (2017)
14. Chen, F., Wang, L.: EEG signal-based fatigue assessment of controllers under different shift systems. China Sci. Technol. Paper **12**(19), 2198–2203 (2017)
15. Huang, B., Dai, F.: Personality analysis of air traffic controllers. J. Civil Aviat. Univ. China (02), 52–56 (2007)
16. Wang, L., Zhu, M.: Analysis of air traffic controllers' situational awareness based on accident tree. J. Safety Environ. **21**(01), 249–256 (2021)
17. Wang, L., Yang, Y.: Evaluation study of radar controllers' situational awareness. J. Saf. Environ. **19**(02), 554–561 (2019)
18. Stanford Sleepiness Scale. https://www.med.upenn.edu/cbti/assets/user-content/documents/Stanford%20Sleepiness%20Scale.pdf
19. Lu, H., Ye, M.: Research on the competency model of controllers in Civil Aviation Guangzhou Control Center. Oper. Manag. (05), 86–92 (2021)
20. Guo, W., Huang, L.: Analysis of aviation controllers' work pressure. Ind. Technol. Forum **12**(13), 126–127 (2013)
21. Lee, E.H., Chung, B.Y., Suh, C.H., et al.: Korean versions of the Perceived Stress Scale (PSS-14, 10 And 4): psychometric evaluation in patients with chronic disease. Scand. J. Caring Sci. **29**(1), 183–192 (2014)
22. Guo, J., Pan, C., Yang, C.: Research on air traffic control hazard source identification method based on gray correlation analysis. J. Saf. Environ. **15**(06), 157–161 (2015)
23. Dong, Y., Duan, Z.: A new method for determining the gray correlation discriminant coefficient. J. Xi'an Univ. Archit. Technol. (Nat. Sci. Edn.) (04), 589–592 (2008)
24. Su, P., Li, J.H.: Research on gray correlation dynamic resolution coefficient algorithm based on triangular fuzzy number. Electron. Components Inf. Technol. **5**(03), 152–155 (2021)
25. Cui, Y., Zhang, J., Wang, S., et al.: Research on quality evaluation of Qiangwu drinking tablets based on entropy weight method and gray correlation degree method. Chin. Herb. Med. **50**(23), 5724–5730 (2019)
26. Li, F., Li, D.P.: Portfolio evaluation model based on entropy weight method. Inf. Technol. Inf. (09), 148–150 (2021)
27. Chen, J.: Research on portfolio empowerment evaluation method based on game theory. Fujian Comput. (09), 15–16 (2003)
28. Han, L., Men, B.: Evaluation of water resources carrying capacity in Haihe River Basin based on combinatorial game theory method. Hydropower Energy Sci. **39**(11), 61–64 (2021)

Human Cognitive Reliability and R&D Efficiency: A Human Factor Study in Semiconductor Pilot Scale Production Line

Yuanjun Li[1](✉), Mengya Zhu[2], Dengkai Chen[3], and Yiting Yu[3]

[1] Ningbo Institute of Northwestern Polytechnical University, Ningbo, China
yuanjun@nwpu.edu.cn
[2] Ningbo University, Ningbo, China
[3] Northwestern Polytechnical University, Xi'an, China

Abstract. A qualified chip sensor determined for mass production must undergo rigorous development and verification on the pilot line. In this experimental process, the sensor performance, quality, and R&D efficiency deeply impact the subsequent progress in the industry. Most pilot lines rely on human(engineers)-machines collaboration because the full-automatic production line requires extremely high investment and does not meet the demand for flexible technique adjustments. Therefore, the operational differences of individual engineers will directly affect the product's qualification rate. It requires the Process Design/Integration Engineers (PIE, as a manager role of the fab) to update the process flow or management strategies to improve the operator's performance and reduce human error probability, thus lowering the time and economic cost. For exploratory purposes, this study investigated three Semiconductor pilot scale production lines and interviewed 17 participants with multiple roles in the fab. It summarized 10 Common Performance Conditions and the related secondary index for operators' performance evaluation and discussed its results in relation to potential human reliability errors.

Keywords: Human Cognitive Reliability · Human Factor · Semiconductor Production

1 Introduction

Pilot-scale production is crucial in the manufacturing process, situated between laboratory research and mass manufacture. The primary objective of pilot-scale production is to optimize the technical process based on laboratory studies, thereby enabling the transition to realistic full-scale production. This optimization comprehensively analyses time, cost, scaling parameters, and unexpected outcomes. In contrast to the laboratory level, which focuses on controlled conditions and techniques, the pilot line also seeks to replicate the conditions and challenges for large-scale deployment, ensuring a smoother transition to commercial production facilities. The pilot-scale production is multidisciplinary and encompasses diverse fields such as biology, medicine, chemicals, machinery, etc. The lack of a widely accepted standard for defining the scale restriction of a "pilot line" is due to the diverse production objects and purposes. For example, the purposes vary from testing the raw material ratio and stability of preservation in the food industry (Pan et al., 2022) to the cultivation technology for the viability of commercial microalgae production of the bioprocess optimisation (San Pedro et al., 2014), testing nutrient recovery of raw materials or waste for sustainable development (Ovsyannikova et al., 2020) or conducting techno-economic assessment (Lai and Ngu, 2020). In the semiconductor industry, in addition to the above, pilot-scale production also needs to ensure an ultra-high yield, quality and R&D efficiency while controlling the loss caused by failure within an acceptable range. Moore's Law speculates on the progress of semiconductor technology, which has been verified in the past decades, and illustrates the requirements for the development rate of the semiconductor industry. Chip design has become increasingly complex with more transistors, components, or finer micro-electro-mechanical structures, meaning more computing power and higher integration are required. The emergence of IoT and AI has made chip design one of the core hardware supporting new functions and scenarios for sensing, interconnection, and computing applications, making it a crucial aspect of the current global technology competition. In this regard, research is needed to support its operational excellence.

In China, the chip production pilot lines mainly serve the tasks of R&D, small batch production for small and medium-sized enterprises, technical personnel training, teaching and experiments. The chain can be divided into three stages: simulation design (upstream), processing and manufacturing (midstream) and packaging and testing (downstream), involving dozens of procedures. Since the industrial chain of intelligent sensors is extensive, it is unaffordable for a single enterprise to have technical knowledge, labour costs and equipment investment for all industry links. As a result, the industry shows the characteristics of modularity, allowing each link to participate independently. It requires human-machine collaboration to meet the need for flexible technical adjustments, as automation cannot replace it, but individual operational differences will directly affect the qualification rate (Bubb, 2005; Sgarbossa et al., 2020). For some time now, Process Integration Engineers (PIE) have realised that human reliability, as a factor of uncertainty, is difficult to articulate, understand or measure but plays a strategic role in improving operators' performance, decreasing the probability of human error, thus lowering the time and economic cost. However, previous studies have largely overlooked this topic. Thus, this research examined the workflow of three chip pilot lines and the human reliability of multi-role personnel, summarising and organising the factors that affect yield and R&D efficiency from an error perspective and proposing improvement suggestions.

2 Methodology

This study utilised a mixed research approach, enabling the researcher to delve into individual experiences and interpretations to uncover meaning. In a given phenomenon, qualitative research encompasses multiple analyses contributing to the conclusion to address the research question (Ward et al., 2018), with quantitative analysis providing additional support. To address the impact of human reliability on R&D efficiency, the study is divided into three sub-questions and is structured according to the procedures outlined in Fig. 1.

1. What human operation is involved in chip production?
2. What possible human errors will cause?
3. What are the factors that cause the errors?

Fig. 1. Research Procedures

This study delved into the complex system of chip manufacturing and investigated the human factors that can lead to errors or deviations in the process. Previous literature on Human Reliability Analysis (HRA) in the semiconductor industry was extensively reviewed to establish a solid theoretical basis for the study. The preliminary research framework was then proposed.

Next, expert interviews were conducted to gain insights into the measures taken by actual enterprises to reduce human errors. A detailed production procedure map was generated accordingly.

Finally, in-depth interviews and surveys were carried out with 17 multi-role personnel on three pilot lines. Participants were asked to provide feedback about their working environment to evaluate the various influencing factors accurately. This approach enabled us to reconstruct operational details as far as possible and achieve a comprehensive understanding of the topic at hand.

3   Literature Review

3.1   Human Reliability Analysis (HRA)

The UK's Health and Safety Executive (HSE) defines human factors as: "Human factors refer to environmental, organisational and job factors, and human and individual characteristics, which influence behaviour at work in a way which can affect health and safety". It consists of three interrelated aspects: work (what people are asked to do), individual (who does it) and organisation (where they work), all of which are influenced by broader societal concerns. Previous studies on human error mainly focused on working safely and reliably, emphasising accident investigation rather than deviation tracing. The iconic event in 2012, for example, the Society of Petroleum Engineers (SPE) reached a consensus on managing future oil and gas exploration and production operations and presented ten key points about human and organisational factors, drawing lessons from the 2010 Deepwater Horizon disaster in the Gulf of Mexico. Some scholars argue that purely following safety guidelines may lead to a "blinders of dominant logic" effect (Prahalad, 2004). It occurs when a management community that prioritises profit above all else (Neumann and Dul, 2010), ironically overlooking opportunities for improvement. In the semiconductor industry, exposure to health hazards during production usually occurs at low levels, with a meager rate of physical accidents. The use of chemicals may lead to cancer or miscarriage (Kim et al., 2014), but the effects of the toxins may take decades to surface. Therefore, from the feasibility perspective, this study will emphasise work behaviour and performance.

The standard HRA methods such as Technique for Human Error Rate Prediction (THERP), Accident Sequence Evaluation Program (ASEP), Human Error Assessment and Reduction Technique (HEART), Human Event Repository and Analysis (HERA), Nuclear Computerized Library for Assessing Reactor Reliability (NUCLARR), Cognitive Reliability and Error Analysis Method (CREAM), etc. have been developed for assessing human errors' sources, types, and strengths to identify their specific impact on performance and propose solutions (Williams, 2015). These methods also aim to detect and measure error-inducing conditions in order to prevent potential human errors (Williams and Bell, 2015) and predict the likelihood of human errors through performance-shaping factors (Blackman et al., 2008). Additionally, new applications have been proposed based on the task complexity (Rasmussen et al., 2015) and capture the context of human accidents for the cause tracing (Ekanem et al., 2016). The availability and reliability of human-robot collaboration performance are also interpreted (Barosz et al., 2020), and it has been demonstrated that a soft control environment can reduce the probability of basic human errors caused by omissions, providing valuable insights into soft control design and operator training methods (Jang et al., 2014).

3.2 Human Cognitive Reliability in the Semiconductor Industry

Even so, the human factors in practice are frequently disregarded. Human operators are treated as quasi-technical elements of the production system, mistaken for machines. Despite the increased electronic control and protection implemented in systems, they remain susceptible to human errors, as "some errors are slips or lapses, often are actions that were not as planned or unintended actions (HSE)". A relatively small percentage of errors result from wrong judgment or decision-making, typically attributed to inadequate training.

In chip processes, most material handling, such as bonding wire and lead frame, requires operator assistance and judgment. Some measures have been proposed to strengthen the effective control of human-machine interaction to reduce error probabilities (Eng et al., 2006). Fabricating these miniature devices on silicon wafers is a complicated manufacturing process involving hundreds of specialised processes, nearly half requiring complex chemical plasma processes, such as etching and deposition. These fundamental processes rely on human engineers using their intuition and experienced skills to affect R&D efficiency and mass production stability, so research trends tend to introduce AI and Deep Learning to avoid repeated trial and error (Kanarik et al., 2023; O'Leary et al., 2020). At the inspection stage, subjective and time-consuming eyeball analysis is required to assess Wafer Bin Map (WBM) patterns - the specific defect pattern for diagnosing root causes of low yield (Chien et al., 2013). Thus, innovative approaches have been developed to improve the recognition efficiency (Chang et al., 2009; Hsu, 2015). Quality control has been shown to correlate with operator fatigue (Givi et al., 2015a, 2015b), including cognitive fatigue, physical fatigue and visual fatigue (Yung et al., 2020). At the same time, the daily work experience of operators, such as trust, stress, good teamwork, and social relationships, has been shown to positively affect a clean and error-free semiconductor production environment (Wurhofer et al., 2014).

The quality of HRA depends on human performance insights, is built on a human factor's foundation field (Boring, 2010) and is reflected in product quality. The quality management system is a systematic strategic decision-making organisation in which "5M1E" - Man, Material, Method, Machine, Measurement, Environment, are highly mentioned as the influencing factors for manufacturing reliability in the Scene Management (Li et al., 2018). Human error can occur in all six dimensions, as shown in Table 1.

Table 1. Probable Human Errors in Semiconductor Industry based 5M1E

5M1E	Probable Human Errors
Man	Engineer's knowledge of quality, technical proficiency, physical condition, operating habits, experience, etc.
Material	Engineers's material selection, material pretreatment and protection, parameter settings, etc.
Method	PIE's design of processes and task flow, etc.
Machine	Engineer's interaction with machine, logical understanding, data reading, equipment maintenance, etc.
Measurement	Engineer's methods of quality testing, specifications and standard applied, etc.
Environment	Engineer's degree of adaptation, concentration, and the impact of environmental conditions (comfort) on the operation in the fab environment, etc.

The interdependent relationships among the six elements necessitate the recalibration of other correlations whenever a single element undergoes a change. This demands the expertise of production operators or quality management personnel, who must maintain error stability, swiftly identify and address anomalies, and implement superior quality management standards and measures. Given its broad applicability, this study utilises this framework to examine the reliability of human factors in manufacturing processes systematically.

3.3   The Framework of CREAM

When conducting an HRA, the probability of human error is determined based on the anticipated impact of various performance factors. Due to the infrequency of such incidents, obtaining sufficient relevant data to confirm the potential for failure is limited. This analysis may be ineffective in predicting preinitiating events or avoiding events that may not have occurred. Relatively, CREAM (Hollnagel, 1998) is suitable for systematically summarising the parts, tasks or actions of operation that require human cognition in specific scenarios. It uses a classification scheme consisting of several groups that describe the phenotypes (error modes) and genotypes (causes) of the erroneous actions to predict, quantify and trace human errors. It considers the factors related to individuals and the relationship with technology, organisation, and the context in which error occurred, which can describe the cause and effect of error in a completed storyline.

Nonetheless, CREAM's approach necessitates a larger investment of resources than other methods, requiring a considerable amount of time to develop a solid background knowledge before conducting a thorough analysis. In semiconductor manufacturing, each process technique can be examined as a distinct subject, and it is impractical to undertake a comprehensive exploration in a preliminary study. As a result, this study aims to simplify CREAM's structure and procedures to outline the fundamental principle.

CREAM raised nine Common Performance Conditions (CPC), a minimum number of essential factors to describe the context. Each CPC has a finite number of levels, such as improved, insignificant, and reduced. After learning the importance of materials through preliminary research and expert interviews, with modifications made based on the research, this study proposes ten CPCs by combining the CREAM and 5M1E framework (Table 2).

Table 2. CPCs Description in the Semiconductor Industry

CPC	Description
#1	Adequacy of organization
#2	Working conditions
#3	Adequacy of MMI and operational support
#4	Availability of procedures/plans
#5	Number of simultaneous goals
#6	Available time
#7	Time of day (Circadian rhythm)
#8	Adequacy of training and experience
#9	Crew collaboration quality
#10	Materials

4   Research Procedures

4.1   Expert Interview - Pilot Line Work Flow and Management System

To efficiently gather comprehensive and reliable information about the pilot production line's operation, management, and production process planning, this study conducted open-ended interviews with five experts from the chip manufacturing industry. These experts included integration engineers, scholars, production principals and product managers from the design, production, packaging, and testing stages. With the assistance of data induction and expert reconfirmation, the study obtained a detailed process map of pilot line chip production, as depicted in Fig. 2.

Fig. 2. Pilot Production Line Workflow Map (Appendix 1)

The pilot production line consists of four stages: Design, Manufacture, Packaging and Test. Tasks are undertaken by different processing fabs. In most cases, the Design and Manufacturing are completed by the same fab, which negotiates with the customer to produce a Technical Process Manual (TPM). TPM is the core and is used as a guidance for the entire production line. The customer has the discretion to use the manual for the packaging and testing fabs for subsequent process design and failure tracing. The TPM is determined after a complete discussion between the customer and PIE and will not be randomly changed unless unplanned issues cannot be solved in actual operation. Sample production will be carried out before the process starts to test the process design, but it does not guarantee that the subsequent formal production will be foolproof. Even though the process design error is a small probability event, it costs high. After summarising the interview content, the current pilot line production mainly has the following characteristics.

Multiple-Job Holding. The team responsible for the pilot line comprises fewer individuals than the automated mass production line. The personnel requirements rely heavily on a wealth of knowledge and experience, resulting in a high recruitment threshold and greater autonomy in decision-making. As a result, the responsibilities on the pilot line are more adaptable and multifaceted. For example, PIE would assume dual responsibilities as both customer managers and heads of production lines; the process lead engineers are accountable for overseeing production, facilitating handovers, and maintaining equipment related to the manufacturing process. The inter-communication among roles is not exclusively confined to specific communication channels. The problem during processing can be easily traced to individuals. Additionally, the lead Process Engineer (PE), the first-line operator, can directly communicate with the customer to adjust the process design so that the customer needs can have timely feedback.

TPM Dominate the Flow of Production. Before production, the PIE will meet with the PE leaders to discuss the manufacturing details and highlight potential processing challenges. The TPM will be provided in a hard copy along with the wafer during the process flow. PEs will check the situation of wafer pieces from the previous process and the processing requirements on the manual, then formally enter the responsible processing step. In certain cases, micromachinery structures are found to be fragile and require careful handling during subsequent processes. PEs would clearly mark the handling instructions on the process sheet or convey them orally to ensure their safe operation. The TPM is a crucial point of reference for designing the appropriate packaging and testing solution, which connects the independent production, packaging, and testing processes.

High Customer Engagement. In order to effectively manage expenses and schedules, the customer will work closely with various facilities, including design, production, packaging, and testing, to place orders. They play a vital role in both creating the initial program and refining it as needed. The customer designates a dedicated team member to oversee the chip processing status and adjust plans accordingly. This individual serves as a liaison between the front and back processes, ensuring clear communication of technical specifications and requirements. In cases where the chip requires oxygen isolation, a vacuum package is necessary. If the device fails to meet standards during testing, a thorough investigation must be conducted throughout the fabs to pinpoint the cause of the issue. This involves coordinating the process plan before and after, organising the process leader of the processing and packaging foundry for negotiation, and ultimately achieving the desired performance.

4.2   Engineer Survey – the Influencing Factors of R&D Efficiency

The second procedure conducted a questionnaire survey on 17 multi-identity roles in three pilot lines according to the obtained process map. The functions of the participants are shown in Table 3.

Table 3. Participants' Responsibilities

Participant No.	Process Integration Engineer (PIE)	Process Engineer (Lead)	Process Engineer (Operator)	Product Engineer/ Manager	Yield Enhancement Engineer (YE)	Test Engineer (TE)	Quality Engineering (QE)	Material Handler	Process Inspector	Responsibility Description
1	√			√						Process design, process supervision, project progress follow-up, customer communication, etc.
2	√			√						Engineer and customer communication, etc.
3		√			√					wet clean, etching, etc.
4			√			√				Defect diagnose by optical microscope, analysis of anomaly, component analysis, etc.
5		√	√							Photoetching, bonding, etc.
6	√			√						Process design, project development, customer communication, device fabrication, etc.
7		√	√							Chemico-mechanical polishing (CMP), optical filming, etc.
8		√	√							Photoetching, bonding, process development, customer communication, etc.
9		√	√							Cleaning, etching, scribing, oxidizing, annealing, etc.
10		√	√		√					Dry cleaning, etching, wafer saw, etc.
11	√			√			√			Factory affair, customer communication, process design
12			√							Pressure welding, photoetching, etc.
13			√				√			Product quality administration, surface-mount technology machine operation
14			√							Pressure welding, etc.
15								√		Allocation of machine, material and tasks, etc.
16						√				Test programming, program debugging, etc.
17									√	Production line inspection, continuous production improvement, etc.

Participants were requested to rate the factors affecting R&D efficiency based on their personal work experience. The factors listed for evaluation were sourced from a comprehensive review of existing literature, and inputs from subject matter experts were also taken into account. In total, 17 participants were selected for the study, and the results were based on the 15 valid scores obtained (refer to Table 4 for details). The participants were invited to make additions.

Table 4. Influencing Factors of R&D Efficiency

No.	Influencing Factors	Analysis				
		Average	Standard Deviation	Confidence	Confidence Interval	
1	Process design of production line	5.857	2.070	1.048	4.809	6.905
2	Coordination between processes	4.733	1.792	0.907	3.827	5.640
3	Communication and feedback between PIE and operators	5.467	2.295	1.161	4.305	6.628
4	Process improvement procedures	6.067	2.052	1.038	5.028	7.105
5	Organization and management of production line leader	5.400	1.595	0.807	4.593	6.207
6	Project plan and management	5.714	1.729	0.875	4.839	6.589
7	Errors and deviation	6.067	2.374	1.202	4.865	7.268
8	R&D Investment (financial and manpower resources)	6.357	2.307	1.168	5.189	7.525
9	Operators' quality, team work and post division	6.333	1.633	0.826	5.507	7.160
10	Supporting tools and software utilization	4.933	2.219	1.123	3.810	6.056
11	Operation specification and technical standard	6.667	2.320	1.174	5.493	7.841
12	Effective customer participation	4.357	1.946	0.985	3.373	5.342
13	Inspection and quality assessment	6.000	2.646	1.339	4.661	7.339
14	Schedule pressures	5.000	2.035	1.030	3.970	6.030
15	Comfortable work space and reasonable task assignment	5.333	2.193	1.110	4.224	6.443
16	Machine capacity	6.857	2.214	1.120	5.737	7.977

Score 0:none; 1-3:low impact; 4-6: high impact; 7-10: significant impact   Alpha=0.05; Sample size=15

The 16 influencing factors are considered to impact R&D efficiency greatly. However, it was found that participants with different responsibilities had varying degrees of understanding and rating of these factors, which was reflected in the standard deviation. Given the small sample size, it was deemed insignificant to rank the priority of these influencing factors. Therefore, confidence intervals were selected to represent the distribution and trend of the data. The result reports that the impact of process design is less than other objective premises such as machine capability, Operation specification and technical standards and R&D Investment. Participants' cognition on the high impact of Operators' quality, teamwork work, and post-division on R&D efficiency is consistent. This is followed by Errors and deviation, Process improvement procedures and Inspection and quality assessment, three factors that can lead to rework or loss.

In the subsequent phase of the study, the participants were instructed to indicate the possible causes of errors. As a result, fifteen additional valid responses were collected, as summarized in Table 5. It is worth noting that two of the participants in this phase were distinct from those mentioned in Table 4.

Table 5. Potential Cause of Errors

No.	Cause of failure or error	Participant No.														
		1	2	3	4	5	6	7	8	9	10	11	12	13	14	15
1	Misunderstanding of TPM	√	√			√	√		√		√	√	√	√		
2	Deficiencies in machine design that cause unintentional errors	√		√			√		√	√						
3	Overcomplicated process design		√			√	√			√						
4	Lack of concentration leads to performance below the required level	√	√		√		√	√		√			√	√		√
5	Mishear, misread or misthink	√	√				√	√	√			√	√	√	√	
6	Omissions due to memory error	√	√	√			√						√			√
7	Information transfer error	√	√	√	√		√		√		√	√	√		√	

Sample Size: 15

Ensuring accurate information delivery is a top priority for most personnel, but simply having an explanation meeting or following up with a written TPM is not enough to guarantee effective transmission of commands. Previous studies identified the capabilities that promote teamwork's efficiency (Sycara and Sukthankar, 2006), including an overall intention to execute a plan (joint intention), sharing of goals, plans and knowledge of the environment (common ground), and awareness of the roles and responsibilities, as well as the capabilities and limitations of one's teammates (team awareness). Judging from the personnel responsibilities and the differentiated feedback on reliability risks it is clear that the current pilot line teamwork needs to establish a cognitive common ground to support effective collaboration. Information transfer is a key area where errors can easily occur, especially under time pressure, which is consistent with participants' feedback on "mishear, misread and misthink" and "overcomplicated process design". Given the different linguistic and grammatical patterns of individuals with various cognitive capabilities, the production line can achieve a uniform description of the same event or instruction, such as the sentence length, diction, etc., to reduce the level of cognitive load (Khawaja et al., 2012).

From the management perspective, due to the overlap of responsibilities, the personnel in charge pays more attention to information transmission and task allocation at the technical level. However, this approach overlooks the importance of non-technical skills such as leadership, situation awareness, decision-making, teamwork, and communication in avoiding errors and enhancing operational performance (Flin et al., 2002). This may explain the shared concerns expressed by PIE, PE leaders, and operational engineers about the information delivery through TPM because, as teammates but in the independent process, they lack channels to anticipate each other's needs or share understanding, hindering collaboration (Baker et al., 2006). While the pilot line achieves person-to-person task tracking and repeated confirmation with a small output and simple personnel composition, this level of performance is insufficient for ensuring a low risk of error on a large-scale production line.

Some participants raised concerns regarding a lack of concentration, leading to lower performance levels. However, the machine's long-term iterative interaction design is quite reasonable and has settings to prevent misoperation. Following parameter input, sustained attention is not required. Therefore, the interaction primarily occurs through the interface operation, 1) wrongly thinking of misoperation as correct, 2) omission in parameter setting and 3) inadequate altering attention control for multitasking. In human information processing, senses are captured by eyes and ears, with attention recourses and long-term memory determining an individual's perception and affecting the decision-making and response selection (Wickens, 1992). Although the fab has safety and operation warning signs in place to provide visual cues, participants generally reported that the effect was minimal. The operator has confidence in the action and does not rely on the instructions. While the basic safety regulations of laboratory construction were met, the content of the warning signs only provides routine tips and has limited significance in guiding the avoidance of errors. The multiple dimensions of factors would impact operational performance (Chen et al., 2023). Aside from regular breaks, the current fab management method allows operators to rest freely and briefly away from the cleanroom of yellow LED lamps or a workplace of continuous noise. Lighting affects emotion, circadian rhythms and manifests as eye strain (Oh et al., 2015). Noise in the workplace has been shown to affect heart rate and blood pressure (Leather et al., 2003; Lusk et al., 2002). The process operators of the participants conveyed their perception concerning several environmental factors, including lighting, noise, screen dark light, temperature, and humidity, among others. While the situation is not entirely comfortable, they have expressed their willingness to tolerate it, citing the priority of the production environment. Rare studies have directly demonstrated the reliability impact of semiconductor production line environmental requirements such as the Lithography area for working long hours, but its potential impact on health can be anticipated.

4.3   Engineer Interview – the Secondary Index of CPCs

Participants then were instructed to respond to a set of well-organized questions derived from CPCs (which measure dimensions indicated in Table 1 with the aim of identifying, analysing, and reporting patterns (Braun and Clarke, 2006). The interview organized 46 primary questions and random follow-up questions. 10 CPCs were used as the initial codes to group participants' conductive answers and identify the sub-themes (Table 6).

The above CPCs and their secondary index can be used as a reference framework to evaluate R&D efficiency, predict potential human errors from the perspective of situational cognitive reliability, and further analyse the influencing factors of R&D efficiency and their interrelationships. According to the above conditions, an improvement plan is proposed to Develop and specify modifications to reduce risk.

Table 6. The Secondary Index of CPCs and Performance

CPC		Secondary Index		CPC level/description	Expected effects on performance
#1	Adequacy of organization	1.1	Process workflow management (Method of task handover, problem report, supervision, etc.)	Very efficient Efficient Inefficient Deficient	Positive Neutral Negative Negative
		1.2	Responsibility assignment and Quality of work (Clearly defined responsibilities, problem-solving ability, teamwork, etc.)	Very efficient Efficient Inefficient Deficient	Positive Neutral Negative Negative
		1.3	Communication system (Efficient information delivery, etc.)	Very efficient Efficient Inefficient Deficient	Positive Neutral Negative Negative
		1.4	Safety management system (Production safety, chemical safety, fab affair management, etc.)	Very efficient Efficient Inefficient Deficient	Positive Neutral Negative Negative
		1.5	Technical Process Manual (Highlight of processing difficulties, risks, process record, failure tracking, etc.)	Very efficient Efficient Inefficient Deficient	Positive Neutral Negative Negative
		1.6	Customer engagement (Exposition needs, participative decision making, etc.)	Very efficient Efficient Inefficient Deficient	Positive Neutral Negative Negative

(*continued*)

Table 6. (*continued*)

CPC		Secondary Index		CPC level/description	Expected effects on performance
#2	Working conditions	2.1	Fab environment (Lightening, noise, screen glare, humiture, etc.)	Advantageous Compatible Incompatible	Positive Neutral Negative
		2.2	Fine work environment (Clean, dust-free, light colour, etc.)	Advantageous Compatible Incompatible	Positive Neutral Negative
		2.3	Supporting facility (Worktop, rest zone, switch handle, etc.)	Advantageous Compatible Incompatible	Positive Neutral Negative
		2.4	Work space layout (Machine operation logic, work space, etc.)	Advantageous Compatible Incompatible	Positive Neutral Negative
#3	Adequacy of MMI and operational support	3.1	Man-machine operation (Interface, operation panel, support, computer workstation, etc.)	Supportive Adequate Tolerable Inappropriate	Positive Neutral Neutral Negative
		3.2	Technical condition (Operator's skills, machine capability, etc.)	Supportive Adequate Tolerable Inappropriate	Positive Neutral Neutral Negative
		3.3	Operational condition (Machine layout, machine-operator allocation, etc.)	Supportive Adequate Tolerable Inappropriate	Positive Neutral Neutral Negative
		3.4	Machine monitoring (Mistake-proofing system, etc.)	Supportive Adequate Tolerable Inappropriate	Positive Neutral Neutral Negative

(*continued*)

Table 6. (*continued*)

CPC		Secondary Index		CPC level/description	Expected effects on performance
#4	Availability of procedures/plans	4.1	Process design (Production schemes, project plan, etc.)	Appropriate Acceptable Inappropriate	Positive Neutral Negative
		4.2	Individual process operation (Particular process operation, standard, specification, etc.)	Appropriate Acceptable Inappropriate	Positive Neutral Negative
#5	Number of simultaneous goals	5.1	Multi-tasking (Arrangement of tasks, evaluation of workload and quality, etc.)	Fewer than capacity Matching current capacity More than capacity	Neutral Neutral Negative
		5.2	Simultaneous processing of pieces (Number of wafers being processed at one time, etc.)	Fewer than capacity Matching current capacity More than capacity	Neutral Neutral Negative
#6	Available time	6.1	Required processing time (Time plan for technical processes, management, communication, etc.)	Adequate Temporarily inadequate Continuously inadequate	Neutral Neutral Negative
#7	Time of day (Circadian rhythm)	7.1	Working hours (Certain time of work, operator's daily schedule, etc.)	Day-time (adjusted) Night time (unadjusted)	Neutral Negative
		7.2	Work break (Continuous working hours, rest period, work burnout, etc.)	Very efficient Efficient Inefficient Deficient	Positive Neutral Neutral Negative

(*continued*)

Table 6. (*continued*)

CPC		Secondary Index		CPC level/description	Expected effects on performance
#8	Adequacy of training and experience	8.1	Training level and quality (Training content setting, training results, etc.)	Adequate, high experience Adequate, limited experience Inadequate	Positive Neutral Negative
#9	Crew collaboration quality	9.1	Teamwork (Trust, collaboration, task flow, etc.)	Very efficient Efficient Inefficient Deficient	Positive Neutral Negative Negative
		9.2	Social climate (Interpersonal relationship, familiarity, etc.)	Very efficient Efficient Inefficient Deficient	Positive Neutral Negative Negative
#10	Material	10.1	Raw material quality (Wafers, chemical agent, etc.)	Very efficient Efficient Inefficient Deficient	Positive Neutral Neutral Negative
		10.2	Material processing (Selection, inspection, specifications, required precision, etc.)	Very efficient Efficient Inefficient Deficient	Positive Neutral Neutral Negative

5   Conclusions

Given the rapidly evolving and highly specialized nature of the chip industry, coupled with the interdisciplinary characteristics of the work involved, there exists a pressing need to bridge the gaps in reliability-related research within the realm of semiconductor pilot-scale production lines. Such research is essential for ensuring future chip development efforts' continued precision and efficacy.

This exploratory study found that the personnel on the pilot line lacked a cohesive cognitive foundation, such as PIE should have a correct understanding of the operating environment and possible failures of each process and would overestimate or underestimate the risk of error. Typically, an experienced PE operator will attempt to solve problems independently and only report them if they cannot be resolved. However, this approach can lead to hidden risk factors that are always present. In addition, the unreasonable division of identity responsibilities may be a challenge that needs to be overcome in the current pilot line. PIE combines production line management with frequent communication but does not necessarily guarantee quality or improve performance (Marlow et al., 2018). It is possible that team familiarity could help mitigate the negative consequences of this issue, but it should not be considered a satisfactory solution.

Understandably, the pilot line, normally as a startup, is inexperienced in personnel organization or management, but placing too much trust in individual engineer's abilities may hinder the company's future development. For example, the management system may stagnate and fail to grow with the company due to a lack of well-structured training. Last but not least, there is still a knowledge gap in the research of semiconductor production lines for human reliability, which is ignored because of the high degree of automation in the industry. Nevertheless, the efficiency and yield of the R&D stage affect the innovation system architecture. This multidisciplinary knowledge requires attention to support the agenda that defines future research.

Appendix 1- Pilot Production Line Workflow Map

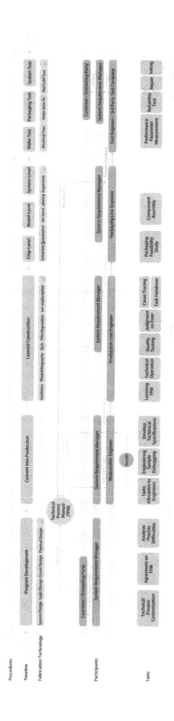

References

Baker, D.P., Day, R., Salas, E.: Teamwork as an essential component of high-reliability organizations. Health Serv. Res. **41**, 1576–1598 (2006). https://doi.org/10.1111/j.1475-6773.2006.00566.x

Barosz, P., Gołda, G., Kampa, A.: Efficiency analysis of manufacturing line with industrial robots and human operators. Appl. Sci. **10**, 2862 (2020). https://doi.org/10.3390/app10082862

Blackman, H.S., Gertman, D.I., Boring, R.L.: Human error quantification using performance shaping factors in the SPAR-H method. Proc. Hum. Fact. Ergon. Soc. Ann. Meet. **52**, 1733–1737 (2008). https://doi.org/10.1177/154193120805202109

Braun, V., Clarke, V.: Using thematic analysis in psychology. Qual. Res. Psychol. **3**, 77–101 (2006). https://doi.org/10.1191/1478088706qp063oa

Bubb, H.: Human reliability: A key to improved quality in manufacturing. Hum. Fact. Ergon. Manuf. Serv. Ind. **15**, 353–368 (2005). https://doi.org/10.1002/hfm.20032

Chang, C.-Y., Li, C., Chang, J.-W., Jeng, M.: An unsupervised neural network approach for automatic semiconductor wafer defect inspection. Expert Syst. Appl. **36**, 950–958 (2009). https://doi.org/10.1016/j.eswa.2007.10.033

Chen, D., Zhu, M., Qiao, Y., Wang, J., Zhang, X.: An ergonomic design method of manned cabin driven by human operation performance. Adv. Des. Res. **1**, 12–20 (2023). https://doi.org/10.1016/j.ijadr.2023.05.001

Ekanem, N.J., Mosleh, A., Shen, S.-H.: Phoenix – a model-based human reliability analysis methodology: qualitative analysis procedure. Reliab. Eng. Syst. Saf. **145**, 301–315 (2016). https://doi.org/10.1016/j.ress.2015.07.009

Eng, T.C., Sani, A.M., Yu, P.K.: Methods to achieve zero human error in semiconductors manufacturing. In: 2006 8th Electronics Packaging Technology Conference. Presented at the 2006 8th Electronics Packaging Technology Conference, pp. 678–683 (2006). https://doi.org/10.1109/EPTC.2006.342795

Flin, R., O'Connor, P., Mearns, K.: Crew resource management: improving team work in high reliability industries. Team Perform. Manage. Int. J. **8**, 68–78 (2002). https://doi.org/10.1108/13527590210433366

Givi, Z.S., Jaber, M.Y., Neumann, W.P.: Modelling worker reliability with learning and fatigue. Appl. Math. Model. **39**, 5186–5199 (2015). https://doi.org/10.1016/j.apm.2015.03.038

Givi, Z.S., Jaber, M.Y., Neumann, W.P.: Production planning in DRC systems considering worker performance. Comput. Ind. Eng. **87**, 317–327 (2015). https://doi.org/10.1016/j.cie.2015.05.005

Hollnagel, E.: Cognitive Reliability and Error Analysis Method (CREAM). Elsevier (1998)

Hsu, C.-Y.: Clustering ensemble for identifying defective wafer bin map in semiconductor manufacturing. Math. Probl. Eng. **2015**, e707358 (2015). https://doi.org/10.1155/2015/707358

Jang, I., Kim, A.R., Jung, W., Seong, P.H.: An empirical study on the human error recovery failure probability when using soft controls in NPP advanced MCRs. Ann. Nucl. Energy **73**, 373–381 (2014). https://doi.org/10.1016/j.anucene.2014.07.004

Kanarik, K.J., et al.: Human–machine collaboration for improving semiconductor process development. Nature **616**, 707–711 (2023). https://doi.org/10.1038/s41586-023-05773-7

Khawaja, M.A., Chen, F., Marcus, N.: Analysis of collaborative communication for linguistic cues of cognitive load. Hum. Factors **54**, 518–529 (2012). https://doi.org/10.1177/0018720811431258

Kim, M.-H., Kim, H., Paek, D.: The health impacts of semiconductor production: an epidemiologic review. Int. J. Occup. Environ. Health **20**, 95–114 (2014). https://doi.org/10.1179/2049396713Y.0000000050

Lai, J.Y., Ngu, L.H.: The production cost analysis of oil palm waste activated carbon: a pilot-scale evaluation. Greenhouse Gas. Sci. Technol. **10**, 999–1026 (2020). https://doi.org/10.1002/ghg.2020

Leather, P., Beale, D., Sullivan, L.: Noise, psychosocial stress and their interaction in the workplace. J. Environ. Psychol. Restorative Environ. **23**, 213–222 (2003). https://doi.org/10.1016/S0272-4944(02)00082-8

Li, H., Huang, H.-Z., Yin, Y., Zhang, K., Huang, P.: Product quality evaluation method based on product gene theory. J. Shanghai Jiaotong Univ. (Sci.) **23**, 438 (2018). https://doi.org/10.1007/s12204-018-1946-5

Lusk, S.L., Hagerty, B.M., Gillespie, B., Caruso, C.C.: Chronic effects of workplace noise on blood pressure and heart rate. Arch. Environ. Health Int. J. **57**, 273–281 (2002). https://doi.org/10.1080/00039890209601410

Marlow, S.L., Lacerenza, C.N., Paoletti, J., Burke, C.S., Salas, E.: Does team communication represent a one-size-fits-all approach?: a meta-analysis of team communication and performance. Organ. Behav. Hum. Decis. Process. **144**, 145–170 (2018). https://doi.org/10.1016/j.obhdp.2017.08.001

Neumann, W.P., Dul, J.: human factors: spanning the gap between OM & HRM. ERIM Report Series Research in Management, ERIM Report Series Research in Management (2010)

Oh, J.H., Eo, Y.J., Yang, S.J., Do, Y.R.: High-color-quality multipackage phosphor-converted LEDs for yellow photolithography room lamp. IEEE Photonics J. **7**, 1–8 (2015). https://doi.org/10.1109/JPHOT.2015.2415674

O'Leary, J., Sawlani, K., Mesbah, A.: Deep learning for classification of the chemical composition of particle defects on semiconductor wafers. IEEE Trans. Semicond. Manuf. **33**, 72–85 (2020). https://doi.org/10.1109/TSM.2019.2963656

Ovsyannikova, E., Kruse, A., Becker, G.C.: Feedstock-dependent phosphate recovery in a pilot-scale hydrothermal liquefaction bio-crude production. Energies **13**, 379 (2020). https://doi.org/10.3390/en13020379

Pan, L., et al.: Pilot-scale production of exopolysaccharide from Leuconostoc pseudomesenteroides XG5 and its application in set yogurt. J. Dairy Sci. **105**, 1072–1083 (2022). https://doi.org/10.3168/jds.2021-20997

Prahalad, C.K.: The blinders of dominant logic. Long Range Plan. **37**, 171–179 (2004). https://doi.org/10.1016/j.lrp.2004.01.010

Rasmussen, M., Standal, M.I., Laumann, K.: Task complexity as a performance shaping factor: a review and recommendations in standardized plant analysis risk-human reliability analysis (SPAR-H) adaption. Saf. Sci. **76**, 228–238 (2015). https://doi.org/10.1016/j.ssci.2015.03.005

San Pedro, A., González-López, C.V., Acién, F.G., Molina-Grima, E.: Outdoor pilot-scale production of nannochloropsis gaditana: influence of culture parameters and lipid production rates in tubular photobioreactors. Biores. Technol. **169**, 667–676 (2014). https://doi.org/10.1016/j.biortech.2014.07.052

Sgarbossa, F., Grosse, E.H., Neumann, W.P., Battini, D., Glock, C.H.: Human factors in production and logistics systems of the future. Annu. Rev. Control. **49**, 295–305 (2020). https://doi.org/10.1016/j.arcontrol.2020.04.007

Sycara, K., Sukthankar, G.: Literature Review of Teamwork Models (2006)

Ward, J.K., Comer, U., Stone, S.: On qualifying qualitative research: emerging perspectives and the "deer" (descriptive, exploratory, evolutionary, repeat) paradigm. Interchange **49**, 133–146 (2018). https://doi.org/10.1007/s10780-018-9313-x

Wickens, C.D.: Engineering Psychology and Human Performance, 2nd edn. HarperCollins Publishers, New York (1992)

Williams, J.: Heart—a proposed method for achieving high reliability in process operation by means of human factors engineering technology. Safety Reliab. **35**, 5–25 (2015). https://doi.org/10.1080/09617353.2015.11691046

Wurhofer, D., Buchner, R., Tscheligi, M.: Research in the semiconductor factory: insights into experiences and contextual influences. In: 2014 7th International Conference on Human System

Interactions (HSI). Presented at the 2014 7th International Conference on Human System Interactions (HSI), pp. 129–134 (2014). https://doi.org/10.1109/HSI.2014.6860461

Yung, M., Kolus, A., Wells, R., Neumann, W.P.: Examining the fatigue-quality relationship in manufacturing. Appl. Ergon. **82**, 102919 (2020). https://doi.org/10.1016/j.apergo.2019.102919

A Non-contact Vital Signs Retrieving Method for Aviation Safety Personnel Using TVF-EMD

Xiaoguang Lu, Xiao Ma, Chenhao Suo, and Zhe Zhang[(✉)]

College of Electronic Information and Automation, Civil Aviation University of China,
Tianjin 300300, China
cauc_2012@163.com

Abstract. Conducting real-time monitoring of aviation safety personnel's vital signs during their duty, like respiration and heart rate, is essential for ensuring the safety of civil aviation operations, especially in promptly detecting fatigue-related anomalies. Traditional contact or wearable measurement systems are inevitably inconvenient and even bring new operational hazards when applied in working scenarios. The Linear Frequency Modulated Continuous Wave Radar (FMCW) provides a non-contact vital signal monitoring means for pilots and air traffic controllers in their working environments. The Empirical Mode Decomposition (EMD) method is a typical time domain solution to retrieve time-varying vital sign signals. However, this method is subjected to the modal aliasing effect due to the respiration rate and heartbeat rate being close in frequency. The Time-Varying Filtered Empirical Mode Decomposition (TVF-EMD) method is then introduced to address this issue, which enhances signal separation performance by adaptively adjusting the local cutoff frequency of the signal. This method successfully resolves the issue of modal aliasing in retrieving respiration and heartbeat signals from mm-wave radar echoes. In addition, heartbeat waveforms are effectively reconstructed using the Instantaneous Mode Functions (IMFs) decomposed by TVF-EMD. This enables precise estimation of Inter-Beat Interval (IBI) and various Heart Rate Variability (HRV) metrics. Simulations and experiment results validate the effectiveness of the TVF-EMD method in accurately extracting vital sign information from millimeter-wave radar measurement signals.

Keywords: Non-contact measurement · Millimeter wave radar · Vital sign monitoring · Time-varying filter empirical mode decomposition · Heart rate variability

1 Introduction

In the new era of intelligent air traffic management systems, human-machine integration is becoming progressively more significant, for the vital signs monitoring of civil aviation personnel on duty is a critical component in ensuring aviation safety. By monitoring the vital signs, including respiratory and heartbeat rates, abnormal physical conditions that may affect the performance of pilots and air traffic controllers can be detected promptly. This immediate physiological status feedback helps to ensure the operational personnel

© The Author(s), under exclusive license to Springer Nature Switzerland AG 2024
D. Harris and W.-C. Li (Eds.): HCII 2024, LNAI 14693, pp. 243–258, 2024.
https://doi.org/10.1007/978-3-031-60731-8_17

maintain their best condition in a high-pressure and high-load work environment, thereby enhancing the safety of the entire civil aviation operation.

Compared to traditional contact or wearable methods for measuring respiration and heartbeat, millimeter-wave FMCW radar for non-contact vital signs detection is more suitable for practical working environments [1-6]. This technology enhances monitoring convenience for operational personnel, making continuous monitoring more feasible in actual operations. For analyzing radar signals, the Empirical Mode Decomposition (EMD) method, proposed by Norden E. Huang and others [7] in 1998, is an essential one conducted in the time domain of nonlinear and non-stationary signals. It has also been applied to processing various other signals, including biomedical ones. Approaches like EMD have been employed by researchers such as Wanling Hou [8], who reconstructed respiratory and heartbeat signals by analyzing the energy spectrum characteristics of each Intrinsic Mode Function (IMF) in the time domain. Zhu and others [9] have adaptively decomposed and reconstructed vital signs signals using the PE-EMD algorithm and acquired breathing and heart rate data through ultra-wideband radar. However, in the experiments, the EMD algorithm still has issues such as modal aliasing and difficulty in determining the number of iterations for decomposition, which prevents it from decomposing and obtaining high-accuracy breathing and heart rate signals. Jinzhao Lin and others [10] used Ensemble Empirical Mode Decomposition (EEMD) to extract baseline drift signals from noisy electrocardiographic signals, reconstructing clean electrocardiographic signals through effective Intrinsic Mode Functions. Hu et al. [11] combined Continuous Wavelet Transform (CWT) with EMD to separate and extract cardiorespiratory signals. However, this method faces the modal aliasing effect. To address this issue, Zheng et al. [12] proposed Partially Ensemble Empirical Mode Decomposition (PEEMD), partially resolving the problem in EMD but introducing new noise components, potentially causing amplitude changes and reconstruction errors. In 2017, Li H [13] proposed the Time-Varying Filter Empirical Mode Decomposition algorithm (TVF-EMD), an adaptive algorithm that improves the modal aliasing issue in EMD. Yang Z and others [14] applied the TVF-EMD algorithm to Ultra-wide Band (UWB) radar signal processing. Furthermore, the modal functions decomposed using the TVF-EMD method can effectively reconstruct the time-domain waveform of heartbeats. This enables the accurate estimation of the Interbeat Interval (IBI) and Heart Rate Variability (HRV).

This paper uses the TVF-EMD method to retrieve the vital signals from FMCW millimeter-wave radar echoes. Using the IMF components derived from the TVF-EMD method, the time-domain signals corresponding to respiration and heartbeat were reconstructed, and through the reconstructed heartbeat signals, related HRV indicators were estimated. This paper also involves numerical simulation for analyzing differences between the TVF-EMD and EMD methods in terms of modal aliasing and signal decomposition performance. Moreover, through measurements of actual human targets, we obtained respiratory and heartbeat rates using the TVF-EMD method. Experiment results show that the rates obtained are consistent with the measurements of contact detection instruments. We extracted IBI data from the reconstructed original heartbeat signals and calculated HRV parameters. Simulation and experiment results demonstrate that the TVF-EMD method can effectively overcome the modal aliasing issues in using the EMD method to process radar echoes. The extracted IMF signals can accurately reconstruct the time-domain signals corresponding to the heartbeat, providing accurate time-domain information for estimating IBI and analyzing HRV.

2 Millimeter-Wave Radar for Heartbeat Detection

2.1 Radar Echo Signal Model

FMCW radar transmits signal $X_T(t)$ through the transmitting antenna [15] is:

$$X_T(t) = A_T \cos(2\pi f_c t + \pi k t^2 + \varphi(t)) \tag{1}$$

where, A_T represents the amplitude of the transmitted signal, $\varphi(t)$ is the phase noise, f_c indicates the initial frequency of the linear frequency modulation, $k = \frac{B}{T_c}$ is the linear frequency modulation slope, B is the bandwidth of the transmitted signal, and T_c is the duration of a single chirp waveform.

The reflected signal $X_R(t)$ received by the radar is:

$$X_R(t) = A_R \cos[2\pi f_c(t - t_d) + \pi \frac{B}{T_c}(t - t_d)^2 + \varphi(t - t_d)] \tag{2}$$

where, A_R represents the amplitude of the received signal, and $t_d = \frac{2R(t)}{c}$ is the time delay between the transmitted and received signals, where c is the speed of light, and $R(t)$ is the radial distance between the radar and the human body.

The received echo is mixed coherently with the transmitted signal, and after I/Q demodulation, the IF signal is obtained:

$$y(t) = A_R e^{j\left(2\pi\left[\frac{B}{T_c}t_d\right]t + 2\pi f_c t_d + \pi \frac{B}{T_c}t_d^2 + \Delta\varphi(t)\right)} \tag{3}$$

The frequency of the intermediate frequency signal obtained from the mixing process is denoted as f_b, and the phase change resulting from the time delay caused by the distance is denoted as $\varphi_b(t)$:

$$\varphi_b(t) = 2\pi f_c t_d + \pi \frac{B}{T_c}t_d^2 \tag{4}$$

$\Delta\varphi(t) = \varphi(t - t_d)$ represents the residual noise in the signal, which can be considered negligible when the distance is short. Additionally, some parts of equation $\pi \frac{B}{T_c}t_d^2$ are very small in practical applications, so they can also be omitted in $\varphi_b(t)$.

The obtained radar echo signal is further simplified:

$$y(t) = A_A e^{j\left(4\pi \frac{BR_0}{cT_c}t + 4\pi \frac{f_c}{c}R_0 + \left(\frac{2B}{cT_c} + \frac{4f_c}{c}\right)x(t) + \Delta\varphi(t)\right)} \tag{5}$$

$$f_b = \frac{2BR_0}{cT_c} \tag{6}$$

where, the distance function $R(t) = R_0 + x(t)$, $x(t)$ is the distance corresponding to chest wall of the target. The frequency $(B/T_c)t \ll f_c$ within the entire period of the duration, thus the $(2B/cT_c)x(t)$ component can be considered negligible in $y(t)$.

Therefore, the intermediate frequency signal can be simplified:

$$y(t) = A_R e^{j\left(2\pi f_b t + \frac{4\pi}{\lambda}(R_0 + x(t)) + \Delta\varphi(t)\right)} \tag{7}$$

By performing a Fourier transform on the echo signal obtained from the equation, the phase value of the signal can be determined. The FMCW radar measures the phase changes of the echo signal within a target distance unit to represent very minor vibrations. When the chest displacement caused by breathing and heartbeat is ΔR, and the phase difference of the intermediate frequency signal is $\Delta\varphi_b$, the relationship between the minute changes in distance and phase is expressed as follows:

$$\Delta\varphi_b = \frac{4\pi f_c}{c}\Delta R \tag{8}$$

Therefore, the displacement caused by breathing and heartbeat can be estimated from this phase difference, which is used to characterize the respiratory and heartbeat signals of the human body [17].

2.2   Radar Signal Preprocessing

Figure 1 shows the five main steps of radar signal preprocessing: Range FFT, Phase Extraction, Phase Unwrapping, and Phase Differencing. Firstly, a spectrogram is generated and the target distance is determined by performing a range FFT on M sweep signals. Then, phase information is extracted using arctan demodulation, reflecting the micro-motions of the target due to breathing and heartbeats. Finally, time-varying phase information is obtained by differentiating the phases of adjacent sweep signals to remove constant phase offsets. To resolve heartbeat signals from the phase difference, frequency domain or time domain methods can be used. The obtained phase difference signal is shown in Fig. 2.

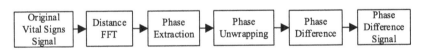

Fig. 1. Signal preprocessing flowchart

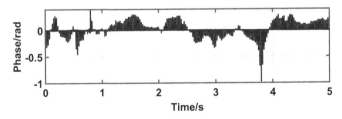

Fig. 2. The phase difference of different chirps

3   Estimation of IBI Based Using TVF-EMD Method

3.1   The EMD Method

The EMD method adaptively decomposes the radar echo signal into several IMF components to achieve adaptive separation of respiratory and heartbeat signals. IMF components can reflect the frequency components present in the signal. In the EMD method, IMF components need to satisfy the following conditions:

1. The number of extrema and zero-crossings in the signal must differ by no more than one;
2. The average of the upper and lower envelope of the signal is zero.

The EMD method process is illustrated in Fig. 3.

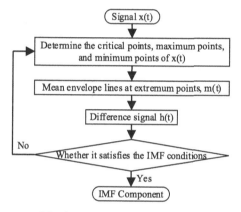

Fig. 3. EMD algorithm flowchart

The n IMF components obtained from the EMD decomposition must meet the following criteria:

$$x(t) = \sum_{i=1}^{n} IMF_i(t) + r_n(t) \tag{9}$$

where $r_n(t)$ represents the residual component obtained after the n-th decomposition. The EMD decomposition concludes when this component becomes a monotonic function.

EMD can decompose relatively complex signals into IMF signal components with a single frequency component, and each component has a specific physical meaning [17]. However, in practical decomposition, EMD is highly sensitive to noise. When the signal is disturbed by noise, it can affect the selection of extreme points, leading to the occurrence of different frequency components in the same IMF or the presence of the same frequency component in different IMFs. This phenomenon is known as modal aliasing, as illustrated in Fig. 4. Figure 4 (a) shows the IMF components obtained from EMD decomposition and (b) shows the corresponding spectrum, revealing the presence of two frequency components at 0.3 Hz and 1.2 Hz. Modal aliasing causes the IMF components obtained from EMD decomposition to lose specific physical meanings.

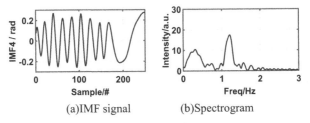

(a)IMF signal   (b)Spectrogram

Fig. 4. Modal aliasing in EMD decomposition

3.2 TVF-EMD Method

To address the issue of modal aliasing in the EMD method, this study employs the TVF-EMD method to enhance the temporal decomposition performance of the heartbeat signal. The TVF-EMD method utilizes instantaneous amplitude and frequency information to design local cutoff frequencies $\varphi'_{bis}(t)$ adaptively, employing non-uniform B-spline approximation as a time-varying filter. The cutoff frequencies are re-ordered during iterations to resolve the modal aliasing problem. Therefore, TVF-EMD is suitable for analyzing linear and non-stationary signals, contributing to improved frequency separation performance. The decomposition process of TVF-EMD is illustrated in Fig. 5.

The decomposition process of the TVF-EMD method can be roughly divided into three steps: estimating the local cut-off frequency $\varphi'_{bis}(t)$, constructing a time-varying filter to obtain the local mean function $m(t)$, and calculating the criterion value $\theta(t)$ to determine if the residual signal meets the stopping criteria.

The instantaneous amplitude $A(t)$ and instantaneous frequency $\varphi'(t)$ of the signal $x(t)$ can be obtained through the Hilbert transform:

$$R(t) = R_0 + r_1 \sin(2\pi f_1 t) + r_2 \sin(2\pi f_2 t + \varphi) \tag{10}$$

$$A(t) = \sqrt{x(t)^2 + \hat{x}(t)^2} \tag{11}$$

$$\varphi'(t) = d(\arctan[\hat{x}(t)/x(t)])/dt \tag{12}$$

The local minimum t_{min} and maximum t_{max} of $A(t)$ are identified.

The variable $z(t)$ can be considered as the sum of two components of $z(t) = a_1(t)e^{j\varphi_1(t)} + a_2(t)e^{j\varphi_2(t)}$, with $\beta_1(t)$ and $\beta_2(t)$ representing the degrees of change in the instantaneous amplitude, therefore:

$$\begin{aligned} \beta_1(t) &= |a_1(t) - a_2(t)| \\ \beta_2(t) &= a_1(t) + a_2(t) \end{aligned} \tag{13}$$

For $A(\{t_{min}\})$ and $A(\{t_{max}\})$, interpolation operations are carried out to obtain:

$$\begin{aligned} a_1(t) &= [\beta_1(t) + \beta_2(t)]/2 \\ a_2(t) &= [\beta_2(t) - \beta_1(t)]/2 \end{aligned} \tag{14}$$

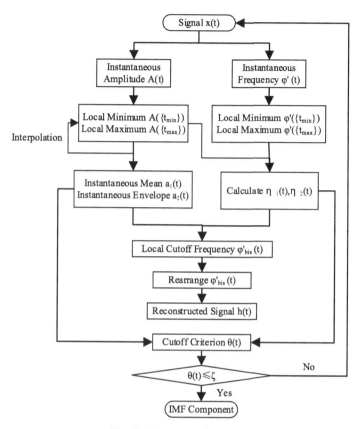

Fig. 5. TVF-EMD flowchart

Using the same interpolation algorithm, calculate $\varphi'(\{t_{min}\})$ and $\varphi'(\{t_{max}\})$:

$$
\begin{aligned}
\varphi'(\{t_{min}\}) &= \frac{\eta_1(t)}{2a_1^2(t) - 2a_1(t)a_2(t)} + \frac{\eta_2(t)}{2a_1^2(t) + 2a_1(t)a_2(t)} \\
\varphi'(\{t_{max}\}) &= \frac{\eta_1(t)}{2a_2^2(t) - 2a_1(t)a_2(t)} + \frac{\eta_2(t)}{2a_2^2(t) + 2a_1(t)a_2(t)}
\end{aligned}
\tag{15}
$$

To calculate the local cutoff frequency, use:

$$
\varphi'_{bis}(t) = \frac{\varphi'(\{t_{min}\}) + \varphi'(\{t_{max}\})}{2} = \frac{\eta_2(t) - \eta_1(t)}{4a_1(t)a_2(t)}
\tag{16}
$$

To address the intermittency issue, adjust the cutoff frequency $\varphi'_{bis}(t)$, find the local maximum values of the signal $x(t)$, denoted as $u_i (i = 1, 2, 3...)$. If u_i satisfies Eq. 17, it is denoted as $e_j = u_i (j = 1, 2, 3...)$.

$$
\frac{\max(\varphi'_{bis}(u_i : u_{i+1})) - \min(\varphi'_{bis}(u_i : u_{i+1}))}{\min(\varphi'_{bis}(u_i : u_{i+1}))} > \rho
\tag{17}
$$

If $\varphi'_{bis}(u_{i+1}) - \varphi'_{bis}(u_i) > 0$, e_j is identified as an ascending edge, otherwise it is a descending edge. For each e_j, determine if it is on an ascending edge then $\varphi'_{bis}(e_{j-1} : e_j)$ is the base; if it is on a descending edge then $\varphi'_{bis}(e_j : e_{j+1})$ is the base, and the rest part $\varphi'_{bis}(t)$ is identified as the peak. Interpolation is performed between two peak values to obtain the final cutoff frequency $\varphi'_{bis}(t)$.

Through $h(t) = \cos[\int \varphi'_{bis}(t)dt]$, calculate $h(t)$, take the extremum points of $h(t)$, and apply B-spline approximation to finally obtain the node $m(t)$.

Calculate the stopping criterion according to the formula. If $\theta(t) \leq \xi$ meets the parameter $\xi = 0.05$ set in this experiment, then $x(t)$ is considered as a local narrow band. If not satisfied, reset $x(t) = x(t) - m(t)$ and repeat the above steps.

$$\varphi_{avg}(t) = \frac{a_1^2(t)\varphi_1'^2(t) + a_2^2(t)\varphi_2'^2(t)}{a_1^2(t) + a_2^2(t)} \qquad (18)$$

$$B_{Loughlin}(t) = \sqrt{\frac{a_1'^2(t) + a_2'^2(t)}{a_1^2(t) + a_2^2(t)} + \frac{a_1^2(t)a_2^2(t)(\varphi_1'^2(t) - \varphi_2'^2(t))^2}{(a_1^2(t) + a_2^2(t))^2}} \qquad (19)$$

$$\theta(t) = \frac{B_{Loughlin}(t)}{\varphi_{avg}(t)} \qquad (20)$$

3.3 Simulation Signal Decomposition and Performance Analysis

To assess the signal decomposition performance of the EMD and TVF-EMD methods, a fixed-frequency sinusoidal signal is employed to simulate the displacement caused by respiration and heartbeat [18]. When the target under measurement is relatively stationary with the radar, the distance $R(t)$ between them satisfies:

$$R(t) = R_0 + r_1 \sin(2\pi f_1 t) + r_2 \sin(2\pi f_2 t + \varphi) \qquad (21)$$

where R_0 represents the distance between the radar and the target, f_1 denotes the frequency of the respiratory signal, f_2 represents the frequency of the heartbeat signal, r_1 represents the displacement amplitude caused by heartbeat, r_2 represents the displacement amplitude caused by respiration, and φ is the initial phase difference between the two.

When $R_0 = 0.6$ m, $f_1 = 0.3$ Hz, $f_2 = 1.2$ Hz, $r_1 = 1$ mm, $r_2 = 0.22$ mm, $\varphi = 0$ is chosen, under the condition of Gaussian white noise with SNR $= 15$ dB, the phase difference

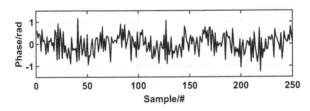

Fig. 6. Phase difference time-domain signal representing vital signs

representing vital signs in the radar echo is $\Delta\varphi_b = \frac{4\pi f_c}{c}\Delta R$, and the time-domain signal is shown in Fig. 6.

The signal is temporally decomposed using both the EMD and TVF-EMD algorithms to analyze their respective performances.

The IMFs obtained from the EMD algorithm within the frequency range of 0.3 Hz to 1.2 Hz and the corresponding spectrum are shown in Fig. 7.

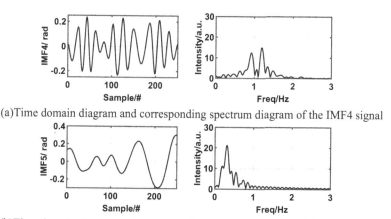

(a)Time domain diagram and corresponding spectrum diagram of the IMF4 signal

(b)Time domain diagram and corresponding spectrum diagram of the IMF5 signal

Fig. 7. The vital sign signals decomposed using the EMD method

After processing with the EMD method, two key IMF signals were obtained, namely IMF4 and IMF5, with their peak frequencies determined to be 1.2 Hz and 0.312 Hz, respectively. The time-domain analysis of these two functions indicates significant differences from standard single-frequency sinusoidal signals. This difference is primarily manifested in the waveform of the signal, showing more complex and variable characteristics than a single-frequency sinusoid. In the frequency domain observation, it can be seen that IMF4 is not a strict single-frequency signal. It displays two main frequency peaks at 0.924 Hz and 1.2 Hz, a phenomenon that points directly to a key issue: significant modal aliasing occurs in the EMD process, which severely affects the quality of signal resolution.

The IMFs obtained from the TVF-EMD algorithm within the frequency range of 0.3 Hz to 1.2 Hz and the corresponding spectrum are shown in Fig. 8.

Using the TVF-EMD method, the peak frequencies of IMF8 and IMF9 are 1.2 Hz and 0.3 Hz, respectively, matching the simulation signal parameters. From the time domain perspective, IMF8 and IMF9 appear almost as standard single-frequency sine signals. This indicates that the TVF-EMD method can effectively separate respiratory and heartbeat signals. Under the same signal-to-noise ratio conditions, there is no modal aliasing in the TVF-EMD decomposition results, and its performance is superior to the EMD method.

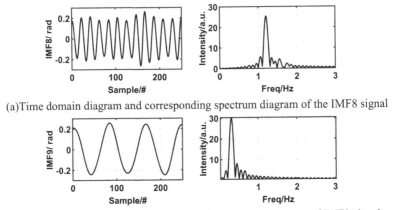

(a)Time domain diagram and corresponding spectrum diagram of the IMF8 signal

(b)Time domain diagram and corresponding spectrum diagram of IMF9 signal

Fig. 8. The vital sign signals decomposed using the TVF-EMD algorithm

4   Experiment Results and Analysis

4.1   Experiment Setup

The experiment utilized the TI's IWR6843 radar evaluation board, and data acquisition was performed using the DCA1000 acquisition board. For monitoring air traffic controllers' and pilots' vital signs in working scenarios, the targets remain in a relatively fixed position and quasi-static. Therefore, in the experiment, the experimental subjects were seated approximately 0.6 m in front of the radar, with their chests aligned horizontally, trying to keep steady breathing. Subjects simultaneously wore contact wristbands to collect average heartbeat and respiratory rate values as reference values during experiments. The radar operated at a carrier frequency of 60 GHz, a frequency modulation slope of 70 MHz/μs, a sampling time of 5 s, a linear frequency modulation pulse (chirp) signal period of 56 μs, with each frame comprising 16 chirps and a frame period of 25 ms. A single chirp comprised 200 sampling points, and the ADC sampling rate was

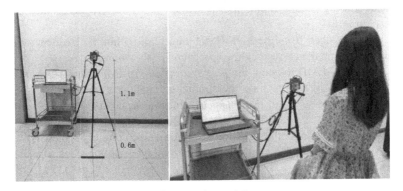

Fig. 9. Experimental Setup

4 MHz. The experiments were conducted when the subjects perceived themselves as highly alert and mentally clear. The experimental setup is illustrated in Fig. 9.

After echo preprocessing, the TVF-EMD method is employed to separate the time-domain signals of respiration and heartbeat. By reconstructing the time-domain signal of the heartbeat, it can be utilized to assess the HRV index. Figure 10 illustrates the process of signal separation and vital signs detection.

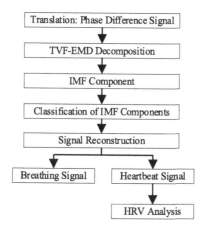

Fig. 10. Signal separation and vital sign detection

4.2 Experimental Signal Separation Results

The TVF-EMD algorithm is employed to decompose the temporal information of respiration and heartbeat from the phase difference signal, as shown in Fig. 11.

The decomposition yields 22 IMF signal components, with IMF20, IMF21 and IMF22 signal components falling within the frequency range of both respiratory and heartbeat signals with the upper-frequency limit of 2 Hz. Figure 12 (a) shows that IMF20 has a peak frequency of 1.176 Hz, (b) shows that IMF21 has a peak frequency of 0.948 Hz, and (c) shows that IMF22 has a peak frequency of 0.192 Hz. The IMF22 corresponds to the respiratory signal (12 Cycles/min), and IMF20 corresponds to the heartbeat signal (71 BPM). The frequency domain plots for these IMF signal components are shown in Fig. 12.

The contact wristband measured the corresponding average heart rate of 70 BPM and respiratory rate of 12 breaths per minute. The separation results for different experimental subjects are shown in Table 1.

It can be seen that the TVF-EMD separation results are consistent with the measurements from the contact wristband.

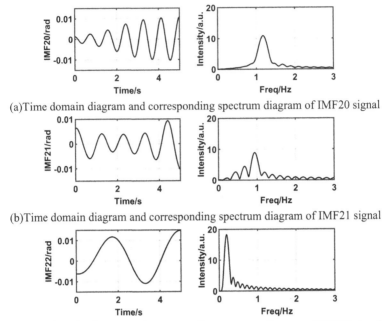

(a)Time domain diagram and corresponding spectrum diagram of IMF20 signal

(b)Time domain diagram and corresponding spectrum diagram of IMF21 signal

(c)Time domain diagram and corresponding spectrum diagram of IMF22 signal

Fig. 11. Signal decomposition using TVF-EMD algorithm

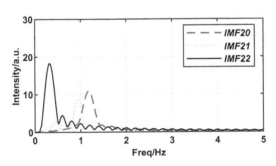

Fig. 12. IMF component frequency

4.3 Signal Reconstruction

The TVF-EMD method extracts a series of IMF components from the phase difference signal. Based on the typical frequency range of resting state breathing and heartbeat signals, components below 2 Hz were categorized. Specifically, these IMF components were divided into three categories: the first category of IMF components with frequencies between 0.1 and 0.5 Hz, representing breathing signals; the second category with frequencies between 0.8 and 2 Hz, representing heartbeat signals; and the third category consisting of redundant IMF components, including those with frequencies above 2 Hz and DC components.

Table 1. Measured respiratory and heartbeat signals.

Target ID	Heart rate detected from radar/BPM	Heart rate detected by the band/BPM	Respiration rate detected by radar Cycles/min	Respiration rate detected by band Cycles/min
man #1	72	75	13	13
man #2	84	82	19	20
woman #1	93	90	15	16
woman #2	65	69	17	17

Different strategies were adopted in determining the number of IMF components. If the number of components is less than or equal to 2, then all IMF components will be used for signal reconstruction. If the number of IMF components exceeds 2, then two IMF components whose combined energy accounts for more than 70% are selected for signal reconstruction.

Taking the separation results shown in Fig. 12 as an example, there is one IMF signal component within the 0.1 to 0.5 Hz range, so this component is directly used for reconstructing the breathing signal. In the 0.8 to 2 Hz range, there are two IMF signal components, specifically the ones with frequencies of 1.176 Hz and 0.948 Hz (corresponding to IMF20 and IMF21 in Fig. 12). These two components are selected for reconstructing the heartbeat signal. The reconstructed heartbeat signal is displayed in Fig. 13. Through this method, breathing and heartbeat signals that are closer to the real physiological state can be more accurately reconstructed, providing a reliable basis for further analysis of heart rate variability.

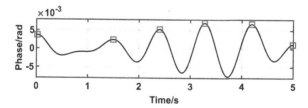

Fig. 13. Reconstructed heartbeat signal

The peaks in the reconstructed heartbeat signal waveform are identified as R-peaks of the QRS waveform. Subsequent IBI calculations and HRV estimations will utilize these R-wave peaks.

4.4 HRV Estimation

Based on the R-wave peak positions in Fig. 13, the temporal intervals between adjacent peaks, known as Inter-Beat Intervals, are calculated. HRV indicators are then estimated from these IBIs. Typical HRV estimations include calculating the MEAN value, SDNN value, and rMSSD value [19]. MEAN: The average value of adjacent R-R intervals throughout the entire recording, reflecting the average level of heart rate variability.

$$MEAN = \sum_{i=1}^{N} \frac{RR_i}{N} \tag{22}$$

SDNN: The standard deviation of R-R intervals, reflecting the variability of all cyclic variables within the recorded time period.

$$SDNN = \sqrt{\frac{\sum_{i=1}^{N} (RR_i - \overline{RR})^2}{N}} \tag{23}$$

rMSSD: The root mean square of the differences between adjacent R-R intervals, used to calculate the variability of successive heartbeats and reflect the rapid changes in HRV.

$$rMSSD = \sqrt{\frac{\sum_{i=1}^{N} (RR_i - RR_{i-1})^2}{N}} \tag{24}$$

where N is the total number of normal heartbeats; RR_i is the i-th R-R interval; $\overline{RR}$ is the average of R-R intervals for N heartbeats.

The following values are obtained upon performing time-domain analysis on the reconstructed heartbeat signal: MEAN = 994.6 ms, SDNN = 102.5 ms, rMSSD = 29.5 ms. The HRV of different experimental subjects is shown in Table 2. The results accurately reconstruct the original heartbeat signal, and the estimated HRV parameters align with the subjective fatigue perception of the individuals under test.

Table 2. Measured heartbeat signal HRV.

Target ID	MEAN/ms	SDNN/ms	rMSSD/ms
man #1	883.4	88.9	14.1
man #2	1098.1	111.7	32.1
woman #1	983.8	98.7	12.2
woman #2	1123.1	114.2	35.1

5 Conclusion

In this paper, the TVF-EMD method is used to extract the vital signs signals encoded in echoes of FMCW millimeter-wave radar. To improve the separation performance, B-spline approximation is adopted as a time-varying filter in the TVF-EMD method, effectively solving the problem of modal aliasing. This allows for the accurate separation of breathing and heartbeat signals. The various IMF components are categorized and reconstructed during the signal decomposition process, thereby obtaining the time-domain signals for breathing and heartbeat separately. Subsequently, an in-depth analysis of the reconstructed heartbeat time-domain signal is conducted, estimating the heartbeat frequency, IBI, and related HRV indicators. This research has significant practical implications for understanding the physiological state of civil aviation personnel and ensuring the safe operation of intelligent air traffic management systems.

Acknowledgments. This study was funded by Graduate Research Innovation Program of Civil Aviation University of China (grant number 2015/1455001024).

Disclosure of Interests. The authors have no competing interests to declare that are relevant to the content of this article.

References

1. Muñoz-Ferreras, J.M., Peng, Z., Gómez-García, R., et al.: Random body movement mitigation for FMCW-radar-based vital-sign monitoring. In: 2016 IEEE Topical Conference on Biomedical Wireless Technologies, Networks, and Sensing Systems (BioWireleSS), pp. 22–24. IEEE (2016)
2. Ernst, R., Nilsson, E., Viberg, P.A.: 60GHz vital sign radar using 3D-printed lens. IEEE Sens. 1–3 (2016)
3. Lee, H., Kim, B.H., Park, J.K., et al.: A resolution enhancement technique for remote monitoring of the vital signs of multiple subjects using a 24 GHz bandwidth-limited FMCW radar. IEEE Access **8**, 1240–1248 (2019)
4. Ren, W., Hou, K., Wang, G., Liu, Q., et al.: Multi-target respiration detection using FMCW MmWave radar. J. Signal Process **37**(9), 1581–1588 (2021)
5. Ernst, R., Nilsson, E., Viberg, P A.: 60GHz vital sign radar using 3D-printed lens. In: 2016 IEEE Sensors, pp. 1–3 (2016)
6. Lee, H., Kim, B.H., Park, J.K., et al.: A resolution enhancement technique for remote monitoring of the vital signs of multiple subjects using a 24 GHz bandwidth-limited FMCW radar. IEEE Access **8**, 1240–1248 (2019)
7. Huang, N.E., Shen, Z., Long, S.R., et al.: The empirical mode decomposition and the Hilbert spectrum for non-linear and non-stationary time series analysis. Proc. A **54**(1971), 903–995 (1998)
8. Hou, W.: Research on Detecting Driver's Fatigue Based on Millimeter Wave Radar. Dalian University of Technology (2020). (in Chinese)
9. Zhu, Z., Yang, D., Zhao, R., et al.: Vital sign signal extraction method based on permutation entropy and EMD algorithm for ultra-wideband radar. In: Proceedings of the 2019 3rd International Conference on Electronic Information Technology and Computer Engineering, Piscataway, NJ, pp. 1268–1273. IEEE (2019)
10. Lin, J., Liu, L., Li, G., et al.: A method for removing baseline drift in ECG signal based on improved EEMD. J. Data Acquis. Process. **33**(05), 880–890 (2018)
11. Hu, W., Zhao, Z., Wang, Y., et al.: Noncontact accurate measurement of cardiopulmonary activity using a compact quadrature dopple radar sensor. IEEE Trans. Biomed. Eng. **61**(3), 72535 (2014)

12. Zheng, J.D., Cheng, J.S., Yang, Y.: Partly ensemble empirical mode. Decomposition: An improved noise-assisted method for eliminating modal aliasing. Signal Process. **96**, 362–374 (2014)

13. Li, H., Li, Z., Mo, W.: A time varying filter approach for empirical mode decomposition. Signal Process. **138**, 146–158 (2017)

14. Yang, Z., Ma, C., Qi, Q., et al.: Applications of TVF-EMD in vital signal detection for UWB radar. J. Sens. (2021)

15. Chuang, H., Kuo, H., Chou, C.: A simple muscle-sphere model to approximate the radar cross section of the man heart for vital-signs detection range problem at different RF frequencies. In: 2019 IEEE MTT-S International Microwave Biomedical Conference (IMBioC), Nanjing, China, pp. 1–3. IEEE (2019)

16. Jing, C. H., Bai, Y.J., Zeng, K., et al.: Destiny detection method based on 77 ghz millimeterwave radar perception. Electron. Measur. Technol. **45**(22), 55–63(2022)

17. Jha, C., Kolekar, M.: Empirical mode decomposition and wavelet transform based ECG data compression scheme. IRBM **42**(1), 65–72 (2021)

18. Lee, H., Kim, B., Yook, J.: Path loss compensation method for multiple target vital sign detection with 24-GHz FMCW radar. In: 2018 IEEE Asia-Pacific Conference on Antennas and Propagation (APCAP), Auckland, pp. 100–101. IEEE (2018)

19. Fang, Y.Y., Zhang, Y.J.: Application of heart rate variability in acute coronary syndrome. Modern Pharmaceut. Hygiene **39**(6), 1011–1014 (2023)

Comparative Analysis of Remote Tower Controllers and Traditional Physical Tower Controllers Based on Human Ergonomics in China

Ting-Ting Lu[1], Zhixuan An[2(✉)], Haiming Shen[2], Yanqing Wang[2], and Wen-Chin Li[3]

[1] College of Air Traffic Management, Civil Aviation University of China, Tianjin 300300, China
[2] College of Safety Science and Engineering, Civil Aviation University of China, Tianjin 300300, China
14747405753@163.com
[3] Safety and Accident Investigation Centre, Cranfield University, Cranfield, Bedfordshire, UK

Abstract. The purpose of this paper is to establish the safety operation evaluation standard of remote towers and provide reference for the safety evaluation of remote tower technology. From the perspective of human ergonomics, this paper takes the controllers of Qiandaohu General Airport in Jiande, China as an example to compare and analyze whether there are significant differences between the controllers in workload, allocation of attention and situational awareness under two different control modes: remote tower and traditional physical tower. The results showed that Mean HR, SDNN, RMSSD and pNN50 had no significant difference in the time-domain indexes of heart rate variability and total mental load when the controllers of Jiande Airport carried out control and command tasks under two different control modes. There were significant differences in the number of fixation points, the average fixation duration, and the average saccade duration. In the SART scale of situational awareness, there were significant differences in the four dimensions of situational complexity, situational variability, mental arousal, and the quantity of acquired information, while there were no significant differences in the other dimensions and the total score. Therefore, the experimental results measured at Jiande Airport in China validate the validity of the research method used in this paper, and the safety evaluation criteria established provides a reference index measurement method for future studies on remote tower operation safety related to human ergonomics at other airports in China.

Keywords: Remote Tower · Traditional Physical Tower · Workload · Allocation of Attention · Situational Awareness

1 Introduction

As an emerging control technology, the remote tower is also known as the digital tower or virtual tower [1]. The basic idea of its operation is to transmit real-time images of the airport back to the screen of the remote tower control room using remote high-definition digital cameras, weather sensors, audio and video access equipment. Utilizing these visual and aural stimuli, the controllers are capable of controlling and commanding aircraft in real time. Therefore, the control environment and command mode are different from the traditional physical tower control, and the workload of the controller will change accordingly. When carrying out remote tower control command tasks, controllers need to obtain effective information from multiple electronic screens at the same time, and accurately issue control instructions; accurately listen to the crews' call content, synchronously record and fill in the process sheet. Therefore, controllers must have good allocation of attention and management capabilities. At the same time, the level of situational awareness of controllers will directly affect the safe and efficient operation of air traffic control. As remote tower technology has certain advantages in terms of cost effectiveness, operation efficiency and technical means [2], it has been continuously applied and developed around the world.

At present, the research on remote tower operation safety mainly focuses on the principle of human ergonomics. In 2020, Peter Kearney et al. [3] compared the workload of controllers between physical tower operations and multi-remote tower operations by using the human error template and NASA-TLX scale, with results showing that there were significant differences in controllers' psychological needs, time demands, effort and frustration. In 2022, Reuschling Fabian et al. [4] proposed to realize remote control in non-ATC airports with low income based on a simplified camera setup and virtual reality headset, which were discussed from three aspects: perceptual ease of use, virtual reality-induced motion sickness and operator acceptance. In 2023, Oliver Ohneiser et al. [5] studied a wireless telephone communication system for air traffic control based on assisted voice recognition in a multi-remote tower control environment to evaluate the workload, situational awareness, and availability of controllers. In China, Tong Fang et al. [6] proposed the fusion method of civil aviation ASTERIX data and airport video surveillance information in 2023 to solve the problem that remote tower video data is single and discrete, where real-time flight information of aircraft cannot be obtained. In the same year, Sun Rui et al. [7] sorted out the research status of remote tower at home and abroad, application scenarios, applicable conditions, key technologies, and problems to be solved, to finally put forward perfect countermeasures. In the same year, scholars Xuan Weijian and Xu Shuang [8] analyzed the future development of remote tower for airport control based on the study of remote tower technology.

To sum up, China's remote tower started relatively late. In addition, the research is relatively concentrated on technical system and operation, and the research on the remote tower based on human factors and ergonomics is relatively scarce. Comparative research on traditional physical tower and remote tower controllers are few to date. Therefore, this paper mainly studies and analyzes controllers with two different control modes based on workload, allocation of attention, and situational awareness from the perspective of human factors and ergonomics, so as to provide reference for the subsequent safety assessment of remote tower technology.

2 Method

2.1 Experimental Scenes and Participants

The experimental scene selected in this paper is Qiandaohu General Airport, located in Jiande City, Hangzhou City, Zhejiang Province, China. Since Jiande General Aviation Airport has the advantage of synchronous operation of traditional physical tower and remote tower dual control mode, Jiande General Aviation Airport is selected as the test scene of this study for test design, relying on advanced test equipment and platform to collect data and carry out statistical analysis.

The participants of this paper were selected front-line controllers from Jiande Qiandaohu General Airport. All controllers voluntarily participated in the experiment, and the whole experiment ensured that each controller had been informed in advance and had the right to know and be anonymous.

2.2 Data Acquisition and Data Processing Methods

Workload. The study of controller workload used an Inner Balance device to capture heart rate data: the Inner Balance application uses ear sensors to capture heart rate variability (HRV) consistency data. The tester needed to wear the device throughout the control command test process, and the impact of the device on the controller's control command task was negligible. In addition, combined with the NASA-TLX scale, the scale was modified according to the actual work situation of controllers, with subsequent reliability and validity analysis carried out, with the results showing that it had certain use value. The scale required the subjects to score the load of six dimensions, namely mental demand, physical demand, time limit demand, self-expression, effort level and frustration, according to their actual situation after completing the control task.

Kubios HRV software and IBM SPSS Statistics 27 software was used for data processing in this test. The Kubios HRV software is a scientifically proven heart rate variability analysis software, designed for research and professional use. Kubios HRV software has achieved gold standard status in scientific research and is used in approximately 149 universities in 1,800 countries and has been used in more than 5,900 scientific publications. At the same time, through consulting the relevant literature, many high-level SCI and EI papers at home and abroad will use this software to carry out relevant research topics. Meanwhile, IBM SPSS Statistics 27 software was used to collect, organize, and analyze the test data.

Allocation of Attention. The device used in the controller attention allocation research test was the Tobiipro eye tracker, with subjects needing to wear the eye tracker throughout the control test. The subjects are less restricted, and the gaze position error is less than $0.5°$ under effective sampling conditions.

ErgoLAB 3.0 software and IBM SPSS Statistics 27 software was used for data processing in this test. Among them, ErgoLAB 3.0 software uses radio frequency physiological recording technology, behavior editing and analysis technology, human-machine environment synchronization technology, combined with human factors engineering, ergonomics, psychology, cognitive neuroscience and other professional theoretical knowledge to record users' physiological, psychological and behavioral changes in real time. Synchronous analysis of the operator's behavior, cognitive behavior, fatigue state, etc., was conducted to understand the causal relationship between all internal and external changes, complete real-time synchronous recording, tracking and analysis of human-machine-environment data at the same point in time or within the same time period, to realize interactive synchronization data visualization and interactive optimization and ergonomic evaluation.

Situational Awareness. The Situation Awareness Rating Technique (SART) was used to study situational awareness of controllers. The scale consists of three parts, namely: attention demand degree D, attention resource supply S and situation understanding degree U. The test content of attention demand degree D includes situation instability, situation complexity and situation variability. The content of attention resource supply S test includes the degree of mental arousal, the degree of distribution of attention, the degree of concentration of attention and the degree of residual energy. The content of situation understanding U test includes the familiarity of the situation, the quality of information obtained, and the quantity of information obtained. The scale used in this test was optimized on the original scale content based on the working state of the controller; and the reliability and validity analysis was carried out at the same time, with the results showing that the scale had certain use value.

IBM SPSS Statistics 27 software was used for data processing in this test.

3   Data Results and Analysis

3.1   Workload

Descriptive statistical analysis was represented by mean $\pm$ standard deviation ($\overline{x} \pm s$). The difference of measurement data between the two groups was analyzed by t test. Analysis of variance was used to analyze the difference between two or more groups of measurement data. Test level $= 0.05$, that is, $P < 0.05$ was considered statistically significant.

1) HRV data analysis.

As can be seen from Table 1, the P-values of the above four indicators are all greater than 0.05. Therefore, there is no significant difference in the time domain indexes of Mean HR, SDNN, RMSSD and pNN50 when controllers carry out control and command tasks under two control modes: traditional physical tower and remote tower. The results show that there is no significant difference in the workload of controllers under the two control modes.

Table 1. Difference analysis of time-domain indexes under different control modes.

Time-domain indexes	Control modes	$\bar{x} \pm s$	t	P
Mean HR(bpm)	1	76.81 ± 6.97	0.173	0.865
	2	76.18 ± 8.37		
SDNN (ms)	1	52.70 ± 11.35	0.462	0.650
	2	49.99 ± 13.43		
RMSSD(ms)	1	50.05 ± 10.46	0.331	0.745
	2	48.11 ± 14.03		
pNN50 (%)	1	25.41 ± 8.25	0.785	0.444
	2	22.17 ± 9.23		

Note: "1" indicates the traditional physical tower control mode. 2 indicates the remote tower control mode

2) data analysis of NASA-TLX scale.

Table 2. Difference analysis of total mental load of controllers under different control modes.

Dimension	Control modes	$\bar{x} \pm s$	t	P
Total mental load	1	41.30 ± 11.15	0.090	0.929
	2	40.83 ± 10.50		

Note: "1" indicates the traditional physical tower control mode. 2 indicates the remote tower control mode

According to Table 2, the P value is greater than 0.05, so there is no significant difference in the total mental load value of controllers when they carry out control command tasks under the two control modes of traditional physical tower and remote tower, indicating that there is no significant difference in the workload of controllers under the two control modes.

After the experiment, the controllers all indicated that there was no significant difference in workload perception between the two control methods.

3.2 Allocation of Attention

In this paper, four eye movement parameters, including the number of blinks, the number of fixation points, the average fixation duration and the average saccade duration, are selected, covering the parameters of fixation behavior and saccade behavior. Statistical analysis methodology was used to test the significance of the eye movement indicators on controllers in the traditional physical tower and remote tower control test scenarios, so as to judge the difference of the influence of different control methods on the attention allocation of controllers. The analysis results are shown in Table 3.

Table 3. Difference analysis of eye movement index data under different control modes.

Eye movement index	Control modes	$\bar{x} \pm s$	t	P
Number of blinks	1	1186.64 ± 741.08	1.508	0.147
	2	1042.36 ± 636.95		
Number of fixation points	1	2464.27 ± 1108.60	−4.514	<0.001
	2	4628.36 ± 1139.64		
Average fixation duration	1	0.24 ± 0.06	−2.147	0.044
	2	0.30 ± 0.05		
Average saccade duration	1	0.04 ± 0.004	−2.659	0.015
	2	0.05 ± 0.003		

Note: "1" indicates the traditional physical tower control mode. 2 indicates the remote tower control mode

According to Table 3, the P values corresponding to the three eye movement indicators: the number of fixation points, the average fixation duration, and the average saccade duration, are all less than 0.05. Therefore, there are significant differences in the eye movement indicators of the number of fixation points, the average fixation duration and the average saccade duration during the control and command of the traditional physical tower and the remote tower. The P value corresponding to the number of blinks is greater than 0.05, so there is no significant difference between the number of blinks of controllers in the traditional physical tower and the remote tower control and command process.

To sum up, the higher the number of fixation points, the faster the reading of brain information in this area, and the more concentrated the attention; indicating that compared with the traditional physical tower control mode, the controller's attention is more concentrated when commanding under the remote tower control mode. There are two possible reasons for the longer gaze time: first, the information is difficult to extract and requires greater cognitive effort. Second, it takes more time to read the rich information source [9], indicating that compared with the traditional physical tower control mode, the controller needs greater cognitive effort and longer time to extract the dynamic information of the aircraft from the screen when commanding the remote tower control mode. The shorter the average saccade duration, the greater the attention span, that is, the larger the amount of information observed. It indicates that when controllers perform control and command tasks in traditional physical towers, the attention span is larger, and the amount of information observed is larger.

3.3 Situational Awareness

1) Analysis of each test dimension

Table 4. Mean scores of each test dimension ($\bar{x} \pm s$).

Test dimension	Control modes	$\bar{x} \pm s$
Situational instability	1	3.86 ± 2.97
	2	3.29 ± 2.36
Situational complexity	1	6.29 ± 1.11
	2	2.71 ± 1.50
Situational variability	1	5.57 ± 1.51
	2	3.57 ± 1.62
Mental arousal	1	8.00 ± 1.16
	2	5.71 ± 1.11
Allocation of attention	1	7.57 ± 2.30
	2	7.71 ± 0.95
The level of concentration	1	8.14 ± 1.68
	2	6.57 ± 0.98
Energy surplus	1	7.71 ± 2.14
	2	6.43 ± 1.62
Situational familiarity	1	9.29 ± 1.11
	2	8.00 ± 1.41
Quality of acquired information	1	8.14 ± 1.35
	2	7.14 ± 0.69
Quantity of acquired information	1	8.86 ± 0.90
	2	6.71 ± 1.11
Total score of situational awareness	1	42.00 ± 7.44
	2	38.71 ± 6.65

Note: "1" indicates the remote tower control mode. 2 indicates the traditional physical tower control mode

According to Table 4, the mean scores of controllers in the aspects of situational instability, situational complexity, situational variability, mental arousal, allocation of attention, energy surplus, situational familiarity, quality of acquired information and quantity of acquired information in the remote tower are higher than those in the traditional physical tower. In terms of the allocation of attention, the average score of controllers in the remote-control tower is lower than that in the traditional physical tower.

2) Significance analysis

Table 5. Difference analysis results of each test dimension under different control methods.

Test dimension	t	P
Situational instability	0.399	0.697
Situational complexity	5.068	0.000
Situational variability	2.389	0.034
Mental arousal	3.771	0.003
Allocation of attention	−0.152	0.883
The level of concentration	2.144	0.053
Energy surplus	1.269	0.229
Situational familiarity	1.890	0.083
Quality of acquired information	1.750	0.106
Quantity of acquired information	2.795	0.016
Total score of situational awareness	0.871	0.401

As can be seen from Table 5, the P values corresponding to the four aspects of situational complexity, situational variability, mental arousal, and the quantity of acquired information are all less than 0.05. Therefore, when controllers conduct control and command tasks under two different control modes: remote tower and traditional physical tower, there were significant differences in the complexity of the situation, the variability of the situation, mental arousal, and the quantity of acquired information; but there was no significant difference in the total score of situational awareness.

3.4 Establishment of Evaluation Criteria

Taking the experimental results of Jiande Airport in China as an example, the evaluation criteria were established based on the three aspects of workload, allocation of attention and situational awareness, with reference to the Evaluation Specifications for Remote Tower Operation issued by the Civil Aviation Administration of China, as shown in Table 6. If there is no significant difference in the test indicators during the evaluation of the above three dimensions, it is acceptable or tolerable; If there is very significant difference, it is not acceptable and risk mitigation measures need to be developed subsequently. After the development of risk mitigation measures, the risk level after mitigation should be evaluated again. If there is always a risk that the change is not reduced to an acceptable or tolerable level, then the change does not meet the safety requirements and the original objective needs to be modified or even the proposed change abandoned; If the risk is unacceptable, the change cannot be implemented. After modifying the original objectives or abandoning the proposed changes, the hazard sources will be further identified, and the safety assessment process repeated according to the new protocol.

Table 6. Operation Safety evaluation standard of remote tower system (Based on Jiande Airport).

Dimension	Acceptable	Tolerable	Unacceptable
Workload	There were no significant differences in Mean HR, SDNN, RMSSD and pNN50 in the time-domain indexes of heart rate variability and total mental load (P > 0.05)	There were significant differences in Mean HR, SDNN, RMSSD and pNN50 in the time-domain indexes of heart rate variability and total mental load (P < 0.05)	There were very significant differences in Mean HR, SDNN, RMSSD and pNN50 in the time-domain indexes of heart rate variability and total mental load (P < 0.01)
Allocation of attention	There were no significant differences in the number of blinking, the number of fixation points, the average fixation duration and the average saccade duration (P > 0.05)	There were significant differences in the number of blinking, the number of fixation points, the average fixation duration and the average saccade duration (P < 0.05)	There were very significant differences in the number of blinking, the number of fixation points, the average fixation duration and the average saccade duration (P < 0.01)
Situational awareness	There was no significant difference in SART score of situational awareness (P > 0.05)	There was significant difference in SART score of situational awareness (P < 0.05)	There was very significant difference in SART score of situational awareness (P < 0.01)

4 Conclusion

4.1 Research Conclusion

1. Taking Jiande Airport controllers as an example, the experimental results verified the validity of the research methods used in this paper, namely, the controller workload research method based on the heart rate variability index and NASA-TLX scale, the allocation of attention research method based on eye movement index, and the situational awareness research method based on the Situational awareness SART scale. The above research methods can be used as test methods in the safety evaluation of remote tower system trial operation in the future, so as to ensure the safe and efficient operation of air traffic control.

2. Based on the real and reliable experimental data and experimental methods, the remote tower system operation safety evaluation standards are established. If there is no significant difference in the test indicators selected in the evaluation process, it is acceptable or tolerable. If there is very significant difference, it is unacceptable and risk mitigation measures need to be developed in the future. The evaluation criteria established in this paper are expected to provide a certain reference for the preliminary systematic safety assessment process of remote tower systems.

4.2 Research Prospect

In the future, with the continuous development and application of remote tower system in China, and the enrichment of scenario cases and data, the authors will continue to follow up the research, add more effective human ergonomics indicators, and design a large number of effective tests based on objective data. In addition, the authors will establish a more complete comprehensive evaluation method and safety operation evaluation standard, conduct relevant safety evaluation during the trial operation of remote tower systems of different types of airports, evaluate the safety of remote tower systems from a multi-dimensional perspective, and then improve the research level of human factors and ergonomics of remote tower systems in China. This paper provides reference for the remote tower operation evaluation of Civil aviation in China.

Acknowledgments. The authors would like to express special thanks to all the controllers who participated in this experiment. Their love for work and serious and responsible attitude provides valuable help for the authors' relevant research.

Disclosure of Interests. The authors have no competing interests to declare that are relevant to the content of this article.

References

1. EUROCAE. ED240, Minimum. Aviation System. Performance-Specification for-Remote-Tower Optical Systems[S] (2016)
2. Feng, X.: Application prospect analysis of remote tower technology in China. J. Civ. Aviation Flight Coll. China **34**(06), 27–30 (2023)
3. Kearney, P., Li, W., Zhang, J., et al.: Human performance assessment of a single air traffic controller conducting multiple remote tower operations. Hum. Factors and Ergon. Manuf. Serv. Indust. **30**(2) (2020)
4. Fabian, R., Jörn, J.: Remote AFIS: development and validation of low-cost remote tower concepts for uncontrolled aerodromes. CEAS Aeronautical J. **13**(4) (2022)
5. Ohneiser, O., Helmke, H., Shetty, S., et al.: Assistant based speech recognition support for air traffic controllers in a multiple remote tower environment. Aerospace **10**(6) (2023)
6. Tong, F., Zhang, X., Qiao, Y., et al.: A fusion of civil aviation ASTERIX data and remote tower video surveillance. Sci. Technol. Eng. [6], **23**(07), 2916–2921 (2023)
7. Rui, S., Tao, H., Ning, S.: Technology and application analysis of remote tower. Modern Navig. **14**(01), 31–37 (2023)
8. Xuan, W., Xu, S.: Application of remote tower technology in ramp control direction. China Airlines (6), 52–55 (2023)
9. Liu, Z., Yuan, X., Liu, W., et al.: Eye movement index analysis based on simulated flight mission. China Safety Sci. J. (02), 47–51+145 (2006)

Response to Acoustic Sounds and Synthesized Speech in an Automated Cockpit Checklist

Niall Miranda[1]([✉]) [ID], Tendai Rukasha[2] [ID], and Wojciech Tomasz Korek[3] [ID]

[1] Safety and Human Factors in Aviation MSc, SATM, Cranfield University, Cranfield, UK
NiallMiranda@outlook.com
[2] Centre for Safety and Accident Investigation, SATM, Cranfield University, Cranfield, UK
Tendai.Rukasha@cranfield.ac.uk
[3] Dynamics, Simulation and Control Group, SATM, Cranfield University, Cranfield, UK
W.T.Korek@cranfield.ac.uk

Abstract. Acoustic sounds have been reasonably effective as brief aural cues within cockpit systems, serving to alert pilots about the configuration and performance of the aircraft. However, these sounds do not establish an intuitive connection between the alert and its intended function, leading to an initial learning curve in grasping their auditory significance. In contrast, synthesized speech is more pliable for comprehension and has gained popularity in applications such as virtual assistants and sat-nav communication. With cockpit automation advancing towards single-pilot operations, communication by cockpit systems requires consideration. Therefore, it is crucial to thoroughly investigate and validate the impact of both acoustic sounds and synthesized speech in this setting. A human-in-the-loop experiment was conducted in an aircraft simulator environment, involving participants with diverse ages and levels of experience, to evaluate the response time for an automated checklist annunciating callouts in the form of acoustic sounds and synthesized speech. The results indicated that the response time, for the aural checklist callouts, had been influenced by anticipation, habituation, and familiarity with a scenario rather than the type of aural alert. Anticipation and habituation in unfamiliar scenarios had led to inappropriate responses to spurious alerts irrespective of the type of alert.

Keywords: Response Time · Synthesized Speech · Acoustic Sound

1 Introduction

1.1 Aural Alerts in Cockpit Systems

Aural alerts in cockpit systems assist pilots in performing a varied range of functions particularly by providing situation awareness of the environment. In an environment that demands constant shuffling to perceive information from displays and instruments in the cockpit, the use of appropriate aural alerts to supplement visual information can alleviate pilots' mental workload and improve situation awareness leading to enhanced flight safety [1]. Modern cockpit systems have two distinctive types of aural alerts classified as

© The Author(s), under exclusive license to Springer Nature Switzerland AG 2024
D. Harris and W.-C. Li (Eds.): HCII 2024, LNAI 14693, pp. 269–284, 2024.
https://doi.org/10.1007/978-3-031-60731-8_19

acoustic sounds and synthesized speech. Acoustic sounds function as transient auditory signals and have been a typical form of aural communication to alert pilots of the aircraft's configuration and performance. These sounds, however, do not impart an intuitive link between the alert and its intended function. Cognizing the aural taxonomy of acoustic sounds used in cockpit systems requires an initial learning curve to comprehend the aural taxonomy. On the contrary, synthesized speech is nimble to be assimilated and provides a direct and intuitive link to its intended function [2].

Considering the multitude of alerts in a cockpit environment required to keep pilots informed about the various modes and states of aircraft systems, several studies have aimed to enhance the efficacy of aural alerts. [3] determined that the information processing times are shorter when acoustic alerts are combined with synthesized speech. [4] determined that response times to aural alerts were quicker when sounded with haptic cues by means of seat vibration to alert vehicle drivers of a crash threat. [5] demonstrated the importance of annunciating alerts in tandem with visual elements in a cockpit environment to prevent accidents attributed to failure in controlling the aircraft. [6] presented a use case with an augmented reality device in a cockpit by supplementing visual cues in tandem with voice recognition and aural communication to optimize the efficiency of pilots' performance.

1.2 Response Time

One of the critical determinants of the effectiveness of aural alerts lies in their impact on human performance, particularly response time. The response time is an outcome of the urgency perceived from the alerting system [7]. The response time for unexpected acoustic sound alerts was found to decrease after participants got accustomed to it over a period of time [8]. When an acoustic sound was added to a synthesized speech, the response time increased; however, when the synthesized speech had been lengthened, the response time decreased [9]. Further studies suggested that the response time to synthesized speech improved with a decrement in the rate of speech [10], thereby indicating response time as a function of aural cognition. The ability of synthesized speech to provide shorter response times through deeper cognition of critical events was also determined in a study on an air traffic alerting system that compared the use of acoustic sounds and synthesized speech [11]. However, other studies described that habituation and prior exposure to an aural alert influenced response time more than from decisions based on cognizing the alert [12]. Therefore, the current research has investigated the effects of the two types of aural alerts on participants' response times.

1.3 Decision-Making

Human performance can also be evaluated based on the decisions made by cognizing information from the environment. Decision-making in a dynamic cockpit environment is propagated by the saliency of information [13]. Studies indicate that monotone and urgent tones provided saliency of aural alerts, leading to significantly faster response times [14]. However, studies also determined that responses to alerts had been driven by familiarity in recognizing the alerts. Familiarization had not just improved responses to authentic alerts but increased responses to spurious alerts as well [15]. A study on decision-making in automated cockpits indicated that pilots used cues from automated systems as a heuristic replacement for tangible information, leading to automation bias [16]. With the advancements in cockpit automation, particularly to support single-pilot operations, appropriate cognition of alerts is essential for precision in decision-making in the cockpit. In a study on the cognition of acoustic alerts, the perception of urgency and annoyance were determined to be influenced by the duration and interval of acoustic sounds [17]. However, analyses of accident reports determined that self-induced time pressure on perceived urgency impeded the quality of decision-making in a cockpit environment [18]. Therefore, the current research has investigated participants' decision-making by evaluating their response to mistimed or spurious aural alerts when presented with tangible visual cues.

2 Method

2.1 Participants

The research involved eighty-two participants categorized into four levels of experience. Participants in the first level had no familiarity with the cockpit environment; participants in the second level had experience in gaming applications; the third level consisted of participants from an aviation background who possessed knowledge related to basic aircraft systems relevant to the experiment or who had had experience in a flight simulator environment; while the fourth level consisted of pilots with flying experience on any type of aircraft. The first and second levels had nineteen participants each, while the third level had thirty-eight participants, and the fourth level had six participants. The age of the participants ranged between 19 and 64 years ($M = 27$, $SD = 6.75$). The approval of the Cranfield University Research Ethics System was obtained prior to conducting the research. All data obtained from the experimental trials were only available to the research team and were stored in accordance with the Ethical Code and the Data Protection Act of the university.

2.2 Apparatus

A human-in-the-loop experiment was conducted in a high-fidelity cockpit simulator, developed by Cranfield University, Rolls-Royce, and DCA Design, called the Future Systems Simulator [19] as shown in Fig. 1. FlightGear application was used to develop the visual scenarios for the experiment [20], while MATLAB and Unity game engine were used to develop the aircraft flight dynamics model and Human-Machine Interface, respectively. The setup aurally, visually, and functionally represented a Gulfstream G500 twin-engine business jet. Cameras positioned around the simulator captured the participants' response to the aural alerts during the experimental scenarios. The acoustic sounds used in this experiment were obtained from pixabay.com (a royalty-free stock media database) and were in the form of beeps. The synthesized speech was generated on a speech synthesizer application RHVoice for annunciating the alerts in a female voice in an American English accent.

Fig. 1. The Future Systems Simulator - a high-fidelity cockpit simulator used in the research.

2.3 Scenarios

Participants were presented with two scenarios in a high-fidelity setting. Both scenarios started with the aircraft at 1800 feet above ground level and in a clean configuration, that is, flaps and landing gear retracted. The aircraft would also be aligned to runway 27L of London's Heathrow Airport, with the autopilot engaged and descending at 600 feet per minute, which provided approximately 180 s to touchdown. To avoid the effects of glare and shades on the westerly approach, the two scenarios were designed to represent mid-day sunlight, however, the scenarios varied visually in weather and visibility. Prior to attempting the two scenarios for the experiment, the participants had been provided with a familiarization scenario that closely represented the experimental scenarios. Calm winds ensured that the flight dynamics and performance were not altered in any scenario.

Scenario 1 presented the participants with receding rain supplemented by thunderstorms in surrounding areas (configured in FlightGear, so the effect was visual); however, the weather was not present along the flight path to ensure a negligible effect of the scenario on the participants' performance. The visibility in this scenario was set to 9999 m with calm winds and broken clouds at 2500 feet above ground level. This scenario had been designed to alert the participants to extend the flaps and landing gear 30 s from the start of the trial. At 60 s from the start of the trial, the pilots would be alerted to disengage the autopilot, providing them 120 s to hand-fly the aircraft until touchdown. The sequence and timing of the alerts in this scenario were identical to the familiarization scenario. Figure 2 is an illustration of Scenario 1.

Scenario 2 presented the participants with fog and overcast conditions, the cloud base set at 1300 feet and the visibility at 3500 m. The approach and runway lights were lit to enable the participants to participants to acquire a visual reference to the runway in poor visibility conditions. The sequence of the alerts remained the same; however, the timings of the alert to disengage the autopilot were delayed by 60 s from Scenario

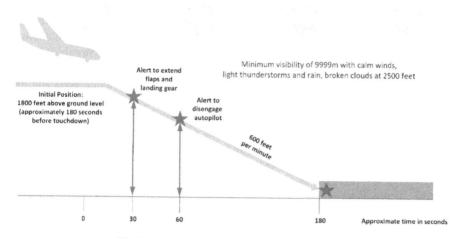

Fig. 2. Schematic Representation of Scenario 1.

1, that is, at 120 s from the start of the scenario, to accommodate the reduced visibility due to fog. However, participants could acquire a visual reference to the runway only after 130 s, thereby making the alert to disengage the autopilot spurious. Figure 3 is an illustration of Scenario 2.

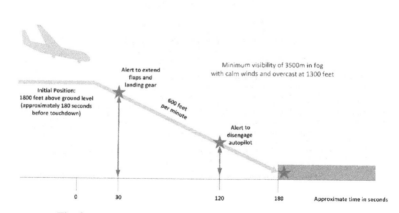

Fig. 3. Schematic Representation of Scenario 2.

2.4   Procedure

The aural alerts used in this experiment had been designed to emulate the operational setting for single pilot operations with the computer performing the functions of a co-pilot annunciating checklist callouts. The synthesized speech had been annunciating

"FLAPS" and "LANDING GEAR" to direct the participant to configure the aircraft, and "AUTOPILOT" to disengage the autopilot. The acoustic alerts were producing two distinct beeps, one to configure the aircraft and the other to disengage the autopilot. The two acoustic alerts were similar in characteristics of sound with only the pitch of the sound distinguishing the alerts for configuration and autopilot. Participants were provided with a briefing video to familiarize themselves with the aural alerts and the simulator environment prior to the experiment.

The participants had been tasked with an objective of performing a successful landing on the simulator while following instructions from an automated aural landing checklist. The participants were presented with an aircraft in a clean configuration and with the autopilot engaged. The computer would perform checklist callouts in the form of aural alerts to guide the participants to configure the aircraft for landing, that is, to extend the flaps, deploy the landing gear, and finally to disengage the autopilot to hand-fly the aircraft. The response time obtained from the recordings measured the duration taken by the participants from the activation of an alert until a correct response to the alert. All responses from participants required in this experiment were obtained prior to the participants hand-flying the aircraft. Participants had been instructed to execute the callouts only upon hearing the aural alerts. Additionally, participants were instructed to confirm visual reference to the runway prior to disengaging the autopilot. However, the outcome of the landing was not used as a crucial determinant for this experiment.

To establish the homogeneity of the data collection, a simple randomization allocated participants to two patterns in the experiment. Pattern 1 ensured participants had experienced synthesized speech in Scenario 1, followed by acoustic sounds in Scenario 2. Pattern 2 ensured the converse, that is, acoustic sounds in Scenario 1 followed by synthesized speech in Scenario 2. The allocation of participants over the two aural alerts and the two scenarios forms a 2×2 matrix, as shown in Table 1, thereby obtaining a mixed between-subjects and within-subjects study group.

Table 1. Pattern × Scenario matrix.

	Scenario 1	Scenario 2
Pattern 1	Synthesized Speech	Acoustic Sound
Pattern 2	Acoustic Sound	Synthesized Speech

3   Results

Table 2 show the descriptive statistics and Fig. 4 shows a box-plot for the response time for configuring the aircraft in scenarios 1 and 2.

3.1   Research Design

A full factorial design was implemented while evaluating interactions among factors. For all analyses, significance level (α) was selected to be 0.05 for strong evidence and

Table 2. Descriptive Statistics for Response Time in Scenarios 1 and 2.

	Mean	Median	Standard Deviation	Range	Min	Max
Scenario 1						
Synthesized Speech	7.9	7	5.1	34	4	38
Acoustic Sound	12.0	9	7.1	29	5	34
Scenario 2						
Synthesized Speech	8.0	7	4.8	26	5	31
Acoustic Sound	11.0	8	10.6	57	3	60

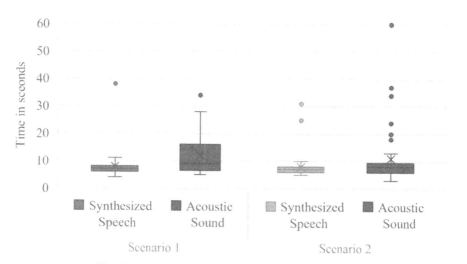

Fig. 4. Box-plot for Response Time in Scenarios 1 and 2.

0.1 for weak evidence and the effect size of the ANOVA was measured by the partial eta square (η^2).

3.2 Between Subjects Design

The response time in the between-subjects design was analyzed for variance with one-way interactions between the type of alert and the level of experience for each of the two scenarios. The results indicated no significant simple main effect for alert type within Scenario 1, $F(1,75) = 1.88$, $p = 0.17$; and within Scenario 2, $F(1,75) = 0.02$, $p = 0.89$. The results also indicated no significant simple main effect for experience within Scenario 1, $F(3,75) = 0.48$, $p = 0.70$; and within Scenario 2, $F(3,75) = 0.55$ $p = 0.65$. There was no significant interaction between alert-type and experience within Scenario 1, $F(2,75) = 0.61$, $p = 0.55$; however, the results indicated weak evidence for a statistically significant interaction between alert-type and experience within Scenario 2, $F(2,75) = 2.58$, $p = 0.08$, $\eta^2 = 0.064$. Table 3 shows the analysis of variance for alert-type and experience level for each of the two trials.

Table 3. Analysis of Variance for Alert-Type and Experience.

Source	df	SS	MS	F	p	η^2
Scenario 1						
Alert-Type	1	72.92	72.92	1.88	0.17	0.024
Experience	3	55.24	18.41	0.48	0.70	0.019
Alert-Type × Experience	2	47.33	23.67	0.61	0.55	0.016
Residual	75	2906.73	38.76			
Scenario 2						
Alert-Type	1	1.35	1.35	0.02	0.89	<0.001
Experience	3	109.69	36.56	0.55	0.65	0.022
Alert-Type × Experience	2	342.34	171.17	2.58	0.08	0.064
Residual	75	4981.36	66.42			

3.3 Within Subjects Design

The response time in the within-subjects design had been analyzed with the two patterns for variance, with the type of aural alert serving as the within-subjects factor while participants' level of experience and the scenarios served as within-subject factors. The results indicated weak evidence for a statistically significant simple main effect for the alert-type within Pattern 1, $F(1,38) = 3.57, p = 0.07, \eta^2 = 0.086$; however, there was no significant simple main effect within Pattern 2, $F(1,37) = 0.38, p = 0.54$. The results also indicated no significant simple main effect for the experience within Pattern 1, $F(2,38) = 0.36, p = 0.70$; and within Pattern 2, $F(3,37) = 1.06, p = 0.38$. There was no significant interaction between alert-type and experience within Pattern 1, $F(2,38) = 1.60, p = 0.21$; and within Pattern 2, $F(3,37) = 1.61, p = 0.20$. Table 4 shows the analysis of variance for alert-type and experience level for each of the two trials.

3.4 Spurious Alert

The mistimed alert to disengage the autopilot in Scenario 2 have been termed as spurious alerts in this experiment. Scenario 2 alerted the participants to disengage the autopilot at 120 s from the start of the scenario. However, the participants were required to not disengage the autopilot prior to 130 s from the start of the scenario due to limited visibility and inability to establish a visual reference to the runway. Therefore, the participants who disengaged the autopilot after the first 10 s of activation of the alert were considered to have responded appropriately to the spurious alert. The results indicate that thirty-one of the eighty-two participants responded appropriately to the spurious alert, that is, disengaged the autopilot after 10 s (M = 16.6, SD = 4.0). Forty-nine participants responded inappropriately to the spurious alert, that is, disengaged the autopilot within the first 10 s (M = 3.8, SD = 2.3). However, two participants did not respond to the alert to disengage the autopilot. Figure 5 shows the distribution of response time for disengaging the autopilot, and Fig. 6 shows the descriptive statistics on a box plot.

Table 4. Analysis of Variance for Alert-Type and Experience for Patterns 1 and 2.

Source	df	SS	MS	F	p	η^2
Pattern 1						
Within-Subjects Factor						
Alert-Type	1	229.29	229.29	3.57	0.07	0.086
Alert-Type × Experience	2	205.74	102.87	1.60	0.21	0.078
Residual	38	2440.46	64.22			
Between-Subjects Factor						
Experience	2	53.45	26.72	0.36	0.70	0.019
Residual	38	2832.46	74.54			
Pattern 2						
Within-Subjects Factor						
Alert-Type	1	13.43	13.43	0.38	0.54	0.010
Alert-Type × Experience	3	168.97	56.32	1.61	0.20	0.116
Residual	37	1291.98	34.92			
Between-Subjects Factor						
Experience	3	113.80	37.93	1.06	0.38	0.079
Residual	37	1323.20	35.76			

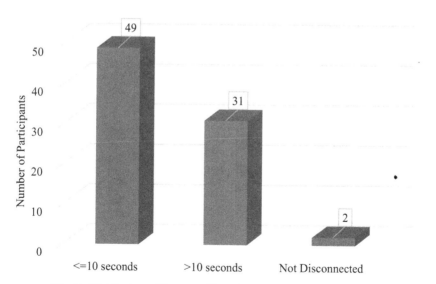

Fig. 5. Distribution of Response Time for Disengaging the Autopilot.

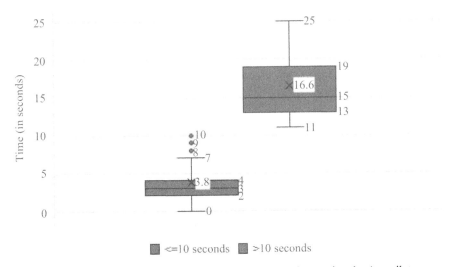

Fig. 6. Descriptive Statistics for Response Time for Disengaging the Autopilot.

4   Discussion

4.1   Response Time for Configuration Alerts

This human-in-the-loop experiment validated the response times while using synthesized speech and acoustic sounds when used in the form of automated checklist callouts. Figure 7 shows the mean response times for configuring the aircraft in Scenarios 1 & 2 based on the type of aural alert and participants' level of experience.

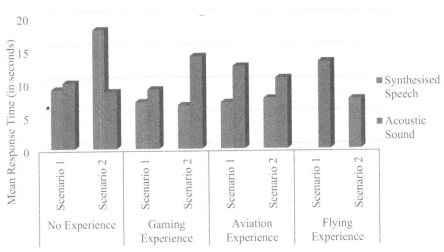

Fig. 7. Mean Response Times for Configuring the Aircraft in Scenarios 1 and 2.

Among the two aural alerts, neither presented strong evidence for significantly quicker response time to configure the aircraft. Despite the role of synthesized speech in providing deeper cognition and quicker response times when compared to acoustic sounds, the results from this experiment showed that habituation and prior exposure to the alert had a greater influence on the response time to checklist callouts. In an automated cockpit checklist where callouts had been anticipated, the decision-making was influenced by the anticipation of the alerts rather than a decision-based on cognizing the alert. The role of anticipation was emphasized when participants had responded inappropriately to spurious alert irrespective of the type of aural alert.

The duration of the aural alert had been considered in evaluating participants' response times. All checklist callouts used in the experiment were iterated until the correct response was obtained from the participant. The accuracy of the recorded response time was taken to be one second. The duration between each iteration had been one second for all callouts. While acoustic sounds had a duration of one second per iteration, the synthesized speech had a duration of two seconds for "LANDING GEAR" and "AUTOPILOT" and one second for "FLAPS." The longer duration of the synthesized speech corresponded to its characteristic ability to provide deeper cognition of the alert to participants. The response time had been measured from the initial activation of the alert till participants responded appropriately to the alert. The results showed that despite the shorter duration of acoustic alerts in this experiment and deeper cognition by the synthesized speech, the response time had not indicated significant variance.

Apart from the characteristics of the alert, participants' experience in a cockpit environment was examined as a factor in this experiment. Despite participants having diverse levels of experience, specifically, flying experience, aviation experience, gaming experience, and no experience, the level of experience had not been a significant factor in participants' response time. By presenting participants with a briefing video and a familiarization scenario, participants were able to not just familiarize themselves with the aural alerts but also with the cockpit environment and the tasks and procedures required for the experiment. Therefore, the results did not indicate significant variance in the response time among the participants with diverse levels of experience. The nonappearance of the effect of participants' levels of experience on the experiment data suggested the generalizability of the experiment and its usability in the context of aviation cockpits.

Figure 8 shows the mean response time for configuring the aircraft based on participants' level of experience for the two scenarios. This Figure indicates that participants with higher levels of experience provided lower response times in Scenario 2 as compared to Scenario 1, signifying that the response time of these participants had been influenced by anticipation and habituation. However, the participants with lower levels of familiarization to a cockpit simulation environment provided higher response times in Scenario 2. Although the procedures and sequence of tasks in Scenario 2 remained the same as in Scenario 1, the effect of external factors, that is, the low visibility due to fog, affected participants' anticipation of the alerts. These findings are consistent with other studies [15] that familiarization of a scenario affects response times.

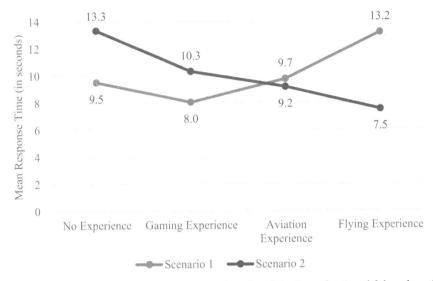

Fig. 8. Mean Response Times for Configuring the Aircraft in Scenarios 1 and 2 based on the participants' level of experience.

4.2 Response Time for Spurious Alerts

Both experimental scenarios required participants to extend the flaps, deploy the landing gear and disengage the autopilot upon hearing the respective alerts. However, participants were required to establish a visual reference to the runway prior to disengaging the autopilot. In the scenarios preceding Scenario 2, that is, the familiarization scenario and Scenario 1, the alert to disengage the autopilot was activated 30 s after the activation of the alert to configure the aircraft. In Scenario 2, the alert to disengage the autopilot was activated 90 s after the activation of the alert to configure the aircraft. The delayed yet anticipated alert activated 10 s before participants could establish a visual reference to the runway. The decision-making under time pressure investigated in this scenario determines that the 60-s delay in time for sounding the alert to disconnect the autopilot after the alert for configuration had an impact on the participants' temporal demand. The mistimed reaction to the alert to disengage the autopilot indicated ineffective decision-making developed on a factor of self-induced time pressure within a dynamic environment that was coupled with an externally induced time pressure. The finding of self-induced time pressure on perceived urgency impeding the quality of decision-making corresponded to the study conducted by [18].

Figure 9 shows the distribution of participants' reaction to the spurious alert based on the type of aural alert. The figure also shows that reaction to spurious alerts had not been dependent on the type of aural alert for both appropriate and inappropriate responses. However, only participants who experienced acoustic sounds did not provide any response to the alert to disengage the autopilot. This finding is consistent with previous studies on aural alerts and sustains that synthesized alerts provide deeper cognition for decision-making [11], which in the current research corresponded to the failure of acoustic sounds from prompting participants to respond to the alert to disengage the autopilot in an unfamiliar scenario.

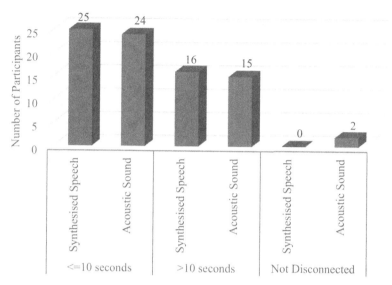

Fig. 9. Distribution for Disengaging the Autopilot Based on Alert-Type.

Figure 10 shows the distribution of participants' reaction to the spurious alert of disengaging the autopilot based on the participants' level of experience. The figure also shows that majority of participants with higher levels of experience mistimed their response to the alert to disengage the autopilot. This effect indicated that reaction times reflect participants prior experience rather than the presence of any determining factors in the scenario, which is consistent with the studies conducted by [12]. Participants who mistimed their reaction were queried for their actions. While some participants admitted to having forgotten to establish visual reference to the runway, the other participants indicated that they were familiar with the terrain and therefore affirmed that they were approaching the runway and were safe to disengage the autopilot. The response obtained from the participants is consistent with the reports on automation bias [16], where participants reported additional cues that did not exist in addition to automation bias, thereby developing a scope of confirmation bias [21].

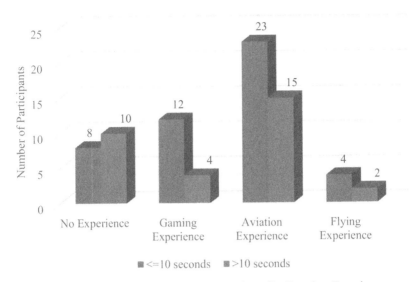

Fig. 10. Distribution for Disengaging the Autopilot Based on Experience.

5 Conclusion

The study on analyzing aural alerts in cockpit systems presented in this paper has determined that the type of aural alert did not provide significant differences in response time and decision making while following callouts from an automated checklist. Factors such as anticipation and habituation driven by biases, such as automation bias and confirmation bias, had greater influence on the results which were noticeable with spurious alerts. This paper also presented that familiarity with a scenario influenced response time and decision making more than participants' level of experience prior to the study. The findings in this study could be used to contribute to the design considerations of automated assistance, to support single pilot operations, where aural alerts are communicated in the form of checklist callouts. Further analysis of unfamiliar and emergency checklists can provide better insights into the effect of the two types of aural alerts on response time and decision-making.

Acknowledgments. The authors would like to thank Rolls-Royce Plc for allowing this research to be carried out in the Future Systems Simulator.

References

1. Mumaw, R.J., Haworth, L.A., Feary, M.S.: The Role of Alerting System Failures in Loss of Control Accidents. Technical Memorandum, NASA, Ames Research Center, Moffett Field, California (2019). NASA/TM—2019–220176
2. Edworthy, J., Hards, R.: Learning auditory warnings: the effects of sound type, verbal labelling and imagery on the identification of alarm sounds. Int. J. Ind. Ergon. **24**(6), 603–618 (1999). https://doi.org/10.1016/S0169-8141(98)00066-3

3. Forster, Y., Naujoks, F., Neukum, A., Huestegge, L.: Driver compliance to take-over requests with different auditory outputs in conditional automation. Accid. Anal. Prev. **109**, 18–28 (2017). https://doi.org/10.1016/j.aap.2017.09.019

4. Fitch, G.M., Kiefer, R.J., Hankey, J.M., Kleiner, B.M.: Toward developing an approach for alerting drivers to the direction of a crash threat. Hum. Factors: J. Hum. Factors Ergon. Soc. **49**(4), 710–720 (2007). https://doi.org/10.1518/001872007X215782

5. Conner, K., Feyereisen, T., Morgan, J., Bateman, D.: Cockpit displays and annunciation to help reduce the loss of control (LOC) or lack of control (LAC) accident risks. In: AIAA Guidance, Navigation, and Control Conference (2012). https://doi.org/10.2514/6.2012-4763

6. Miranda, N., Bonotaux, J.-B., Li, W.-C.: Augmented design with voice recognition and auditory alerts in the flight deck. In: Golightly, D., Balfe, N., Charles, R. (eds.), Ergonomics & Human Factors 2023, pp. 247–249. CIEHF (2023)

7. Edworthy, J., Loxley, S., Dennis, I.: Improving auditory warning design: relationship between warning sound parameters and perceived urgency. Hum. Factors: J. Hum. Factors Ergon. Soc. **33**(2), 205–231 (1991). https://doi.org/10.1177/001872089103300206

8. Warrick, M.J., Kibler, A.W., Topmiller, D.A.: Response time to unexpected stimuli. Hum. Factors: J. Hum. Factors Ergon. Soc. **7**(1), 81–86 (1965). https://doi.org/10.1177/001872086500700110

9. Simpson, C.A., Williams, D.H.: Response time effects of alerting tone and semantic context for synthesized voice cockpit warnings. Hum. Factors: J. Hum. Factors Ergon. Soc. **22**(3), 319–330 (1980). https://doi.org/10.1177/001872088002200306

10. Simpson, C.A., Marchionda-Frost, K.: Synthesized speech rate and pitch effects on intelligibility of warning messages for pilots. Hum. Factors: J. Hum. Factors Ergon. Soc. **26**(5), 509–517 (1984). https://doi.org/10.1177/001872088402600503

11. Kearney, P., Li, W.-C., Lin, J.J.H.: The impact of alerting design on air traffic controllers' response to conflict detection and resolution. Int. J. Ind. Ergon. **56**, 51–58 (2016). https://doi.org/10.1016/j.ergon.2016.09.002

12. Wong, A.L., Goldsmith, J., Forrence, A.D., Haith, A.M., Krakauer, J.W.: Reaction times can reflect habits rather than computations. ELife 6, e28075 (2017). https://doi.org/10.7554/eLife.28075

13. Endsley, M.R.: Situation Awareness in Dynamic Human Decision Making: Theory and Measurement. University of Southern California, Faculty of the Graduate School (1990)

14. Arrabito, G.R.: Effects of talker sex and voice style of verbal cockpit warnings on performance. Hum. Factors: J. Hum. Factors Ergon. Soc. **51**(1), 3–20 (2009). https://doi.org/10.1177/0018720808333411

15. Greene, R.L.: The role of familiarity in recognition. Psychon. Bull. Rev. **6**(2), 309–312 (1999). https://doi.org/10.3758/BF03212335

16. Mosier, K.L., Skitka, L.J., Heers, S., Burdick, M.: Automation bias: decision making and performance in high-tech cockpits. Int. J. Aviat. Psychol. **8**(1), 47–63 (1998). https://doi.org/10.1207/s15327108ijap0801_3

17. Marshall, D.C., Lee, J.D., Austria, P.A.: Alerts for in-vehicle information systems: annoyance, urgency, and appropriateness. Hum. Factors: J. Hum. Factors Ergon. Soc. **49**(1), 145–157 (2007). https://doi.org/10.1518/001872007779598145

18. Orasanu, J., Strauch, B.: Temporal factors in aviation decision making. Proc. Hum. Factors Ergon. Soc. Ann. Meet. **38**(14), 935–939 (1994). https://doi.org/10.1177/154193129403801431

19. Korek, W.T., Li, W.-C., Lu, L., Lone, M.: Investigating pilots' operational behaviours while interacting with different types of inceptors. In: D. Harris & W.-C. Li (Eds.), Engineering Psychology and Cognitive Ergonomics, vol. LNAI 13307 (EPCE 2022, pp. 314–325). HCI International 2022 (2022). https://doi.org/10.1007/978-3-031-06086-1_24

20. Barrio, L.D., Korek, W., Millidere, M., Whidborne, J.: Analysis of Visualization Systems in Flight Simulators. AIAA AVIATION 2023 Forum (2023). https://doi.org/10.2514/6.2023-3476

21. Nickerson, R.S.: Confirmation bias: a ubiquitous phenomenon in many guises. Rev. Gen. Psychol. **2**(2), 175–220 (1998). https://doi.org/10.1037/1089-2680.2.2.175

Using Flight Quick Access Recorder (QAR) Data to Examine the Effect of Sun Glare on Landing Performance: An Initial Attempt

Weiwei Qiu[1,2], Ziyue Cao[1], Xing Chen[3], Jingyu Zhang[1,2(✉)], Xianghong Sun[1,2], Yinger Zheng[4], and Haofeng Wang[4]

[1] Institute of Psychology, Chinese Academy of Sciences, Beijing 100101, China
zhangjingyu@psych.ac.cn

[2] Department of Psychology, University of Chinese Academy of Sciences, Beijing 100101, China

[3] Flight Technology College, Civil Aviation Flight University of China, Guanghan 618307, China

[4] Big Data Application Center, China Academy of Civil Aviation Science and Technology, Beijing 100028, China

Abstract. Flight safety during the landing phase is crucial, and many environmental factors may undermine this process. Sun glare has been identified as an important environmental factor affecting operation performance, but the empirical evidence concerning its effects requires further exploration. This study investigates the effect of sun glare on flight landing performance based on real flight QAR data. Five landing performance indicators were extracted from the QAR data encompassing 1235 flights at an east-west runway airport during clear weather conditions. We examined whether landing performance can be undermined when sun glare is more likely to happen, specifically during westward landing in the late afternoon and eastward landing in the early morning. The general linear model analysis findings reveal a marginally significant interaction effect between runway direction and time period on touchdown distance. Notably, in the morning, eastward landings exhibited longer touchdown distances compared to westward landings, while during the late afternoon, the opposite trend was observed with westward touchdown distances being longer. This study offers a novel perspective on how environmental factors can influence flight performance. The findings hold promise in devising strategies to mitigate the adverse effects of sun glare on flight operation performance, thereby enhancing overall flight safety standards.

Keywords: Quick Access Recorder (QAR) Data · Flight Landing Performance · Sun Glare · Aircraft Safety

1 Introduction

Flight safety is paramount in the aviation industry, with the landing phase being of utmost criticality. According to flight statistics reported by Boeing, spanning from 2007 to 2016, the landing phase accounted for 24% of total fatal accidents, despite comprising

---

The original version of the chapter has been revised. The author affiliations 1 and 2 have been swapped. A correction to this chapter can be found at
https://doi.org/10.1007/978-3-031-60731-8_25

only 1% of average flight time [1]. Specifically, the touchdown phase, typically from a height of 50 feet to touchdown, is considered the most hazardous. While accidents often result from a complex interaction of multiple factors, it remains valuable to identify the contribution of individual factors. Various environmental factors have been implicated in impacting flight safety, including wind, temperature, and sun glare [2, 3].

While wind and temperature have been extensively examined, research on sun glare is rather lacking. However, sun glare may have a small but nonnegligible impact on aviation safety. The FAA reported that in just the year 1998, there were 130 incidents in which sunlight glare played a role [3]. Nevertheless, due to the challenges associated with simulation and real-world data collection, the precise extent of its effect remains unclear, highlighting the need for further research into the effects of glare on flight approaches.

Glare, defined as the impact of bright light on visibility in the visual field, is attributed to light scattering in the ocular media, resulting in a veiling effect on the retina's image. Disability glare occurs when this veiling obstructs the view of the target. Previous research identifies two types of disability glare: Real-time Glare, caused by intense light scattering on the retina, and Delayed Glare, occurring during transitions between light and dark conditions [4]. Factors influencing glare include light source brightness, background brightness, light source size, viewing angle, and light source angle [5].

While flying towards the sun, glare can cause disturbances. However, to date, there are no methods for evaluating the level of sun glare. Although various quantification methods for glare, such as UGR and CGI, have been proposed by organizations like the International Commission on Illumination (CIE) and researchers, they are primarily designed for assessing indoor or artificial light glare and may exhibit significant deviations when applied to outdoor sunlight glare conditions [6, 7].

Solar elevation angles and azimuth, in combination with human visual direction, can be used to assess the potential for glare [8, 9]. In the context of driving, researchers have suggested that sun glare can occur when the angular distance between the line of sight and the glare source is below 19° for 40-year-old drivers or 25° for 60-year-old drivers [9]. In another study involving driving safety, researchers found a larger criterion, indicating that sun glare can occur when the absolute difference between solar azimuth and the vehicle's heading was less than 45° [8].

Since the line of sight typically aligns with street direction in the context of driving, and solar elevation angles and azimuth are jointly determined by the latitude of the location, the day of the year, and the time of day, it is feasible to mathematically calculate the potential for sun glare on each street given this information, which generally remains constant. Indeed, scholars have successfully used time periods and street orientations to assess the susceptibility of each street to sunrise and sunset glare in Cambridge, MA [10].

A similar situation arises in flight landing scenarios, where the direction of the runway typically remains fixed. Technically, we can calculate the potential for sun glare on each runway at any given time on a given day, provided the weather is clear. However, providing direct evidence of the effects of sun glare on flight performance remains challenging. One reason is that it is hard and expensive to simulate sun glare in laboratory settings. Even if light simulation is feasible, ensuring ecological validity may be challenging as sun glare may affect operations unexpectedly. Pilots may also adaptively respond to sun glare, such as shifting to instrument flight. Therefore, the adverse effects of sun glare on flight performance may be relatively small and only observable with large datasets when other confounding factors, such as wind conditions, are fully taken into account. These factors are challenging to examine using simulations.

Quick Access Recorder (QAR) data provide a novel approach to analyzing flight incidents and human performance [11], offering a comprehensive solution to address environmental influences on flight safety. QAR is an essential onboard electronic device designed to continuously record various flight parameters. With the capability to record raw data continuously for up to 600 flight hours, it accumulates hundreds to thousands of distinct flight parameter data points at any given moment. These data encompass a wide array of crucial aircraft flight metrics, spanning from latitude, longitude, and altitude to wind speed, direction, airspeed, fuel consumption, temperature, pressure, and beyond [12, 13].

Despite the richness of QAR data, the challenge arises from its vastness. To address this challenge, various methods have been employed, and the most pertinent factors influencing safety have been initially identified. Within the context of the Implementation and Management of Flight Operational Quality Assurance (FOQA) [14], various flight parameters are systematically monitored during the landing phase to detect potential exceedances. These parameters include touchdown distance, maximum vertical acceleration at touchdown, pitch angle at touchdown, and heading angle, among others. Notably, touchdown distance and maximum vertical acceleration at touchdown have received significant attention in prior research due to their association with long and hard landing incidents—two abnormal events frequently encountered during the landing phase [15–17]. A long landing incident occurs when the touchdown distance exceeds the normal touchdown area on the runway, while a hard landing occurs when the monitored maximum vertical acceleration at touchdown exceeds safety thresholds. Both occurrences increase the likelihood of aircraft damage and the incidence of flight accidents, such as runway excursions. Consequently, these parameters, namely touchdown distance and maximum vertical acceleration at touchdown, were deemed pivotal for our investigation. Additionally, the pitch angle at touchdown, also a monitored parameter within FOQA and a subject of previous research, was included in our study [15–19]. Given that aircraft must adhere to a precise glide path profile during the final landing phase, even minor deviations in heading angle can significantly impact the aircraft's flight dynamics. Hence, the heading angle during the landing phase was analyzed.

Regarding environmental factors, sun glare presents a multifaceted association with flying direction, geographical location, weather conditions (particularly sunny weather), date, and time. Furthermore, variations in wind and temperature are known to affect flight performance. Consequently, our study also takes into account various factors such as wind direction, wind speed, and temperature to comprehensively evaluate their impact on flight performance.

This study aimed to examine the effects of sun glare on landing performance based on real flight QAR data. As acquiring adequate QAR data was difficult due to institutional barriers, we examined only a limited number of flights (1235 flights during July 2023) at a given airport. Nonetheless, we selected the airport (Dalian, China), which has two runways (an eastward one and a westward one, see details in the method section) to maximize comparison effects. Five important landing performance indicators were calculated from the QAR data, and we evaluated how these indicators would differ when the potential for sun glare varies. Specifically, if the runway faces east, glare tends to occur during the sunrise and morning time, whereas if the runway faces west, glare tends to occur during the late afternoon and sunset.

2 Methods

2.1 Data Collection

A total of 2276 Quick Access Recorder (QAR) data samples documenting flight landings at Dalian Zhoushuizi International Airport in China during July 2023 were collected. These data include flights landing on runways oriented in two directions: RWY10, facing eastward, and RWY28, facing westward. After filtering for clear weather conditions and limiting the analysis to the five designated daytime periods, comprising the period from sunrise to sunset, a total of 1235 flight landing cases were retained. Among these, 661 samples were directed westward, while 574 samples were directed eastward.

2.2 Performance Indicator Extraction

A total of five performance indicators were used in the current study.

Heading direction deviation (HDD). This indicator measures the aircraft's heading direction relative to the magnetic bearing angle of the runway during landing. The instant HDD is calculated using the formula:

$$\text{HDD} = \text{HEAD angle} - \text{Magnetic Bearing of the Runway} \tag{1}$$

Subsequently, the average of absolute HDD values and the standard deviation of HDD during the landing phase from 50 feet to touchdown point were determined.

Touchdown Distance. This represents the horizontal distance from the radio altitude of 50 feet to the touchdown point during landing, directly obtained from the original QAR data file (CP_DIST_50TD).

Maximum Vertical Acceleration at Touchdown. This signifies the maximum acceleration of the aircraft on the vertical axis at touchdown, directly obtained from the original QAR data file (CP_VRTG_MAX_TD).

Pitch Angle at Touchdown. This refers to the rotation angle around the aircraft's front-to-back axis at the main wheel touchdown, directly obtained from the original QAR data file (CP_PITCH_MTCHDN).

The details of each indicator are presented in Table 1.

Table 1. The variables derived from QAR Parameters in the present study.

Variables	Description	Used parameter in QAR data file	Unit
Dependent Variables			
1. Touchdown distance	The horizontal distance from the radio altitude of 50 feet to the touchdown point in landing	CP_DIST_50TD	Feet
2. Maximum vertical acceleration at touchdown	The maximum acceleration of aircraft on the vertical axis at touchdown	CP_VRTG_MAX_TD	g
3. Pitch angle at touchdown	Rotation angle around the aircraft front-to-back axis at main wheel touchdown	CP_PITCH_MTCHDN	degree
4. Average heading direction deviation (HDD)	Average of the absolute aircraft's heading direction relative to the magnetic bearing angle of the runway during landing	HEAD	degree
5. The standard deviation of HDD	/	HEAD	degree
Control Variables			
6. Crosswind speed	The component of wind that blows perpendicular to the direction of motion of an aircraft	WIND_SPD, WIND_DIR	knot
7. Tailwind speed	The component of wind that blows in the same direction as the movement of an aircraft	WIND_SPD, WIND_DIR	knot
8. Total air temperature	/	TAT	Celsius degree
Independent Variables			
9. Runway direction	RWY10, RWY28	RUNWAY	/
10. Time period	/	DATE, TIME	/

2.3 Time Period Categorization Based on Sun Glare Potential

In our study, we investigated the effect of sun glare by categorizing the daytime into five groups, wherein the likelihood of sun glare varies with the changing sun elevation over time.

First, we checked the sunrise and sunset times for each day in July 2023 in Dalian. We defined the sunrise and sunset time periods using the 19° criteria proposed by Jurado-Piña and Mayora [9]. Accordingly, these two time periods spanned a duration of no less than 107 min and up to a maximum of 110 min following sunrise and preceding sunset each day.

Second, we defined morning and afternoon periods to be after the sunrise or before the sunset period but within 2 h before/after noon. Consequently, the daylight hours were segmented into five distinct intervals: sunrise, morning, noon, afternoon, and sunset. For example, on July 21st, sunrise occurred at 4:45, and sunset at 19:15. There were two specific instances when the sun's elevation reached 19°: at 6:33 after sunrise and at 17:27 before sunset. Therefore, for July 21st, the sunrise period was delineated as "From sunrise to 108 min after sunrise," while the sunset period was defined as "From 108 min before sunset to sunset." Glare incidents may occur during the sunrise period when landing towards the east and during the sunset period when landing towards the west (see Fig. 1 and Table 2).

The flight distribution throughout a 24-h period (refer to Fig. 2) illustrates varying levels of activity, with tens to hundreds of flights occurring in each hour, notably fewer before 7 am. Consequently, each segmented time period encompasses more than 200 landing samples, with the exception of the sunrise period.

2.4 Covariates Calculation

The crosswind and tailwind components were computed using the QAR wind speed and wind direction parameters according to the following formulas:

$$CROSSWIND = WIND\_SPD * sin(A) \tag{2}$$

$$TAILWIND = WIND\_SPD * cos(A) \tag{3}$$

Here, A represents the relative angle between the wind direction and the landing direction (QAR HEAD angle). Since the impact of crosswind from both the left and right sides of the aircraft is comparable during landing along a glide slope, absolute values of crosswind were initially computed. Subsequently, the mean of all absolute crosswind values during the landing phase from 50 to 0 feet was calculated (referred to as CROSSWIND_MEAN_50TD). Similarly, the mean of tailwind values during the same descent phase was determined (designated as TAILWIND_MEAN_50TD) for each flight. Additionally, the temperature value was extracted from the original QAR data.

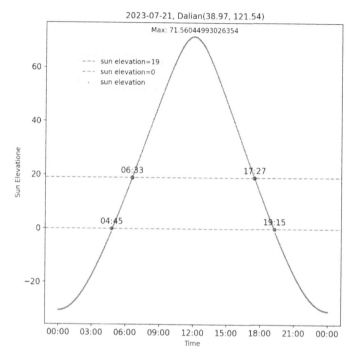

Fig. 1. Sun elevation angles by hours of the day July 21st 2023

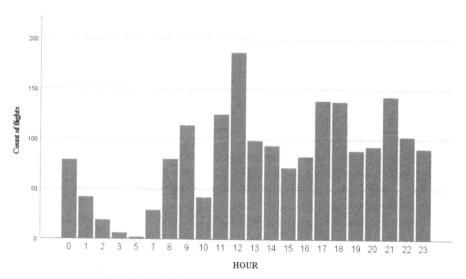

Fig. 2. Distribution of flights by hour in the entire July

2.5 Statistical Analysis

The study regarded runway direction and time period as between-subjects factors, functioning as independent variables, while all flight performance variables were regarded as dependent variables. General Linear Model analysis was conducted, with total air temperature, crosswind, and tailwind serving as covariates (see Table 1).

Table 2. The segmentation of five time periods during the day and example

Time Period	Definition	An example of time range when sunrise time is 4:45, noon is 12:00, and sunset time is 19:15 at Dalian on July 21st of 2023		Count of flights
		From (sun elevation)	To (sun elevation)	
1 Sunrise	From sunrise to 108 min after sunrise	4:45 (0°)	6:33 (19°)	3
2 Morning	From 108 min after sunrise to 120minuts before noon	6:33 (19°)	10:00 (58.4°)	225
3 Noon	From 120minuts before noon to 120 min after noon	10:00 (58.4°)	14:00 (58.3°)	457
4 Afternoon	From 120 min after noon to 108 min before sunset	14:00 (58.3°)	17:27 (19°)	288
5 Sunset	From 108 min before sunset to sunset	17:27 (19°)	19:15 (0°)	262

3 Result

The results reveal a marginally significant interaction effect between runway direction and time period on touchdown distance ($F(4, 1231) = 2.19$, $p = 0.088$) (see Fig. 3).

Further examination of this interaction concerning touchdown distance indicates that landings towards the east exhibit significantly longer touchdown distances compared to those towards the west in the morning (95% CI [11.93, 208.33], $p = 0.028$) and at noon (95% CI [9.14, 149.43], $p = 0.027$). Conversely, during the sunset period, the reverse trend is observed, albeit approaching significance.

Regarding average HDD, the interaction effect between runway direction and time period on average HDD only approaches significance ($F(4, 1231) = 1.93$, $p = 0.123$). The trend suggests that westward landings exhibit more deviations during the afternoon and sunset, while eastward landings display more deviations in the morning (see Fig. 4).

No significant interaction effect between runway direction and time period exists for all other performance indicators.

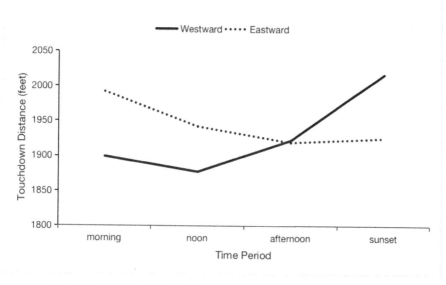

Fig. 3. Average touchdown distance by time period by runway direction

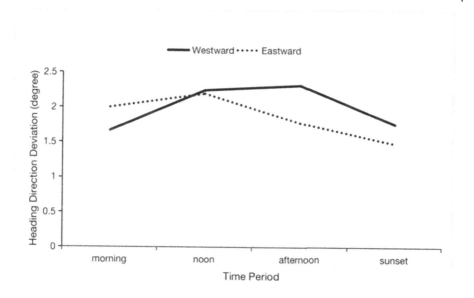

Fig. 4. Average heading direction deviation from 50 feet to touchdown by time period by runway direction

4 Discussion

In this study, we proposed a new approach to examine the small but potentially detrimental effects of environmental factors, such as sun glare, on flight performance. Utilizing QAR data from 1253 real flights at an airport with east-west runways, we uncovered preliminary evidence suggesting that sun glare may indeed influence flight performance.

Specifically, we observed that touchdown distance and heading direction deviation were longer during eastward landings in the morning and westward landings during sunset, albeit with the latter showing only a trend. This provides initial empirical evidence aligning with pilots' reports that heading towards the sun is problematic. However, it's worth noting that the observed effects appeared to be relatively minor, as we did not observe statistically significant results of substantial magnitude.

Nevertheless, these findings underscore the importance of acknowledging such effects and implementing preventive measures. Future research endeavors could benefit from employing larger datasets and more sophisticated modeling techniques to better control for confounding factors.

Firstly, our study employed an approximate categorization of sun glare potential based solely on time periods, which may underestimate the statistical effect and fail to detect smaller impacts. Future studies could consider utilizing more direct metrics, such as the distribution of sun magnitude in the visual field.

Secondly, there is a need to investigate the combined effects of various environmental factors. While we treated wind and temperature as simple covariates, their interactions with each other may be more complex. For instance, sun glare may have minimal influence under normal weather conditions, but in the presence of rapidly changing winds, even brief periods of visual interference could pose significant challenges for pilots.

Additionally, our analysis focused solely on five performance indicators during the final touchdown phase. While these indicators are crucial for flight safety, they may not fully capture the overall impact of glare. Visual impairment might exert greater influence during the transition from automated to manual control, which typically occurs at higher altitudes.

5 Conclusion

This study investigated the influence of sun glare on flight performance during the landing phase. It was observed that encountering sun glare while flying towards the sun could potentially affect flight performance. This underscores the need for more comprehensive research utilizing real data to explore the effects of environmental factors. Such research is crucial for identifying remedies and preventative techniques.

Acknowledgments. This study was supported by Natural Science Fundation of China (T2192932, U2133209, 52072406), the Fundamental Research Funds of CAST (x242060302218), and the key project of Chongqing Technology Innovation and Application Development (grant no. Cstc2021jscx-dxwtBX0020).

References

1. Boeing. Statistical Summary of Commercial Jet Airplane Accidents, Worldwide Operations, 1959–2016. Boeing Commercial Airplanes, Seattle, WA (2017)
2. Zhu, Y., Wang, J., Chen, Y., Wu, Y.: Calculation of takeoff and landing performance under different environments. Int. J. Mod. Phys. Conf. Ser. **42**, 1660174 (2016). https://doi.org/10.1142/S2010194516601745
3. Nakagawara, V.B., Wood, K.J., Montgomery, R.W.: Natural sunlight and its association to civil aviation accidents. Optom. – J. Am. Optom. Assoc. **75**, 517–522 (2004). https://doi.org/10.1016/S1529-1839(04)70177-3
4. Aslam, T.M., Haider, D., Murray, I.J.: Principles of disability glare measurement: an ophthalmological perspective. Acta Ophthalmol. Scand. **85**, 354–360 (2007). https://doi.org/10.1111/j.1600-0420.2006.00860.x
5. Aguirre, R.C., Colombo, E.M., Barraza, J.F.: Effect of glare on reaction time for peripheral vision at mesopic adaptation. J. Opt. Soc. Am. A, JOSAA. **28**, 2187–2191 (2011). https://doi.org/10.1364/JOSAA.28.002187
6. Wienold, J., Christoffersen, J.: Evaluation methods and development of a new glare prediction model for daylight environments with the use of CCD cameras. Energy Buildings **38**, 743–757 (2006). https://doi.org/10.1016/j.enbuild.2006.03.017
7. Wang, T.-H., Huang, Y., Park, J.: Development of daylight glare analysis method using an integrated parametric modelling approach: a comparative study of glare evaluation standards. Buildings **12**, 1810 (2022). https://doi.org/10.3390/buildings12111810
8. Hagita, K., Mori, K.: The Effect of Sun Glare on Traffic Accidents in Chiba Prefecture, Japan. Asian Transp. Stud. **3**, 205–219 (2014). https://doi.org/10.11175/eastsats.3.205
9. Jurado-Piña, R., Mayora, J.M.P.: Methodology to predict driver vision impairment situations caused by sun glare. Transp. Res. Rec. **2120**, 12–17 (2009). https://doi.org/10.3141/2120-02
10. Li, X., Cai, B.Y., Qiu, W., Zhao, J., Ratti, C.: A novel method for predicting and mapping the occurrence of sun glare using Google Street View. Transp. Res. Part C: Emerg. Technol. **106**, 132–144 (2019). https://doi.org/10.1016/j.trc.2019.07.013
11. Gavrilovski, A., et al.: Challenges and opportunities in flight data mining: a review of the state of the art. In: AIAA Infotech @ Aerospace. American Institute of Aeronautics and Astronautics. https://doi.org/10.2514/6.2016-0923
12. Chen, J., Zhang, X., Zhao, M., Xia, Y.: Research on extraction of QAR key parameters during approach phase of civil aviation. In: Presented at the Advances in Materials, Machinery, Electrical Engineering (AMMEE 2017) June (2017). https://doi.org/10.2991/ammee-17.2017.46
13. Gao, X., Cheng, Z., Huo, W.: Anomaly location method for QAR data based on principal component analysis hierarchical clustering. IOP Conf. Ser.: Mater. Sci. Eng. **790**, 012085 (2020). https://doi.org/10.1088/1757-899X/790/1/012085
14. Civil Aviation Administration of China. Implementation and management of flight operation quality assurance. Advisory circular: 121/135-FS-2012–45. CAAC: Beijing, China (2012)
15. Wang, L., Wu, C., Sun, R.: An analysis of flight Quick Access Recorder (QAR) data and its applications in preventing landing incidents. Reliab. Eng. Syst. Saf. **127**, 86–96 (2014). https://doi.org/10.1016/j.ress.2014.03.013
16. Wang, L., Ren, Y., Wu, C.: Effects of flare operation on landing safety: a study based on ANOVA of real flight data. Saf. Sci. **102**, 14–25 (2018). https://doi.org/10.1016/j.ssci.2017.09.027
17. Wang, L., Zhang, J., Dong, C., Sun, H., Ren, Y.: A method of applying flight data to evaluate landing operation performance. Ergonomics **62**, 171–180 (2019). https://doi.org/10.1080/00140139.2018.1502806

18. Li, C., Sun, R., Pan, X.: Takeoff runway overrun risk assessment in aviation safety based on human pilot behavioral characteristics from real flight data. Saf. Sci. **158**, 105992 (2023). https://doi.org/10.1016/j.ssci.2022.105992
19. Zhang, H.: A review of the research of quick access recorder data. Acad. J. Sci. Technol. **5**, 95–101 (2023). https://doi.org/10.54097/ajst.v5i1.5395

Human Factors Association Mining for Controlled Flight into Terrain Based on QAR Data

Feiyin Wang[✉] and Xiaochen Liu

College of Safety Science and Engineering, Civil University of China, Tianjin, China
feiyinwang@126.com

Abstract. Background: The International Civil Aviation Organization (ICAO) has identified Controlled Flight Into Terrain (CFIT), Runway Excursion (RE), Loss of Control In-flight (LOC-I), Mid-Air Collision (MAC), and Runway Incursion (RI) as the five core risks in the 2020–2022 Global Aviation Safety Plan. Airbus mentioned in the *2022 Commercial Aviation Accident Statistical Analysis Report* that the top three causes of fatal accidents in the past 20 years were Loss of Control In-flight (LOC-I), Controlled Flight Into Terrain (CFIT), and Runway Excursion (RE), with CFIT accounting for 17% of the total, which is the second most fatal type of accident. Therefore, it is crucial to study the causation of CFIT accidents to reduce the fatal accident rate of airlines and improve the safety management level. However, the existing accident causation analysis methods are highly generalized and lack human factor causation analysis for CFIT accidents; moreover, the existing human factor causation analysis indexes are mostly descriptive indexes and lack data indexes. **Purpose:** The purpose of this study is to summarize the human factor causation pattern of CFIT accidents by analyzing historical CFIT accident investigation reports; combine with the flight data monitoring indicators, further refine the analysis level on the basis of the existing causation analysis methods, and put forward an optimized human factor analysis method based on the flight data of CFIT, so as to provide assistance for the safe and efficient operation of the safety company. **Methods:** First, a total of 73 CFIT accidents from 2008 to 2021 were collected and counted, and the investigation reports of the 73 CFIT accidents were analyzed in two dimensions, horizontal and vertical, using the SHELL model and the HFACS model. The horizontal dimension refers to the human-aircraft-environmental-management causal factors based on the SHELL model, and the vertical dimension refers to the human factors causal factors based on the HFACS model. Second, based on CFIT accidents investigation report, a combination of literature research and correlation analysis was used to correlate the indicators of the HFACS model with the Quick Access Recorder (QAR) data monitoring program and to refine the analysis level of the HFACS model. In particular, the levels of unsafe behaviors in the HFACS model are further refined on the basis of errors and violations to establish the correlation between human factors and QAR data monitoring items. Finally, based on the above findings, an optimized human factors analysis method for Controlled Flight Into Terrain (CFIT) based on flight data is proposed. **Results:** 1) The optimized HFACS model can refine the analysis of crew error violations in CFIT accidents and provide specific behavioral level qualitative analysis for CFIT accidents; 2) The correlation between crew error violations and QAR data monitoring items can mine out the behaviors that may lead to the occurrence of CFIT accidents and the QAR data monitoring items that need to be paid attention to, and provide specific behavioral level qualitative analysis for CFIT accidents. The correlation between crew errors and violations and QAR data monitoring items can be used to identify the behaviors that may lead to CFIT accidents and the QAR data monitoring items that need to be focused on, so as to provide a specific behavioral level quantitative analysis for CFIT accidents and provide support for the airlines to formulate flight training plans.

Keywords: Accident Causation Analysis · Controlled Flight Into Terrain (CFIT) · Human Factors · Flight Data

1   Introduction

1.1   Literature Review of Controlled Flight into Terrain

Junjie Liu, Yinghao Ye, et al. [1] based on the CFIT events collected by the Civil Aviation of China from 2017–2019 and the CFIT event data in the Aviation Safety Network in the last 20 years as a sample, utilized the Bayesian network event consequence layer and predisposing factor layer, as well as the sample overall Bayesian network quantification results, and concluded that the key risk links based on the sample data are "flight altitude control, crew loss of situational awareness, and flight security". Based on the analysis of CFIT accidents, Wei Yanming et al. [2] analyzed the causal relationship of CFIT using explanatory structural model, and summarized and analyzed the main causal factors leading to CFIT. Sun Ruishan and Zhan Xin [3] based on 30 general aviation controlled flight into terrain that occurred during 2006–2015 in the insecurity database of the Civil Aviation Safety Office of China, analyzed them using the primitive event analysis method, established the system of general aviation controlled flight into terrain influencing factors, and used the explanatory structural model to analyze the influencing factors in a two-by-two comparison, and established a 3-layer The stepwise directional model is used to calculate the weights of the influencing factors and rank them using the CRITIC method. Guo Chaochao and Zhao Huibing [4] used hierarchical analysis to determine the weights of different overrun events based on controlled flight into terrain of an airline from 2015 to 2018, combined with the risk index evaluation method and Heinrich's law to establish a controlled flight into terrain risk evaluation method based on the QAR overrun events, and utilized the model to evaluate and validate the risk of controlled flight into terrain of an airline from 2015 to 2018. Evaluation and validation are carried out. Zhu Hai [5] analyzed the interrelationship between angle of attack and pilot operation, and the pilot's cognitive process of aircraft angle of attack by analyzing the cognitive process of angle of attack in a typical stall accident based on the situational awareness model to establish a civil aviation pilot's angle of attack cognitive model in an airborne loss-of-control accident. The complex state with sequential precursor model represents the complex state accident as a sequence characterized by "precursor events", and the in-flight accidents are all the accidents experienced by the aircraft in the in-flight loss-of-control accidents. Zuo Pengchong [6] analyzed the probability of various precursor events based on 30 complex state accidents.

1.2 Literature Review of Human Factor Causation Analysis of Aviation Accidents

Wenjun et al. [7] based on the original data of the flight requisition 10,000-h rate of transport aviation from 2003 to 2015, used the long- and short-term memory neural network model (LSTM) and the autoregressive sliding average model (ARMA) as a single model to make a prediction, and utilized the induced ordered geometric weighted average operator (IOWGA) to determine the weight of the single prediction model in the combined prediction model, to construct the flight requisition 10,000-h rate of flight requisition The combined prediction model is used to determine the weights of the single prediction model in the combined prediction model to construct the flight sign 10,000-h rate, and the single prediction model is compared with the combined prediction model in order to improve the prediction accuracy of the flight sign 10,000-h rate of transport aviation. Wang Jianhui et al. [8] proposed a transportation aviation flight safety risk evaluation method based on the investigation report of unsafe events and Quick Access Recorder (QAR) data, and based on the severity of the consequences of the risk source events and the average contribution to the classification of the transportation aviation flight safety risk, and then establish the transportation aviation flight safety risk evaluation index system and risk evaluation model. Haojun Xu et al. [9] developed a virtual test flight safety analysis system for multi-factor coupled flight scenario research based on the aircraft six-degree-of-freedom full-volume equations of motion, the mathematical model of unfavorable factors, and the maneuvering mode of human-machine loop. Si-Xuan Yu [10] used a sparse noise reduction self-coding model to predict general aviation risks and constructed the SDAE aviation safety risk framework system. Wang et al. [11] constructed a discrete gray model based on time polynomials based on the rate of serious accidents in air transport per 10,000 h from 2014–2019 and predicted the rate of serious accidents per 10,000 h of air transport. Yu Jiayang et al. [12] proposed the Bow-tie-DT-FTA model to analyze the causes of accidents, proposed preventive measures, and mined the key influencing factors through the sensitivity analysis of influencing factors. Luo Yuchuan et al. [13] statistically analyzed the occurrence patterns and main causes of 56 accidents and 2,196 signs that occurred in China's civil aviation from 2006 to 2015. Chen Nongtian [14] used a gray Markov model to predict approach landing unsafe events. Graham Wild et al. [15] classified and coded flight information based on more than 200 transport aviation accidents and incidents during 2000–2016, and used the Pearson Chi-Squared test to verify whether the human factor had an effect on the accidents and incidents between the Marina Efthymiou et al. [16] used the HFACS framework to categorize the human factors of accident causes based on 50 controlled flight into terrain accidents during 2007–2017. Pang Bing et al. [17] calculated and evaluated the correlation between the underlying factors based on 100 aviation accidents during the period 2009–2011 using association rules and the Human Factors Analysis and Classification System (HFACS) model, and refined the correlation between the underlying factors of the model using GeNIe software. Guo Q. et al. [18] proposed the THERP + CREAM model based on NASA recommendations to determine the cognitive control model of aircraft maintenance personnel and improve the accuracy of aircraft human factors reliability prediction. Lv Tao [19] combined ATC-related aviation accident reports with expert experience to identify major human factors, constructed a Bayesian network assessment model of controller performance, and utilized the (Noise-Max) algorithm to calculate conditional probabilities among model nodes and derive the importance ranking of human factors affecting controller performance through sensitivity analysis. Don Harris [20] and Wen-Chin Li [21] classified human errors by analyzing 523 Air Force flight accidents, and used a combination of artificial neural networks and HFACS to construct a model of the relationship between the prerequisites of unsafe behaviors and unsafe behaviors. Wang Lei et al. [22] mined key flight parameter characteristics of far-landing events by analyzing Quick Access Recorder (QAR) data and proposed human factor preventive measures from the perspective of pilot operations.

2   Analysis of the Cause of the Incident

The SHELL model is used to analyze the causes of controlled flight into terrain from the perspectives of Software, Hardware, Environment, Liveware and Other Liveware. Taking the crew as the core, liveware refers to the crew; other liveware refers to other people other than pilots; the environment is subdivided into cockpit environment, airport terrain environment, meteorological environment, airspace traffic environment, corporate operation environment, and human and social environment, and the results are shown in Table 1.

Table 1. SHELL model influence factor statistics

Incident Triggers	Software	Hardware	Cockpit Environment	Airport Terrain Environment	Meteorology Environment
Number of incidents	14	6	1	6	26
Percentage	19.2%	8.2%	1.4%	8.2%	35.6%
Incident Triggers	Airspace Traffic Environment	Corporate Operational Environment	Human and Social Environment	Crew	Others
Number of incidents	1	2	1	67	19
Percentage	1.4%	2.7%	1.4%	91.8%	26.0%

Firstly, the frequency of crew factor in controlled flight into terrain is as high as 67 times, which means that 91.8% of controlled flight into terrain are directly caused by pilots. Secondly, meteorological environment factor appears 26 times, accounting for 35.6% of the total number of incidents, other liveware factor other than crew factor appears 19 times, accounting for 26.0%, and software factor appears 14 times, accounting for 19.2%, which are largely triggering controlled flight into terrain. The software factor appears 14 times, accounting for 19.2%, to a large extent, they could induce controlled flight into terrain; airport terrain environmental factor and hardware factor appears 6 times, accounting for 8.2%, which is important factor affecting controlled flight into terrain. Finally, the corporate operational environment factor appears 2 times, and airspace traffic environmental factor, cockpit environmental factor and human and social environmental factor appears once, which are also influential factors that could not be ignored.

Based on the results of the statistical analysis, it is concluded that human factors (Liveware) are the most important factor inducing controlled flight into terrain, and the meteorological environment also has a great influence on controlled flight into terrain, followed by the influence of software factor.

3 Analysis of Human Factors

This study provides an in-depth analysis of human factors in controlled flight into terrain based on the HFCAS model. Statistical analyses are conducted in terms of direct, indirect, fundamental and root causes of the pilots' unsafe acts, precondition for unsafe acts, unsafe supervision, and organizational factors.

3.1 Analysis of Direct Causes

Among the direct causes of pilots, see Table 2, the skill-based errors with the highest frequency of poor flight skills occurred 32 times (43.8% of the total number of incidents), followed by exceptional violations of orders, regulations, and procedures, which occurred 20 times, (27.4% of the total number of incidents). In addition, the unsafe acts that occurred frequently were, in order, insufficient control of the aircraft (9 times, 12.3% of the total number of incidents), lack of experience (7 times, 9.6% of the total number of incidents), and multiple, prolonged violations of orders, rules, and procedures (7 times, 9.6% of the total number of incidents).

3.2 Analysis of Indirect Causes

Among the indirect causes, see Table 3, the most frequent occurrence was the failure of crew teamwork in crew resource management, which occurred a total of 18 times, accounting for 24.7% of the total number of incidents; followed by the loss of situational awareness in the adverse mental states, which occurred a total of 11 times, accounting for 15.1% of the total number of incidents; and then the mental fatigue in the adverse mental states, the poor communication with ATC in the crew resource management and the problems communicating with the crew, all occurred 9 times, accounting for 12.3% of the total number of incidents.

3.3 Analysis of Fundamental Causes

Among the fundamental causes, see Table 4, the most frequent occurrence was failure to provide adequate technical data or procedures in inadequate supervision, which occurred a total of 18 times, accounting for 24.7% of the total number of incidents; followed by inadequate supervision by the supervisor, which occurred a total of 8 times, accounting for 11.0% of the total number of incidents; and then inadequate training provided by the

Table 2. Frequency statistics of direct causes

Pilot's direct causes/ unsafe act	Errors	Skill-based errors	Poor flight skills	32
			Missed flight maneuvers	0
			Inadequate control of the aircraft	9
		Decision errors	Lack of experience	7
			Lack of training	4
			External pressures	7
			Emergency situations	5
		Perceptual errors	Misjudging distance, altitude, airspeed, etc.	5
			Visual errors	1
	Violations	Routine violations	Multiple, prolonged violations of orders, rules, procedures	7
			Multiple poor preflight preparations	1
			Multiple violations of the workbook	1
			Multiple failures to use or misuse of equipment	3
		Exceptional Violations	Exceptional violations of orders, rules, procedures	20
			Exceptional violations of the workbook	4

organizer, which occurred a total of 7 times, accounting for 9.6% of the total number of incidents. Based on the results of the statistical analysis, the fundamental causes were mostly focused on inadequate supervision, and the frequency of fundamental causes of incidents caused by inadequate supervision accounted for 85% of the total frequency of fundamental causes.

3.4 Analysis of Root Causes

Among the root causes, see Table 5, the most frequent occurrence is the lack of safety procedures/risk management procedures in organizational processes, which occurred 11 times in total, accounting for 15.1% of the total number of incidents; followed by the failure to develop standard operating procedures/lack of procedures, which occurred 6 times in total, accounting for 8.2% of the total number of incidents. Based on the results of the statistical analysis, the root causes were mostly focused on organizational processes, with the frequency of incidents caused by organizational processes accounting for 76.9% of the total frequency of root causes.

Table 3. Frequency statistics of indirect causes

Indirect causes/ Precondition for unsafe acts	Environmental factors	Physical environment	Extravehicular environment (weather, altitude, terrain)	3
			Cabin environment (temperature, vibration, lighting, toxic gases)	0
		Technological environment	Control design of equipment	1
			Display design and interface features of the equipment	1
			Checklist Programming	0
			Fatigue fracture	0
			Equipment failure	1
	Conditions of operators	Adverse mental states	Mental fatigue	9
			Loss of situational awareness	11
			Complacency	2
		Adverse physiological states	Low flight alertness	1
			Illness, physical fatigue	2
		Physical/mental limitation	Side effects of medication (side effects include hallucinations, disorientation, etc.)	0
			Operational requirements beyond personal ability	2
			Visual limitations	1
	Personnel factors	Crew resource management	Inadequate physical fitness	0
			Poor communication with ATC	9

(*continued*)

Table 3. (*continued*)

		Personal readiness	Problems communicating with the crew	9
			Failure of crew teamwork	18
			Inadequate rest	1
			Inadequate training	0
			Pre-flight tasks that interfere with individual cognitive accuracy	0

Table 4. Statistics on the frequency of root causes

Fundamental causes/ Unsafe supervision	Inadequate supervision	Failure to provide professional guidance by organizer	1
		Inadequate training provided by the organizer	7
		Inadequate supervision by the supervisor	8
		Failure to provide adequate technical data or procedures	18
	Planned inappropriate operations	Unreasonable staffing	0
		Unreasonable tasks/workload	2
	Failure to correct problem	Managers knew inadequate personnel training but took no actions	0
		Failure to address safety hazards	4
		Failure to correct incorrect documentation	0
	Supervisory violations	Allowing unqualified personnel to perform related work	0
		Allowing unlicensed pilots to fly	0
		Failure to effectively monitor preflight preparation	0
		False Records	0

Table 5. Frequency statistics of root causes

Root causes/ organizational factors	Resource management	Improper allocation of staff resources	1
		Inappropriate allocation of funds	0
		Inappropriate allocation of equipment	1
	Organizational climate	Inappropriate organizational setup	0
		Lack of safety climate	0
		Organizational policies	1
		Inappropriate allocation of responsibilities	0
		Inappropriate values and attitudes	3
	Organizational processes	Slow organizational work rate	0
		Deficiencies in work procedures standards	2
		Failure to develop standard operating procedures/lack of procedures	6
		Systems, regulations not enforced	0
		Lack of safety procedures/risk management procedures	11
		Lack of supervision and inspection of resources, climate and procedures	1

4 Conclusion

(1) The causal analysis based on the SHELL model concludes that human factors are the most direct cause of inducing controlled flight into terrain, and that meteorological environmental factors and software factors have a greater impact on inducing controlled flight into terrain.

(2) The human factor analysis based on the HFACS model shows that among the factors of unsafe pilot acts, poor flight skills and exceptional violation of orders, rules and procedures have the highest frequency and are the most important unsafe acts inducing controllable flight into terrain. In particular, when the two factors occur simultaneously, they are more likely to induce controlled flight into terrain. Failure of crew teamwork and loss of situational awareness are important precondition of unsafe acts influence; failure to provide adequate technical data or procedures is an important unsafe supervision influence; and lack of safety procedures/risk management procedures is an important organizational processes influence that has a significant impact on inducing controlled flight into terrain when the above influences occur.

(3) Based on the results of SHELL and HFACS analysis, it is concluded that the unsafe acts of the crew is an important influence factor that can easily lead to the occurrence of controlled flight into terrain. Based on the result, this study refined an optimized HFACS model, whose refined analysis of the influencing factors combined with the QAR data helps to quantitatively study the unsafe acts of pilots.

Acknowledgments. This study was funded by the Scientific Research Program of the Tianjin Education Commission (grant number 2023KJ230).

References

1. Liu, J., Ye, Y.H., Du, Y.L.: Quantification of controlled flight into terrain event based on Bayesian network. J. Civ. Aviat. Univ. China **41**(02), 21–26 (2023)
2. Wei, Y., Gan, X., You, W., et al.: Inducement relationship analysis of controlled flight into terrain based on ISM model. Fire Control Command Control **43**(02), 172–176 (2018)
3. Sun, R., Zhan, X.: Analysis on influence factors of controlled flight into terrain of general aviation based on ISM-CRITIC method. J. Saf. Sci. Technol. **14**(01), 129–135 (2018)
4. Chaochao, G.U.O., Huibing, Z.H.A.O.: Study on risk analysis and countermeasures of controlled flight into terrain based on QAR over-limit events. J. Anyang Inst. Technol. **19**(04), 1–4 (2020). https://doi.org/10.19329/j.cnki.1673-2928.2020.04.001
5. Zhu, H.: Construction of a cognitive model of civil aviation pilots' angle of attack in airborne loss-of-control accidents. Sci. Technol. **26**(36), 217–219 (2016)
6. Pengchong, Z.: Analysis of Aircraft Upset Accident and Research on UPRT Scheme. Civil Aviation Flight University of China (2022).https://doi.org/10.27722/d.cnki.gzgmh. 2021.000030
7. Wen, J., Chen, J.Q., Luo, X.Y., et al.: Combined prediction of air transport flight accident symptoms based on IOWGA. J. Saf. Environ. **22**(01), 256–262 (2022)
8. Jianhui, W.A.N.G., Wei, D.E.N.G., Zhenghong, X.I.A., et al.: Flight risk assessment method of transport aviation. China Saf. Sci. J. **29**(12), 110–116 (2019)
9. Liu, D., Xu, H., Zhang, J.: Quantitative risk evaluation methods for multi-factor coupling complex flight situations. Acta Aeronautica et Astronautica Sinica **34**(03), 509–516 (2013)
10. Si-Xuan, Y.: Risk Analysis for Gernal Aviation Safety. Nanjing University of Aeronautics and Astronautics (2019).https://doi.org/10.27239/d.cnki.gnhhu.2019.001151
11. Yuanying, W., Jue, L.: Research on air transportation accident symptoms based on polynomial discrete grey model. In: 2022 IEEE 4th International Conference on Civil Aviation Safety and Information Technology (ICCASIT), Dali, China, pp. 400–403 (2022)
12. Jiayang, Y.U., Jiansheng, G.U.O., Chuhan, Z.H.O.U., et al.: Decision-making analysis of preventive measures for aviation safety accidents based on bow-tie-DT-FTA. Fire Control Command Control **47**(08), 158–164 (2022)
13. Luo, Y., Han, X., Luo, X.: Statistic analysis based on accidents and incidents of China civil aviation during 2006–2015. J. Civ. Aviat. Flight Univ. China **29**(03), 21–24+29 (2018)
14. Chen, N., Zhang, H., Cao, Y.: Prediction of approaching landing unsafe events based on gray markov method. Math. Pract. Theor. **50**(04), 306–314 (2020)
15. Kharoufh, H., Murray, J., Baxter, G., et al.: A review of human factors causations in commercial air transport accidents and incidents: from to 2000–2016. Progress Aerosp. Sci. **99**, S0376042117302154 (2018)
16. Kelly, D., Efthymiou, M.: An analysis of human factors in fifty controlled flight into terrain aviation accidents from 2007 to 2017. J. Saf. Res. **69**, 155–165 (2019)
17. Bing, P., Wenyu, Y.: On the improvement of HFACS model based on the association rules and GeNle. J. Saf. Environ. **18**(05), 1886–1890 (2018)
18. Guo, Q., Guan, D.: Human factor reliability prediction model for civil aircraft maintenance task analysis. Acta Aeronautica et Astronautica Sinica **44**(16), 163–173 (2023)
19. Lu, T.: Human Factors Analysis of Air Traffic Safety Based on HFACS-BN Model. Shanghai Jiaotong University (2020)

20. Don, H., Wen-Chin, L.: Using neural networks to predict HFACS unsafe acts from the pre-conditions of unsafe acts. Ergonomics **62**(2), 181–191 (2019)
21. Li, W.-C., Harris, D.: Identifying training deficiencies in military pilots by applying the human factors analysis and classification system. Int. J. Occup. Saf. Ergon. **19**(1), 3–18 (2013)
22. Wang, L., Wu, C., Sun, R.: An analysis of flight Quick Access Recorder (QAR) data and its applications in preventing landing incidents. Reliab. Eng. Syst. Saf. **127**, 86–96 (2014)

Future Flight Safety Monitoring: Comparison of Different Computational Methods for Predicting Pilot Performance Under Time Series During Descent by Flight Data and Eye-Tracking Data

Yifan Wang, Wen-Chin Li(✉), Arthur Nichanian, Wojciech Tomasz Korek, and Wesley Tsz-Kin Chan

SATM, Cranfield University, Cranfield, Bedford, UK
{Yf.Wang,wenchin.li,a.nichanian,W.T.Korek,
Wesley.Chan}@cranfield.ac.uk

Abstract. Introduction. Effective and real-time analysis of pilot performance is important for improving flight safety and enabling remote flight safety control. The use of flight data and pilot physiological data to analyse and predict pilot performance is an effective means of achieving this monitoring. **Research question.** This research aims to compare two forecasting methods (XGBoost and Transformer) in evaluating and predicting pilot performance using flight data and eye tracking data. **Method.** Twenty participants were invited to fly an approach using Instrument Landing System (ILS) guidance in the Future Systems Simulator (FSS) while wearing Pupil-Lab eye tracker. The deviation to the desired route, the pupil diameter and the gaze positions were selected for forecasting the flight performance indicator: the difference between the aircraft altitude and the reference altitude corresponding to the ideal 3-degree glide path. Utilize XGBoost and the Transformer forecasting technique to develop a forecasting model using the data from this research, and conduct a comparative analysis of the accuracy and convenience of both models. **Results & Discussion.** The result demonstrates that using XGBoost regression model had a higher prediction accuracy, (RMSEXGBoots = 42.29, RMSETransformer = 102.10) and its easier to achieve a high prediction accuracy than Transformer as Transformer forecasting method placed a high demand on debugging model and computing equipment. The deviation to desired route and the pupil diameter were more important in the XGBoost model. **Conclusion.** The use of machine learning and deep learning methods enables the monitoring and prediction of flight performance using flight data and pilot physiological data. The comparison of the two methods shows that it is not necessarily the newer and more complex technology that can build more accurate and faster prediction models, but building the right model based on the data is important for real-time flight data monitoring and prediction in the future.

Keywords: data analysis · human-machine interactions · eye-tracking data · pilot performance monitoring

D. Harris and W.-C. Li (Eds.): HCII 2024, LNAI 14693, pp. 308–320, 2024.
https://doi.org/10.1007/978-3-031-60731-8_22

1 Introduction

How to effectively monitor and predict flight performance and pilot behaviour is a major topic in future aviation safety research [1]. Remote monitoring of flight status and pilot performance with time series has become possible with improvements in transmission technology and aircraft computer power [2]. This paper aims to utilize machine learning methods to analyse flight data and eye tracking data, the goal is to predict and monitor pilot performance during landings effectively. Descent angle deviation was used as a criterion for evaluating landing performance as inadequate vertical position awareness during the approach phase was known to be a large contributor to inadequate situation awareness and approach-and-landing accidents [3]. Throughout this process, the paper will compare the advantages and disadvantages of two different computational approaches in handling the data.

Analysing remote flight data and pilot status data is essential to improve aviation performance, efficiency, and safety. Firstly, the analysis of remote flight data and pilot status data is critical for a high level of flight safety [4]. Continuous monitoring of aircraft parameters such as altitude, speed and system health, as well as monitoring of pilot status such as eye tracking, HRV, etc. helps in early detection of anomalies and timely intervention to reduce the likelihood of potential accidents and human error. Additionally, optimising flight operations and enhancing fuel efficiency are possible with the aid of remote flight data analysis. Airlines can find solutions to reduce emissions, optimise routes, and increase fuel efficiency by monitoring weather patterns, engine performance, and flight paths.

It is essential to approach flight safety monitoring from two angles to achieve successful monitoring: first, by monitoring and processing flight data; and second, by monitoring the pilot's condition [5]. Flight Data Monitoring (FDM) has evolved into an important tool for analysing aviation safety and performance. Continuous monitoring and analysis of FDM data provides a comprehensive view of an aircraft's dynamic behaviour, including pitch, roll and altitude angles. Most current flight data monitoring analyses are based on monitoring deviations from acceptable parameter ranges, such as low speeds for two pilots with dual flight control inputs [6]. Fewer studies have focussed on FDM in conjunction with external or physiological data to further speculate on flight data variations and assess pilot performance and actions. In this context, the introduction of eye tracking data can effectively complement the flight data, addressing the lack of pilot monitoring data [7]. Eye tracking on the flight deck has the potential to improve our understanding of pilot conduct and cognitive processes as the technology continues to advance [8].

Eye tracking techniques provide an objective measurement on understanding attention distribution and measuring pilot cognitive workload [9, 10]. Eye tracking allows for the non-intrusive, real-time monitoring of a pilot's gaze patterns, reaction speeds, and visual attention [11]. These measurements offer a special perspective on the mental strain that pilots experience during crucial stages like descent and landing. Pilot attentional patterns and reaction times to visual inputs can be used to measure workload, decision-making effectiveness, and situation awareness in general [8, 12, 13]. Studies using ocular features such as pupil diameter and blink frequency to assess cognitive load have been conducted in many application areas [9]. Van et al. observed a strong linear relationship between the time derivative of pupil diameter and task performance measures [14]. Researchers found that in a numerical task in noise, the larger the pre-stimulus pupil diameter, the worse the task performance [15]. In addition, in studies with fixations, researchers have found that the distribution of fixations can effectively reflect the distribution of human attention and may affect the pilot's decision-making process [16]. All these indicate that it is possible to realise the quantitative analysis of pilot performance by supplementing flight data with eye-tracking parameters.

The selection of appropriate data analysis models is important for improving the accuracy and efficiency of data analysis and prediction. XGBoost is a powerful and widely used machine learning algorithm known for its efficiency and performance in various predictive modelling tasks [17]. It uses gradient boosting techniques to minimise the loss function by iteratively adding new models that focus on the errors of existing models. XGBoost is known for its scalability, speed, and ability to handle a wide range of data types and feature engineering techniques, making it a popular choice for regression and classification problems in machine learning [18]. XGBoost is not an artificial neural network, but a collection of decision trees. In addition, XGBoost is more efficient in dealing with large datasets and generates more accurate results because it uses decision trees to identify the most important variables and construct the model, whereas artificial neural networks can be computationally expensive and require more training time [19]. The general architecture of XGBoost is as follows (Fig. 1):

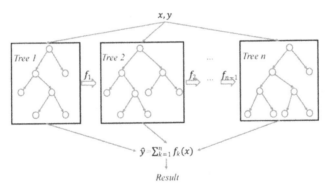

Fig. 1. The general architecture of XGBoost [20]

Transformer is a state-of-the-art architecture originally designed for natural language processing but has been adapted for time series forecasting [21]. In contrast to tradi-tional Recurrent Neural Networks (RNNs) and Convolutional Neural Networks (CNNs), Transformer relies on a self-attention mechanism to capture long-range dependencies in the input sequence. This self-attention mechanism allows the model to dynamically attend to different parts of the input sequence and thus learn complex temporal patterns efficiently [22]. In terms of time series prediction, Transformer processes historical input sequences and directly predicts future values [23]. The general Transformer-based forecasting model is as follows.

XGBoost excels in feature engineering, interpretability and scalability, while Trans-former excels in capturing long-range dependencies, adaptation and end-to-end learning

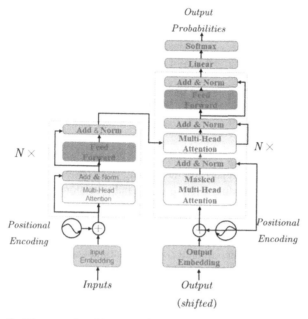

Fig. 2. The general architecture of Transformer forecasting model [24]

[25]. The choice between the two methods depends on the specific requirements of the forecasting task, the characteristics of the time series data, and the trade-offs needed between interpretability, performance, and computational efficiency.

2 Methodology

2.1 Participants

Twenty participants (15 males, 5 females) were invited to participate in this research. The participants had an average fixed-wing flying experience of 74.4 h (mean = 74.4, *s.d.* = 93.9). In accordance with Cranfield University's Research Ethics System approval (CURES/14853/2021), data for this paper was collected from participants only for research purposes. Before the study began, a contract was given to each participant; only if they signed it could the experiment proceed, and they retained the right to terminate the trial at any time and have all of their data deleted. The participants' demographics are as follows (Table 1):

2.2 Data Collection and Pre-processing

The Rolls-Royce Future System Simulator (FSS) at Cranfield University was used for this study. The FSS is a highly integrated future flight deck simulator with four big programmable touchscreens and two small side touchscreens. Using this simulator, researchers and pilots can investigate optimal procedures for a single-pilot operation flight deck with highly autonomous engines and novel technologies in the future [26].

Table 1. Participants' demographics

	Mean	SD
Age	32.15	10.70
Fix-wing flight hours	74.35	93.91
Simulator flight hours	64.5	221.60
Gender	15 male	5 female

Participants were asked to perform the landing task following the cues displayed to them by the Instrument Landing System (ILS) and precision approach path indicator (PAPI) while wearing the eye tracker. The weather was clear, no turbulence. The starting point is at five miles final approach to the runway, at an altitude of 1400 feet and speed of 150 knots. The landing gear and throttle lever were all automated to maintain a constant approach speed. The simulator would automatically record all of the flight data, including flight path, altitude, and calibrated airspeed (CAS), which allowed to calculate the deviation from the desired route post-trial. Throughout the experiment, the environment was stabilized and well illuminated to increase the accuracy of the eye tracking data that was gathered (Fig. 3).

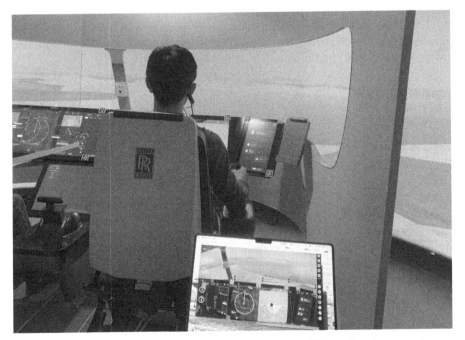

Fig. 3. Participant performing the landing task in the FSS while wearing the eye tracker.

Data on eye-tracking were gathered for this study using the Pupil-Labs eye tracker. The components of this eye tracker include an eye camera that is fixed in a plastic frame to monitor eye characteristics and movement, and a world camera that synchronizes user viewpoints. The sample rate was 60 frames per second and the resolution was 1280×720 pixels. The eye camera would watch each participant's right eye in order to measure the pupil's diameter and gazes.

The altitude difference between the aircraft altitude and the reference altitude corresponding to the ideal 3-degree glide path was selected as a marker for evaluating the flight performance to be used as a target for prediction in this study. This variable is called 'ΔGP' and determined is as follows:

$$GP = \tan(3) \times x_{thr} \times 6076.12 + CH_{thr}$$

$$\Delta GP = Altitude - GP$$

The parameters:

x_{thr}, representing the aircraft distance to the runway threshold in NM;

CH_{thr}, representing the crossing height, which is 50ft above the runway threshold height.

There were three factors used for GP prediction: Root mean square of deviation from the desired route (RMS), pupil diameter and the gaze position. Gaze is the basic unit of fixation, which contains not only the information of fixation, but also the information of saccade, which can fully reflect the participant's visual attention changes. And in 3D space, the gaze position is decomposed into three vectors under the XYZ axis. Then the data was cleaned to only keep the 4.5 NM to 1 NM to the runway threshold to exclude the possibility that the results varied too much due to large differences in the experience level of participants, affecting the accuracy of the predictions. Finally, the data were normalised: the data were scaled to a standard normal distribution with mean 0 and standard deviation 1:

$$X_{norm} = \frac{X - \mu}{\sigma}$$

2.3 Statistical Tools Used

The XGBoost regression prediction model and the Transformer time series prediction model used in this study are two of the more representative approaches in machine learning and Artificial Neural Networks (ANN).

The XGBoost is an ensemble machine learning technique based on trees that generates several decision trees (a weak learner) and merges them into a prediction model (a strong learner). In each iteration, it develops a new tree greedily in order to lower the residuals of the previous model. This technique is a type of gradient-boosted tree approach. The 'Sklearn' package was used in the Python for the XGBoost algorithm.

$$\hat{y}_i = \sum_{k=1}^{K} f_k(x_i), \ f_k \in F \tag{1}$$

In the formulas, the f_k is a function of an independent tree with the specific tree structure and leaf weight. K represents the total number of additive functions. The space of the classification and regression trees (CART) is represented by F. At the t-th iteration, the objective function $\mathcal{L}^{(t)}$ that has to be optimized can be written as follows:

$$\mathcal{L}^{(t)} = \sum_{i=1}^{n} \ell(y_i, \hat{y}_i) + \Omega(f_t) \tag{2}$$

In the formulas, l is the loss function that measures the truth y_i and the prediction $\hat{y}_i$. The regularisation term, $\Omega(f_t)$, penalizes the model's complexity to prevent overfitting.

$$\Omega(f_t) = \gamma T + \frac{1}{2}\lambda||\omega||^2 \tag{3}$$

The basic principle of Transformer's time series prediction is to convert the time series data into a sequence format, then capture the correlation between different positions in the sequence through a self-attention mechanism, and finally make the prediction through a multilayer feedforward neural network based on positional encoding. In this research, the 'PyTorch' package was used for the Transformer algorithm in Python. By debugging the Transformer model, the optimiser was set to RMSprop, which adaptively adjusts the learning rate for each parameter, thus avoiding the problem of learning rates decaying too quickly. The learning rate was initially set to 0.0001 and the epochs was set to 25. The Self-Attention formulas is as follows:

$$Attention(Q, K, V) = softmax\left(\frac{QK^T}{\sqrt{d_k}}\right)V \tag{4}$$

In the formulas, the Query (Q) is the vector used to calculate the attention score. The Key (K) is the vector that measures the similarity between Query and Value. The Value (V) is the vector used to calculate the weighted average value.

3   Results and Discussion

3.1   Comparing for Two Forecasts Methods

The transformer time series forecasting model and the XGBoost forecasting model were used to predict the 'ΔGP' representing the flight performance in this research. The gaze position in X axis (gaze_x), gaze position in Y axis (gaze_y), gaze position in Z axis (gaze_z), RMS and pupil diameter. The accuracy of the predictions using the two methods is shown in the table below. It is clear to notice that the results for both MAE (mean absolute error) and RMSE values were smaller when using the XGBoost method, meaning that the accuracy of the prediction was higher. And with the higher prediction accuracy of XGBoost, it has advantages that Transformer does not have: fast computation and lower equipment requirements. The length of the computation using Transformer is much longer than that of XGBoost, which is a high requirement for the hardware. The convergence of the Transformer model is difficult due to the large discrete values of the eye tracking data and is subject to large individual differences in participants (Table 2).

Table 2. Participants' performance against XGBoost and Transformer values

	XGBoost	Transformer
RMSE	42.29	102.10
MAE	25.18	78.01

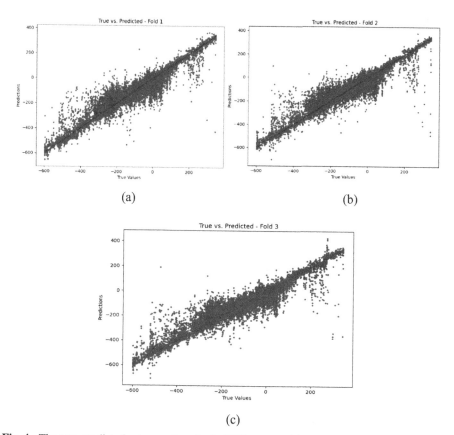

(a)   (b)

(c)

Fig. 4. The true-predicted value scatter plot in XGBoost model. X-axis is the true value and Y-axis is the predicted value. Subfigures (a), (b) and (c) represent the results for each fold in a 3-fold validation set.

The true-predicted value scatter plot for prediction using the XGBoost model is shown in Fig. 4. It can be found that the scatter points are approximately arranged on a diagonal line, indicating a high prediction accuracy. However, it is worth noting that the lower prediction accuracy was found near the extremes in all three folds. Firstly, it may be because these extremes are outliers that are not suitable for prediction. Secondly, these extremes may represent unacceptable deviations (e.g., due to the skill level of the pilots), which affects the accuracy of the prediction.

Based on the comparison between the models built by XGBoost and Transformer, it is observed that XGBoost achieves higher predictive accuracy. This finding suggests several possible reasons. Firstly, XGBoost is a highly optimized ensemble learning algorithm specifically designed for tabular data, which may be more suitable for the particular characteristics of this dataset. Secondly, XGBoost relies on decision trees, which are capable of capturing complex nonlinear relationships in the data, while Transformer may struggle to model certain types of tabular data effectively. Additionally, XGBoost typically requires less data preprocessing and tuning compared to Transformer, which can simplify the modelling process and reduce the risk of overfitting. Therefore, further investigation and experimentation are warranted to better understand the factors influencing the relative performance of XGBoost and Transformer in different scenarios.

3.2 Features Importance Analysis in XGBoost Model.

The importance of different features in forecasting model building is analysed using 3-fold cross-validation. The features are gaze_x (feature 1), gaze_y (feature 2), gaze_z (feature 3), RMS (feature 4) and pupil diameter (feature 5). The importance for the models are shown as follows:

The gaze_y (feature 2) had a significantly high importance in model (weight_1 = 0.3314, weight_2 = 0.2971, weight_3 = 0.3132), indicating that changes in gaze position in the vertical direction are strongly weighted for analysing flight performance during descent. Changes in gaze position in the vertical direction may indicate that the pilot frequently switches attention between the display and out the window, which affects the pilot's performance during landing [27].

The RMS (feature 4) also had a high importance in predicting ΔGP (weight_1 = 0.3061, weight_2 = 0.3237, weight_3 = 0.3125). The RMS deviation to the desired route reflects the accuracy of the piloting actions during descent and it is highly related to the altitude changes, thus, it occupies a higher weight in the prediction of the ΔGP.

Gaze_x (feature 1) and pupil diameter (feature 5) possess similar importance in analysing ΔGP. The correlation between gaze position and performance during landing is mainly due to the pilot's lateral shift of attention between the primary flight display and the navigation display, so the acquired landing-related information may affect the pilot's situation awareness and thus the landing performance. Whilst this lateral shift of attention may be influenced by external factors such as cockpit instrumentation layout, the feature of pupil diameter correlates with the pilot's tension level and workload level, which may affect the flight performance during landing [28] (Fig. 5).

3.3 Limitations

As an exploratory study, this study had the following limitations. Firstly, the sample size was small and not fully representative of all pilots. Data from only 20 participants were retained for analysis due to eye-tracking data accuracy issues. Secondly, although the accuracy of the model was acceptable overall, the extreme ends suffered from lower prediction accuracy which may have been due to the pilots' performance. The homogenisation of the models used results in the Transformer model did not achieve the desired

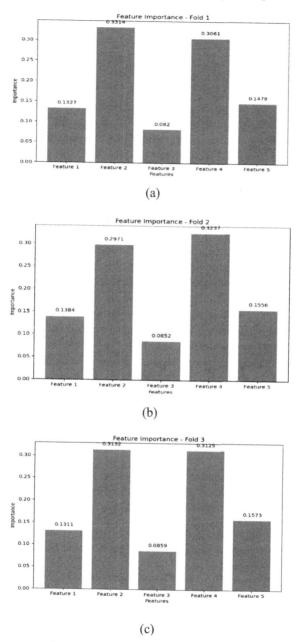

(a)

(b)

(c)

Fig. 5. Feature importance for the XGBoost model. Subfigures (a), (b) and (c) represent the results for each fold in a 3-fold validation set.

accuracy and does not represent its capability in time series prediction of flight performance. Finally, for future studies, a more diverse selection of parameters may help to better represent the flight data and pilot physiological data, which may enhance the predictive potential for pilot performance.

4 Conclusion

Achieving the monitoring and prediction of pilot performance is important for improving flight safety and realising future remote flight safety monitoring. In order to investigate the analysis and prediction of pilot performance, this study analyses the prediction outcomes of two distinct time-series forecasting models, XGBoost and Transformer, using two types of data: flight data and pilot physiological data. The gaze (decomposed into three vectors under the XYZ axis), pupil diameter and the RMS of deviation to desired route were selected to predict the pilot performance indicator: ΔGP, the altitude difference between the aircraft altitude and the reference altitude corresponding to the ideal 3-degree glide path. The results show that the simpler structure of XGBoost has a higher prediction accuracy, and the calculation process is simpler and faster. Factor significance analyses showed that gaze's component on the z-axis and RMS had a more significant effect on predicting ΔGP. On the contrary, this does not mean that neural network algorithms, represented by Transformer, do not have the potential for flight performance analysis and prediction. The parameters selected in this study were small, but with the use of a larger number of parameters (big data) and an increase in the computing power of the computing device, Transformer may have better performance. This study provides an exploration for future analysis and prediction of flight performance by combining flight data with pilot physiological data or other parameters. Future research could consider adding different parameters and selections to improve the algorithm to further enhance the accuracy of the prediction.

References

1. Nguyen, T., Lim, C.P., Nguyen, N.D., Gordon-Brown, L., Nahavandi, S.: A review of situation awareness assessment approaches in aviation environments. IEEE Syst. J. **13**(3), 3590–3603 (2019). https://doi.org/10.1109/JSYST.2019.2918283
2. Wiseman, Y.: Unlimited and protected memory for flight data recorders. Aircraft Eng. Aeros. Technol. **88**(6), 866–872 (2016). https://doi.org/10.1108/AEAT-06-2015-0152
3. Flight Safety Foundation. FSF ALAR Briefing Note 7.1 Stabilized Approach. Flight Safety Foundation (2009)
4. Matalgah, M.M., Alqodah, M.A.: Real-Time Ground-Based Flight Data and Cockpit Voice Recorder: Implementation Scenarios and Feasibility Analysis. John Wiley & Sons, Hoboken (2023)
5. Guo, Y., Ma, C., Jing, Z.: A Hybrid health monitoring approach for aircraft flight control systems with system-level degradation. IEEE Trans. Ind. Electron. **70**(7), 7438–7448 (2023). https://doi.org/10.1109/TIE.2022.3201317
6. Walker, G.: Redefining the incidents to learn from: safety science insights acquired on the journey from black boxes to Flight Data Monitoring. Saf. Sci. **99**, 14–22 (2017). https://doi.org/10.1016/J.SSCI.2017.05.010
7. Hebbar, P.A., Pashilkar, A.A., Biswas, P.: Using eye tracking system for aircraft design – a flight simulator study. Aviation **26**(1), 11–21 (2022). https://doi.org/10.3846/aviation.2022.16398

8. Li, W.C., Zhang, J., Le Minh, T., Cao, J., Wang, L.: Visual scan patterns reflect to human-computer interactions on processing different types of messages in the flight deck. Int. J. Ind. Ergon. **72**, 54–60 (2019). https://doi.org/10.1016/J.ERGON.2019.04.003

9. Chen, S., Epps, J.: Using task-induced pupil diameter and blink rate to infer cognitive load. Hum. Comput. Interact. **29**, 390–413 (2014). https://doi.org/10.1080/07370024.2014.892428

10. Stanton, N.A., Plant, K.L., Roberts, A.P., Allison, C.K.: Use of highways in the sky and a virtual pad for landing head up display symbology to enable improved helicopter pilots situation awareness and workload in degraded visual conditions. Ergonomics **62**(2), 255–267 (2017). https://doi.org/10.1080/00140139.2017.1414301

11. Li, F., Lee, C.H., Chen, C.H., Khoo, L.P.: Hybrid data-driven vigilance model in traffic control center using eye-tracking data and context data. Adv. Eng. Inform. **42**, 100940 (2019). https://doi.org/10.1016/J.AEI.2019.100940

12. Jiang, S., Chen, W., Kang, Y.: Correlation evaluation of pilots' situation awareness in bridge simulations via eye-tracking technology. Comput. Intell. Neurosci. **2021**, 1–15 (2021). https://doi.org/10.1155/2021/7122437

13. Feng Zhou, X., Yang, J., de Winter, J.C.F.: Using eye-tracking data to predict situation awareness in real time during takeover transitions in conditionally automated driving. IEEE Trans. Intell. Transport. Syst. **23**(3), 2284–2295 (2022). https://doi.org/10.1109/TITS.2021.3069776

14. Van Den Brink, R.L., Murphy, P.R., Nieuwenhuis, S.: Pupil diameter tracks lapses of attention. PLoS ONE **11**(10), e0165274 (2016). https://doi.org/10.1371/JOURNAL.PONE.0165274

15. Alhanbali, S., Munro, K.J., Dawes, P., Carolan, P.J., Millman, R.E.: Dimensions of self-reported listening effort and fatigue on a digits-in-noise task, and association with baseline pupil size and performance accuracy. Int. J. Audiol. **60**(10), 762–772 (2020). https://doi.org/10.1080/14992027.2020.1853262

16. Callaway, F., Rangel, A., Griffiths, T.L.: Fixation patterns in simple choice reflect optimal information sampling. PLoS Comput. Biol. **17**(3), e1008863 (2021). https://doi.org/10.1371/JOURNAL.PCBI.1008863

17. Zhang, P., Jia, Y., Shang, Y.: Research and application of XGBoost in imbalanced data. Int. J. Distrib. Sens. Netw. **18**(6) (2022). https://doi.org/10.1177/15501329221106935

18. Asselman, A., Khaldi, M., Aammou, S.: Enhancing the prediction of student performance based on the machine learning XGBoost algorithm. Interact. Learn. Environ. **31**(6), 3360–3379 (2023). https://doi.org/10.1080/10494820.2021.1928235

19. Tarwidi, D., Pudjaprasetya, S.R., Adytia, D., Apri, M.: An optimized XGBoost-based machine learning method for predicting wave run-up on a sloping beach. MethodsX **10**, 102119 (2023). https://doi.org/10.1016/j.mex.2023.102119

20. Wang, Y., Pan, Z., Zheng, J., Qian, L., Li, M.: A hybrid ensemble method for pulsar candidate classification. Astrophys. Space Sci. **364**(8), 1–13 (2019). https://doi.org/10.1007/s10509-019-3602-4

21. Ahmed, S., Nielsen, I.E., Tripathi, A., Siddiqui, S., Ramachandran, R.P., Rasool, G.: Transformers in time-series analysis: a tutorial. Circuits Syst. Signal Process. **42**(12), 7433–7466 (2023). https://doi.org/10.1007/s00034-023-02454-8

22. Tay, Y., Bahri, D., Metzler, D., Juan, D.C., Zhao, Z., Zheng, C.: Synthesizer: rethinking self-attention for transformer models. In: Proceedings of Machine Learning Research (2021)

23. Haugsdal, E., Aune, E., Ruocco, M.: Persistence initialization: a novel adaptation of the transformer architecture for time series forecasting. Appl. Intell. **53**(22), 26781–26796 (2023). https://doi.org/10.1007/s10489-023-04927-4

24. Caosen, X., Li, J., Feng, B., Baoli, L.: A financial time-series prediction model based on multiplex attention and linear transformer structure. Appl. Sci. **13**(8), 5175 (2023). https://doi.org/10.3390/app13085175

25. Cai, Y., et al.: MST++: multi-stage spectral-wise transformer for efficient spectral reconstruction. In: IEEE Computer Society Conference on Computer Vision and Pattern Recognition Workshops (2022). https://doi.org/10.1109/CVPRW56347.2022.00090

26. Korek, W.T., Li, W.C., Lu, L., Lone, M.: Investigating pilots' operational behaviours while interacting with different types of inceptors. In: Harris, D., Li, W.C. (eds.) Lecture Notes in Computer Science (including subseries Lecture Notes in Artificial Intelligence and Lecture Notes in Bioinformatics), vol. 13307 LNAI, pp. 314–325. Springer, Heidelberg (2022). https://doi.org/10.1007/978-3-031-06086-1_24

27. Ziv, G.: Gaze behavior and visual attention: a review of eye tracking studies in aviation. Int. J. Aviat. Psychol. 26(3–4), 75–104 (2017). https://doi.org/10.1080/10508414.2017.1313096

28. Krejtz, K., Duchowski, A.T., Niedzielska, A., Biele, C., Krejtz, I.: Eye tracking cognitive load using pupil diameter and microsaccades with fixed gaze. PLoS ONE 13(9), e0203629 (2018). https://doi.org/10.1371/JOURNAL.PONE.0203629

Multi-rotor eVTOL Safety Interval Assessment Based on Improved Event Model

Xinglong Wang and Youjie Wang[✉]

College of Air Traffic Management, Civil Aviation University of China, Tianjin 300300, China
1419151137@qq.com

Abstract. The rapid development of electric vertical take-off and landing vehicles (eVTOL) is a response to the increasingly congested urban ground traffic, low positioning accuracy, and the many hidden risks of traversing flight. Therefore, the safety interval standard is of great significance in ensuring the safe operation of these vehicles. To investigate the safety interval of multi-rotor eVTOL in low-altitude airspace, we have improved the Event collision model for lateral, longitudinal, and vertical collisions by modifying the shape characteristics. Specifically, we have replaced the original rectangular collision box with a round table body collision box, which reduces computational redundancy. We have also calculated the relative velocity and overlap probability while considering the error distribution. Finally, this text presents an arithmetic analysis using the EH 216-S model as an example to calculate the safety interval under different safety target levels and navigation accuracy. When the safety target level is 1×10^{-7} times/flight hour and the navigation accuracy is high, the minimum longitudinal, lateral, and vertical safety intervals are 42.1 m, 24.5 m, and 14.4 m, respectively. The improved model reduced the longitudinal, lateral, and vertical collision risks by 43.4%, 23%, and 58.4%, respectively, compared to the original model. The study results can serve as a reference for developing eVTOL interval standards for multi-rotor types. If a vehicle smaller than the safety interval standard is detected, it can be promptly displayed on the human-computer interface to alert the supervisors.

Keywords: Multi-rotor eVTOL · Safety Interval · Collision Risk Model

1 Introduction

In recent years, with the accelerating process of urbanization, urban traffic is becoming increasingly congested, and the operational capacity of ground road traffic is now difficult to meet people's travel needs, while urban air traffic resources are still abundant. At the same time, along with the continuous development of 5G new technology, artificial intelligence and other technologies, urban air transportation has become a promising field [1]. Electric Vertical Take-Off and Landing (eVTOL) is a new type of aircraft, which is mainly used for short-distance passenger and cargo transportation services in urban low altitude. It has the characteristics of vertical take-off and landing, distributed propulsion, and air hovering, and compared with helicopters, electric Vertical Take-Off and Landing Vehicle (eVTOL) has the advantages of green energy, simple structure, low noise, and fully automated flight, etc.[2]. eVTOL market is about to usher in explosive growth, and scholars have predicted that from 2020 to 2025, the cargo eVTOL will be hopeful of completing the commercial operation; from 2025 to 2030, the cargo eVTOL will be in commercial operation. 2030, eVTOL freight commercialization to establish relevant infrastructure and improve laws and regulations and rules; after 2030, to carry out the construction of driverless passenger eVTOL [3]. However, the existing safety interval regulations are only applicable to civil passenger airplanes, and there is a lack of regulations related to the safety interval in low-altitude airspace, so it is urgent to study the safety interval problem of eVTOL.

In the field of civil aviation, the earliest research on spacing was conducted by Prof. Reich [4] in the United Kingdom in the 1960s, who modeled the collision risk evaluation of parallel routes on the ocean in the longitudinal, lateral, and vertical directions, respectively; Peter Brooker [5] proposed the Event model to study the collision risk in the lateral direction, and conducted a longitudinal collision risk research; Xu X H et al. [6, 7] used Event model to carry out research on the safety intervals in each direction on the flight path respectively and improved it by using cylindrical collision box; Dai F Q et al. [8] used ellipsoid instead of traditional rectangular collision template to make it more accurate; Huang Jin et al. [9] used spliced quadrangular conic collision box instead of the original rectangular collision box, which improves the accuracy; Zhang Z N et al. [10] established the free improved Event collision risk model under flight, and calculated the minimum safe distance between aircrafts as 10096 m.

In the civil airliner-UAV collision risk and spacing, Zhang et al. [11] established a cylindrical UAV collision risk model under non-isolated airspace, and investigated the conflict risk between manned aircraft and UAVs; Yang Xinjian et al. [12] improved the Reich model, and evaluated the safe spacing between UAVs and civil airliners;

In the collision risk and interval between UAVs, Zhao Zheng et al. [13] improved the interval layer of the classical Event collision model to calculate the collision risk of UAVs and reduced the collision probability; Weinert A et al. [14] conducted a study for the safety interval of small and medium-sized UAVs in low altitude areas, which resulted in a horizontal interval of 2000 ft and a vertical interval of 250 ft; Zhang Honghai et al. [15] used the minimum outer joint sphere of UAV body cylinder as a collision box, established a collision model based on three-dimensional Gaussian distribution, and calculated the minimum safety interval with a safety target level of 5%, whose values are: vertical interval 15 m, horizontal interval 10 m, and vertical interval 5 m.

The above study has discussed the collision between civil airliners and UAVs in detail, with the following two deficiencies: (1) Some scholars at home and abroad directly apply the model and parameters of civil airliners to study the collision of low-altitude small aircrafts, but there are large differences in the body size, speed and operation mechanism between civil airliners and UAVs as well as eVTOL, so directly applying the model and parameters of civil airliners will cause large errors in the safety assessment. Safety assessment. (2) eVTOL undertakes the function of manned transportation, and compared with UAVs, its safety target level is required to be higher, which is not directly equivalent to UAVs, and there is a lack of research on the safety interval of eVTOL.

Therefore, this paper takes the low-altitude airspace as the operation background, adopts the round table body collision box according to the geometric characteristics of the multi-rotor type eVTOL, considers the characteristics of the eVTOL operation automation and the positioning error, establishes the collision model, and takes the multi-rotor type EH 216-S as an example, for the characteristics of the uniform distribution of its velocity magnitude and heading angle, takes into consideration of the velocity error and the pitch angle limitation, and utilizes the Monte Carlo simulation to calculate the relative velocity and obtain the minimum safety interval under different conditions.

2   Event Collision Model and Its Improvement

The basic assumptions of the Event collision model are:

1. The model only considers collisions between two vehicles;
2. The positions between the two vehicles are independent of each other;
3. The longitudinal, lateral, and vertical intervals between the two vehicles are denoted as S_x, S_y, S_z, respectively;

Assuming that there are two vehicles A and B, the fuselage length, width and height of the vehicles are recorded as a, b, h, m respectively; according to the vehicle A to establish the collision box, the size of the collision box is twice the size of the vehicle A. Consider B to be a mass point with a point at the end of the collision box. Consider B as a mass point, and establish a three-dimensional right-angle coordinate system with point B as the origin, and the X-axis, Y-axis, and Z-axis correspond to the longitudinal, lateral, and vertical directions, respectively.

2.1   Event Collision Model

Event Longitudinal Collision Model. Event longitudinal collision model mainly studies the collision before and after the same altitude layer with the same flight path, and defines the plane formed by the Z-axis and Y-axis as the longitudinal spacing layer. When an error occurs, if vehicle A crosses the longitudinal spacing layer, and vehicle B is also in the longitudinal spacing layer at this time, it is regarded as a collision, as shown in the left of Fig. 1. The relative velocities of vehicle A and vehicle B in the three directions are u_x, u_y, u_z, km/h; assuming that the time required for the vehicle to pass through the longitudinal spacer is t, s. When the vehicle traverses the spacer, because of the relative velocities in the three directions, there are three displacements in the three directions, and the position diagram after the collision is represented by a plane diagram as shown in the right part of Fig. 1.

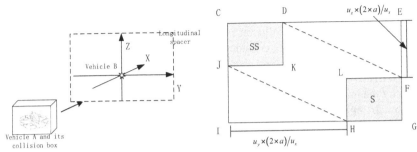

Fig. 1. Event longitudinal collision model (left) and Expansion collision box for longitudinal traversal (right)

The longitudinal spacer layer is set as a quadrilateral CEGI, vehicle A traverses the longitudinal spacer layer, and the projected trajectory on this surface is from entering quadrilateral LFGH(S region) to quadrilateral CDKJ (SS region), if vehicle B is on hexagonal CDFGHJ at this time, collision occurs, but due to the more complex shape of the hexagon, it is not convenient to calculate, and give the rectangle CEGI is defined as an extension of the collision box [16], so the collision risk is the frequency of the collision box crossing the spacer multiplied by the probability that vehicle B is located on the rectangular CEGI.

$$P(C/O) = P_z(0) \times P_y(0) \times \left(1 + \frac{u_z}{u_x}\frac{2a}{2h}\right) \times \left(1 + \frac{u_y}{u_x}\frac{2a}{2b}\right) \tag{1}$$

where P(C/O) is the probability of collision between the two machines in the event of a longitudinal crossing. $p_z(0)$ is the vertical overlap probability, $p_y(0)$is the lateral overlap probability.

$$P(O)=E(S) \times P_x(S_x) \tag{2}$$

where P(O) is the longitudinal crossing rate, E(S) is the longitudinal proximity rate, and $P_x(S_x)$ is the longitudinal overlap probability. A collision is regarded as two accidents, so the longitudinal collision risk N_x is:

$$N_x = P(C/O) \times P(O) \tag{3}$$

Event Lateral Collision Model. Event lateral collision model mainly studies the collision of adjacent parallel flight paths in the same altitude layer, and defines the plane formed by the Z-axis and Y-axis as the lateral spacing layer. When an error occurs, if vehicle A crosses the lateral spacing layer and vehicle B is also in the lateral spacing layer at this time, it is regarded as a collision, as shown in Fig. 2.

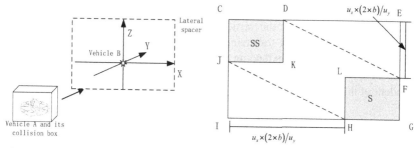

Fig. 2. Event lateral collision model (left) and Expansion collision box for lateral traversal (right)

The risk of collision is the frequency of the collision box crossing the lateral separation layer multiplied by the probability that vehicle B is located in the rectangular CEGI, and that aircraft in the same altitude layer are flying the same heading. Therefore

$$N_y = 2 \times P_y(S_y) \times P_z(0) \times E(S) \times \left(\frac{u_y}{2b}\right) \times \left(\frac{a}{S_x}\right) \times \left(1 + \frac{u_z}{u_y}\frac{b}{h}\right) \times \left(1 + \frac{u_x}{u_y}\frac{b}{a}\right)$$

(4)

where N_y is the lateral collision risk and $P_y(S_y)$ is the lateral overlap probability.

Event Vertical Collision Model. Event vertical collision model mainly studies the collision of two aircraft on the same trajectory, adjacent altitude layer, defining the plane XOY formed by the X-axis and Y-axis is the vertical spacing layer, the vertical collision model and the extended collision box is shown in Fig. 3.

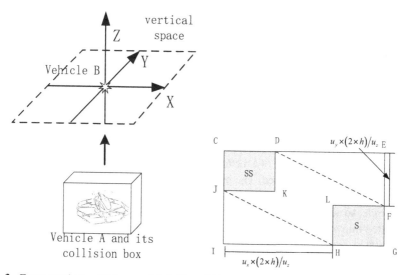

Fig. 3. Event vertical collision model (left) and Expansion collision box for vertical traversal (right)

Let the vertical spacing loss rate be SL, the vertical spacing loss rate is the frequency of the collision box traversing the vertical spacing layer, and the collision risk is the frequency of the collision box traversing the vertical spacing layer multiplied by the probability that the vehicle is extending the collision box. The vertical collision risk is N_Z, since a collision is regarded as two accidents and the lateral overlap probability is independent of the longitudinal overlap probability, there are

$$N_z = 2 \times SL \times E(O) \times \frac{a}{S_x} \times \left(1 + \frac{u_x}{u_z}\frac{2h}{2a}\right) \times P_y(0) \times \left(1 + \frac{u_y}{u_z}\frac{2h}{2b}\right) \qquad (5)$$

The vertical overlap probability $P_z(S_z)$ can be obtained by multiplying the vertical spacing loss rate SL with the time taken to cross the spacer.

$$N_z = 2 \times P_z(S_z) \times E(O) \times P_y(0) \times \frac{a}{S_x} \times \frac{u_z}{2h} \times \left(1 + \frac{u_x}{u_z}\frac{2h}{2a}\right) \times \left(1 + \frac{u_y}{u_z}\frac{2h}{2b}\right) \qquad (6)$$

2.2 Improved Circular Platform Model

Multi-rotor eVTOL tend to have a fuselage attached to a rotor with a circular structure, and common models are shown in Fig. 4.

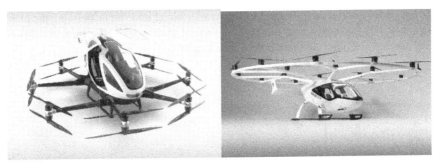

Fig. 4. Common multi-rotor eVTOL (EH-216 and Volocopter VoloCity)

As can be seen from Fig. 4, the shape of the multi-rotor eVTOL does not conform to a rectangular shape, and the use of a rectangular collision box will have a large redundant space, so it needs to be improved. The plane where the rotor of the multi-rotor eVTOL is located is a circle, and the top (or bottom) of the fuselage part can be regarded as a smaller circle, so according to the characteristics of the shape of the multi-rotor eVTOL will be fitted into a round platform, the bottom of the platform fits the plane where the rotor is located, and the top of the platform fits the fuselage part, and the improvement of the original collision box into the new round platform shape of the collision box can effectively improve the accuracy of the calculations and reduce the risk of collision. Risks. Multi-rotor eVTOL usually have tapered or conical fuselages, and their fuselage contours are usually one of their most prominent features, such as wider at the bottom and tapering at the top. Compared with traditional cylinders or rectangles, the rounded body is more in line with the shape of the vehicle, and it can better capture these features, so that the collision model more accurately describes the vehicle's shape; since the rounded body shape is better adapted to the vehicle's shape, using the rounded body shape can improve the accuracy of the calculation and reduce the risk of collision. Since the shape of the dome is better adapted to the shape of the vehicle, the use of a dome as a collision box provides a more accurate representation of the spatial extent, which is essential for accurately assessing the collision risk of a vehicle, especially in complex spatial environments such as urban areas or dense air traffic.

The diameter of the small circle of the round table body collision box is 2c, m; the diameter of the large circle is 2a, at this time 2a = 2b; the height is 2h. If vehicle A traverses the vertical spacing layer, vehicle B is in the projection plane of the vertical spacing layer of the flight path of the dome body, then a collision occurs, and the dome body collision box is shown in Fig. 5.

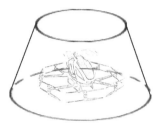

Fig. 5. Round table collision box

Although the collision box has been improved, resulting in a change in the graph projected into the vertical spacing layer, the actual calculation method and calculation process have not changed, because the size of the collision probability is directly related to the size of the area of the extended collision box, so only the change in the area of the extended collision box needs to be taken into account again. In the original model, the quadrilateral CEGI is defined as the extended collision box; in the present improved model of the circular table body, the extended collision box is the figure enclosed by the irregular figure OSQRTP, and it is only necessary to calculate the ratio of this area to the area of the original extended collision box, which is called the collision probability relation ratio R(O).

For longitudinal traversal, the longitudinal collision probability relation ratio is written as R(O)$_X$, and the improved extended collision box for longitudinal traversal is shown in Fig. 6

The new extended collision box is the figure enclosed by the OSQRTP, denoted as S$_c$, and the area of the original extended collision box rectangle CEGI is denoted as S$_r$. From Fig. 1

$$S_r = EG \times GI = \left(2b + u_y\frac{2a}{u_x}\right) \times \left(2h + u_z\frac{2a}{u_x}\right) \quad (7)$$

Calculate the area of the new extended collision box S$_c$ by making the auxiliary line ST, ST = CO = a-c, the rectangular area minus the areas of the triangles PCO, PRI,

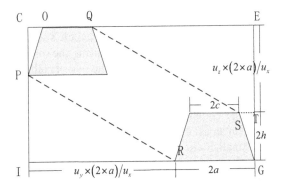

Fig. 6. Improved expansion collision box for longitudinal traversal

STG with the trapezoid STEQ is S_c, then we have

$$S_{\Delta PCO+\Delta PRI+\Delta STG} = \frac{1}{2} \times (a-c)(2h) \times 2 + \frac{1}{2}\big(u_y \times (2a)/u_x\big)\big(u_z \times (2a)/u_x\big) \quad (8)$$

$$S_{STEQ} = \frac{1}{2} \times (ST+QE) \times ET = \frac{1}{2}(a-c+u_y \times (2a)/u_x)\big(u_z \times (2a)/u_x\big) \quad (9)$$

$$S_c = S_r - S_{\Delta PCO+\Delta PRI+\Delta STG} - S_{STEQ} \quad (10)$$

Then from the above equation, the longitudinal collision probability relation ratio is:

$$R(O)_x = \frac{S_c}{S_r} = 1 - \frac{\big(u_y(2a)/u_x\big)\big(u_z(2a)/u_x\big) + \frac{1}{2}(a-c)\big(\big(u_z(2a)/u_x\big)+4h\big)}{\big(2b+u_y\frac{2a}{u_x}\big) \times \big(2h+u_z\frac{2a}{u_x}\big)} \quad (11)$$

The lateral collision relationship ratio $R(O)_y$ is calculated in the same way as for the longitudinal direction described above, which gives

$$R(O)_y = \frac{S_c}{S_r} = 1 - \frac{\big(u_x(2b)/u_y\big)\big(u_z(2b)/u_y\big) + \frac{1}{2}(a-c)\big(\big(u_z(2b)/u_y\big)+4h\big)}{\big(2a+u_x\frac{2b}{u_y}\big) \times \big(2h+u_z\frac{2b}{u_y}\big)} \quad (12)$$

For vertical traversal, the collision probability relation ratio is noted as $R(O)_z$, and the improved extended collision box for vertical traversal is shown in Fig. 7.

The new extended collision box is the graph enclosed by the OSQRTP, denoted by the area S_c. For the rectangle CEGI in the original model, it is not difficult to derive the lengths of its two sides EG and GI from Fig. 3, and the area of the rectangle CEGI:

$$S_r = EG \times GI = \left(2b+u_y\frac{2h}{u_z}\right) \times \left(2a+u_x\frac{2h}{u_z}\right) \quad (13)$$

S_c decomposed into two semicircles OPT and SQR and a trapezoid OSRT, two semicircle radius are a and c, G point as the origin of the coordinates to establish a right-angled coordinate system, GE direction for the direction of the x-axis, the direction of

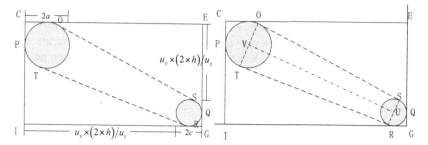

Fig. 7. Improved expansion collision box for vertical traversal

the y-axis direction of the GI direction; it can be known that the coordinates of the U point for the (c, c), the coordinates of the V point for the (c + u_yt, c + u_xt), then there are

$$S_{OPT} + S_{SQR} = \frac{1}{4}\pi a^2 + \frac{1}{4}\pi c^2 \tag{14}$$

$$S_{OSRT} = \frac{1}{2} \times (OT + SR) \times UV = (a + c) \times t \times \sqrt{u_x^2 + u_y^2} \tag{15}$$

$$S_c = S_{OSRT} + S_{OPT} + S_{SQR} \tag{16}$$

$$R(O)_z = \frac{S_c}{S_r} = \frac{(a + c) \times t \times \sqrt{u_x^2 + u_y^2} + \frac{1}{4}\pi a^2 + \frac{1}{4}\pi c^2}{\left(2b + u_y\frac{2h}{u_z}\right) \times \left(2a + u_x\frac{2h}{u_z}\right)} \tag{17}$$

Since the magnitude of the collision risk is directly related to the size of the area of the extended collision box, the three R(O) expressions derived in the above equation, multiplied with the collision risk of the Event collision model in the corresponding directions, give the Event collision risk equation based on the modified circular table body

$$N'_i = N_i \times R(O)_i (i = x, y, z) \tag{18}$$

3   Calculation of Collision Risk

3.1   Longitudinal, Lateral and Vertical Overlap Probabilities

Let the longitudinal positioning error of the multi-rotor type eVTOL obey a normal distribution

$$L_x = (I_A + M_A) - (I_B + M_B) = S_x + (M_A - M_B) \tag{19}$$

where, L_x is the actual distance between vehicle A and vehicle B in the longitudinal direction, m; S_x is the longitudinal distance (i.e., the interval standard) of the two vehicles, m; M_A, M_B are random variables obeying the normal distribution, there are $M_A \sim N\left(0, \sigma_{A1}^2\right)$, $M_B \sim N\left(0, \sigma_{B1}^2\right)$, from the knowledge of probability theory, two positively distributed random variables are subtracted from each other, and their differences also obey the normal distribution, and their means subtract from each other but their variances add up to each other, $M_A - M_B \sim N\left(0, \sigma_1^2\right)$, $\sigma_1^2 = \sigma_{A1}^2 + \sigma_{B1}^2$, Therefore, the probability density function is

$$f_X(x) = \frac{1}{\sigma_1 \sqrt{2\pi}} \times \exp\left(-\frac{(x - S_x)^2}{2\sigma_1^2}\right) \tag{20}$$

Longitudinal overlap occurs when the actual distance is less than a.

$$P_X(S_X) = P(|L_X| < a) = \int_{-a}^{a} \frac{1}{\sigma_1 \sqrt{2\pi}} \times \exp\left(-\frac{(x - S_x)^2}{2\sigma_1^2}\right) dx \tag{21}$$

Similarly, assuming that the lateral deviation of each eVTOL follows a normal distribution, there are

$$P_Y(S_Y) = P(|L_Y| < a) = \int_{-b}^{b} \frac{1}{\sigma_2 \sqrt{2\pi}} \times \exp\left(-\frac{(x - S_Y)^2}{2\sigma_2^2}\right) dx \tag{22}$$

where $\sigma_2^2 = \sigma_{A2}^2 + \sigma_{B2}^2$, σ_{A2}, and σ_{B2} are the standard deviations of vehicles A and B, respectively. The Required Navigation Performance (RNP) is the RNAV with on-board navigation performance monitoring and alerting capability, and the RNP n is the navigation performance accuracy of n nautical miles that the aircraft is expected to achieve at least 95% of the time. This standard deviation is solved for by borrowing the concept of RNP from civil aviation, with n in meters

$$\int_{-n}^{n} \frac{1}{\sigma_{A2} \sqrt{2\pi}} \times \exp\left(-\frac{x^2}{2\sigma_{A2}^2}\right) dx = 0.95 \tag{23}$$

When n is 15, 10, and 5, the corresponding standard deviations are 7.65, 5.1, and 2.55, respectively.

Vertical overlap can be caused by two types of errors: operational errors and technical errors. Operational errors are errors caused by pilot or controller errors during the operation of the vehicle. Technical errors are the errors caused by abnormal altitude measurement capability of the vehicle or the display capability of the altimeter. In this paper, we study a multi-rotor eVTOL, which operates in urban low-altitude airspace, relying on pre-set flight procedures and unified scheduling and commanding by the control room, so we mainly consider its technical error here, i.e., the study of the vertical overlap probability, $P_Z(S_Z)$ is mainly considered in terms of the altitude measurement capability. Let the altitude error of the multi-rotor type eVTOL obeys a normal distribution, similarly, there are

$$P_Z(S_Z) = P(|L_Z| < h) = \int_{-h}^{h} \frac{1}{\sigma_3 \sqrt{2\pi}} \times \exp\left(-\frac{(x - S_Z)^2}{2\sigma_3^2}\right) dx \tag{24}$$

3.2 Relative Velocity

Let the velocity error of eVTOL obeys $\varepsilon_v \sim N\left(u_v, \sigma_v^2\right)$; let the angle between vehicle A and the XOY plane be α, rad; the angle between vehicle B and the XOY plane be β, rad; the angle between A's projection in the XOY plane and the x-axis be θ, rad; the angle between B's projection in the XOY plane and the x-axis be φrad; assuming that the multicopter-type eVTOL has a maximal pitch angle of 25° [15], then α, β obey $(-5\pi/36, 5\pi/36)$ uniform distribution, and θ, φobey $(0, 2\pi)$ uniform distribution [17, 18]. Let the cruising speed of the vehicle be Va, Vb, respectively, and its value obeys $[0.3V_{max}, 0.7V_{max}]$ uniform distribution of [15], so there are

$$u_x = V_A \cos\alpha \cos\theta - V_B \cos\beta \cos\varphi \tag{25}$$

$$u_y = V_A \cos\alpha \sin\theta - V_B \cos\beta \sin\varphi \tag{26}$$

$$u_z = V_A \sin\alpha - V_B \sin\beta \tag{27}$$

In longitudinal and lateral collision models, where aircraft in the same altitude stratum are travelling in opposite directions and the velocity components in the x-axis direction are in the same direction, there should be constraints on the relative velocities $\cos\theta \cos\varphi > 0$; In the vertical collision model, the velocity components in the x-axis direction are in opposite directions, so there are $\cos\theta \cos\varphi < 0$. At the same time, according to the above model derivation, in the longitudinal, lateral and vertical models, respectively, there needs to be the possibility of vehicle A traversing the longitudinal, lateral and vertical spacer layers, so corresponding to the direction of the x, y and z axes, respectively, vehicle A should have a positive relative velocity with respect to vehicle B, so that u_x, u_y and u_z, respectively, are greater than 0. Monte Carlo simulation was carried out by using MATLABR2019b.

4 Example Simulation and Analysis

At present, the multi-rotor eVTOL manufactured by EH is in the world leading level, and its latest product EH216-S is taken for example analysis. Let vehicle A and B are both this type of eVTOL, and the relevant parameters of this type of multi-rotor electric vertical take-off and landing vehicle are shown in Table 1.

Defining n = 15, 10 and 5 for the route positioning accuracy (i.e. 95% of the time the navigation performance accuracy that can be expected to be achieved is n meters) corresponds to low, medium and high accuracy, respectively, and other relevant parameters of the collision risk model are shown in Table 2. Defining n = 15, 10 and 5 for the route positioning accuracy (i.e. 95% of the time the navigation performance accuracy that can be expected to be achieved is n meters) corresponds to low, medium and high accuracy, respectively, and other relevant parameters of the collision risk model are shown in Table 2.

Table 1. EH216-S parameters

Parameter	value
a	5.63 m
c	5.63 m
h	3.2 m
σ_{A1}	1.855 m
σ_{A3}	5 m
V_{max}	130 km/h
u_v	0
σ_v	2 km/h

Table 2. Collision risk parameters

Parameter	value
E(O)	0.01
E(S)	0.2
$P_z(0)$	0.4881
$P_y(0)$	0.5382 (low Acc)
	0.7304 (medium Acc)
	0.9739 (high Acc)
U_x	22,22,80 km/h
U_y	51,51,51 km/h
U_z	9,9,21 km/h

The TLS is an acceptable probability maximum of collision risk, which is expressed in units of sub-accidents per flight hour. ICAO, the International Civil Aviation Organization, stipulates that the safety target level for collisions of aircraft in airspace in any of the three directions, namely longitudinal, lateral and vertical, is 5×10^{-9} collisions/flight hour. To calculate the changes in collision risk corresponding to changes in the interval between the three directions with different navigation accuracies, the relative speed unit km/h was converted to m/s in the calculation. The results are shown in Fig. 8.

In Fig. 8, the horizontal axis is the vertical separation in meters; the vertical axis is the collision risk in times/flight hour; the horizontal dotted line is the safety target level of 5×10^{-9} stipulated by ICAO, and the solid, double-dotted and dashed lines in the curves are the longitudinal collision risk curves under the conditions of low-precision, medium-precision, and high-precision navigation, respectively. It can be seen that the minimum longitudinal, lateral, and vertical intervals are 45.9 m, 26.4 m, and 15.8 m, respectively, under high-precision navigation conditions. The increase of the interval

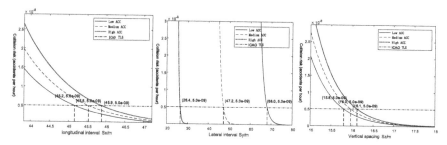

Fig. 8. The minimum interval in different directions at the ICAO TLS.

will lead to the decrease of the collision risk, in Fig. 10(b) lateral, with the improvement of navigation accuracy, the lateral collision risk decreases with it, and the lateral interval can be reduced; however, in Fig. 10(a) longitudinal and (c) vertical, the improvement of the navigation accuracy has instead led to a certain increase of the collision risk, and after analyzing, assuming that the two aircrafts are operated on the same airway in both the longitudinal and the vertical collision models. The improvement of the lateral navigation accuracy increases the ability of the aircraft to stay in the center of the flight path, so the lateral overlap probability increases, so the collision risk has a certain growth.

The safety target level specified by ICAO has strong authority, but it is proposed for civil airliners, and the one studied in this paper is the multi-rotor eVTOL, referring to Part CS-27 and EASA SC-VTOL-01, another safety target level can be set as 1×10^{-7} flights/flight hour [19, 20], and the interval change under this safety target level is calculated as shown in Fig. 9

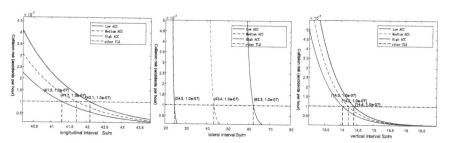

Fig. 9. The minimum interval in different directions at other TLS

The dotted line at the level in Fig. 9 is the other safety target level (1×10^{-7} flights/hour), and the rest of the meaning is the same as in Fig. 8, and the same, the risk of collision grows when the navigation accuracy is increased in the longitudinal and lateral models. It can be seen that the minimum longitudinal, lateral, and vertical intervals are 42.1 m, 24.5 m, and 14.4 m, respectively, for the high-precision navigation condition at this safety target level. Comparing with Fig. 8, the minimum safety intervals in all three directions have been reduced to a certain extent, so the increase in the value of the safety target level, i.e., the decrease in the safety target level will lead to the decrease in the minimum vertical interval, so the appropriate safety target level should be determined to reduce the intervals on the basis of guaranteeing the safety and to increase the airspace utilization rate.

The results of the comparative analysis of the changes in collision risk between the improved model and the original model in the three directions under high navigation conditions are shown in Fig. 10.

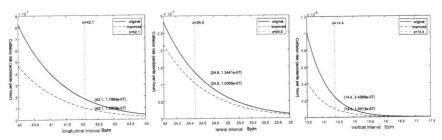

Fig. 10. The risk of collision between the original model and the improved model

In Fig. 10, the upper solid line is the collision risk curve of the original Event collision model, and the lower double-dotted line is the collision risk curve of the improved Event collision model, and the dotted lines perpendicular to the x-axis represent the longitudinal $Sx = 42.1$ m, the lateral $Sy = 24.5$ m, and the vertical interval $Sz = 14.4$ m, respectively. It can be seen that at the same interval, the collision risk of the improved Event model has a significant reduction compared with that of the original model, with the longitudinal interval of 42.1 m, the longitudinal collision risk is reduced by 43.4% compared with that of the original model; with the lateral interval of 24.5 m, the lateral collision risk is reduced by 23% compared with that of the original model; with the vertical interval of 14.4 m, the vertical collision risk is reduced by 58.4% compared with that of the original model. 58.4%.

5 Conclusions

1. In this paper, with the background of neighboring altitude layers in low-altitude airspace, and with the multi-rotor eVTOL as the research object, the Event collision model is established and the collision box is improved according to its shape characteristics, adopting the circular table body collision box, considering the position error and characteristics of eVTOL, the parameters are derived, and the three-direction collision risk calculation formula is obtained, which is more suitable for the multi-rotor eVTOL, and the collision risk can be calculated 43.4%, 23% and 14.4% lower than the original model under the high Under the condition of navigation accuracy, when the three directions are separated by 42.1,24.5 and 14.4 m respectively, it can be calculated that the collision risk of the improved Event collision model is reduced by 43.4%, 23% and 58.4% compared with the original model collision risk.

2. Take EH 216-S eVTOL as an example, plot the relationship between vertical spacing and collision risk under different navigation conditions, and calculate the minimum safety spacing under different safety target levels, in which the minimum spacing in

the longitudinal, lateral, and vertical directions can be shrunk to 42.1 m, 24.5 m, and 14.4 m when the safety target level is 1×10^{-7} flights/flight hour and the navigation accuracy is high. The calculation method and results can provide some references for the development of safety interval standards for multi-rotor eVTOL under low altitude airspace.

Acknowledgments. The authors would like to thank the Key Laboratory of Flight Networking of Civil Aviation University of China for its support to this study. This research was partially supported by the National Natural Science Foundation of China: The National Natural Science Foundation of China Youth Program Fund (52102419), the National Natural Science Foundation of China General Project (62173332), and the National Natural Science Foundation of China Key Project (U2133207).

Disclosure of Interests. All authors disclosed no relevant relationships.

References

1. Zhang, H.H., Zou, Y.Y., Zhang, Q.Q., et al.: Review of research on future urban air mobility (UAM) management. Acta Aeronautica et Astronautica Sinica **42**(07), 82–106 (2021)
2. Du, W., Sun, N.: Research on development status of eVTOL. Aeron. Sci. Technol. **32**(11), 1–7 (2021)
3. Lineberger, R., Hussain, A., Rutgers, V.: Change is in the air: the elevated future of mobility: what's next on the horizon. Deloitte Insights (2019)
4. Reich, P.G.: Analysis of long-range air traffic systems: separation standards—I. J. Navig. **19**(1), 88–98 (1966)
5. Brooker, P.: Lateral collision risk in air traffic track systems: a 'post-Reich' event model. J. Navig. **56**(3), 399–409 (2003)
6. Xu, X.H., Li, D.B., Li, X.: Research on safety assessment of flight separation. Acta Aeronautica et Astronautica Sinica **06**, 1411–1418 (2008)
7. Xu, X.H., Wang, Z.Y., Zhao, H.S.: Improved lateral collision risk model based on event. J. Civil Aviat. Univ. China **03**, 1–4 (2008)
8. Dai, F.Q., Zhou, Q.: Study on improved vertical collision risk model based on Event. J. Civil Aviat. Univ. China **29**(06), 4–7 (2011)
9. Huang, J., Jiao, Y.Y., Liu, H.R., et al.: Cross route collision risk analysis based on improved event model. Aeron. Comput. Techn. **53**(01), 11–15 (2023)
10. Zhang, Z.N., Shi, R.J.: Study on free flight collision risk based on improved event model. China Saf. Sci. J. **25**(07), 35–40 (2015)
11. Zhang, Z.Y., Zhang, J., Wang, P., et al.: Research on operation of UAVs in non-isolated airspace. CMC-Comput. Mater. Continua **57**(1), 151–166 (2018)
12. Yang, X.S., Ren, Z.: Research on assessment of longitudinal safety separation between UAV and civil aircraft based on trailing vortex intensity. J. Saf. Sci. Technol. **14**(10), 64–69 (2018)
13. Zhen, R., Zhao, Z.: Kang J Research on collision risk based on improved EVENT model. Hebei J. Ind. Sci. Technol. **38**(01), 7–11 (2021)
14. Weinert, A., Campbell, S., Vela, A., et al.: Well-clear recommendation for small unmanned aircraft systems based on unmitigated collision risk. Air Traffic Control Q. **26**(3), 113–122 (2018)

15. Zhang, H.H., Li, B.W.: Demarcation method of safety separation for multi-rotor UAV in free airspace. Syst. Eng. Electron. **45**, 1–11 (2023)
16. Xu, X.H., Li, D.B., Li, X., et al.: Research on collision risk of vertical separation minima based on EVENT model. J. Civil Aviat. Univ. China (04), 1–5+17 (2008)
17. Meng, X.W., Zhang, P.: Research on aircraft mid-air collision risk in low-altitude uncontrolled airspace. In: 2010 Annual Conference on Airworthiness and Air Traffic Management. Beijing, China, pp. 127–134 (2010)
18. Wang, L.L., Yang, J.: A collision risk model for small UAVs based on velocity random distribution in low-altitude airspace. J. Transp. Inf. Saf. **40**(04), 64–70 (2022)
19. Royal, N.: Safety targets for UAM vehicles (2021)
20. Easa. Special condition Vertical Take-Off and Landing (VTOL) Aircraft (2019). Accessed 20 Jan 2024. SC-VTOL-01.pdf (europa.eu)

FEMAS: A Method to Establish Workload Evaluation Scenarios in Aircraft Certification Phase

Yiyuan Zheng[✉] and Yuwen Jie

Shanghai Aircraft Airworthiness Certification Center of CAAC, Shanghai, China
zhengyiyuan@saacc.org.cn

Abstract. Pilot workload has always been one of the most crucial safety-related factors in flight. In airworthiness regulation, the minimum flight crew in flight deck should be determined based on the workload on individual crew members. In order to establish the comprehensive flight scenes to demonstrate the workload, a method called FEMAS was proposed, which including five dimensions (FHA based, experience of similar models, abnormal procedures, MMEL requirements, and specific environment conditions) and one integration process. The method was implement in one type of aircraft airworthiness certification phase, and 27 scenarios were determined to be carried out in total.

Keywords: Flight crew · Workload · Scenarios

1 Introduction

Pilot workload has always been one of the most crucial safety-related factors in flight. Either excessive or insufficient workload could lead to unexpected performance, or even the unacceptable consequences [1]. On the one hand, if pilot was exposed in an undue workload condition, he/she might be force to deal with emergencies with confusion. On the other hand, if the workload was extremely low, the essential situation awareness might be lost. Therefore, in aircraft design phase, it is necessary to demonstrate that the flight crew workload is in an acceptable level, neither too high, nor too low. In airworthiness regulation, CS 25.1523, also prescribes the minimum flight crew in cockpit should be established based on the workload on individual crew members [2].

The research on pilot workload evaluation mainly concentrated on three aspects, task performance, subjective evaluation and psychophysiological measurement [3]. Task performance analysis has been divided into Measures of Performance (MOPs) and Secondary Task Measures [4]. For the former one, as the term suggests, they are directly qualitative or quantitative measures of human or system capabilities or characteristics. Speed, accuracy, reaction time and error rates are typically used as indictors. Although MOPs are effective when the needs exceed the operator's capacity resulting in performance deteriorating, they are more a measure of what the system can achieve rather than an estimate of the operator's achievement [5]. Otherwise, secondary task measures predict the remaining capacity of operator while performing primary tasks. For

D. Harris and W.-C. Li (Eds.): HCII 2024, LNAI 14693, pp. 337–346, 2024.
https://doi.org/10.1007/978-3-031-60731-8_24

instance, Wester et al. examined the impact of an auditory oddball task performance (secondary task) on lane keeping (primary driving task) [6]. The most challenging issue is secondary task measures might produce an undesired change of strategy, distorting performance on the primary task. Therefore, an embedded task, which is part of the operator's responsibilities, might be more appropriate [7].

Subjective evaluation has a long history for measuring effort, fatigue, etc., and is most wildly used in workload measurement for its convenience, including NASA-TLX, Bedford Scale, and SWAT [8, 9]. During application, the properly designed rating scales are specifically sensitive measurement instruments, especially with highly-trained populations. For instance, NASA-TLX, a multi-dimensional rating procedure providing an overall score, has been applied successfully in flight deck workload evaluation [10]. Nevertheless, the repeatability and validity of subjective techniques are sometimes not convincing. They are also subject to operator biases and preconceptions, and can only be based on what is remembered or abstracted from an experience. Besides, the intrusiveness to the task and frequency of use have been controversial, with no definitive result in sight [11].

Psychophysiological measures, which attempt to capture and explicate the workload influences on physiological changes, are continual and objective. Heart rate and its variability are constantly used as indictors to represent mental workload, since the cardiovascular responses are stronger if task demands are larger. Mansikka etc. stated that HR and HRV could distinguish the level of pilot mental workload after which the subjects were no longer able to cope with the increasing task demands in an instrument landing [12]. In addition, eye movement parameters can also be implemented as workload indices. Higher fixation frequency, fewer blink duration and decreased saccadic amplitude have been found associated with increased workload [13]. However, contextual effects, such as operator's background state and environment issues, should be considered in psychophysiological measures [14].

Almost all workload studies have focused on evaluation methods, operator's performance or physiological changes. There lacks a logical method to construct flight scenes to demonstrate the workload of flight crew is acceptable, especially in aircraft certification phase. Therefore, a method called FEMAS, including five dimensions (Fault Hazard Analysis (FHA) based, Experience of similar models, Abnormal procedures, Master Minimum Equipment List (MMEL) requirements, Specific environment conditions), and one integration process, was developed to not only satisfy the airworthiness regulations requirements, but also cover the actual operating scenarios as realistic as possible.

2   Methods

Five dimensions and one integration process were included in workload evaluation scenarios establishment as following:

2.1 FHA Based

System failure usually occurs in an unexpected condition, which requires pilot's immediately attention or actions, could result in an instantaneous increase in workload. Consequently, the results of Fault Hazard Analysis should be considered. The aircraft functional hazard assessment is a process that allows the identification and evaluation of potential hazards related to an aircraft regardless of the details of its design or implementation. Normally, system failure conditions are classified into five levels, shown as in Table 1. On the one hand, since class I is belonged to catastrophe, in the process of system design, the failure probability is required to be less than $1 * 10^{-9}$, which is an extremely unlikely event and cannot be considered. On the other hand, class IV and V failure states have little impact on flight crew operating, monitoring, navigating or other responsibilities, and would be covered in other dimension (MMEL requirements). Therefore, only level II and III were selected.

Table 1. Failure Condition Severity Classification

Effect on Aircraft	Effect on Flight Crew	Classification
Loss of aircraft	Crew unable to accomplish required tasks, or required crew strength or skill in excess of crew capability, or crew incapacitation, or crew fatalities	I Catastrophic
Large reduction in aircraft functional capability or safety margin	Excessive crew workload increased, crew unable to fully accomplish required tasks, or crew physical distress	II Hazardous
Significantly reduced aircraft functional capability or safety margin	Significant crew workload increased, or conditions impairing crew efficiency, or crew physical discomfort	III Major
Slightly reduced aircraft functional capability or safety margin	Slight crew workload increased	IV Minor
No effect or aircraft functional capability or safety margin	No effect on crew workload or physiology	V No Safety Effect

2.2 Experience of Similar Models

The most frequently used basis for deciding that a new design is acceptable is a comparison of a new design with a previous design proven in operational service [15]. Therefore, operating experience on similar models, from both subjective choices of senior captains, and incident/accident investigating reports, is an important source for determining scenarios with high workload. Six Chinese male captains, ranging in age from 39 to 52 (Mean = 45.6 ± 5.24), with 9420 ± 3637 mean total flight hours (range from 5500 to 15000 h), were participated in this dimension determination.

These pilots, based on their own flight experience and subjective evaluation, screened the typical task scenarios of the reference model, especially the abnormal ones. Then the generality of the target model was analyzed and compared from the aspects of control interface, display mode and operation procedures, and finally determined the scenarios of this dimension.

2.3 Abnormal Procedures

Normally, the system failure or malfunction occurs in unexpected circumstances, which requires the pilot to transfer his/her attention from the normal flight to the abnormal state in time, and take the corresponding measures according to standard operation procedures. Some procedures could be executed by referring to the checklists when the alert prompt appears, while others are mandatory memory items for pilots, which require them to deal with the fault in a timely manner under high pressure. Therefore, complex procedures, or procedures with more memory items, should be carefully considered in the workload assessment.

To reflect the difference from the second dimension, only abnormal procedures corresponding to novel design features are considered. The novel design features are determined from the aspects of novelty, complexity and integration through reference of guidance material such as advisory circulars, at the initial stage of the cockpit design.

2.4 MMEL Requirements

MMEL determines which equipment items could be in an inoperative state while the aircraft still maintaining an acceptable safety level. The goal of MMEL is to provide additional dispatch capabilities, and to impose additional restrictions following in-service feedbacks or design changes.

Although states under MMEL could ensure the safety, they usually bring certain operating restrictions and increases the flight crew workload. For some equipment items in MMEL, operating (O) procedures or maintenance (M) procedures are required. In this dimension, only the influence of operating procedures on workload is considered.

2.5 Specific Environment Conditions

The operational environment characteristics, which including internal and external environment of the cockpit, would significantly influence flight crew system. The external environment, such as turbulence and ambient light might affect readability of displays. The internal environment, for instance flight deck noise, might affect audibility of aural alerts. There are also some characteristics that might both come from the outside of the aircraft and from the inside of the aircraft, such as vibrations (may result from ice or fan blade loss). These specific environment condition may have an impact on flight crew workload, and need to be taken into account when determining the test scenarios.

2.6 Integration Process

Due to the inevitable repetition of the test scenarios determined by different dimensions, for example, some scenarios come from both the level III failure state in FHA based, and the experience judgment of the similar models, it is necessary to synthesize the scenarios.

The integration process consists of three steps. Firstly, eliminating the extremely unlikely scenes which normally defined in system level functional hazard assessment report, such as, losing all brakes and dual engines failure. Secondly, integrating the repeated scenarios or mutually inclusive tasks of crew operation procedures. For instance, engine fire, engine overheating and engine fire alarm are combined into engine fire. Last but not least, selecting more rigorous one in similar scenes. In the case of cabin pressure changing rate exceeds the limitation, the flight crew only needs to manually adjust the cabin pressure. However, when facing high-altitude pressure, in addition to controlling the cabin pressure, rapidly lowering the altitude is also required. Therefore, the latter scenario is selected.

3 Case Study

Taking an airworthiness verified large transport aircraft as an example, FEMAS method was used to establish the verification scenarios when demonstrating airworthiness compliance. The specific analysis results by each dimension are as follows.

3.1 Results of FHA Based

As same aircraft level function may contain multiple failure states, the state with higher functional hazard level was preferred. While for the same level, the failure state with more complicate or more urgent handling procedures was considered, shown as Table 2. Under these two principles, 41 scenarios were selected on the basis of the results of safety analysis. The typical scenes included Incorrected Horizontal / Vertical Guidance, Loss of Landing Lighting function, Rotor Bursting due to APU Failure, and etc.

Table 2. One example of FHA based scenarios selection

Failure State	Level	Analysis		Selected or Not
All the landing gear cannot be retracted - announced	III	lower level	/	Not
All the landing gear cannot be retracted - unannounced	II	higher level	Sufficient reaction time	Not
All the landing gear cannot be lowered or not locked - announced	II	higher level	Immediate reaction	Selected

3.2 Results of Experience of Similar Models

According to the actual flight experience, six captains had sorted out 13 typical scenarios with relatively higher workload, especially in abnormal and fault conditions. Then, the applicability of those scenarios to aircraft to be approved was confirmed by comparing and analyzing the characteristics from the perspective of control interface, display mode and operation procedures. Consequently, all 13 scenarios were selected in this dimension, including Emergency Descent, Dual Hydraulic Systems Failure, Unreliable Airspeed and etc.

3.3 Results of Abnormal Procedures

By comparing with the reference model, the abnormal procedures for novel design features of this model were sorted out. Subsequently, analyzing and selecting the procedures with large number of actions, urgent handling time or complex logic judgement required. Therefore, a total of 15 scenarios were captured, including thrust control loss of left (right) engine, total/static pressure sensor heating failure, insufficient wing anti-ice heating and etc.

3.4 Results of MMEL Requirements

111 non-work items, which contained crew operation procedures in the minimum equipment list were analyzed based on operating frequency, task duration and procedure steps. Finally, 7 scenarios were determined in this dimension, including Flight Director not working, one display control panel not working, TAWS not working and etc.

3.5 Results of Specific Environment Conditions

This dimension consisted of five representative aspects, including turbulence, noise, ambient lighting conditions, smoke and vibration. The specific descriptions are as follows in Table 3.

Table 3. Specific environment conditions and relevant scenarios

Environment condition	Scenarios	Brief description
turbulence	Non-precision approach	approaching and conducting a go-around
noise	High noise circumstance	take-off with landing gear not retracted
ambient lighting	Flying at night	conducting landing at night
smoke	Smoke in cabin	cabin smoke caused by air conditioner
vibration	Cockpit vibration	left engine overrun

3.6 Results of Integration

After analyzing the above 5 dimensions, 81 scenes were sorted out. Furthermore, 20 scenarios were deleted according to the aircraft safety assessment report, as the probability of occurrence is extremely unlikely, such as "losing all the brakes", and "two-engine failure". Of the remaining 61 scenes, 18 scenarios were either identical to other scenarios or contained the similar operating procedures. Moreover, according to the severity of similar scenarios, 31 scenes were retained. Finally, there were 4 scenarios related to the functional assessment of aircraft systems that could be integrated, shown as in Table 4. Totally, 27 scenarios were determined at last.

Table 4. Four integrated scenes

Scenes Description	Integration Scenes
Error indication of two engines	Error indication of two engines resulting in takeoff interruption
One display control panel malfunction	The normal lighting function of the cockpit is lost, and the crew uses the backup display control panel during the approach
Inconsistent indication of approach decision height	Combined with terrain warning, inconsistent indication of approach decision height is triggered first, and then the terrain warning
Using backup tuning page	The normal lighting function of the cockpit is lost, and the crew uses the backup tuning page during the approach

4   Discussion

In airworthiness regulations, six basic workload functions, including flight path control, collision avoidance, navigation, communication, operation and monitoring of aircraft engines and systems and command decisions, should be considered in determining the minimum flight crew [16]. Nevertheless, these functions seem make few contributions in defining necessary demonstrating flight scenarios. Besides, when analyzing and evaluating the flight crew workload, ten factors are considered significant. Some of the factors would be the guidance to build the flight scenes. For instance, "Incapacitation of a flight-crew member whenever the applicable operating rule requires a minimum flight crew of at least two pilots" which clearly points out that a scenario of one pilot incapacitation should be included. However, other factors are too general to select appropriate scenarios directly, such as, "System Failures", "Emergency and Non-normal Situations".

As generally accepted, the more rigorous conditions, the great the workload of flight crew [17]. However, the verification scenarios should be possible during normal operation. The extremely unlike events, although might cause the unacceptable results, the failure probability is less than $1 * 10^{-9}$, should not be concerned when determining the scenarios [18]. Thus, class II and class III failure states should be paid more attention to. In addition, some failure states have continuity, which may induce multiple type of alerts, therefore, the severity of similar scenarios also need to be considered comprehensively, and more stringent conditions should be selected as far as possible.

Furthermore, whether the similar design features, or the pilots' operating experience, the reference of similar models is also important. From the overall layout of the flight deck to the installation and operation of specific systems, different models have similarities. Such similar designs can result in similar crew errors, or workload distributions. At the same time, complex fault scenarios lead to abnormal procedures, such as under unreliable airspeed condition, which gives rise to the relatively high crew workload on almost all models. Because in the dimension of experience of similar models, the pilots could give many common abnormal scenarios, so we only consider procedures related to novel design features in the dimension of abnormal procedure.

The novelty of design feature is an important factor should be carefully considered. However, the judgment principles of novelty are various. Normally, some characteristics could be used when determining the degree of novelty, for instance, a new function; a new technology, a new design item that may affect flight crew task, and unusual procedures needed. Similarly, the system design complexity could also be considered from several aspects. For example, the number, the accessibility and the level of integration of information that the flight crew has to use; the number, the location and the design of the flight deck controls associated with each system; and the number of steps required to perform a task.

A MMEL, intended to permit operation with inoperative items of equipment for a period of time until repairs can be accomplished, is developed by the TC holder and approved by the authority, to improve aircraft utilization and thereby provide more convenient and economic air transportation for the public [19]. For some certain items, a requirement for a specific operations procedure would be accomplished by flight crew. These are different from normal operations, which usually lead to the increase of workload. Otherwise, the environment characteristics should also be taken into account. Both the conditions in the cockpit and the external environment of the aircraft will affect the workload of the pilots [20].

Although this method has already been successfully implemented in the process of aircraft type certification, and in the same compliance test comparison with other aircraft types, the scenarios coverage is wider and the workload impact factors are more fully considered. But it still has some aspects that need to be perfected. Firstly, the participation of the end users is insufficient, and only in dimension 2. Scenarios selected from other dimensions, or the final integration results should also be confirmed by pilots to adequately represent the intended usage. Secondly, the method proposed involves many aspects knowledge such as system safety analysis, operating system requirements, flight operation, etc., which requires certain skills of users to ensure the adequacy and effectiveness of the analysis. Last but not least, the novelty and complexity of the devices varies from aircraft manufacturer to manufacturer. Especially in term of system integration, large and experienced manufacturers are able to provide better management and control. So the maturity of the manufacturer might also be considered.

In sum, FEMAS was proposed to systematically established workload evaluation scenarios, which contains five dimensions, Fault Hazard Analysis (FHA) based, Experience of similar models, Abnormal procedures, Master Minimum Equipment List (MMEL) requirements, and Specific environment conditions. In total, 27 scenarios were determined to be carried out in the certification phase.

Acknowledgement. This study was funded by National Natural Science Foundation of China (U2033202).

Disclosure of Interests. The authors have no competing interests to declare that are relevant to the content of this article.

References

1. Farmer, E., Brownson, A.: Review of workload measurement, analysis and interpretation methods. Eur. Organ. Saf. Air Navig. **33**, 1–33 (2003)
2. EASA: Certification specifications for large aeroplanes CS-25 (2009)
3. Cain, B.: A review of the mental workload literature. DTIC Document (2007)
4. Gawron, V.J.: Human Performance, Workload, and Situational Awareness Measures Handbook. CRC Press (2008)
5. Meshkati, N., et al.: Techniques in mental workload assessment (1995)
6. Wester, A., et al.: Event-related potentials and secondary task performance during simulated driving. Accid. Anal. Prev. **40**(1), 1–7 (2008)
7. Tsai, Y.-F., et al.: Task performance and eye activity: predicting behavior relating to cognitive workload. Aviat. Space Environ. Med. **78**(5), B176–B185 (2007)
8. Roscoe, A.H., Ellis, G.A.: A Subjective Rating Scale for Assessing Pilot Workload in Flight: A decade of Practical Use. A Subjective Rating Scale for Assessing Pilot Workload in Flight A Decade of Practical Use (1990)
9. Yiyuan, Z., et al.: Using NASA-TLX to evaluate the flight deck design in design phase of aircraft. Procedia Eng. **17**, 77–83 (2011)
10. Hart, S.G.: NASA-task load index (NASA-TLX); 20 years later. In: Proceedings of the Human Factors and Ergonomics Society Annual Meeting. Sage Publications (2006)
11. Lee, Y.-H., Liu, B.-S.: Inflight workload assessment: comparison of subjective and physiological measurements. Aviat. Space Environ. Med. **74**(10), 1078–1084 (2003)
12. Mansikka, H., et al.: Fighter pilots' heart rate, heart rate variation and performance during instrument approaches. Ergonomics **59**(10), 1344–1352 (2016)
13. Ahlstrom, U., Friedman-Berg, F.J.: Using eye movement activity as a correlate of cognitive workload. Int. J. Ind. Ergon. **36**(7), 623–636 (2006)
14. Wilson, G.F.: An analysis of mental workload in pilots during flight using multiple psychophysiological measures. Int. J. Aviat. Psychol. **12**(1), 3–18 (2002)
15. Stickdorn, M., Schneider, J: This is Service Design Thinking: Basics, Tools, Cases. Wiley (2012)
16. FAA, Advisory Circular (AC) 25.1523-1, Minimum Flightcrew (1993)
17. Moray, N.: Mental Workload: Its Theory and Measurement, vol. 8. Springer, New York (2013)https://doi.org/10.1007/978-1-4757-0884-4
18. De Florio, F.: Airworthiness an Introduction to Aircraft Certification: A Guide to Understanding JAA, EASA and FAA Standards. Access Online via Elsevier (2010)

19. Cini, P.F., Griffith, P.: Designing for MFOP: towards the autonomous aircraft. J. Qual. Maint. Eng. **5**(4), 296–308 (1999)
20. Karavidas, M.K., et al.: The effects of workload on respiratory variables in simulated flight: a preliminary study. Biol. Psychol. **84**(1), 157–160 (2010)

Correction to: Using Flight Quick Access Recorder (QAR) Data to Examine the Effect of Sun Glare on Landing Performance: An Initial Attempt

Weiwei Qiu, Ziyue Cao, Xing Chen, Jingyu Zhang, Xianghong Sun, Yinger Zheng, and Haofeng Wang

Correction to:
Chapter 20 in: D. Harris and W.-C. Li (Eds.): *Engineering Psychology and Cognitive Ergonomics*, **LNAI 14693,**
https://doi.org/10.1007/978-3-031-60731-8_20

In the originally published version of chapter 20, the author affiliation order had been rendered incorrectly. This has been corrected.

The updated version of this chapter can be found at
https://doi.org/10.1007/978-3-031-60731-8_20

Author Index

Printed in the United States
by Baker & Taylor Publisher Services